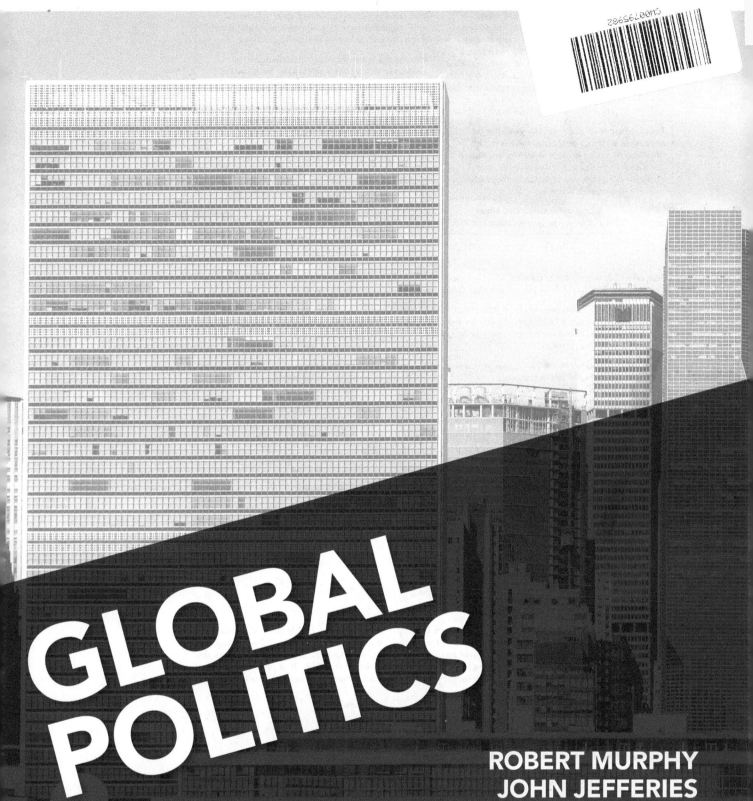

PEARSON EDEXCEL A LEVEL

GLOBAL POLITICS

ROBERT MURPHY
JOHN JEFFERIES
JOSIE GADSBY

Boost

Endorsed for
**Pearson Edexcel
Qualifications**

HODDER
EDUCATION
AN HACHETTE UK COMPANY

In order to ensure that this resource offers high-quality support for the associated Pearson qualification, it has been through a review process by the awarding body. This process confirms that this resource fully covers the teaching and learning content of the specification or part of a specification at which it is aimed. It also confirms that it demonstrates an appropriate balance between the development of subject skills, knowledge and understanding, in addition to preparation for assessment.

Endorsement does not cover any guidance on assessment activities or processes (e.g. practice questions or advice on how to answer assessment questions), included in the resource nor does it prescribe any particular approach to the teaching or delivery of a related course.

While the publishers have made every attempt to ensure that advice on the qualification and its assessment is accurate, the official specification and associated assessment guidance materials are the only authoritative source of information and should always be referred to for definitive guidance.

Pearson examiners have not contributed to any sections in this resource relevant to examination papers for which they have responsibility.

Examiners will not use endorsed resources as a source of material for any assessment set by Pearson.

Endorsement of a resource does not mean that the resource is required to achieve this Pearson qualification, nor does it mean that it is the only suitable material available to support the qualification, and any resource lists produced by the awarding body shall include this and other appropriate resources.

Every effort has been made to trace all copyright holders, but if any have been inadvertently overlooked, the Publishers will be pleased to make the necessary arrangements at the first opportunity.

Although every effort has been made to ensure that website addresses are correct at time of going to press, Hodder Education cannot be held responsible for the content of any website mentioned in this book. It is sometimes possible to find a relocated web page by typing in the address of the home page for a website in the URL window of your browser.

Hachette UK's policy is to use papers that are natural, renewable and recyclable products and made from wood grown in well-managed forests and other controlled sources. The logging and manufacturing processes are expected to conform to the environmental regulations of the country of origin.

Orders: please contact Hachette UK Distribution, Hely Hutchinson Centre, Milton Road, Didcot, Oxfordshire, OX11 7HH. Telephone: +44 (0)1235 827827. Email education@hachette.co.uk Lines are open from 9 a.m. to 5 p.m., Monday to Friday. You can also order through our website: www.hoddereducation.co.uk

ISBN: 978 1 3983 4506 5

© Robert Murphy, John Jefferies and Josie Gadsby 2022

First published in 2017. This edition published in 2022 by
Hodder Education,
An Hachette UK Company
Carmelite House
50 Victoria Embankment
London EC4Y 0DZ

www.hoddereducation.co.uk

Impression number   10 9 8 7 6 5 4 3 2

Year   2026 2025 2024 2023 2022

All rights reserved. Apart from any use permitted under UK copyright law, no part of this publication may be reproduced or transmitted in any form or by any means, electronic or mechanical, including photocopying and recording, or held within any information storage and retrieval system, without permission in writing from the publisher or under licence from the Copyright Licensing Agency Limited. Further details of such licences (for reprographic reproduction) may be obtained from the Copyright Licensing Agency Limited, www.cla.co.uk

Cover photo © MissKlik – stock.adobe.com

Illustrations by Integra Software Services Pvt. Ltd., Pondicherry, India

Typeset in Integra Software Services Pvt. Ltd., Pondicherry, India

Printed and bound by CPI Group (UK) Ltd, Croydon, CR0 4YY

A catalogue record for this title is available from the British Library.

Get the most from this book

This new edition of our best-selling textbook covers the key content of the Edexcel A-level Government and Politics specification for teaching from September 2017.

Special features

Learning outcomes
A summary of the learning objectives for each chapter.

Key terms
Concise definitions of key terms where they first appear.

Topic links
Links between different topics on the specification.

Synoptic link
Synoptic links with core political ideas are highlighted. This is a requirement in Section B exam questions.

Activity
Activities to cement your learning.

Distinguish between
A clarification of the difference between two commonly confused concepts or institutions.

Debate
The two sides of a controversial question set out to hone evaluation skills.

Further reading
Websites, books and articles that are relevant to the chapter.

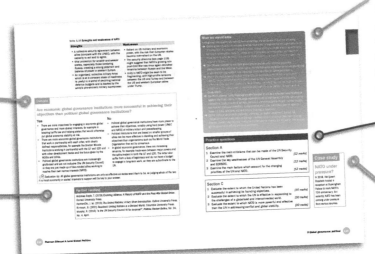

What you should know
A summary at the end of the chapter against which you can check your knowledge.

Practice questions
Revision questions at the end of each chapter.

Case study
Topical examples to use in essays.

Contents

Answers to practice questions can be found at:
www.hoddereducation.co.uk/GlobalPolitics2022

1 Theories of global politics

Learning outcomes

By the end of the chapter you should understand:
- ➜ what global politics is
- ➜ what the challenges of modern global politics are
- ➜ what realism is and whether states behave in a realist way
- ➜ what liberalism is and whether there is a liberal world order
- ➜ the main ideas of the anarchical society and society of states theory
- ➜ how realism and liberalism explain recent developments in global politics

Getting you started

This chapter introduces the key theories of global politics. In doing so, it also covers many themes and debates that are covered in depth in later chapters.

A world order or world in disorder?

In the twenty-first century's second decade, global politics faces significant challenges. Increasingly, the world order feels disorderly. The world is grappling with a climate emergency, with collective action needed and time running out. There is an increasingly multipolar distribution of power, with the US, China and Russia all competing for influence and becoming bolder in their actions. Since 2020, states face a difficult global recovery from the Covid-19 pandemic which devastated economies worldwide and brought our globalised, interconnected world to a standstill.

It is a reasonable question to ask whether the current global world order is able to respond to these challenges. Are states willing to cooperate and make necessary sacrifices to advance global progress? Or are states becoming increasingly willing to distance themselves from the institutions of globalisation and defend their national interest?

There is some evidence that in recent years the world's most significant powers – the US, Russia and China – became increasingly willing to challenge that liberal world order of cooperation. Under President Trump, the US withdrew from several key international agreements and openly challenged the world order of globalism supported by the United Nations. The project of re-engaging the US in a more cooperative approach was an immediate challenge for President Biden. Russia has become increasingly willing to use its military power using conventional and unconventional methods, from Ukraine to Syria to Salisbury. And China has been busily building a global infrastructure network costing trillions of dollars, continuing its economic rise and modernising its military power.

States tend to prioritise their own national interests. Has this made the world safer and helped to resolve the many pressing collective action problems? There has been some progress on tackling climate change, but it is still far from keeping pace with the scale of the problem. Major abuses of human rights are still too often outside the control of global governance, with those responsible not held accountable or facing justice. Global efforts to reduce poverty have had some success, but there is growing inequality within and between states and still too many areas where poverty has yet to be significantly reduced. Some regional organisations have grown in membership and influence and attempt to advance shared interests at a regional level that struggle to be advanced at the global level.

A wildfire in Manavgat, Turkey, July 2021. The world is grappling with a climate emergency

National politics is about the ability to resolve disputes, share resources and take decisions legitimately within agreed structures, laws and institutions. However, unlike in national politics, such as that in the UK or the US, global politics has no central world government or authority. Global politics has a far more complex and multilayered range of structures, laws and institutions at regional and international level. Getting things done requires leadership, negotiation, compromise and imagination.

Ultimately, this responsibility for getting things done and meeting the challenges of the moment rests with states, as they are the most legitimate and powerful actors in global politics. Agreements are made and achievements realised because states have negotiated them and stick to their commitments. Progress can be made when states' interests and the international interests are similar or aligned. But, ultimately, states are in the driving seat of global politics and the actions of some states matter more than others.

This chapter examines the different lenses through which states view global politics and how these viewpoints translate into policies and actions. Ultimately, whether the world is orderly or disorderly depends on the actions and behaviours of states.

What is global politics?

To begin to understand global politics, it is useful to compare global with national politics. Both relate to:

- taking decisions legitimately
- accountability and holding those in power to account
- solving shared problems, such as a global threat of terrorism
- resolving disputes, such as disagreements over ownership of territory
- sharing resources fairly and peacefully.

The differences between national and global politics

There are important differences between national and global politics in terms of power, legitimacy and authority.

Power in global politics is the ability to achieve desired outcomes and to influence others. In national politics, a national or sub-national government, such as Her Majesty's Government in the UK, exercises power. It is legitimately elected by the people with a mandate to implement the manifesto promises that a political party made during an election campaign. In global politics, there is no form of world government nor any single authority to govern a world composed of multiple nation-states. Institutions such as the United Nations (UN) carry some authority, but only as much as individual member states allow. Therefore, states can choose to ignore or defy these attempts at **global governance**.

Legitimacy is the ability to do things fairly and lawfully. This can be achieved through complying with or creating a form of legislation or law. For example, one way of undertaking military action lawfully is through a UN Security Council (UNSC) Resolution, which in itself is a statement of international law. In national politics there is usually a legislature, which holds the legitimacy and powers to create laws, and a judiciary and police force, which apply and enforce the law (see Table 1.1). In global politics, there is rarely such clear authority. Laws are created only when states agree to them. Laws often apply only to those states that have signed up to them. And laws are often enforced only when states permit it.

Authority comes from the possession of both power and legitimacy. The UK Parliament has authority because it is democratically elected and so possesses legitimacy. For example, in 2018, when the UK Parliament persistently refused to vote in support of Theresa May's European Union withdrawal agreement, the prime minister certainly felt the effects of Parliament's authority and was unable to get her Brexit plan approved. The same applied to Parliament's rejection of David Cameron's proposals for military action against the Assad regime in Syria in 2013.

In global politics, there is no comparable structure of world government with such clearly defined powers and scope. There is certainly no government structure that has comprehensive power over every state and region of the world. This is often referred to as a state of global anarchy, in the literal sense of there being no single authority that can bring order to a world of multiple nation-states. There are institutions that have some authority over certain states or regions, but this authority is not absolute, because states can decide to ignore or withdraw from these institutions. Some states are not even members of these institutions to begin with.

> ### Key term
>
> **Global governance**
> Attempts to bring government structures and authority to world politics in order to deal with common interests and challenges, such as climate change or global terrorism.

Table 1.1 Examples of sources of power and authority in UK and US national politics

Source	UK authority	US authority
Legislature: amends and votes on laws	The UK Parliament has the power and authority to make and unmake laws.	The US Congress has the power and authority to approve presidential appointments and budgets, pass laws and impeach or try federal officers (including presidents).
Executive: proposes laws	Her Majesty's Government in the UK is made up of the prime minister and his/her cabinet, supported by the civil service. It can propose laws and policies for Parliament to vote on.	The US president is head of state and commander-in-chief of the armed forces, has powers to negotiate treaties with other states and executes the laws created by Congress.
Judiciary: interprets and upholds the law	A key role is ensuring the executive does not exceed its powers. For example, the UK's Supreme Court in 2017 declared that the UK Parliament, rather than the executive, must trigger Article 50 to begin the process for leaving the EU. In 2019, the Supreme Court ruled that Prime Minister Boris Johnson's prorogation of Parliament had been unlawful.	The Supreme Court is the US's highest court and takes decisions on issues of major constitutional significance. For example, the 1973 *Roe vs Wade* decision ruled that women had the right to decide whether or not to terminate their pregnancy.

Activity

1 Looking at Table 1.1 and the separation of powers it summarises, are there institutions in global politics that have similar powers and responsibilities to:

(a) an executive? (b) a legislature? (c) a judiciary?

2 What differences do you see between the powers of these branches of government in national politics compared with global politics?

Distinguish between

National and global politics

Global politics

- There is no single world government with a clear mandate or authority. States are the most powerful and authoritative actors and, ultimately, a higher authority cannot force states to do anything against their will.
- International law may be written down and codified but often it applies only to states that have formally agreed to these laws (normally by signing and ratifying treaties).
- International law is hard to enforce, particularly if powerful states refuse to comply. Enforcement is possible only through sanctions or military action, and is inconsistent.
- There are many institutions capable of making decisions, but none can do so without the consent of member states. Summits and intergovernmental organisations (IGOs) offer states a means of resolving disputes and opportunities to work together (for example, in the UN, the EU, the Group of Seven (G7) and at the Paris Climate Change Conference 2015). They have varying legitimacy and authority, and states can ultimately choose whether or not to join and remain part of these institutions. States can also ignore their decisions or opt out of joint action.

National politics

- There is a government with a clear mandate and authority. Political parties usually compete in elections, are legitimately elected by a defined electorate within the state and then govern with clear authority.
- National laws are usually clearly written down, codified and set out in law, and apply to all citizens without exception.
- Courts and police enforce national laws and have clear and legitimate authority to do so.
- There are usually clear and authoritative institutions for taking decisions, such as voting on laws and resolving disputes fairly and legitimately, for example national parliaments or assemblies, such as the UK Parliament or the US Congress. A vote in one of these institutions carries clear authority and results in laws being debated, amended and, ultimately, approved or not.

Who is involved in global politics?

By the nature of its much larger geographical scope, there are more actors involved in global than national politics. The powers, impact and limitations of each of these actors are covered in greater depth in later chapters.

States are the primary actors in global politics, as they have the most authority and legitimacy to take decisions. States differ widely in terms of their power, which impacts on the amount of authority they have on the world stage and their ability to achieve their desired outcomes and influence other states. Powerful states, such as China, Russia and the US, are more likely to achieve their own goals and also to dominate and limit the choices available to less powerful states.

In addition to states, there are a number of non-state actors that contribute towards global decision making. These include:

- IGOs such as the UN and the Bretton Woods Institutions (the International Monetary Fund (IMF), the World Trade Organization (WTO) and the World Bank)
- regional organisations such as the EU and the Association of Southeast Asian Nations (ASEAN)
- non-governmental organisations (NGOs) such as Oxfam and Human Rights Watch.

Realism and liberalism

Two of the key theories in global politics are **realism** and **liberalism**. They represent different ways of approaching international problems.

Realism and an anarchical world order

Realism is governed principally by the belief that nation-states are the most legitimate and powerful actors in global politics. The realist viewpoint includes the following:

- Global politics takes place in an anarchical society, with no world government that can impose authority and order, since nation-states retain the exclusive right to act in whatever way they wish. Although nation-states may decide to work through and with other non-state actors, they do not abandon their sovereign right to advance their own self-interest and the authority of IGOs, such as the EU and the UN, should be limited. (Anarchy, in this context, should be understood in its literal sense as the 'absence of authority or government' rather than necessarily a state of chaos and disorder.)
- Realism starts from a conservative, pessimistic view of human nature as fundamentally selfish. Since nation-states exist in a state of global anarchy, states live in a self-help system in which they must build up their own security apparatus through military power and alliances and must always be watchful and suspicious of others. This creates a **security dilemma**, because they can only rely upon themselves for their own protection. Security comes before any other considerations, such as human rights.
- All states are ultimately trying to find ways of increasing their power and influence within the global political order. They can be thought of as power maximisers, where no power is enough to meet the challenges of a disorderly, selfish global political system.
- The natural state of the world order is for states to compete with each other, making the most of their power. Therefore, states are often in conflict with each other.

Activity

Consider the difference between national politics and global politics.
1 Why might it be more difficult to reach agreement in global politics than in national politics?
2 In global politics, which actors are:
   (a) the most powerful?
   (b) the most legitimate?

Key terms

Realism States are the most important and authoritative actors in global politics, and their primary goal is to protect their own national interests. The world is anarchical and selfish, with no single authority above states that is able to impose order.

Liberalism States' interests in global politics are linked and interdependent, and best advanced through states cooperating with each other and with intergovernmental organisations in order to achieve common political objectives. Democracy and human rights are seen as essential.

Security dilemma The idea that as one state builds up its defences, others will respond by building up theirs, thereby increasing tensions between the two states or even provoking conflict. This risks becoming a competitive cycle of events.

See Box 1.1 for more information on the theories of key realist thinkers.

Key terms

Anarchical society The term used by Hedley Bull in his 1977 book of the same name. It is the idea that global politics is in a state of disorder because there is no higher authority than nation-states with the power to control global politics.

Box 1.1

Important realist thinkers

The titles of the following texts from key realist thinkers all question some of the assumptions of liberalism, and emphasise the inevitable competition for power that exists between states and the idea of an **anarchical society** where there is no higher authority in global politics above nation-state level.

Kenneth Waltz, *Theory of International Politics* (1979)

Waltz was a defensive realist thinker. Bipolarity, where two major powers are competing for power, is more stable than multipolarity, where many rival powers are competing with each other (see page 269). Two major powers can negotiate their way to stability more easily than many competing powers. The international system is in a state of anarchy, with no central authority above nation-state level.

Stephen Walt, *The Origins of Alliances* (1987)

Walt put forward the idea of a 'balance of threats' whereby states develop friendly relations with other states in order to counter a threat that they see from a rival state. Walt also defended the 2021 US withdrawal from Afghanistan arguing that it allowed the US to focus on more relevant and significant security threats.

Hans Morgenthau, *Politics Among Nations* (1948)

Morgenthau is a classical realist thinker. Political man is a naturally selfish creature and will always try to dominate and have power over others. Moral considerations in global politics are less important than the national interest.

John Mearsheimer, *The Tragedy of Great Power Politics* (2001)

Mearsheimer is an offensive realist thinker. He explained that conflict and competition for power between the great world powers will continue. States are trying to secure hegemony, meaning they want to dominate all other states within a region.

Synoptic link

In your study of Political Ideas in Component 1, you learn about **conservatism** in which **Thomas Hobbes (1588–1679)** who put forward his view of the 'state of nature' in his most important work *Leviathan* (1651) as inherently selfish, motivated by greed and suspicion of others. In the absence of a powerful higher authority to tame human nature, a 'leviathan' as Hobbes termed it, there would be anarchy. In the international system there cannot be an authority above the nation state. We can see this conservative viewpoint linking closely with realists' views of human nature leading to an anarchical world order in which states cannot trust others and maximise their power.

Synoptic link

In your study of Political Ideas in Component 1, you learn about the conservative thinker **Edmund Burke (1729–97)** – one particularly important idea that links conservatism and realism is of society operating in 'little platoons', seeing a benefit to society from hierarchical structures. Burke continued the conservative (and realist) analysis of human nature as flawed and imperfect.

Anarchical world order in action

The Iraq War, 2003

Believing that Iraq still owned, and was prepared to use, weapons of mass destruction (WMD), the US and a limited number of allies, including the UK, invaded the country in March 2003. The stated objective was to disarm Iraq and its leader, Saddam Hussein, of these weapons.

However, the US launched military action without a clear UNSC Resolution authorising the use of force. In fact, the last resolution before the invasion (UNSC Resolution 1441) offered Iraq 'a final opportunity to comply with its disarmament obligations', and Russia and France did not support US invasion plans and urged UN weapons inspectors (who reported that Iraq was partially cooperating with inspections) to be given more time for assessments.

In March 2003, a combination of a ground assault and air strikes brought Saddam Hussein's regime to an end within days. Saddam Hussein fled, but was later captured and tried by an Iraqi Special Tribunal. He was executed on 30 September 2006. After the invasion, UN weapons inspectors concluded that there were no WMDs in Iraq.

In March 2003, US soldiers invaded Iraq during the War on Terror

The 2003 Iraq War is an example of realism in US and UK foreign policy because of the following.

- **The US was prepared to 'go it alone', without international support:** military action was launched without clear UNSC approval or wider international agreement and support. The coalition consisted of the US as the lead player and military forces from Australia, Poland and the UK.
- **The war's legality was highly questionable:** the UK's Chilcot Inquiry into the Iraq War concluded in 2016 that the case for war was 'unjustified' and that Saddam's regime posed 'no imminent threat'. The UN secretary-general at the time, Kofi Annan, said in 2004 that the invasion did not conform to the laws of the UN's founding Charter and was, 'from our point of view, illegal'.

● **The US and its allies were acting in what they perceived, and argued, was their national interest:** the US saw the UN Security Council as an obstacle to successfully carrying out action it believed to be in its national interest. Prime Minister Tony Blair said that Iraq represented 'a current and serious threat to the UK national interest' because the UK government believed that WMDs were a threat to the middle east region.

However, many realist thinkers opposed the Iraq War. For example, US political scientist John Mearsheimer believed that it was not in the US's national interest to invade.

China's Belt and Road Initiative since 2013

A key element of China's rising power since 2013 has been its 'One Belt, One Road' project, also known as the Belt and Road Initiative (BRI). The project, spanning over 70 countries and costing as much as $4 trillion in direct investments and other projects, aims to improve and secure infrastructure connectivity, energy supplies and key maritime shipping routes. The network stretches from China's borders as far as western Europe and East Africa (see Figure 1.1).

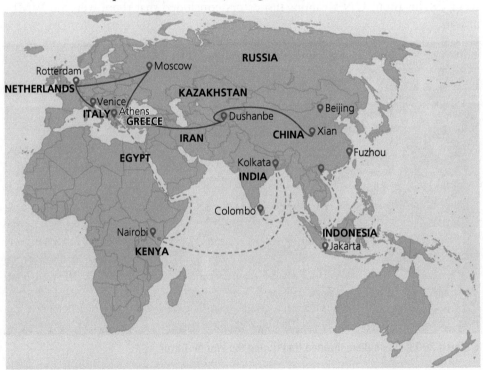

Figure 1.1 China's Belt and Road initiative

Realists would interpret China's actions as a means to seek to maximise power in its ambitions to cement China as a global superpower and exert influence far beyond its borders. A key benefit will be to enable China to project economic power across the region and to invest in a huge number of states. It will build new markets for Chinese goods, strengthening its domestic economy through higher incomes and consumer spending. The wider ambition is to build China's global economic power in its race to overtake the US as the world's largest economy, which some forecasts estimate might happen within this decade.

The project poses a challenge to US power, with both President Trump and President Obama struggling to respond effectively to China's growing economic power.

Obama tried a 'pivot to Asia', essentially an attempt to reassert US investment and military power in the South Asia region, whereas under Trump economic relations escalated into a trade war. Ultimately, the US has been unable to propose tempting enough economic offers of its own to states participating in the BRI.

Critics also argue that weaker states end up in a debt trap with China, where infrastructure projects constructed using Chinese contractors create long-term financial liability for poorer states. Other analysts see the BRI as a potential network through which growing Chinese military power could eventually be deployed.

The Russian annexation of Crimea, 2014

In 2014, Russian-backed militia entered the Crimea region in Ukraine and, within months, Crimea was declared independent and subsequently voted in a referendum to become part of Russia. Ukraine, formerly part of the Soviet Union, has long been torn between the West (potentially joining the EU and even NATO) and the East (Russia offered Ukraine very favourable gas prices and, since the break-up of the Soviet Union, an agreement with Ukraine allowed Russia to continue to operate from the Sevastopol port in Crimea's Black Sea region, Russia's only warm-water port).

Russia did not invade Ukraine with conventional military forces, but reports suggested the presence of special forces wearing uniforms without any identifying insignia (see page 251). Pro-Russian rebel groups then became active in the predominantly ethnically Russian eastern regions of Ukraine, some with Russian government backing.

Russia's actions in Crimea are an example of realism for the following reasons.

- **Russia put military forces into Ukraine unilaterally:** it did not discuss the move with IGOs or gain justification through international law. The UNSC was unable to pass a resolution condemning Russia because, as a permanent member, Russia vetoed this (see page 10).
- **Russia argued that it was acting in its national interest:** from a Russian perspective, there were worrying signs that Ukraine might be tilting decisively towards closer ties with the West and, in particular, the EU and NATO. Since the end of the Cold War in 1991, ten former Soviet Union and Warsaw Pact states, including Estonia, Latvia and Lithuania, all of which share a direct border with Russia, had joined the North Atlantic Treaty Organization (NATO, see page 117), the pro-Western military alliance founded as a means of countering the military might of the Soviet Union. Moscow judged this as a threat to its national interest and in 2008 declared the prospect of Ukraine and Georgia joining NATO as a 'hostile act'.
- **The primary objective was to regain territorial control of Crimea** and, from a Russian perspective, to protect a majority ethnically Russian population. In particular, Russia wanted to secure the warm-water port of Sevastopol, a key strategic objective of the annexation. In terms of maintaining its maritime military power, Russia wanted to keep its main, and historically significant, Black Sea naval base.
- **In July 2014, an international passenger plane was shot down over Ukraine** with 298 lives lost. An EU joint investigation team concluded that the plane had been shot down by a missile which had been transported from Russia the same day. A UNSC Resolution aiming to establish an international tribunal into the incident was vetoed by Russia, highlighting the challenges of holding states accountable in an anarchical world order.

Activity

Research other events in global politics and examine how they can be explained using the theories and ideas of realism. Did states act unilaterally? Were states acting in their national interest or the wider international interest? You could start with the following examples:

- the Syrian civil war (2011–)
- war in Afghanistan (2001–20)
- the UK's decision to leave the EU, known as 'Brexit' (2016)
- US–China relations under President Trump (2016–2021).

Distinguish between

Realism and liberalism: human nature

Realism

- Human nature is naturally selfish and egoist and therefore states are interested in their own (national) interests.
- Human nature is fixed and driven, and cannot be changed, so states too are motivated by a desire to dominate and have power over others.
- States are also motivated by a need to survive, especially in a global 'self-help' system where there is no guarantee that any other state or actor in global politics will help them.

Liberalism

- Liberals believe in a more optimistic vision of human nature than realists. Human nature is not fixed and states can therefore improve and develop.
- Humans, and therefore states, are committed to individual liberty and freedom (for example, human rights).
- Humans, and therefore states, prefer to work in partnership with others and look for opportunities to do so. International cooperation, through IGOs, is therefore possible and desirable.
- It is possible to impose order on humans and states from above, for example through a rules-based system of international law.

International anarchy and its implications

The concept of a world that is in a state of anarchy is worth clarifying. The literal meaning of anarchy is that there is a lack of authority. Anarchy is frequently associated with the idea of conflict or chaotic social unrest, for example riots and lawlessness. In global politics, the realist viewpoint of anarchy may mean both:

- a simple lack of authority, and
- the potential for conflict between states in the absence of a higher authority above states.

An analogy frequently used to explain realism and the idea of **international anarchy** is the so-called 'billiard ball model'. The billiard balls in the game represent nation-states. The balls, like states, have a hard outer shell which represents the national sovereignty of individual states and is difficult to break through or penetrate. Realists want global politics to work this way, for example through clearly defined borders. Global politics, just like a game of billiards, is a competitive environment in which the states knock against each other and a collision between two states might have a knock-on effect on others. The billiard balls dominate the table, in the same way that realists would see states as the key actors in global politics.

It is important to note that the 'billiard ball model' is a way of explaining and visualising realism and is not a theory in its own right. Therefore, it is better to refer to the theory as 'realism' rather than the 'billiard ball model'.

Key term

International anarchy
The notion that states are self-contained units that frequently clash with each other, in a world system where there is no authority such as a 'world government' that is as legitimate, powerful or authoritative as nation-states.

Consequences of international anarchy

In the eyes of realists, international anarchy and the absence of any authority above nation-state level leads to the following.

- IGOs such as the EU and the UN will be limited in their impact and effectiveness. This is because states determine the success or failure of these international efforts. IGOs cannot force states to do anything, and any authority they do have has been granted by the member states themselves (such as the powers given to the UN Security Council in the UN Charter which was approved by UN member states, not by some other authority beyond the states themselves). States have created IGOs, and IGOs ultimately serve state interests. When they no longer do this, they collapse – such as the League of Nations – or states leave, as seen in the UK's decision to leave the EU.

- States will also want to prevent IGOs from making decisions that are not in their national interest. This is often most clearly seen in the veto powers that the five UNSC permanent members (China, France, Russia, the UK and the US) wield, which frequently prevent coordinated action on matters ranging from the Israel and Palestine conflict to the Syrian civil war.

- Unlike national law, rules in global politics – known as international law – are not always enforceable. In an anarchical world system, no international body can force states to sign up to international law. Customary international law, which in theory applies to states regardless of whether or not they have signed and ratified a law, does exist for abuses of humanitarian law. The Geneva Conventions, for example, are customary international law and apply to all states, but the decision to enforce the law is ultimately the political decision of international bodies, such as the UN, or individual, especially powerful, states. Many important international laws, such as the UN's human rights covenants or the Rome Statute, are completely optional for states to sign up to.

- International courts may be ignored, or may not have decisive powers to investigate at all. The International Criminal Court (ICC, see page 52) has limited powers to hold states to account for the most serious crimes against humanity. But, in reality, states that have not fully agreed to the ICC's founding Rome Statute (see page 112) are able to escape justice, as there is no authoritative global force to bring states and those responsible for international crimes before the court. The European Court of Human Rights (ECtHR, see page 52) experiences similar difficulties. So, even when states have signed up to international laws, we have to examine whether international courts have sufficient power to uphold those laws.

- The absence of any authority above nation-state level means that states are able to breach international law or to commit human rights abuses within their state without fear of being held accountable or stopped from doing so. This happens all too frequently in global politics. For example, human rights abuses by the Assad regime and ISIL (also known as Islamic State or Daesh) in Syria have persisted for over a decade without any sustained international intervention to prevent this. Combined with the realist view that states mirror the selfish behaviours inherent in human nature, this lack of constraints drives conflict both internally and between states.

- If world order is without authority, the most powerful states will try to gain enough power to become that authority and exert their own control over global politics. A hegemon or hegemony is where extremely powerful states dominate regions or even globally with military and economic power and may force other states to subscribe to their rules and world view. The desire to become a global or regional hegemon is in itself a further source of tension.

Realism and states as key actors

Realists believe that states are the most important actors in global politics, and that they are more powerful and significant than other actors, such as IGOs, NGOs and multinational corporations (MNCs). In terms of IGOs, realist states might still join them if it is in their national interest to do so and if they can defend and promote that national interest within the IGO.

Ultimately, however, realists see IGOs as driven by state actions, for the following reasons:

- **IGOs exist only because states created them:** this further reflects the power of states. States have the ultimate power to decide to join or leave IGOs. It is rare, but not unprecedented, for states to decide to leave IGOs. The most obvious example is the UK deciding to trigger Article 50 of the Treaty of Lisbon, enabling it to leave the EU in 2020. In 1966, France withdrew its troops from NATO (but remained a member state of NATO) in protest against perceived US dominance of the alliance. More recently, African Union states threatened to withdraw from the ICC (see page 170) in protest at a perceived bias against African states in the court's investigations and judgments. States are, therefore, the fundamental building blocks of IGOs.

- **IGOs succeed or fail based on member state actions:** the success or failure of IGOs is down to the decisions and agreement of their member states on matters large and small. Most IGOs are intergovernmental forums in which state governments conduct and negotiate business and only agree what the member state governments are prepared to accept. When a UNSC Resolution is passed on matters of international peace and security, this is because states have negotiated the text between them, made amendments and then a majority of states has agreed to it. Equally, when the UNSC fails to agree a resolution, this is because a majority of states has not agreed to it. Criticism of the UN for 'failing to act' – for example, in the Syrian conflict – may be considered unfair. The UNSC is able to act only when a majority of its member states agrees to a particular course of action.

- **States often act outside IGOs:** states often make agreements with each other outside IGOs, by negotiating treaties with each other. These treaties are each individually pieces of international law. States have complete freedom to agree to or opt out of these treaties. For example, the New Strategic Arms Reduction Treaty (START) in 2021 is the latest of many treaties signed between Russia and the US whereby both states agree to limits on nuclear warheads.

- **Free trade exists only because states have agreed to it:** it is states that control tariff (taxes on imports from other states) and non-tariff barriers (such as limits or quotas) at their territorial borders. As with IGOs, states are the 'building blocks' (see page 302) of the global system of international trade. States are able to create protectionist measures that could make trade more difficult, for example by raising national taxes on foreign imported goods. States also have the power to abolish or reduce the amount of measures, making trade easier, for example by granting tariff-free access to another state that wishes to export to the other. States have the power to enter into free-trade agreements with groups of countries. An example of this is the Trans-Pacific Partnership or TPP trade agreement with mostly Pacific states, which fell through in 2018 when

President Trump withdrew from the treaty, leading to a replacement treaty excluding the US later the same year. States can also negotiate individual trade agreements with individual states, for example the new free-trade agreements signed by the UK with other states – such as Japan – when it left existing EU trade agreements after leaving the EU in 2020. Since it left the EU, the UK had to negotiate new trade agreements with many other states (including Japan and Australia), since it was no longer part of EU-wide trade agreements with many non-EU states.

- **States still have the power to act unilaterally and to ignore IGOs or treaties:** for example, Russian action in Crimea (2014) and UK and US action in Iraq (2003) went ahead without clear UNSC mandates. These actions show the overwhelming power of nation-states to act alone. When states do this frequently, it is called isolationism.

Realists view the state to be superior to MNCs, such as Amazon or Facebook, NGOs and other non-state actors (which might include violent non-state actors such as al-Qaeda or ISIL; and non-violent non-state actors such as social movements like Extinction Rebellion), for the reasons given in Table 1.2.

Table 1.2 Relationships between states and non-state actors

States vs MNCs	States vs NGOs	States vs violent non-state actors
MNCs operate in an economic environment that is controlled by states, for example through taxation, which can either help or hinder MNCs according to the wishes of states. States' power to control tariff and non-tariff barriers is another state-driven reality with which MNCs have to cope and adapt.	NGOs can try to influence states' behaviour with advocacy campaigns but ultimately hold no decision-making power, which rests with states. Access and safe passage for aid or human rights inspections can be blocked at the whim of states.	If states are vigilant to the emergence of violent non-state actors, they can possess more and higher-tech military power than violent non-state actors and, ultimately, defeat them. This would be the sensible, realist foreign policy to adopt in terms of being uncompromising in military campaigns against such insurgencies or terrorist groups.

Realism and the inevitability of conflict

Realists agree that conflict is an important feature of global politics and is the most natural, or usual, state of affairs in global politics. This is because they believe the following:

- States are likely to try to maximise their power and influence, resorting to, or provoking, conflict if necessary.
- States are inherently selfish and are likely to promote their own national interest, even if that means resorting to conflict.
- The world system is anarchical, so there is no authority capable of preventing conflict unless states judge that conflict is not in their interests. For example, international efforts through the UN and Geneva peace talks failed to restrain the various actors from pursuing their perceived interests during the Syrian conflict.
- States put their own security at risk and make conflict more likely when they build up their own military defences to counter a perceived threat. This in turn encourages the opposing state to increase its own security or military infrastructure. This is known as the 'security dilemma'.

Realism and liberalism: order, security and the likelihood of conflict

Realism

- Conflict is an unavoidable feature of global politics.
- Conflict is sometimes necessary, both to defend vital national interests and to increase a state's power and influence.
- Defending internal security and stability is crucial. This is best done through well-defended borders, and clear and enforced laws.
- Every state is potentially a threat to other states.

Liberalism

- Conflict is avoidable and efforts should be made to prevent and reduce conflict.
- IGOs, such as the UN, offer a forum for conflict resolution.
- States being bound together in deep economic cooperation reduces the likelihood of them fighting each other. The EU is a good example of economic cooperation leading to limited conflict (for this it was awarded the Nobel Peace Prize in 2012).

The security dilemma

Realists view global politics as an arena in which states cannot trust each other and cannot reliably predict the actions of other states. In this scenario, states can rely only on themselves for protection against attack. The world is a 'self-help' system where there is no other power that can be relied on to come to states' rescue when things go wrong.

Consequently, all states want to protect themselves against threats from other states and, increasingly, non-state actors.

In this case, states may:

- decide to invest in their military power, by increasing the number of troops, warships or aircraft that they are able to deploy
- keep or acquire nuclear weapons (for example Iran, North Korea). Others may want to acquire new technology to gain a strategic advantage, such as missile-firing drones.

However, other states may see this military build-up as a threat and respond by building up their own military resources or they may even respond with aggression. It is difficult for other states to trust the intentions of states which have built up their military resources, and states will not risk being inferior to another state. The net result is that states can become locked in a pattern of continually building up their security and no state can ever feel safe for long.

The dilemma is that by trying to act defensively, states risk acting aggressively and provoking conflict. But, if states do nothing to protect themselves and enhance their security, they may also invite conflict through apparent weakness. Trying to achieve a non-threatening balance of power (see page 16) may be a more desirable strategy. But this is a precarious process, where states may misread each other's intentions or mistakenly exceed (rather than match) their rival's military resources and become sucked into the security dilemma's downward spiral of increased tension.

One means of avoiding the security dilemma is to agree international treaties to try to deliver a more transparent and verifiable balance of power. For example, the US and Russia have agreed several treaties to gradually decrease their nuclear weapons at similar rates. The most recent (New Strategic Arms Reduction Treaty – or New START) was signed in 2021 and limits the amount of nuclear missiles, warheads and launchers to a specific number for each state. This is a means of delivering greater predictability, backed up by international law, helping both states to avoid the suspicion and misjudgement of the security dilemma. It gives confidence that both sides are reducing their weapons by similar amounts, increasing the chances of a balance of power emerging.

Case study

NATO and Russia tensions

Russian president Vladimir Putin

President Vladimir Putin has repeatedly declared NATO to be a threat to Russian interests. NATO enlargement, now numbering 30 states, has seen the alliance reach Russia's borders with troops deployed in the Baltic states of Lithuania, Latvia and Estonia (formerly in the Soviet Union). Russia has said that the build-up of NATO forces in these countries was not consistent with international law and that Russia's foreign policy had triggered a 'counter-action' from the US and its allies.

With the end of the Cold War in 1991, it might have been expected that relations between Russia and the NATO member states would ease. During the immediate aftermath of the Cold War, with Russia's territory much decreased and its power significantly weakened, NATO expanded to include ten former Soviet Union and Warsaw Pact (the Moscow-led military alliance during the Cold War) states. Some analysts suggest that Western powers missed an opportunity to reassure Russia and to try to influence it to seek greater partnership with its European neighbours. Instead, the conclusion is that NATO and the West decided to expand their power and influence when Russia was at its weakest.

From a Russian perspective, NATO's military build-up is the security dilemma in action. As Russia rebuilt after its defeat in the Cold War, and attempted to regain its power and influence in global politics, so it has increased its military power and influence in its immediate neighbourhood.

Both NATO and Russia remain highly vigilant against potential threats from each other. NATO's Exercise Trident Juncture in 2018 saw 50,000 personnel practise for an Article 5 scenario where an attack on a member state required the bloc to come to the defence of another. For its part, Russia has been taking part in military exercises with China, with troops numbering as many as 300,000. These exercises act as both an opportunity to rehearse and also to demonstrate capability to their opponents.

NATO has, for the most part, weathered the storm of President Trump's open scepticism of the alliance. Faced in 2018 with the first nerve agent attack by Russia on a NATO member in the Salisbury novichok poisonings, the alliance responded by coordinated expulsions of Russian diplomats (the US expelled 60 and closed two embassy outposts in Seattle and San Francisco). Tensions remain high, but responses are carefully measured so as not to escalate tensions.

Balance of power

Given that a key goal of realists is to protect their own security from rival state attacks, it is no surprise that realists are preoccupied with how power is distributed in the global system. Is there one state that is much more powerful than all the others (a unipolar system, see page 254)? Are there lots of states and actors competing for power (a multipolar system, see page 254)? Or are there only two major powers, which are roughly equal to each other, with no other potential rivals (a bipolar system, see page 254)?

Realists believe that a balance of power in a bipolar world order is best for security and that the most stable outcome is for the powerful states to roughly match each other's power. In this scenario, realists believe that the states will balance each other out. This is sometimes called defensive realism, because the idea is to maintain enough power to match the rival state's power, as opposed to maximising state power relentlessly as offensive realists would want. It is a key theory of international relations put forward by Kenneth Waltz in his 1979 book *Theory of International Politics.*

Neither state in a balance of power will want to risk attacking or challenging the other, because they would run the risk of retaliation by a state with similarly threatening military resources to their own. This could lead to the following:

- States may try to balance power by trying to match the military and economic resources of their rival. There may be an arms race, with both states trying to acquire similar amounts of weapons or types of technology.
- Smaller states may try to join alliances with these powerful states. This is known as 'band wagoning' as states jump on the 'bandwagon' of the state they think is most likely to serve their interests.

A world order in which there is a balance of power is not necessarily without risk. There is the chance that states will misread the other's intentions and the security dilemma (see page 115) might emerge, where some believe that when states try to match each other in terms of their military power, they can actually risk provoking the other state by appearing to represent more of a threat.

The most obvious example of a balance of power in global politics was between the US (including its NATO allies) and the Warsaw Pact during the Cold War. With the knowledge that both were equally matched and that a nuclear weapons attack would only result in deadly retaliation, the two states engaged in a nuclear weapons arms race. This concept of mutually assured destruction (MAD) successfully ensured that there was no nuclear confrontation between the US and the Soviet Union during this period. Neither did the two rivals fight each other on the battlefield – both instead engaged in proxy wars using other actors to fight each other (for example, the US arming the mujahideen in Afghanistan to fight the Soviet Union, without actually deploying troops of its own).

It is important to note that balance of power does not necessarily mean a bipolar world order dominated by only two powers. Another way of thinking about balance of power is that states seek 'equilibrium'. So, there may be more than one balance of power in the world order with, say, the US trying to find equilibrium with China and Russia. There may also be regional powers trying to seek a balance of power within a region, such as Saudi Arabia and Iran. This world order of balances of power is more common within the current multipolar distribution of power.

Activity

Using the information provided in this chapter and Box 1.2, what evidence is there that there is a balance of power between China and the US? Base your assessment on:
- their respective military resources and their willingness to use them
- their respective economic power resources
- the extent to which they are seeking to maintain or, rather, maximise their power.

How is this balance of power consistent with a multipolar order in today's global politics?

Box 1.2

China and the US: a balance of power?

Table 1.3 compares the balance of power between China and the US by examining types of power and tactics in response to recent global crises.

Table 1.3 China vs the US: a balance of power?

	China	US
Military power	Annual defence spending of $208 bn (2020), second only to the US. Greatest number of regular armed forces at just over 2 million. Chinese naval power has been growing and modernising steadily; China's navy has a battleship capacity of approximately 350 ships. Its global reach is limited but a first overseas base opened in East Africa in 2017 and the Belt and Road Initiative offers the potential for more.	Annual defence spending of $778 bn (2020). Ranks third behind China and India with 1.3 million regular armed forces. US navy has an impressive 11 aircraft carriers, but fewer battleships overall than China at approximately 293, but arguably US ships are still technologically superior. The US military's global reach surpasses China's, with bases across the world.
Nuclear warheads	Estimated at 320 warheads (2020) and growing. Twelve submarines with nuclear weapons and building more.	Estimated at 5,800 (2020). US stockpiles are decreasing, as a result of arms control treaty agreements with Russia.
Willingness to use military power	China's military power is building within its own region, acting as an increasing counterweight to US military presence especially in the South China Sea. It has been increasing its contribution to UN peacekeeping operations.	Under Presidents Trump and Obama a new era of US reluctance to use military force developed, with a preference for using air power as opposed to 'boots on the ground' military campaigns such as those in Iraq and Afghanistan. In spite of this, US forces still carried out operations in over ten countries between 2010 and 2020 (including Libya, Somalia, Iraq and Syria).
Cyber power	China's cyber power derives from its control of the internet domestically and its powerful commercial telecommunications companies, notably Huawei. President Trump banned US firms from doing business with Huawei, arguing it could be used by China for spying.	With a budget of $17 bn it has impressive offensive and defensive cyber capabilities. In 2019, Huawei accused US agencies of hacking its servers.
Economic power	China's economy has been steadily narrowing the gap with the US. Some forecasters estimate it will overtake the US in 2028–29 as the world's biggest economy. China continues to rank poorly, however, compared to the US on the share of wealth (gross domestic product, GDP) per capita.	Losing ground to China on size of the economy, the US performs much better in terms of wealth as a share of the population with approximately $65,000 GDP per capita compared with approximately $10,500 for China, indicating much higher living standards and less poverty in the US.
IGOs	China has been increasingly using the veto in the UN Security Council since 2007. As well as pledging more action on climate change within the UN system, it has set up its own economic institutions including the Asian Infrastructure Investment Bank (AIIB).	President Trump's 'America first' stance saw the US clash with several IGOs of which it was a founding and, traditionally, leading member – including NATO and the G7.
Conclusion	Rising in military power and increasingly balancing the US within Asia if not globally. China's most impressive feat is that it is on track to overtake the US economically perhaps within a decade. The Belt and Road Initiative will further extend China's power beyond its borders.	Still with unparalleled military experience and global reach and a leading role in key global governance institutions. The Trump presidency has arguably damaged the US role in global leadership. Although its population will remain wealthier for some time, losing its place as the world's richest economy will be a significant reverse.

Activity

Spend some time thinking about the realist viewpoint on global politics.
1 Do you agree that conflict between states is an inevitable, even natural, state of affairs?
2 To what extent was Donald Trump a realist president?
3 Do all states try to become as powerful and influential as possible, or does this only apply to states that are already powerful?

Distinguish between

Realism and liberalism: power

Realism

- The primary goal and motivation of states is to increase their power in order to feel more secure.
- Having more power than other states is important because, in an anarchical world order, states cannot trust each other and cannot rely on other states to help them.
- Hard power threats and the use of force are particularly important power tactics (see page 247) to be able to deploy, as they are most likely to achieve a state's goals.

Liberalism

- The use and accumulation of power, particularly military, can often be counterproductive (the security dilemma, see page 115).

- Military power is not the only form of significant power. Economic power and free-trade links can enable states to become richer, and also more stable and secure. As states become more economically interdependent, the risk of conflict decreases. In this way, economic interdependence makes the entire global system more stable and peaceful.
- When power is shared equally between states it can create stability (the balance of power, see page 16).
- States are aware of the limits of soft power (see page 247), though they may use smart power (see page 249) by combining hard and soft power to achieve their intended outcomes.
- Soft power and smart power are important means by which states can achieve their intended outcomes. They should be the first option, with hard power used only as a last resort.

Liberalism and a cooperative world order

Liberalism is governed principally by the belief that states can, and should, work together, and that international agreements, laws and institutions are both helpful and possible. The liberal viewpoint includes the following:

- States are not the only actors in global politics — a wider range of non-state actors have a positive role to play, including IGOs and NGOs. They can help states become aware of different viewpoints and policy choices, adding to a richness of ideas and debate.
- International law is possible and desirable. Global politics and world order should be based in clearly agreed international rules. These can help to hold states accountable for their actions and ensure that all states conform to basic standards. For example, the Universal Declaration of Human Rights (UDHR) sets out basic principles of human rights that all states should respect.
- A state's primary aim should not merely be to become more powerful, particularly not at the expense of other states. Liberals reject the idea of a zero-sum game, where global politics is a question of one state winning and another losing.
- On the contrary, there is mutual benefit in states cooperating and working together on matters such as security, trade and development. IGOs, such as the EU and the UN, offer clear rules and forums within which cooperation can be organised and deepened.

- Democracy plays a key role in keeping states safe and peaceful. Democratic states are less likely to fight each other.
- International trade binds states together in common interests, making them more dependent on each other and reducing the likelihood of conflict.

The significance of morality and optimism on human nature

Liberalism in global politics shares the optimistic view of human nature of liberal key thinkers studied in Component 1, such as John Stuart Mill. It rejects the pessimistic view of human nature as inherently selfish and leaning always towards conflict, competition and confrontation.

Liberalism in global politics therefore has the following views of morality and human nature:

- Human beings are rational and reasonable and are therefore able to solve problems that occur in global politics if they work together.
- This ability to solve problems rationally means that it is desirable to create dispute resolution forums, such as the United Nations, and to keep working on collective action problems with other states through treaty agreements.
- While optimistic about human nature and its capacity for cooperation, liberals including John Locke agreed that clashes would occur within a 'state of nature', which is the natural order if no rules or government is organised in its place. For this reason, liberals in global politics see a need for international law and human rights protections just as liberals see a need for state structures in national politics.
- Given liberalism's optimism about human nature, liberals see a vital need to protect the human rights of the individual, wherever they may live in the world. When individuals are sufficiently protected from those in power, they are more likely to reach their potential. This is also reflected in the idea of a 'social contract', in which individuals should have certain rights protected as well as responsibilities to abide by the laws of the state.
- In terms of morality, the 'harm principle' applies in global politics just as it should in national politics. It provides a useful guide to striking a balance between freedom of states and freedom of the individual, both of which are important ideas for liberals but need closely defined limits.
- The liberal view of 'foundational equality' is a moral view that individuals are born equal and should have the same opportunities to flourish and achieve their aspirations. In global politics, liberals attach great importance to reducing inequality between states and reducing poverty.
- Democracy offers the best chances for the individual to flourish freely and fairly. Liberals in global politics view a world of democracies to be safest, both for individuals within states and to reduce the likelihood of inter-states conflict. Liberals are suspicious of non-democratic and autocratic states.

Synoptic link

In your study of 1 Political Ideas in Component 1, you learn about the **liberal thinker John Rawls (1921–2002)**. The argument of an 'enabling state' was put forward by Rawls, in which the state actively helps individuals to achieve their social and economic potential. For liberals, this translates into global politics through the global governance structures which aim to reduce poverty, such as the UN's development goals. It also features in international human rights laws which affirm and protect economic and social (also known as 'positive') rights.

Synoptic link

In your study of 1 Political Ideas in Component 1, in **liberalism** you learn about **John Stuart Mill (1806–73)** and the 'harm principle' that the state should not interfere with the freedom of the individual unless that individual is causing harm to others. Similarly, the liberal view in global politics is that individual states should exist in freedom, unless they are harming their citizens. This idea has gained ground in global politics with the adoption of the Responsibility to Protect (also known as R2P) principle that other states should intervene in another state to protect individuals from human rights abuses.

Liberalism, complex interdependence and globalisation

Complex interdependence is the idea that states and their fortunes are inextricably linked. An economic crisis in one state has the potential to impact other states because economies are tied together through trade. A civil war in one state has the potential to impact other states if refugees flee that conflict in fear for their safety. Globalisation is seen as a key factor in increasing these types of links between states and their dependence on each other.

Globalisation can be thought of as increased links between and dependence on states and all other non-state actors in global politics. It has primarily occurred due to improved communications links and technology. Liberals are convinced that globalisation is a reality that needs to be managed through increased cooperation. They believe that greater interconnectedness and cooperation is the direction of travel for global politics.

- **Economic:** much-improved communication and transportation have increased trade between states. There is greater economic interconnectedness because more states are trading with each other as it becomes easier to do so. International economic organisations, such as the WTO (see page 132), have played their part in this expansion of new trade agreements. Developed economies have invested heavily in many developing economies.
- **Political:** political decision making has become increasingly globalised, through the growth in international and regional governmental organisations. The number of political challenges that require a collective response has also increased, including climate change, organised crime, health pandemics (such as the Covid-19 crisis which began in 2020) and global terrorism. The number of international and regional political institutions managing shared interests has increased, as has their membership.
- **Social:** communities that were previously relatively self-contained have become increasingly connected in terms of shared media and culture. Increased global immigration has created much more diverse societies, although some argue that this has led to an erosion of national culture. It has also enabled ideas to travel quickly across borders. For example, the speed with which the Arab Spring spread in 2011 from Tunisia to Egypt and other middle eastern and north African states has been attributed to the power of social media (such as Facebook and Twitter) and satellite news channels (such as Al Jazeera).

An analogy often used to explain **complex interdependence** and liberalism is that of a cobweb. In contrast to the 'billiard ball model' (see page 11), the 'cobweb model' represents the links and dependencies between states rather than the competitive clashes between states of the realist model. If one strand breaks, the cobweb may begin to disintegrate. The cobweb can also grow bigger and stronger, connecting more states in more cooperative relationships.

For example, the US's increasing distancing from and even rejection of liberal institutions (such as withdrawing from the Paris climate change agreement or withdrawing from the World Health Organization) meant that, overall, institutions that bind states together, like a cobweb, were weakened and even broken away from during the Trump presidency. On the other hand, the formation of regional organisations such as the EU or the Association of Southeast Asian Nations (ASEAN)

> **Key term**
>
> **Complex interdependence**
> The idea that states and their fortunes are inextricably linked and that states rely on each other. They also share common threats and challenges, which can only be resolved through collective action.

and their expansion to include new members will strengthen the connections within the cobweb of interconnected states.

The global Covid-19 pandemic which began in 2020 is another example of complex interdependence. A virus which was first discovered in Wuhan province in China quickly spread across many continents due to the multitude of human and travel connections in our globalised and interconnected world. The impact of states closing large parts of their economies as societies went into lockdown caused significant damage to global trade. States relied on pharmaceutical companies in other states for the production of vaccines, leading to considerable challenges in terms of ensuring vaccines were distributed widely and quickly. As the phrase suggests, complex interdependence is complex and global governance institutions need to be robust and flexible to resolve challenges fairly. But, as liberals would have it, states acting alone is not an option.

Just as with the 'billiard ball model', it is important to note that the 'cobweb model' is a way of explaining liberalism and complex interdependence, rather than it being a theory in its own right. Therefore, it is better to refer to the theory as 'liberalism', rather than the 'cobweb model'.

Case study

Complex interdependence and the global financial crisis

In 2008–09, a house price crash sparked a lending crisis in US banks, which spread around the world. The effects were felt in the global banking system, as banks became nervous about taking on risk and stopped lending to each other. In some cases, customers began withdrawing their savings, putting banks under even greater pressure. It led to what has been described as the worst global financial crisis since the Great Depression in the 1930s.

Economic growth slowed across the world and unemployment rose. North America and Europe were particularly severely affected. Economic growth in China slowed. A crisis was sparked in the Eurozone single currency area, as several indebted economies, notably Greece, were unable to borrow from international markets and required other Eurozone member states and the European Central Bank (ECB, see page 128) to bail them out.

The financial crisis fallout dominated UK Prime Minister Gordon Brown's time in office. As part of international efforts to deal with an international crisis, in April 2009 Brown hosted a Group of Twenty (G20, see page 140) summit in London. The meeting resulted in national governments and the IMF agreeing a financial stimulus to inject much-needed funds into the international banking system.

The crisis raised questions of whether or not the international financial system needed tighter regulation and if the IMF could have done more to both prevent and react to the crisis (see Chapter 4).

In April 2009, Gordon Brown hosted a G20 summit in London, as part of international efforts to deal with the global financial crisis

Realism and liberalism: states and sovereignty

Realism

- States remain the primary and most powerful actors in global politics.
- Sovereignty is an absolute concept – it should not be violated, limited or given away, except ...
- ... another state's sovereignty may be infringed upon if one's own national interest requires it. For example, the US's unauthorised 2011 operation to assassinate Osama bin Laden was justified as a necessary incursion into Pakistan's sovereign territory.
- States should be wary of giving up too much sovereignty to IGOs. Powers of veto are a useful means of protecting one's national interests while retaining one's ability to use the IGO as a forum for influencing other states towards one's own desired outcomes.

Liberalism

- States are important actors in global politics but they work within a complex web of interdependence and with other non-state actors, such as IGOs and NGOs, which also have important roles to play.
- Sovereignty exists to be used to a state's advantage, not to be protected in a state of isolationism. This may mean pooling sovereignty with other states in an IGO, such as the EU.
- Another state's sovereignty may be infringed if it is necessary to uphold the values and interests of the international community, for example under the doctrine of the UN Responsibility to Protect (R2P, see page 23) if human rights abuses are taking place.

The anarchical society and society of states theory

At the heart of the division between realism and liberalism is the extent to which order and cooperation can be brought to global politics. Is the world order really completely chaotic and unstable? Can the world order really be completely harmonious and free of conflict? The answer comes somewhere in the middle.

Hedley Bull's important book *The Anarchical Society* (1977) set out to explain the nature of world order in global politics. His theory of the 'anarchical society and society of states' argued that the world order is neither completely anarchical nor are there highly authoritative structures that might be deemed to be a 'world government'. But states, selfish though they are, do find a middle ground of cooperation because they recognise:

- it is in their interests to avoid disorder and chaos and the unrestrained aggression and lack of accountability that would result
- it is not in their interest to give up control and sovereignty to a 'world government'.

The possibilities for order in global politics therefore operate on a spectrum as can be seen in Table 1.4 below. It is important to remember that the 'society of states' is still in many ways anarchical. It is prone to periods of stability and instability. An organisation such as the UN is part of this society of states, but it is only capable of doing what states allow it to do.

In this middle ground of the 'society of states' we can find both the successes and disappointments of global governance. Here, we find the humanitarian interventions that did not take place when, morally, they should have – but states failed to agree it. Here, we find the enlightened self-interest of international treaties and organisations where states agree to work together to solve problems that they share and make the most of opportunities for co-operation.

Table 1.4 Key characteristics of the anarchical society, society of states and world government

Anarchical society	Society of states	World government
No global body with any authority, states acting selfishly and independently.	Convergence of realism and liberalism.	States would surrender all sovereignty to a single global authority.
Frequent clashes between states as they compete for power without any authority or law restraining states' behaviour.	States realise they have common interests and values, and will benefit from working together.	A world government would be an authoritative source of power able to impose order on states.
Hobbesian view of the world order: 'nasty, brutish and short'.	This society is built on diplomacy, 'norms' (informal, accepted practices, e.g. R2P) and rules (international law, treaties, IGOs). Many norms have subsequently become international law (e.g. human rights).	All states would be signed up to international law (they wouldn't even have a choice), which would not be selective or unenforceable.
Security dilemma becomes a key risk in an unstable order where states may miscalculate or misread others' intentions.	This society is formed despite states' selfish, realist principles – these tendencies do not disappear, so the society can be stable or unstable.	This model does not exist, could be said to be utopian or idealism.
		States are not prepared to accept this loss of sovereignty, nor to agree on a body which would have the legitimacy to command global power. This is why it does not exist.

Possibility of harmony and balance

Unlike realists, who believe global politics is naturally prone to conflict and competition, liberals believe there is a possibility that relations between states can be harmonious and balanced. There is no need for states to be continuously competing with one another or clashing. There are three key elements that underpin this potential democracy, the existence of IGOs and international trade.

1 **Democracy:** many analysts note that conflict between democratic states is rare and that democracy acts as an important restraint on states fighting each other. Certainly, governments in democratic states are more accountable to their citizens than in undemocratic states. Usually governments of democratic states have to seek the permission of their national legislature to engage in military action. For example, in 2013 the UK Parliament voted against military action against the Assad regime's chemical weapons programme in Syria. It has become increasingly common – but not compulsory – for the UK Parliament to be consulted before UK armed forces are committed to military action. The refusal of the UK Parliament to support military action was considered to be a factor in the Obama administration later deciding not to put possible military action in Syria to a vote in Congress. Leaders and governments in democratic states also have to bear in mind that military action may be unpopular (particularly if there are large numbers of casualties) and that they may be voted out in elections if this is the case. This is not a concern that leaders of undemocratic states necessarily need to worry about. Liberals argue that these democratic constraints lead to more harmonious relations between states.

2 **IGOs:** liberals believe that IGOs encourage harmony and balance because they provide a means of peaceful dispute resolution between states. The UN Security Council, for example, is a forum in which the most powerful states can take action to resolve and stabilise conflict around the world. While IGOs do not have full authority over states (and states can ignore them, opt out of agreements, or can be locked in gridlock when faced with more complex problems), liberals believe they are the closest possible solution to the dangerous notion of an anarchical system of global politics. They may not resolve every dispute, but they offer a forum to defuse some disputes altogether, reduce tensions in some and keep open the possibility of dialogue in others.

Synoptic link

Socialist political thinkers challenge the view that the liberal notions of economic interdependence and trade have brought harmony and balance. For example, Karl Marx (1818–83) gave rise to a Marxist view of international relations which challenged both realism and liberalism. Marxism sees a global capitalist system which perpetuates inequality and class conflict at international level, just as it does at the national level. This is evidenced by dependency theory and world systems theory (see pages 44 and 149) and Marxism prioritises breaking down structures of international capitalism, with the proletariat in all nations acting together. Socialists also criticise globalisation for its tendency for wealthy elites to accumulate economic and political power. Democratic socialist George Orwell (1903–50) commented that 'in all countries, the poor are more national than the rich', highlighting his view that the rich are better able to take advantage of a globalised society.

3 **Economic interdependence and trade:** liberals believe that the more states are trading with each other, the more they are dependent on each other and the more likely it is that conflict would be mutually harmful. Liberals also believe that free trade in a global system governed by rules has formalised and legitimised the global sharing of resources. Previously, states fought each other for territory and resources, but in modern times, global free trade has offered a peaceful means for states to gain from each other's resources.

These three restraints on conflict are visualised through the Kantian Triangle (see Figure 1.2). Even before IGOs and free trade existed in the sense that we know them today, liberal philosopher Immanuel Kant identified that:

> ... republican constitutions [democratic states], commercial exchange [economic interdependence] and a system of international law would help foster peaceful relations between states.

The Kantian Triangle helps us to understand the relationship between the three core elements and how each:

(a) helps to strengthen the others
(b) contributes towards the overall outcome of a more peaceful status quo

For example:

- Membership of IGOs often helps to build democracy within states. The EU, for example, makes it a requirement for member states to meet certain democratic criteria. Turkey has so far failed to be accepted into the EU, partly because of weaknesses that the EU has identified in its democracy.
- Democratic states offer a more stable base with which other states can trade. They are more transparent and less prone to corruption, which is a factor that puts off potential foreign investors. Democratic states are more likely to be peaceful and stable, making them attractive to foreign investment.
- Many IGOs have been founded to make economic interdependence easier. IGOs such as the EU and ASEAN offer their members a framework within which they can trade with each other freely, based on a commonly agreed set of rules. One state can potentially open up more trade links more quickly with other states through joining a bloc of nations, rather than acting alone.

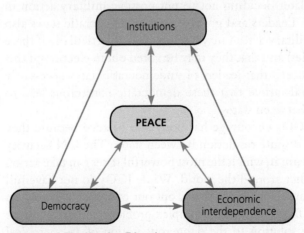

Figure 1.2 The Kantian Triangle

Source: Adapted from Russett, B. & Oneal, J. (2001) 'International Systems: Vicious Circles and Virtuous Circles', *Triangulating Peace*, Norton.

Does democracy contribute to peace?

Yes

- Wars must be seen as legitimate, and governments that initiate conflict are held accountable for the legitimacy, success and failure of military conflicts they initiate.
- Democratic governments need to win elections and are unlikely to enter into conflict if it does not have domestic support.
- Intra-state conflict, or civil war, is less common in states that are internally democratic. Peaceful dispute resolution forums such as democratic parliaments offer an outlet for debate and representation. The rise in the number of democratic states has been accompanied by a fall in global conflict (both civil wars and inter-state conflicts).
- Democratic states are more likely to be plugged into international systems of cooperation (as opposed to 'rogue states') with interdependent relationships with other states through trade or membership of IGOs. These mutually dependent relationships would be mutually harmed by conflict, and tend to discourage confrontation.

No

- During the 2003 Iraq War, two of the most well-respected democratic states (the US with the backing of the UK, commonly known as 'the cradle of democracy') initiated wars that were later declared to have been illegal.
- Both President George W. Bush (in 2004) and Prime Minister Tony Blair (in 2005) won elections despite signs of early difficulty in the Afghanistan and Iraq Wars, though both conflicts became significantly more difficult and unpopular after these elections.
- A democratic decision to avoid conflict may not result in peace. Many suggest that the UK and the US should have initiated military action against President Assad in 2013 and that failure to act also has consequences (specifically, the US's failure to take action against Assad's use of chemical weapons, something that President Obama had called a 'red line').
- No democracy is perfect, so some states that appear democratic may offer insufficient safeguards against conflict or poor decision making. The UK Parliament voted to invade Iraq in 2003 because the government and the opposition agreed on the need for conflict.

⚙ Evaluation prompt: It may seem difficult to argue against democracy contributing to peace, but is there other evidence to suggest that democracies can use their legitimacy to push for conflict?

President Donald Trump: challenging the liberal world order?

In his inauguration speech in 2017, President Donald Trump pledged to put 'America first', promising to prioritise American interests where previous administrations had 'made other countries rich, while the wealth, strength and confidence of our country has dissipated over the horizon'. He pledged to cut overseas aid and military spending, strengthen borders and affirmed 'the right of all nations to put their nations first'.

So, did the Trump presidency challenge the liberal world order?

Military power

Under Trump, the US did not initiate any major new conflicts. The US continued to use air power to bomb ISIL in Iraq and Syria (which had started under President Obama), and declared a quick 'victory' against ISIL, withdrawing troops in 2018. The US did not engage in any new conflict in the middle east. The Syrian regime's further use of chemical weapons was met with two sets of missile strikes but no wider military campaign. In general, this was a quiet presidency in terms of willingness to use military power, judging it was not in the national interest to embroil the US in costly conflict after protracted wars in Iraq and Afghanistan.

Climate change

As promised during his election campaign, Trump announced that he was withdrawing the US from the Paris Climate Change Agreement in 2017, with this finally taking effect in 2020. The US was the only state to sign and then withdraw from the wide-ranging agreement.

→

International organisations

Trump's speech at the UN General Assembly in 2019 was an outright rejection of globalism, declaring that the US 'rejects the ideology of globalism, we embrace the doctrine of patriotism. Responsible nations must defend against threats to sovereignty ... from global governance'. Trump also repeatedly confronted NATO members for not meeting their 2% of GDP budget contributions. At the height of the Covid-19 pandemic, Trump withdrew the US from the World Health Organization, cutting significant funding in the process.

Iran nuclear deal

In 2018, the US withdrew from the Joint Comprehensive Plan of Action (JCPOA), which Obama had signed with the other UNSC permanent members and Germany in 2015. The deal reversed years of economic sanctions in return for closer monitoring and reductions to Iran's nuclear programme.

Unpredictability

A hallmark of Trump's foreign policy was its unpredictability and a tendency to deviate from tougher stances with allies against key opponents, such as Russia and North Korea. In 2018, alongside President Putin at a press conference, Trump disagreed with his own intelligence agencies when he said he could see no reason why Russian intelligence would have interfered in the 2016 US elections. Also in 2018, Trump broke with years of US policy by agreeing to meet North Korean leader Kim Jong-un without preconditions in talks that ultimately collapsed with no agreement.

Conclusion

This brief snapshot of the four years of foreign policy under President Trump demonstrates a significant willingness to challenge the liberal world order that the US had spent decades establishing and leading. The US's traditional allies found the US an unreliable and unpredictable partner. Several key agreements and institutions were abandoned as they did not fit the national interest. Trump was successful in not engaging the US in any new overseas conflicts – defending his perception of the US national interest.

President Donald Trump was inaugurated as the 45th President of the US on 20 January 2017

While realists believe that states should act only when their national interest requires it, there is a strand of liberal thinking that believes states should act regardless of their national interest. The media and political leaders often employ the phrase 'international community' to describe a coordinated response to a crisis, often referring to what the international community believes or what it 'should do'. It is a notoriously vague expression, with no clear definition. Who is the 'international community'? Do those using this term have a defined group of states in mind?

For liberals, the idea of an 'international community' does exist as an aspiration to work towards. They believe states share interests, values and attitudes. For example, human rights apply to all human beings regardless of where they live in the world. Consequently, liberals believe that human rights are worth defending, since they are a globally shared value and interest. Therefore, if a state abuses basic human rights, the 'international community' should do something to prevent the abuse. Why? Because preventing human rights abuses is in the global interest – if human rights abuses go unchecked, the argument runs, the entire global system of human rights would be weakened.

Of course, realists disagree that there are shared global attitudes and values. They believe that attitudes, interests and values come primarily from states themselves and are not always aligned.

Tony Blair's Chicago speech (1999)

The idea of an international community with shared interests and values to be defended was underlined in a key speech given by former UK Prime Minister Tony Blair, in Chicago in 1999. Blair put forward the idea of 'liberal interventionism' and was acting on a liberal analysis of global politics. The speech came during the NATO-led military intervention in Kosovo, in former Yugoslavia, where Serbian forces' expulsion of ethnic Albanians had prompted a humanitarian crisis. Blair argued that such an international community did exist, stating that 'just as within domestic politics, the notion of community – the belief that partnership and cooperation are essential to advance self-interest – needs to find an international echo'. Blair argued that national interest and international interest were increasingly difficult to separate. Military intervention in another state should not be decided purely on whether there was a threat from that state to the outside world, but on the basis of the nature of the threat to the state's own domestic population. Put simply, other states should intervene for humanitarian reasons, in order to prevent human suffering in its own right, rather than for narrow self-interest alone.

The UN and the Responsibility to Protect

In 2005, the UN General Assembly also gave its backing to the idea that states had a responsibility to intervene in other states in order to prevent human suffering. The failure of UN peacekeepers to prevent a genocide from taking place in the African state of Rwanda in 1994 prompted the UN's concern.

There was also agreement that the legitimacy of intervening in other states to protect lives needed to be made clearer. The Responsibility to Protect doctrine, agreed at the UN World Summit that year, confirmed that states had a 'responsibility to protect' (see page 23) the populations of other states if they were suffering, or were likely to suffer, serious harm.

Military action would be justified by several core principles of liberalism:

- The purpose of military action was solely to protect civilians, rather than to pursue narrow self-interest.
- The state/s could only intervene once it/they had made every effort to resolve the situation through non-military means, such as diplomacy and negotiation.
- Intervention could take place only if a UNSC Resolution authorised it (thereby making the intervention legitimate in the eyes of international law).
- The military action must be proportionate, must be likely to succeed and must not make the situation worse.

Liberalism and the likelihood of global governance

Liberals disagree that global politics is naturally without order and instead believe that global governance is possible and desirable. They do not necessarily agree that a form of world government, with full authority to force states to comply, is possible. But they point to the huge number of IGOs that have been created since the end of the Second World War as evidence that a more informal type of governance can indeed work.

Activity

Spend some time thinking about the liberal viewpoint on global politics.

1 Do you agree that states and their fortunes are inextricably linked? What evidence is there for this idea of complex interdependence?

2 What evidence can you find from recent events in global politics that a sense of 'international community' exists?

Impact and growth of intergovernmental organisations

IGOs are a feature of the post–Second World War global order. Before 1945, very few IGOs existed. Apart from the League of Nations, states worked together by agreeing ad hoc treaties with a flexible, rather than fixed, number of partner states.

After the horrors of the Second World War, during which nationalism had once again given rise to global conflict, world leaders believed that security and stability would be best delivered if states tried to find more ways of working together in a more formal and sustained manner.

Several of the world's now most established and influential IGOs emerged during the time immediately after the end of the Second World War. The UN, the IMF and the World Bank were all founded between 1944 and 1945. NATO was founded in 1949, as divisions between the Soviet Union and the US and its allies deepened.

Since the Second World War, international organisations:

- have increased in number
- have increased in the range of policy areas with which they are involved (for example, military, economic, trade and development objectives)
- have seen the number of states joining them (member states) increase
- have prompted the founding of other regional organisations (for example, ASEAN, the AU and the Gulf Cooperation Council). (See Table 1.5 for further information.)

Table 1.5 Post-Second World War IGOs and their impact

Date founded	Organisation and purpose	Impact
1945	The United Nations (UN) was founded to advance international peace and security, human and economic development.	The UN expanded from 52 to 193 states. The UN Security Council (UNSC) has authorised military action, sanctions and peacekeeping missions around the world. The UN agreed and drove forward the most comprehensive and coordinated set of international development targets in the Millennium Development Goals (MDGs) and Sustainable Development Goals (SDGs). It is now considered the most authoritative and legitimate global political institution.
1945	The International Monetary Fund (IMF), founded at the Bretton Woods Conference (see page 123), aimed to create institutions that would stabilise and organise the global economy after the Second World War. A key objective was to move the global economy towards more free trade and greater economic cooperation.	The IMF's role has expanded to make it a key institution in resolving financial crises that have an impact on more than one state, in order to minimise their impact on the global economy. It played an important role in the international response to the 2008 global financial crisis (see Chapter 4).
1944	The World Bank was also founded at the Bretton Woods Conference. Member states contribute to a fund, which provides loans to developing countries.	The World Bank has focused its work increasingly on international development.
1949	The North Atlantic Treaty Organization (NATO) was founded as a collective military alliance to act as a counterweight to the Soviet Union.	NATO has grown from 12 to 30 signatory states. It combines defence of western Europe, including securing the airspace of its Baltic members, with operations outside western Europe, such as in Afghanistan.

→

Date founded	Organisation and purpose	Impact
1957	The European Community (EC) (subsequently the EU) was founded to bind states that had been at the centre of two world wars in an economic and political union.	The EU has spent over 60 years widening its membership (2004 saw the biggest expansion to ten former Soviet states) and deepening the policies on which its members cooperate (notably adopting the euro in 2000) through successive treaties. After four years negotiating its withdrawal and future relationship with the EU, in 2020 the UK became the first EU member state to leave.
1963	The African Union (AU) (established 2001 and launched 2002) was founded as the Organisation of African Unity in 1963 to act as a political and economic union for all African states.	The AU does not compare with the EU in terms of depth of integration and impact on state sovereignty. Instead, it has remained a forum through which African states can speak with greater influence on the world stage. For example, in 2013, the AU threatened to withdraw as a bloc from the founding treaty of the ICC. The AU, with UN funding and training, has carried out mostly successful peacekeeping operations in Somalia and Darfur, Sudan.
1967	The Association of Southeast Asian Nations (ASEAN) was founded primarily to promote economic cooperation and development in southeast Asia.	ASEAN has enabled southeast Asian nations, each economically powerful in its own right, to form a much more powerful bloc in a region dominated by China's economic might. Trade and connectivity between ASEAN states have been made easier. In 2002, the ASEAN bloc negotiated a free-trade agreement with China, which, together, is worth 10% of the global economy, giving the states greater bargaining power and influence than if they had negotiated alone.

Distinguish between

Realism and liberalism: intergovernmental organisations

Realism

- IGOs are useful as a means of enhancing state power and sovereignty, and conducting business with other states, if it is possible to get outcomes that are the same as a state's national interest.
- They are not useful, and are even dangerous, if it is not possible to achieve one's national interest.
- They are very dangerous and undesirable if the IGO has powers to compel states to do things. States should be able to veto decisions that do not fit with their national interest.

Liberalism

- IGOs are a key part of establishing a world order governed by rules. They are the most powerful and authoritative source of international law. They are also likely to be the most comprehensive and even universal source of international law if IGOs have lots of members.
- They offer states a means of peaceful dispute resolution (for example, through the UN). They provide a forum for discussion and negotiation.
- They offer states a means of deepening economic integration and free trade (for example, through the EU and ASEAN).
- They offer states the opportunity to work together and be more powerful than if they acted alone (for example, through NATO).

Debate

Does conflict or cooperation dominate global politics?

Conflict

- Conflict continues to exist in all its forms.
- Civil wars are increasing. The Syrian civil war, which began in 2011, has seen over half a million killed and led to 12 million refugees. Non-state actors, such as the militant organisations Boko Haram, Al-Shabaab and ISIL, have been engaged in struggles against state governments and have seized state territory.
- Conflict between states has reduced significantly but continues, as seen with Russia and Ukraine since 2014. Some states, such as Iran and Saudi Arabia, are not directly fighting each other, but instead engage in proxy wars, for example in Syria and Yemen.
- Since the 9/11 terror attacks in the US, non-state actors, such as al-Qaeda and ISIL, have created significant conflict.

Cooperation

- The number of international and regional governmental organisations has increased, as has the number of states joining them. These bodies offer a means of peaceful dispute resolution.
- States cooperate deeply and are extremely interdependent on matters of trade, which have expanded with the forces of economic globalisation, decreasing regulation, improved technology and communications.
- Extensive international efforts have been made to resolve shared challenges, ranging from climate change (see Chapter 6) to the global financial crisis (see Chapter 4) and global poverty (see Chapter 4). States have chosen to work through IGOs and also through more informal means, such as ad hoc summits like the 2015 Paris Climate Change Conference and groups such as the G7 and G20.

⚙ Evaluation prompt: This question is quite a close call, but consider the overall trends as well as a snapshot of the current situation. Which seems to have been rising and which decreasing?

Case study

President Joe Biden: a return to liberalism?

The election of Joe Biden as US president in 2020 was hailed by many analysts as a return to liberalism in US foreign policy. In the 46th President's words, 'America is back' – a clear rejection of President Trump's 'America first' rhetoric. But what did Biden promise to do, both in tone and concrete policies?

The US rejoined the Paris Climate Agreement just hours after Biden's inauguration. Highly experienced former Secretary of State John Kerry was appointed as Special Envoy for Climate Change, bringing the US back to the forefront of UN climate negotiations.

Biden pledged to re-enter the so-called Iran nuclear deal, along with the remainder of the UNSC permanent members and the European Union, that President Obama agreed in 2015.

Biden has returned to a more confrontational stance with Russia, criticising the arrest of opposition leader Alexei Navalny. In relation to China, Biden has maintained a tough stance on issues such as political freedom in Hong Kong and independent status for Taiwan. In August 2021, Biden followed through on his promise to end America's 'forever wars' and leave Afghanistan, the United States' longest war. However,

he was criticised for doing so by his European allies who felt the US was abandoning cooperation and forsaking the Afghan government, a government they had built since 2001. This move was also interpreted by many as an attempt to move away from fighting terrorism to confronting an assertive China.

President Joe Biden in the Oval Office, January 2021

Activity

Review the key foreign policy actions of President Biden.

1   To what extent is there evidence of a return to liberalism?
2   To what extent is there evidence of maintaining a realist approach?
3   Is Biden proving more or less successful than Trump in foreign policy?

How do liberalism and realism explain recent developments since 2000?

You should always be on the lookout for realism and liberalism influencing events, decisions, successes and failures in the topics that follow. These are covered in more depth in each chapter, but some key issues to look out for in each topic are set out here.

Table 1.6 Realism and liberalism: summary of impact on each topic

	Realism	Liberalism
The state and globalisation (see Chapter 2)	Some might argue that states are now increasingly sidelined in a globalised world and have lost their importance in a crowded space of other actors (such as MNCs, NGOs and IGOs).	Globalisation and the increasing interdependence between states have increased the number of shared challenges that states have to solve together and opportunities they can exploit together.
Global governance: political and economic (see Chapters 3 and 4)	Organisations such as the UN are only as productive as their member states want them to be. In the absence of world government, there is always a risk that nation-states will pursue the national rather than international interest. The hurried withdrawal of US troops from Afghanistan for example left the country in a humanitarian crisis.	The number of political global governance institutions has been growing and the international community has become more focused on reducing poverty, through the Millennium Development Goals and Sustainable Development Goals – indicating liberalism is alive and well?
Global governance: human rights and environmental (see Chapters 5 and 6)	The most significant barrier to human rights remains nation-states which are given almost complete responsibility for protection and enforcement. On climate change, it is not yet clear that enough states view taking action as central to their national interest.	International institutions and laws to protect human rights have increased in recent decades, and the Responsibility to Protect principle offers hope that liberal and moral imperatives will be considered before the national interest.
Power and developments (see Chapter 7)	With a return to a more multipolar world order, global politics is seeing more competition and uncertainty among significant powers (US, China and Russia).	The number of liberal, democratic states increased in the latter half of the twentieth century, but is now under pressure with democracy in some states regressing and becoming less secure.
Regionalism and the EU (see Chapter 8)	There are some signs that realism is creeping into regionalism. The UK's exit from the European Union in 2020 and the US renegotiation of the North American Free Trade Agreement (NAFTA) indicate that states are pushing back against the compromises of sovereignty these organisations involve.	The EU is a significant liberal institution that has been growing in membership and powers, the deepest form of cooperation that might be seen in global politics. Other regional organisations are growing and some are cooperating more easily than might be possible at a global level.

What you should know

Having read this chapter you should have knowledge and understanding of the following:

→ The realist theory of global politics: with its focus on the national interest, a pessimistic view of human nature and the need for states to maximise their power in a global order that is dominated by states and is anarchical.

→ The liberal theory of global politics: with its focus on the international interest, an optimistic view of human nature and the need for states to cooperate through intergovernmental organisations in order to bring order and security to global politics.

→ The key divisions between liberals and realists on fundamental ideas and elements of global politics. These include: power, different ideas on human nature and how it drives states' actions, the likelihood of conflict, the nature of the world order and the impact of IGOs.

→ The nature of our world order: is it truly anarchical or is there scope for cooperation and the establishment of a 'society of states' where international law and norms of behaviour are observed, even if it does lack a world government that has full authority over nation-states?

→ The existence of realism and liberalism throughout your study of global politics. This chapter is the starting point for identifying realist or liberal behaviours or obstacles in all the topics that follow. These theories will help you to understand the successes and failures of global politics.

Further reading

Bridges, W. (2021) 'Realism and Liberalism – comparative theories in global politics', *Politics Review*, Vol. 30, 2020–21, No. 3, February.

Bull, H. (1977) *The Anarchical Society: A Study of Order in World Politics*. Columbia University Press.

Cunliffe, C. (2020) *The New Twenty Years' Crisis: A Critique of International Relations, 1999–2019*. McGill-Queen's University Press.

Marshall, T. (2021) *The Power of Geography: Ten Maps That Reveal the Future of Our World*. Elliott & Thompson.

Reus-Smit, C. (2020) *International Relations: A Very Short Introduction*. Oxford University Press.

Practice questions

Section B

1 Analyse the divisions regarding human nature and morality that exist between realists and liberals. [12 marks]

2 Analyse the differences between the realist concept of the security dilemma and the liberal concept of complex interdependence. [12 marks]

3 Analyse the divisions regarding power that exist between realists and liberals. [12 marks]

4 Analyse how realists and liberals explain the likelihood of conflict. [12 marks]

5 Analyse the divisions regarding the impact of IGOs between realists and liberals. [12 marks]

6 Analyse the differences between the realist concept of international anarchy and the liberal concept of global governance. [12 marks]

The state and globalisation

Learning outcomes

By the end of the chapter you should understand:

→ both the meaning and the significance of the Westphalian nation-state-centred approach to global politics

→ how to define economic globalisation and explain why and in what ways free-trade economic liberalism has impacted the world

→ why economic globalisation is so controversial

→ the ways in which political globalisation has impacted the centrality of the state in global affairs

→ the meaning of 'cultural globalisation' and the way in which it has challenged the nation-state's cultural hegemony

→ why the impact of political and cultural globalisation has been limited

→ contrasting approaches to the impact of globalisation on international relations

→ to what extent globalisation has successfully challenged the fundamental importance of the state in global relations

Getting you started

'The report of my death was an exaggeration'

In 1992, the prominent Japanese-American academic Francis Fukuyama published *The End of History and the Last Man*. Fukuyama argued that war would eventually become a thing of the past due to the rise of liberal democracies and their unwillingness to engage in conflict with each other. He indicated that the close connectivity between democracies could evolve to challenge the primacy of the state and that the European Union (EU) could provide a model for the future relationship between nations. As states worked more closely together, supranational governance would increasingly challenge the absolute authority of the **nation-state**.

Fukuyama provided no time frame for what he termed the 'end of history', but the book's publication, just as the Cold War was ending, persuaded many that Fukuyama was providing a clear insight into what the world of the future could look like. In 1989, the Berlin Wall was torn down, leading to the reunification of Germany as a liberal democracy. Elsewhere, in eastern Europe communist dictatorships were overthrown with extraordinary rapidity to be quickly replaced with democratically elected governments. In 1991, the Soviet Union collapsed and a year later, in Maastricht, the leaders of the European Economic Community (EEC) pledged themselves to a common citizenship and currency. Significantly, the community was renamed a union. The popularity of the economic liberal principles of the Washington Consensus further encouraged trust and cooperation between states.

> ### Key term
>
> **Nation-state** An autonomous political organisation defined by the common ties of a shared nationality and citizenship based upon a recognisable culture manifested through, for example, a common ancestry and language. State borders broadly match a relatively homogenous culture.

Even in China it seemed that free-market reforms would so empower a new middle class that they would demand democratic reforms that would challenge communist rule.

However, history has not moved in the way many liberals predicted. The internet has provided unheard-of opportunities for the integration of peoples across the world through shared online experiences. Global free trade has created greater global wealth than ever before. And yet the internet has also facilitated insularity. The television network RT (formerly Russia Today), for example, deploys its global outreach not to break down barriers but to provide Russian nationalism with a global audience. Fox News is deeply partisan. In 2020 the United Kingdom fully reclaimed its **sovereignty** from the European Union, while EU member states like Hungary and Poland have undergone a dramatic rise in nationalist sentiment. In the US the Trump administration (2017–2021) won huge support among large swathes of Americans with its commitment to put the national interests of the US first. In 2021 emerging powers such as China, India, Turkey and Brazil all had nationalist leaders who boasted of their nation's cultural uniqueness.

Mark Twain is alleged to have remarked on reading his obituary in the newspaper that 'the report of my death was an exaggeration'. The same may be true today of the nation-state. This chapter will therefore explore to what extent **globalisation**, in its diverse forms, has really transformed the world. Are we moving into what has been called the 'post-sovereign state' world or does the nation-state remain the key player in international relations?

Francis Fukuyama, who in the 1990s optimistically predicted the global triumph of liberal democracy and the 'end of history'

The state: nation-state and national sovereignty

Characteristics of a nation-state and national sovereignty

Since the seventeenth century, the state has increasingly become the main player in global relations, providing the foundation for domestic peace and international relations. According to the Dutch scholar Hugo Grotius, the state is 'a complete association of free men, joined together for the enjoyment of rights and for their common interest', while both Jean Bodin and Thomas Hobbes argued that adherence to the authority of the sovereign state provided the most effective way of protecting society from mankind's potential for anarchy. Bodin lived through the St Bartholomew's Day Massacre in 1572, when vengeful Catholics murdered French Protestants in their thousands as royal governance broke down. Hobbes had first-hand experience of the destruction wrought by the English Civil War. Both appreciated that a powerful sovereign state, with the ability to control its subjects, provided the best way of ensuring peace and stability.

The Westphalian state system

The Peace of Westphalia in 1648, which ended the Thirty Years' War, is particularly important in the development of the principle of state sovereignty. It finally ended the Holy Roman Emperor's claim to possess sovereign authority over virtually independent German states. This meant that each individual state would be sovereign

Key terms

Sovereignty The principle of absolute and unlimited power and the defining characteristic of a state. National sovereignty means that a state has absolute authority over all its citizens within its borders.

Globalisation Process by which the world has become so interconnected that a variety of non-state actors, global trends and events challenge territorial borders and state sovereignty.

over its own internal affairs and no other state or, supposedly, superior body could intervene within its borders. By establishing the principle of the territorial integrity of sovereign states, Westphalia also defined the theory of the sovereign equality of states as follows:

- No state has the legal right to intervene in the sovereign affairs of another state.
- All states, whatever their size, possess the same legal right to independence.

The nation-state in the twentieth century

During the twentieth century, Westphalian principles dominated across the globe. In his Fourteen Points (1918), US president Woodrow Wilson established the principle that nation-state sovereignty should be founded upon the right of self-determination based on a shared ethnic heritage. This led to the creation of new states such as Austria, Czechoslovakia, Hungary and Poland after the First World War.

The Montevideo Convention (1933) determined that a sovereign state must possess:

- a defined territory
- a permanent population
- a viable government
- the capacity to enter into diplomatic relations with other states.

A state would possess a monopoly of law-making powers within its borders, while outside interference could not legally change a state's borders.

Post-Second World War decolonisation

Following the end of the Second World War, as the old colonial empires were dismantled, new independent nation-states were established across the developing world. Then, from 1989 to 1991, as communism collapsed throughout eastern Europe, new nation-states, including the 15 constituent parts of the Soviet Union, were established based upon Wilsonian principles of self-determination.

The UN and state sovereignty

The nation-state as a political community bound together by citizenship, nationality and culture therefore became an increasingly powerful force in global politics. It provided states, old and new, with a common identity and determined the main structures by which international relations are still conducted to this day. Article 2 of Chapter 1 of the UN Charter recognises this fact by noting that 'The Organization is based on the principle of the sovereign equality of all its Members'.

No state, however powerful, has the right to intervene in the affairs of another state, since all states can claim the same right to determine policy within their own borders without fear of outside interference. All states can claim equal territorial integrity. Loyalty to the state and the use of its economic, political and military power to achieve its objectives underpin the realist interpretation of global affairs. States act out of self-interest in order to achieve the best possible outcome for themselves.

The legitimacy of a nation-state also derives from its acceptance as a nation-state by other nation-states. Palestinians, Kurds and Catalans, for example, all claim nation-statehood. However, since the UN does not accept their claims, they remain unrecognised.

Synoptic link

Respect for Westphalian principles of state sovereignty is a core element of realism which is covered in Chapter 1.

The process of globalisation

The widening and deepening of interconnectedness and interdependence

Globalisation has had a dramatic impact on the influence of the state. It has created a complex web of **interconnectedness** that challenges the state's sole authority to make decisions affecting the lives of its citizens. This process of growing interconnectedness has manifested economically, financially, politically, technologically and culturally. It has created a world in which nation-states cannot insulate themselves from what is happening elsewhere in the world.

The significance of economic and financial globalisation

Since the end of the Cold War, economic liberalism, often referred to as the 'Washington Consensus', has led to the dominance of free-market principles in global trade. This means that:

- states need to establish the sort of conditions that global investors find attractive, which includes policies of low corporate taxation and light regulation, since too much taxation and/or bureaucracy is likely to repel investment
- any state that seeks to act in defiance of **economic globalisation** will risk loss of investment and capital flight.

Governments can tailor the macro-economic decisions which they make to encourage foreign business. Ireland, for example, achieved striking economic success by dramatically reducing corporation taxation to 12.5% in order to encourage foreign companies to locate there. Apple, consequently, moved its European, middle eastern and African centre of operations to Dublin.

The globalisation of markets

The globalisation of financial markets, facilitated by the instantaneous communication the internet provides, means that global events can affect a state's economic wellbeing. This is seen in a number of ways:

- In 2007–8, the sub-prime mortgage crisis in the US, precipitated by the bankruptcy of US bank Lehman Brothers, provoked a global banking crisis. This led to stock markets throughout the world plummeting and a sudden and prolonged global recession.
- The global impact of the Covid-19 pandemic which began in 2020 impacted every economy in the world. As a result, global merchandise trade declined by approximately 9%.

The influence of non-state actors

Global interconnectedness has also been advanced through the rise of myriad **non-state actors**. As the problems that the world faces become more complex, from climate change to international terrorism, a 'collective security dilemma' is created, which states cannot resolve on their own. Therefore, they increasingly need to work together in intergovernmental organisations (IGOs) in order to try to resolve problems.

Key terms

Interconnectedness
The way in which states become more linked through their shared membership of intergovernmental and regional organisations. Through cooperation, states no longer approach global relations in terms of maximising their own power.

Economic globalisation
Process by which states across the world become more closely connected and interdependent according to the principles of free trade, which leads to the greater transnational flow of goods, services and capital.

Non-state actors
Entities, such as NGOs, IGOs, globally influential individuals, transnational corporations and even criminal and terrorist networks, that wield significant influence over global affairs.

For example, in 2009, the G20 responded to the global financial crisis by implementing a global strategy of reflation and continued commitment to free trade. The Intergovernmental Panel on Climate Change (IPCC) provides an international forum in which recommendations for action are agreed. The International Atomic Energy Agency is designed to ensure that its signatory states abide by the terms of the Treaty on the Non-Proliferation of Nuclear Weapons (NPT).

The influence of intergovernmental organisations

The Bretton Woods Institutions
These are:

- the World Bank
- the International Monetary Fund (IMF)
- the World Trade Organization (WTO)

All of them impact state sovereignty by advancing global free markets and free trade. The structural adjustment programmes (SAPs) that the World Bank and IMF implement are founded on the core premise that economic growth is maximised through free-market reforms and free trade. Governments should encourage foreign investment by adopting economic policies conducive to foreign investment.

In 2021, the WTO had 164 states as members, including both China (2001) and Russia (2012). The WTO is closely associated with globalisation, since it encourages free trade by seeking to persuade nations to reduce import tariffs. It tries to resolve trade disputes between countries and provides a forum for the resolution of trade wars. Economic globalisation has created a neoliberal consensus that free trade creates greater wealth and so all states should engage with this economic model in order to achieve prosperity.

The United Nations
The UN is the most significant of all IGOs. Established in 1945, it is based on the liberal principle that the international community needs to work together to resolve 'collective dilemmas'. Nation-states do not sacrifice their sovereignty as members of the UN. However, by cooperating, nation-states create a more peaceful and prosperous world that they each benefit from.

UN agencies include the following:

- **World Health Organization (WHO):** responsible for the eradication of smallpox and the near total elimination of polio. The WHO also spearheads and coordinates the global response to epidemics such as Ebola and Sars. Its most serious challenge has been responding to the Covid-19 virus, which killed 1.8 million people in 2020.
- **International Atomic Energy Agency (IAEA):** monitors states' fulfilment of the terms of the Treaty on the Non-Proliferation of Nuclear Weapons (1968).
- **United Nations High Commission for Refugees (UNHCR):** the world's most important tool in seeking to alleviate the plight of refugees. In 2020, there were 80 million refugees worldwide: the highest number since the end of the Second World War.

- **United Nations International Children's Fund (UNICEF):** spearheads childhood immunisation programmes in the developing world and globally promotes the rights of the child.
- **World Food Programme (WFP):** the world's biggest humanitarian relief organisation, which provided food relief, income support and free school meals and supported small farmers in 88 countries in the developing world countries in 2020. In recognition of its work it was awarded the Nobel Peace Prize (2020).

The UN has also been responsible for:

- the Millennium (2000–15) and Sustainable Development Goals (2015–30), which have made considerable progress in reducing poverty. The MDGs included eradicating extreme poverty and hunger, achieving universal primary education, reducing child mortality and combating HIV/AIDS, malaria and other diseases. The SDGs built on the MDGs, also including goals such as gender equality, improving sustainability and pushing for action on climate change.
- climate change conferences, which are organised by the UN Framework Convention on Climate Change (UNFCCC) and provide an opportunity for states and non-state actors to work together on limiting carbon emissions and reducing the impact of climate change.

Topic link

The work of the United Nations is fully covered in Chapter 5.

Regional organisations

Many regional organisations have been established in order to take advantage of the opportunities globalisation offers. These include the following.

- **1957:** EEC (the EU since 1993)
- **1967:** ASEAN
- **1991:** Mercosur
- **1994:** NAFTA. This was renegotiated as the United States–Mexico–Canada Agreement (USMCA) by the Trump administration and formally replaced NAFTA in 2020.

These regional IGOs function as mini-free trade areas, encouraging trade and specialisation within them. This cooperation provides these regions with greater influence in international trade. By establishing regional customs unions, or 'fortresses', this also protects them from the rigours of global competition. In the process, economic (and in the case of the EU considerable political) sovereignty is pooled. This means that nation-states accept limits on what their governments can do so that they can achieve a greater collective benefit.

Topic link

Regionalism is fully covered in Chapter 8.

The influence of non-governmental organisations

NGOs can have considerable soft-power influence on the development of international political dialogue by enriching the political debate. They include pressure groups such as:

- Amnesty International
- Greenpeace/Friends of the Earth
- Human Rights Watch.

Internationally respected individuals can also have a huge impact on the way in which global policy develops. The urgency with which the international community is now having to address the issue of climate change has been encouraged by Swedish environmentalist Greta Thunberg, whose principled stance in demanding immediate action on climate change has been called the 'Greta effect'. The famous naturalist David Attenborough has further helped to make climate change a global priority for world leaders, discussing the environment with President Obama in 2015 and presenting his powerful witness statement on the impact of climate change in the documentary 'A Life on Our Planet' (2020). At COP26 in Glasgow he also addressed world leaders, urging them to 'turn tragedy into triumph' and so 'rewrite our story'.

Activity

Vanessa Nakate

Although the first, Greta Thunberg is by no means the only young climate activist who is now shaping world opinion. In Uganda, Vanessa Nakate has established Youth for Future Africa and the Rise Up Climate Movement. Especially concerned with the future of the Congolese rainforest, Nakate is an increasingly powerful voice on social media, raising awareness of the way in which climate change is already impacting Africa.

1 Research other examples of young people raising awareness of climate change.
2 Research examples of business leaders, entrepreneurs and philanthropists who are contributing to the debate on climate change.
3 Do you think that the internet has meaningfully expanded the global political debate about climate change beyond the leaders of nation-states?

The internet's impact

The internet has transformed global communication, impacting states across the world. It has led to the instantaneous trading of shares and movement of capital, creating a global marketplace for business and commerce. It has also created a global marketplace of ideas, in which people anywhere in the world are able to access a limitless supply of information and ideas. The consumer opportunities the internet offers would have been unthinkable even in recent memory.

These technological advances have created the potential for a more global culture in which the same goods, fashions and ideas penetrate anywhere in the world. Coca-Cola, Microsoft, Google, Apple and Facebook are among the most instantly recognisable brands in the world.

Activity

Fridays for Future

Fridays for Future is an online global environmental movement which coordinates international protests and action to encourage urgent action on climate change. On September 24 2021, for example, it organised a climate change strike with support across the world.

● Research examples of other social movements which have created global momentum for progressive change.
● In what ways can the internet be used to encourage the extremism and violence which divides rather than unites people?
● On balance, do you think the internet has been a force for good in terms of encouraging global understanding, unity and cooperation?

Key terms

Political globalisation
Process by which the nation-state no longer solely takes decisions affecting its citizens. Instead, decisions are more polycentric, involving a variety of non-state actors (e.g. IGOs, NGOs and regional organisations).

Global governance The way in which the nation-state increasingly shares decision making with non-state actors, such as IGOs, NGOs and MNCs. Global collective dilemmas have made the principle of global governance increasingly important in international relations.

The internet has transformed global communication, trade and technology

In terms of the spread of ideas, the internet has made it more difficult for states to control the information its citizens receive. Facebook and Al Jazeera played an important role in provoking the 2010–12 Arab Spring by undermining states' ability to control the flow of information to their people. The internet also provides a powerful platform for social movements to determine the global debate. The murder of George Floyd in police custody in the US in 2020 provoked an international response from supporters of Black Lives Matter, making racism a powerful topic of debate especially in Western democracies.

Distinguish between

Economic and political globalisation

Economic globalisation

- Economic globalisation is the process by which the world's economy becomes more closely connected. This leads to the greater transnational flow of goods, services and capital.
- A greater global commitment to free trade and free markets has encouraged this connectivity. This is closely associated with the principles of the Washington Consensus advanced by the Bretton Woods Institutions (the World Bank, IMF and WTO).
- Technological advances, including greater capacity for transportation and instantaneous communication via the internet, have further encouraged economic globalisation, linking most countries in the world into a global supply chain.
- Economic globalisation is closely associated with liberalism. This derives from nineteenth-century liberal thought, which regarded free trade as a moral good, since it encourages cooperation between states. According to liberalism, free trade between nations reduces the risk of war between states.

Political globalisation

- **Political globalisation** refers to the way in which nation-states and non-state actors work together in IGOs such as the United Nations, the World Trade Organization and the International Criminal Court to achieve collective outcomes.
- Political globalisation creates the potential for **global governance** based upon increasing inter-reactions among states and non-state actors.
- Since states still value domestic political hegemony, political globalisation has not penetrated as deeply as economic globalisation.

To what extent does globalisation address and resolve contemporary issues?

The contemporary world faces numerous challenges, such as poverty, climate change, terrorism and extremism, and the role of globalisation in resolving such problems has proved extremely controversial. Some political commentators regard globalisation as part of the solution, while for others it is actually part of the problem.

Poverty

In what ways has economic globalisation reduced poverty?

Supporters of globalisation argue that it has done more than anything else in history to address and resolve the problem of global poverty.

Convergence between the Global North and South

The Brandt Reports in 1980 and 1983 first coined the term 'the North/South divide'. It highlights the economic and social divisions between the developed world (the Global North) and the developing world (the Global South). According to this definition, high living standards, high wages and industrial productivity are mostly to be found in the northern hemisphere. Poverty, low wages, agriculture and structural disadvantage are mostly concentrated in the southern hemisphere.

Supporters of economic globalisation argue that free-trade liberalism has done more than anything else in history to encourage convergence between the Global North and the Global South by creating new opportunities for manufacturing in the developing world. As a result of greater trade than ever between countries, gross world production has dramatically increased, as the following figures show.

- **2000:** US$33,895.94 billion
- **2019:** US$87,552.44 billion.

Consequently, the number of people living in extreme poverty has dramatically decreased, as people across the world gain higher-paid jobs in manufacturing and service-based industries and have access to cheaper mass-produced food and medical equipment. According to the World Bank, the numbers living in extreme poverty (calculated at less than US$1.90 a day) dropped:

- **1980:** 36% of the world's population
- **2019:** 9.2% of the world's population.

As a result of the enhanced trading opportunities that free trade creates, developing countries have been able to break into global markets and use their comparative advantage in cheap labour in order to lift millions of their citizens out of extreme poverty.

Tariffs (protectionism) may seem to provide an immediate answer to domestic prosperity by protecting producers from foreign competition. This means that governments put a tax on foreign imported goods to make them less attractive to domestic consumers. However, this can also encourage domestic producers to charge higher prices in a protected environment. In contrast, free trade encourages countries to specialise in what they produce most cheaply and abandon those sectors in which they lack comparative advantage. As a result, producers are able to take advantage of the opportunities provided by a global marketplace to maximise the potential of their natural resources. Also, global competition requires producers to produce as efficiently as possible, so benefiting consumers by reducing the cost of goods.

The relative success of the Millennium Development Goals (MDGs) can, to a great extent, be attributed to the way in which globalisation has lifted more people out of poverty than ever before in history. By opening up their markets to foreign investment, developing countries have often been able to climb the development ladder to prosperity. In the process, this has significantly altered the global balance of power, with emerging countries, such as China and India, playing an increasingly assertive role in global politics.

- China has used its enormous supply of cheap labour to manufacture low-cost goods, which it sells globally. In 2019, exports from China amounted to US$2.5 trillion, making it the biggest exporting country in the world.
- In 2020, according to the IMF, South Korea had the world's tenth biggest GDP (gross domestic product), specialising in computers, cars and wireless telecommunications equipment. Its companies, including Hyundai, Kia and Samsung, have achieved global brand recognition. In the 1970s the economies of North and South Korea were roughly equal. However, North Korea's ideological commitment to Juche (self-sufficiency) in comparison to South Korea's engagement in global free trade means that its GDP in 2019 was 54 times smaller than that of South Korea.
- Since the 1950s, Taiwan has focused on export markets. Initially, this was in cheap toys and textiles. The capital this created was then used to diversify into more high-price goods. Taiwan is now a high-income country specialising in one of the world's most advanced information technology sectors.
- Vietnam is increasingly focusing on the development of its world export market, specialising in low-cost manufacturing such as footwear and textiles. The EU/Vietnam free-trade agreement (2020) is likely to further boost Vietnam's export market.

Many African countries have also been able to take advantage of new trading opportunities by concentrating on those sectors in which they possess comparative advantage:

- Botswana (diamonds)
- Côte d'Ivoire (cocoa, coffee, palm oil)
- Ethiopia (coffee)
- Ghana (gold, cocoa and oil)
- Kenya (tea).

The population of Africa is also expected to rise from 1.4 billion in 2020 to 1.7 billion in 2030. As a result of this, major companies are increasingly moving their operations to Africa in order to take advantage of its youthful labour market and relatively cheap labour costs. In contrast, as emerging economies in Asia become wealthier so their labour costs increase, making them a less attractive prospect for transnational corporations to open factories in.

- Renault, Peugeot and Volkswagen are moving more of their car production to African plants.
- Toyota manufactures cars in Kenya and South Africa.
- In 2019, Microsoft opened its first Africa Development Centre in Nairobi, Kenya.

Coffee is one of Ethiopia's main exports

China has been especially quick to appreciate the value of the cheap outsourcing of labour in Africa's new urban centres. According to a report by McKinsey in 2017, there were at least 10,000 Chinese companies operating in Africa. These include Chinese mobile phone companies SIMI, which now has a plant in Uganda, and Transsion, which is manufacturing in Ethiopia. By 2020, China had also opened 25 industrial parks in Africa, including the Hawassa Park in Ethiopia which employs 30,000 people.

Globalisation and consumers

Globalisation has also driven down the cost of consumer goods, providing most people in the world with the opportunity to own the sort of sophisticated material possessions that were once confined to only the very wealthiest. In 2020, 45% of the world's population owned a smartphone, with the world's cheapest smartphone, the Freedom 251, launched on the Indian market in 2016 for less than US$3.50.

Globalisation and ideas

Globalisation encourages the international dispersal of ideas, introducing people in different parts of the world to new ways of making products, doing business and innovating. This further benefits people by providing them with access to new commodities and job opportunities in new growth sectors offering higher rates of pay. This is an argument which the economist Johan Norberg explores in *Open* (2020), in which he contrasts the stagnation of closed economies with the progress which globalisation encourages.

Breaking out of the poverty cycle

The employment opportunities that economic globalisation creates also provide people in the developing world with the chance to break out of a cycle of rural poverty. Protected economies stagnate, since markets are restricted, and a lack of competition encourages complacency and inefficiency. Jobs in factories may not, of course, seem very attractive, but they can provide the opportunity for people, for the first time, to enjoy a regular wage, have the potential for career development and accumulate the capital necessary to give their children a better education. As the economist Paul Collier remarks in *The Bottom Billion* (2007): 'Globalisation provides virtually infinite possibilities of expansion ... this expansion creates jobs, especially for youth.'

In what ways has economic globalisation entrenched poverty?

World systems (dependency) theory

Globalisation sceptics, such as the Marxist Immanuel Wallerstein in his 'world systems' theory, argue that globalisation locks developing states into permanent dependency status. This is because if they open their borders to trade too early, the 'dumping' of cheap manufactured products on them means they become 'dependent' on cheap foreign imports and so never develop their own industries. This can be termed 'neocolonialism', since developing countries are condemned to a peripheral status in global trade by core states in the developed world. Developing countries therefore end up providing markets and a workforce for globally dominant MNCs, without developing their own business interests.

The Cambridge economist Ha-Joon Chang suggests that developing countries should embrace globalisation only when they have achieved a sufficient stage of development as to be able to withstand foreign competition and exploit globalisation to their advantage. Indeed, he notes in support of this argument that the US only abandoned Alexander Hamilton's model of subsidies and tariffs when it was strong enough to compete on a level playing field with existing industrial giants like the United Kingdom.

Greater inequality

Critics of economic globalisation argue that although globalisation has created greater wealth than ever before, it has also had dramatically negative consequences. Too often the wealth that is generated through global free trade is concentrated in the hands of the elite. This dramatically increases the gap between the rich and the poor. For example, although China has dramatically increased in wealth since it embraced globalisation, it has also become a much more unequal society, with a huge gap in income and life opportunities between urban and rural areas. It is a similar story in India where in 2019 1% of the population earned 21% of total income compared to just 11% in 1990, the year before India began to open its markets.

Globalisation may be raising all boats, but it is not raising all boats equally. Amy Chua in *World on Fire* (2002) has argued that by obviously concentrating wealth in the hands of a very small number of individuals, resentment and dissatisfaction are created among the majority who, although they may be becoming practically better off, do not feel as though they are better off. This undermines social cohesion and can encourage the rise of destabilising political movements.

The problem is also not confined to the developing world. From 1989 to 2016, the income gap between the poorest and wealthiest households in the US more than doubled. Strikingly, too, the number of middle-income families declined from 61% in 1971 to 51% in 2019. The anger and resentment this has encouraged among working-class and middle-class voters who feel as though they are being excluded from the 'American Dream' provided one of the key reasons for the election of Donald Trump in 2016 and his continued strong support in the 2020 US presidential election.

Case study

Poorer but happier?

The Gini coefficient measures the extent of inequality within a state. Zero represents perfect equality and one represents perfect inequality. The higher the level of income inequality, the higher the number. Critics of economic globalisation suggest that although it increases wealth, it fails to share the wealth fairly. This increasing divide between the rich and the poor can dangerously destabilise society by fuelling resentment.

In the US income inequality has significantly increased from 0.43 in 1990 to 0.48 in 2020. This may help to explain the rise of populist politicians such as Donald Trump, whose support has often come from those who feel that they are being left behind by globalisation. According to President Biden, this is a problem which has to be addressed since, 'When we have income inequality as large as we have in the US today, it brews and ferments political discord and basic revolution.'

However, for right-wing politicians like former UK prime minister Margaret Thatcher, income inequality does not matter, so long as everyone is getting wealthier as a result of free-market reforms. In her last Prime Minister's Question Time in November 1990, the Liberal Democrat MP Simon Hughes asked Thatcher if she regretted that the gap between rich and poor had considerably increased in the UK since 1979. Her reply was unequivocal:

> What the honourable member is saying is that he would rather that the poor were poorer, provided that the rich were less rich. So long as the gap is smaller, they would rather have the poor poorer. You do not create wealth and opportunity that way. You do not create a property-owning democracy that way.

A race to the bottom?

As global capitalism is based upon the maximisation of profit, so it suits the interests of international business to seek the lowest costs at which to do business. This can create a 'race to the bottom', as states compete to attract business by keeping regulations as minimal as possible.

Chinese companies in particular are alleged to have very low standards of corporate social responsibility and to exploit workers in the developing world. Human Rights Watch has accused Chinese mining firms in Africa of countenancing appalling human rights abuses. According to anti-globalisers, globalisation gives too much power to MNCs, which are undemocratic, unaccountable and driven only by profit. It also undermines the ability of the state to protect its own citizens from exploitation. In this way, globalisation takes real power from the people and gives it to MNC directors, who too often wield defining influence over governments, especially in the developing world.

Economic globalisation has even been called a form of violence against the poor through the exploitation of their cheap labour, while MNCs weaken the industrial rights that over generations have been built up to protect people. The way in which global capitalism is driven by profit also means that human rights abuses can be ignored if they interfere with the demands of the market. For example, a coalition of over 180 human rights groups have accused China of putting Uighur

Activity

Use the case study above to answer the following questions.

1 In which nation-states has income inequality increased most in recent years?

2 To what extent do you think that this has been due to the impact of economic globalisation?

3 Do you agree with Margaret Thatcher that growing income inequality does not matter?

Muslims in Xinjiang in forced labour camps where many manufacture cotton. However, since China is the world's biggest supplier of cotton and cotton is vital to the garment trade, many global companies continue to source the bulk of their cotton from China, especially as it is so difficult to determine where in China the cotton comes from.

Activity

'The unacceptable face of capitalism'

In recent years a number of shocking incidents have shown how developing countries can 'cut corners' in order to attract business. For example, 1,129 employees at the Rana Plaza garment factory in Bangladesh were killed when it collapsed in 2013 due to inadequate building regulations. The factory manufactured low-cost garments for the world market, including brands such as Benetton, Monsoon Accessorize, Primark and Walmart. Even though employers had discovered cracks in the building, employees were ordered to carry on working as usual.

Critics claim, too, that MNCs too often fail to adequately investigate the conditions in which their products are being manufactured in the developing world. In 2019 a night-time fire in a Delhi factory manufacturing bags killed 43 workers who slept at the factory where they worked. Since leading clothing brands often sub-contract, this further blurs lines of accountability, making it difficult to ensure that working conditions are monitored effectively.

1 Research other examples of poor and unsafe working conditions in the developing world.
2 In which countries are conditions the worst?
3 To what extent do you think that Western consumers should boycott brands manufactured in countries in which factory workers are often exploited?

Topic link

The Bretton Woods Institutions (the World Bank, IMF and WTO) represent global economic governance and are covered in greater detail in Chapter 4.

Democratic deficit

Economic globalisation gives too much power to intergovernmental bodies such as the IMF, World Bank and the WTO, which are severely lacking in democratic accountability. Too often the free-market/free-trade reforms these agencies encourage damage the interests of the poorest, and yet there are no democratic means of opposing them. For example, IMF and World Bank structural adjustment programmes often require cuts in public spending which impact most negatively on the poorest in society. Austerity was imposed on Greece by the IMF in 2010 in order to try to resolve its debt crisis. Although it created massive popular unrest, the government had no option but to accept the terms of the agreement. Critics also claim that the way in which WTO agreements are made without reference to workers' rights severely undermines the ability of labour unions to protect the rights of their workers.

Destruction of local cultures and the environment

MNCs' success in reducing labour costs and prices can lead to the destruction of traditional local industries, such as rice in Ghana, groundnuts in Sierra Leone or small-scale agriculture in Jamaica. In terms of cost-efficiency, this is economically sound. However, opening up local markets to global competition, as the IMF, World Bank and WTO advocate, can have an appalling social cost. Sudden global challenges to small-scale industry and agriculture lead to the breakdown of communities and the disruption of vulnerable local economies which can encourage crime as traditional hierarchical structures lose their authority.

Foreign competition and the reduction of government subsidies can lead to the destruction of local businesses such as the rice paddy fields of Ghana

The materialism that globalisation encourages also undermines traditional cultural observances. The spread of factories throughout the developing world breaks up families, as young people head for big cities in search of work. In China, a spate of suicides among lonely young workers at Foxconn factories demonstrates how such 'proletarianisation' can have devastating consequences.

MNCs have also been accused of abusing the environment and showing little responsibility towards indigenous cultures. For example, a report by the United Nations (2011) estimated that it will take at least 30 years for the pollution caused by Shell in the Niger Delta to be cleaned up. The way, too, in which economic globalisation encourages a 'throw-away' global consumer culture is having a disastrous impact on the planet's sustainability. In 2020, it was estimated that every year 12.7 million tonnes of plastic waste enter the sea, dramatically reducing its ability to sustain the ecosphere.

Lack of job security

Since global capitalism seeks the cheapest workforce, it can undermine the long-term job security of workers around the world. For example, Chinese firms are increasingly moving operations to lower-cost Africa and Vietnam. In the

2016 US presidential election, both Bernie Sanders and Donald Trump generated massive vocal support among blue-collar workers who felt that they were losing their future to cheaper factories in China and Mexico. In his 2017 inaugural speech, Trump asserted that global competition had created 'carnage' in the US's manufacturing heartlands as 'one by one, the factories shuttered and left our shores, with not even a thought about the millions of American workers left behind'.

Anti-globalisation resentment is also likely to have encouraged some of the extreme nationalistic attitudes deployed towards the EU during the UK's 2016 referendum. Especially among the working class, there was a strong conviction that Brexit would stop the free flow of goods, capital and labour that threatened job security.

Debate

Does economic globalisation resolve the issue of global poverty?

Yes

- Developing countries attract investment by engaging in free trade, so allowing them to break out of a cycle of subsistence agriculture.
- Nation-states use their 'comparative advantage' within a global market, so creating limitless opportunities for expansion.
- Developing countries have an incentive to provide a better-trained and educated workforce in order to attract investment.
- Global capital flows encourage the rise of a job-creating entrepreneurial class.
- Globalisation reduces the global cost of imports, enabling the world's poorest to purchase subsistence and consumer goods more cheaply.
- The internet facilitates global investment and the spread of new knowledge-skills, so creating a commercial environment from which no country needs to be excluded.
- MNCs outsource employment to countries with the lowest labour costs, creating diversification in developing countries that export raw materials and/or manufacture products.
- There has been a dramatic decrease in levels of global poverty since developing countries have engaged in globalisation.
- There is greater convergence between the GDP of the Global North and the Global South.
- The MDGs have been largely successful due to the effect of economic globalisation.

No

- Economic globalisation creates a 'race to the bottom', as governments reduce costs by limiting workers' rights through organised commercial violence against workers.
- Proletarianisation leads to the disintegration of communities, with a corresponding rise in crime.
- Job security in both the developed and developing worlds is threatened, as businesses move production in order to take advantage of the lowest-cost environment in which to produce.
- Social harmony is undermined as the income gap between rich and poor increases both within and between countries.
- Core states 'dump' cheap manufactured products on peripheral/developing states so that they continue producing raw materials. This ensures that they remain in a state of neocolonial dependency (Prebisch–Singer hypothesis), trapping them in low levels of development.
- Global capitalism is volatile, encouraging crises such as the sub-prime mortgage recession of 2007–09 and the euro crisis. Instability threatens stable socioeconomic progress in states.

Evaluation prompt: This is a controversial question which requires a balanced approach. Make sure therefore that your answer is guided by the evidence rather than prejudice. For example, what has happened to life expectancy in the developing world since 1990? How might this guide your conclusion?

Case study

The Dell Theory of Conflict Resolution or the Thucydides Trap?

During the nineteenth century, liberal economists and politicians were keen to point out the close connection between free trade (economic globalisation) and peace. British liberals such as John Bright, Richard Cobden and William Gladstone viewed free trade not only as an economic good but as a moral imperative, according to the principle that 'if goods do not cross borders, armies will'. More recently, Thomas Friedman, in his Dell Theory of Conflict Resolution, has argued that not only does economic globalisation encourage greater global prosperity, it also greatly reduces the risk of conflict between nation-states. This is because such a complex web of economic interconnectedness is established between states that it would be irrational for any state to go to war with another in the same supply chain. The US's and China's reliance on each other for both trade and foreign investment has therefore created such a symbiotic relationship that it would be self-defeating for them to go to war with each other.

However, this theory does not take into account the way in which economic globalisation has made China so powerful that it may choose to challenge the US's hegemonic dominance. According to the Greek historian, Thucydides, the Peloponnesian War broke out because the dominant power, Sparta, was not prepared to tolerate the challenge which Athens represented. The American political scientist, Graham Allison, has coined the term the Thucydides Trap to denote a situation in which an existing hegemon will fight to maintain its dominance against an aspiring hegemon. He warns that the relationship between the US and China today is not dissimilar to that which existed between Sparta and Athens.

Activity

Use the case study above to answer the following questions.
1 Niall Ferguson, a British historian, has coined the term Chimerica to denote the economic relationship between China and the US. In what ways does the theory of Chimerica suggest that conflict between them would be irrational and so unlikely?
2 Explain the concept of power transition. Why do realists argue that it is so destabilising in global relations? Do you think it represents the current relationship between China and the US?
3 Does the evidence suggest that relations between the US and China have deteriorated or improved as a result of economic globalisation?

Human rights

In what ways has international law advanced human rights?
Respect for the rule of law provides the basis for liberal democracy within a nation-state. In the same way, the acceptance of international law is a prerequisite for adherence to a global standard of human rights.

The state as the source of civil liberties
Westphalian principles of non-interventionism enshrine the concept that states determine civil liberties. This means that the cultural heritage of the nation-state influences the rights that its citizens enjoy. Realists support this interpretation, arguing that it is the sole right of national communities to decide these rights. Not only does the diversity of cultural traditions throughout the world justify this, but it also encourages global stability by making states the moral arbiters of what occurs within their borders. This removes any legal justification for outside powers destabilising sovereignty.

Topic link

The extent to which a global culture of human rights protection can ever be achieved is covered in Chapter 5.

The rise of international human rights-based law

Liberals claim that human rights are universal rather than relative. There is such a thing as a global community and there are certain human rights that, by virtue of our common humanity, we all possess. In 1948, the UN, responding to the horrors of the Second World War, issued the Universal Declaration of Human Rights (UDHR). This established certain human freedoms that all human beings have a right to enjoy. The UDHR recognises 'the inherent dignity' and 'equal and inalienable rights of all members of the human family' as 'the foundation of freedom, justice and peace in the world'. It also sets out the core civil, political, social and religious rights that we should all enjoy, whomever we are and wherever we live.

The UDHR does not represent hard international law, since states are not bound to obey it. However, it possesses great moral persuasive power and provides a standard of human rights accountability by which the international community can judge states. Human Rights Watch, for example, uses the UDHR to measure the extent to which governments abuse the rights of their citizens.

The 1950 European Convention on Human Rights (ECHR) also dates from the aftermath of the Second World War. The convention enumerates what rights European citizens may claim by virtue of their humanity rather than by means of their national citizenship. It also established the European Court of Human Rights which all 47 member states of the Council of Europe are signatories to.

The ECHR has established a powerful standard of human rights, which has greatly impacted the development of European domestic law. The ECtHR's rulings on member states are binding (although they are not enforceable). In a number of significant cases, European states have changed their domestic laws to conform to ECtHR rulings:

- In 1981, after the Royal Ulster Constabulary questioned Jeff Dudgeon about his sexual preferences, the ECtHR declared that Northern Ireland's criminalisation of homosexual acts was in violation of the ECHR. Consequently, in 1982, Northern Ireland's domestic law was altered to decriminalise male homosexual sex.
- In 1999, the ECtHR ruled in *Smith and Grady v the UK* that the dismissal of two gay men from the Royal Navy on the grounds of their homosexuality was in breach of their right to a private life. As a result of the ruling, the UK recognised the equal rights of gay people to serve in the UK military.

ECHR judgments have been especially important, too, in encouraging the principles of the rule of law in countries which do not have a history of liberal democracy:

- In 2005 in the case of *I.I. v Bulgaria* the ECtHR ruled that a suspect had been illegally held in prison in unacceptable conditions without his case being properly examined. Consequently, legislation was enacted to limit the circumstances when detention without charge is allowed.
- In 2007 in the case of *Baczkowski and Others v Poland*, the ECtHR stated that the mayor of Warsaw had acted illegally when he refused to allow a march because it included supporters of LGBT groups. As a result, Poland enacted legislation to better protect the freedom to protest.
- The rise of more authoritarian governments in Turkey and Russia, as well as in EU member states such as Poland and Hungary, further demonstrates the ongoing

importance of the ECHR since it provides plaintiffs with the opportunity to achieve justice beyond the confines of the nation-state.

- In 2020, the ECtHR demanded that the Turkish government release Kurdish opposition leader Selahattin Demirtas who was imprisoned following the failed military coup in 2016. In a powerful criticism of the way in which the Erdoğan government has limited democracy, the court stated that Demirtas' detention without trial had 'merely been cover for an ulterior political purpose, which was a matter of indisputable gravity for democracy'.
- In 2021, ECtHR began to investigate claims that the Polish government has put so much political pressure on the judiciary that the separation of powers is breached, so undermining the rule of law in Poland.

The New World Order

The ending of the Cold War, an ideological conflict that had divided the world since the end of the Second World War, provided further impetus for the development of a universal standard of human rights. Dramatic steps were also being taken to resolve seemingly intractable conflicts, such as those in Northern Ireland, Palestine and South Africa. Such optimism was reinforced in 1993, when the UN General Assembly voted unanimously to establish the post of a UN High Commissioner for Human Rights. Globally influential political figures, such as former UN secretary-general Kofi Annan, South African president Nelson Mandela, US president Bill Clinton and UK Prime Minister Tony Blair, also focused the world's attention on human rights as an issue of defining importance in international relations.

Instant news

The internet's globalisation of information has also meant that human rights abuses can be instantly publicised, so that atrocities captured on mobile phones can be flashed around the world in seconds. Global pressure groups, such as Human Rights Watch and Amnesty International, have further raised the profile of human rights abuses. The UN's failure to intervene during the Rwandan genocide in 1994 and its hesitancy over how to react to the Bosnian Civil War (1991–95) also heightened the sense that the global community could and must do more to enforce an international standard of human rights.

UN war crimes tribunals and the International Criminal Court

In the 1990s, several international courts were established to try war crimes. In 1993, the UN Security Council (UNSC) established the International Criminal Tribunal for the former Yugoslavia to deal with war crimes that took place during the Balkan conflict. War crimes tribunals to investigate human rights abuses committed in Cambodia, Rwanda and Sierra Leone followed.

In 2002, following the Rome Statute treaty (1998), the International Criminal Court (ICC) was established as a permanent body prepared to try all those (including heads of state) indicted for either war crimes or crimes against humanity. This court, it was hoped, would dramatically increase the influence of human rights-based law by establishing a global consensus that an internationally recognised court could now challenge the Westphalian principles of state sovereignty. By 2021, 123 nation-states had ratified the Rome statute which means that they recognise the authority of the ICC within their own borders. In the first 18 years of its existence (2002–2020) the ICC made eight convictions and four acquittals.

Activity

In 2021, when the opposition leader Alexei Navalny was sentenced to jail, there were demonstrations in his support across Russia. Navalny, having escaped a poisoning with the nerve agent novichok, had become the key figure leading opposition to Putin's rule. Just before his imprisonment he released the film 'Palace for Putin' which within two weeks gained over 100 million views on YouTube. As well as accusing Putin of corruption on a massive scale, in the film Navalny directly accused Putin of ordering his poisoning and called for mass protests against the government on 23 January. The response of the police was often brutal and was live-streamed so that millions in Russia and beyond could watch online.

1 In what ways did the Alexei Nalvany campaign against the Kremlin demonstrate how the internet is changing politics?
2 Research other examples of the internet challenging governments and stimulating new debate.

In what ways has international law failed to advance human rights?

The rival claim of state sovereignty undermines the scope of international human rights justice. The UN's Universal Declaration of Human Rights only amounts to soft persuasive power, while the authority of the European Court of Human Rights and the International Criminal Court requires the cooperation of nation-states to be effective. This means that international human rights-based law only works if nation-states are prepared to make it work. Too often states will decide to pursue their own perceived best interests, confident that they will not be punished if they act in defiance of international law.

The International Criminal Court

The unwillingness of nation-states to accept the ICC's jurisdiction considerably undermines its authority:

- Three (China, Russia and the US) of the permanent five members of the United Nations Security Council have hardly set a good example of liberal internationalism by refusing to accept the ICC's jurisdiction. India is also not a member even though it is an increasingly influential emerging power.
- In 2014, the ICC withdrew its indictment of President Uhuru Kenyatta of Kenya for inciting ethnic violence because of the Kenyan government's failure to cooperate.
- In 2016, Russia withdrew its signature from the Rome Statute when the ICC claimed the country's forces had illegally annexed Crimea.
- In 2019, the Philippines withdrew from the ICC in response to its investigations into whether the government of Rodrigo Duterte had committed large-scale human rights abuses in its campaign against drugs.

> **Topic link**
>
> The way in which realism undermines the cause of global human rights protection is further covered in Chapters 1 and 5.

The European Court of Human Rights

The influence of the ECtHR is limited because member states may 'derogate' from the ECHR during national emergencies. According to Article 15 of the ECHR in these circumstances, member governments may suspend 'in a temporary, limited and supervised manner' ... 'their obligation to secure certain rights and freedoms under the convention'. The UK government did this in 1975 when it claimed that republican internees arrested during Operation Demetrius in Northern Ireland could not appeal their arrest because the government's actions had been a response to a 'public emergency'.

The ECHR also lacks the coercive powers to enforce its judgments on states if they do not obey its rulings:

- In 2015, Russia asserted the primacy of domestic law over the jurisdiction of the ECHR.
- In 2020, the UK government was criticised by the Council of Europe for failing to comply with ECHR judgments that it must reopen cases involving potentially illegal killings by the security forces in Northern Ireland.

The ECtHR has been highly critical of Turkey's suppression of civil liberties. In 2020 it demanded the release of businessman and philanthropist Osman Kavala who had been held in custody without trial since 2017 on the charge of trying to overthrow the government. However, at the end of 2020, Turkey's highest court refused to comply with the ECtHR's judgment.

The problems that the ECtHR and ICC face in establishing a more rules-based approach to global justice demonstrate the continued importance of the state as the final arbiter of human rights. The increased self-assertiveness of nationalist leaders, such as Vladimir Putin in Russia, Recep Erdoğan in Turkey and Xi Jinping in China, suggests that the centrality of the state in determining the rights of its citizens is likely to continue. This illustrates the limitations of international courts of justice, but also their increasing importance in putting forward the case for human rights when liberal internationalism is more vulnerable than at any time since the end of the Cold War.

Debate

Has the advance of globalisation encouraged global human rights protection?

Yes

- As a result of globalisation there is now greater interconnectivity between nation-states, making human rights abuses more difficult to cover up.
- The internet provides immediate evidence of human rights abuses, so providing the opportunity for immediate global condemnation.
- New institutions of political globalisation such as the International Criminal Court provide a global standard of human rights protection.
- Human Rights NGOs such as Human Rights Watch and mass movements like Black Lives Matter operate globally and provide an instantly accessible record of human rights abuses.

No

- Nation-states frequently still ignore international criticism of alleged human rights abuses.
- As globalisation leads to the balance of global power shifting away from Western powers so they are less likely to be able to take a lead in encouraging global human rights protection.
- Globalisation has led to the emergence of China as a powerful force in global politics. Given its poor record on human rights, China's growing influence is not conducive to better human rights protection.
- The way in which economic globalisation can lead to the exploitation of workers can undermine human rights.

Evaluation prompt: Although the internet can expose human rights abuses, the way in which economic globalisation is shifting the global balance of power away from Western powers suggests that human rights are likely to become a less central issue in international relations.

Conflict

In what ways has the international community attempted to resolve conflict?

Post-Cold War idealism

Since the end of the Cold War, the rise of human rights-based international law has led to several humanitarian interventions in order to protect people from war crimes, ethnic cleansing or crimes against humanity. These include:

- Iraq, 1991
- Somalia, 1992
- Bosnia, 1995
- Kosovo, 1999
- Sierra Leone, 2000
- East Timor, 2000
- Libya, 2011.

By the end of April 1999, half of the 2 million residents of Kosovo were refugees or internally displaced people

Following the First Gulf War, in 1991, UN Resolution 688 condemned Saddam Hussein's retribution against Shia and Kurdish rebels. This led to France, the UK and the US establishing 'no-fly zones' within Iraqi airspace to protect Saddam's opponents from his retribution. In 1992, President George H. W. Bush sent US troops into Somalia 'to stop the starvation'. In 1995, as a result of the escalating humanitarian disaster, the North Atlantic Treaty Organization (NATO) intervened against the Bosnian Serbs during the Bosnian Civil War. In 1999, NATO bombed Serbia in order to stop the 'ethnic cleansing' that Serb forces were carrying out in Kosovo, a constituent part of the Serbian state. During this conflict, former prime minister Tony Blair, who had pushed especially hard for military action, defined the principles of this new internationalism in his Chicago speech in which he stated that mass murder could not be 'a purely internal matter'.

Other such humanitarian, rather than geostrategic, interventions were made by the UN to keep the peace in East Timor when it secured independence from Indonesia in 1999. In 2000, the UK forces intervened in Sierra Leone in order to stop the country's slide into civil war.

In 2005, the UN's World Summit committed member states to the Responsibility to Protect (R2P), a global political commitment declaring that sovereignty is conditional upon a nation-state protecting its citizens from 'genocide, war crimes, ethnic cleansing and crimes against humanity'.

The 2011 NATO-led intervention in the Libyan civil war took place in order to fulfil the UN Resolution 1973 to deploy 'all necessary measures' to protect civilians.

> ## Topic link
>
> The justification for humanitarian intervention and the reasons for its mixed success are covered in Chapter 5.

The decline of humanitarian interventionism

When the Cold War ended in 1991, the future seemed to be one of greater global cooperation. States increasingly embraced the sorts of common values that led US president George H. W. Bush to speak of a 'New World Order' based on a global community increasingly working together to resolve the problems it jointly faced. Former UK foreign secretary Douglas Hurd recalls that there were 'no more enemies – just new friends to be made', while 'out went ideology – in came idealism'. Initially, influenced by liberal idealists like Tony Blair and the dominance of Western power, it had seemed as though a determined effort was being made to create an 'empire of the good'. Westphalian principles of state sovereignty would no longer be used to excuse mass murder within states.

Liberals hoped that increasing economic, political and cultural exchanges between states would establish the UN as the ultimate arbiter of peace and war, and that a newfound global respect for human rights would restrain the brutality of dictators. Yet, even during the euphoria of the immediate post-Cold War period, there were unmistakable signs that the influence of the state in determining the treatment of its citizens, together with its relationship with other states and NGOs, was still paramount.

When the Yugoslav Federation broke up in 1991 and the Balkans were plunged into civil war, both the UN and the EU were paralysed by indecision, only hesitantly intervening to ease the suffering without being seen to take sides. In Chechnya, during two brutal wars, Russian forces succeeded in quelling independence at the cost of, some have estimated, 160,000 lives. In Rwanda, 800,000 Tutsis were killed during the 1994 genocide while the UN dithered. In all these cases the global community failed to confront mass killings, since these were going on within states and so, it could be claimed, were outside the jurisdiction of any other body.

Failings of intervention

- In 2003, the US and UK invaded Iraq without the UN's explicit endorsement, primarily in order to achieve geostrategic objectives in the region. The resulting humanitarian disaster, in which some estimates suggest half a million may have died, together with the rise of militant Islamism and the consequent destabilising of the region, further challenged both the justification and the effectiveness of interventionism.
- The limits of interventionism have been further illustrated by the failure in Afghanistan. In spite of almost twenty years of 'nation-building' by Western powers, the Taliban swept into Kabul in August 2021, re-establishing its control of the country.
- Although it helped to topple Colonel Muammar Gaddafi, NATO's 2011 intervention in Libya has left the country in a state of anarchy.

Failures such as these have undermined much of the practical case for humanitarian interventionism. In addition, the conflicting strategic interests and declining trust between China, Russia and the US have further discouraged Western powers from pursuing a human rights-based agenda. Therefore, even though the civil war in Syria has led to an unparalleled humanitarian disaster, Western powers, scarred by failings in Iraq, Afghanistan and Libya, have been wary of fully committing themselves to the overthrow of the Assad government. The way, too, in which Russia and Iran, sensing Western lack of resolve, then militarily intervened in support of their long-time ally President Assad suggests that great power realism may once again be becoming the most important factor in determining international relations.

It is, of course, too early to say that the post-Cold War age of humanitarian intervention is over. In spite of his claim in his inaugural speech that the US would 'not seek to impose our way of life on anyone', the Trump administration twice bombed Syria when it killed civilians with chemical weapons. President Biden's secretary of state, Antony Blinken, has also acknowledged that more should have been done by the administration to stop the killing in Syria: 'It's something that I will take with me for the rest of my days. It's something that I feel very strongly.'

However, memories of what interventions led to in Somalia, Iraq, Afghanistan and Libya have weakened the impetus for humanitarian intervention. The economic impact of Covid-19 has also made large-scale interventions even less attractive. As Donald Rumsfeld, former US secretary of defence, once put it, 'money is a coward'. Perhaps most importantly the shifting balance of world power which has emboldened Russia and China has made it significantly more risky for Western powers to intervene within nation-states for fear of the consequences. It is unlikely, therefore, that the ideals of UN Responsibility to Protect are going to be fulfilled anytime soon.

Case study

Responding to evil

The use of chemical weapons is forbidden by international law in the Chemical Weapons Convention (1997).

However, Syria has built up large stockpiles of chemical weapons. In 2013, the Assad regime struck Ghouta, a rebel-held suburb of Damascus, with chemical weapons. Many civilians including large numbers of children were killed. It was the most lethal use of a chemical weapon since the Iran/Iraq War (1980–1988).

President Obama had announced that the use of chemical weapons in the Syrian conflict would be a 'red line' for the US. However, in spite of his strong language, Obama eventually decided not to launch military strikes. One of his closest allies, David Cameron, had failed to persuade parliament to support military action. Obama was uncertain of the support of Congress and Americans were concerned that the US could be dragged into a new conflict in which it did not have obvious vital strategic interest. He decided to pursue diplomatic means instead.

In 2017, there was another chemical attack, on Khan Shaykhun, and in 2018 on Douma in which many civilians were killed. As a presidential candidate, Donald Trump had refused to become involved in the conflict, stating, 'Assad's a bad guy, but they're all bad guys.' However, on both occasions he targeted Syria with missiles in response to this breach of international law. On the first occasion he acted unilaterally and on the second occasion with the support of France and the United Kingdom.

1   Do you agree that President Obama was right to be cautious about a military response in 2013 given the risk of provoking conflict with Iran and Russia, which closely support Assad?

2   Was President Trump's more aggressive response in 2017 and 2018 justified even though vital American interests in the region were not affected?

3   To what extent do you think the Biden administration (2021–) is taking a more principled and assertive response to human rights violations? Do you agree with its position?

Case study

The Rohingya Muslims and Myanmar

The Rohingya Muslims are denied citizenship in predominately Buddhist Myanmar. According to the United Nations, Myanmar's government shows 'genocidal intent' towards the Rohingya and in 2017 it launched a military campaign against them forcing 700,000 to flee Myanmar, mostly into neighbouring Bangladesh. In 2020, the International Court of Justice (ICJ) ruled that Myanmar must 'take all measures within its power' to ensure that the remaining Rohingya Muslims in Myanmar are protected from genocide.

According to Myanmar's then leader, Aung San Suu Kyi, the international community had no justification for intervening in 'internal armed conflict' and 'if war crimes have been committed by members of Myanmar's Defence Services, they will be prosecuted through our military justice system, in accordance with Myanmar's Constitution'.

Myanmar also has very strong economic, ethnic and diplomatic links with China. It is a member of China's Belt and Road Initiative and just a week before the ICJ's judgment, Chinese President, Xi Jinping, made the first visit to Myanmar of a Chinese leader since 2001 when he signed a memorandum of understanding with Suu Kyi.

1. What are the arguments in favour of outside powers intervening in Myanmar to enforce compliance with the ICJ ruling?
2. Why is humanitarian intervention in Myanmar to protect the human rights of the Rohingya Muslims unlikely?
3. If nothing is done to help the Rohingya Muslims, does this invalidate the whole principle of humanitarian intervention?

In what way has globalisation impacted environmental issues?

Although economic globalisation has lifted millions of people out of poverty in the developing world, the way in which it has done this through large-scale industrialisation has dramatically increased carbon emissions. The way, too, in which people are now living longer and mortality rates among children are being cut because of better standards of living means that the world's population has undergone an unprecedented increase. In 2000 the global population was 6.1 billion and by 2020 it had increased to 7.8 billion. A larger global population will further contribute to increased carbon emissions, which suggests that, paradoxically, the success of economic globalisation in challenging poverty is creating existential problems for the future of humanity.

'Collective dilemma'

The challenge of 'man-made' climate change provides a classic example of a 'collective security dilemma', which can only be resolved if states cooperate in order to lower carbon emissions and so protect the environment. The way in which the members of the UN's IPCC have worked together to highlight the dangers of a rise in global temperature demonstrates that IGOs have a vital part to play in developing a global response to cross-border shared problems. This therefore suggests that political globalisation can play a powerful role in addressing the environmental problems created by economic globalisation.

However, although the IPCC has focused global attention on the risks of climate change, nation-states remain the key players in determining how to respond to this challenge. For example, at the Paris Agreement nation-states themselves decided what their Intended Nationally Determined Contributions (INDC) to carbon reduction would be rather than having them imposed on them.

Significantly, too, the UN possesses no coercive power if states fail to reduce their promised carbon emissions or abandon the Agreement. The Trump administration

(2017–2021) withdrew from the Paris Agreement because it claimed that it would cost the US US$3 trillion and 6.5 million jobs. As the president put it, 'I was elected to represent the citizens of Pittsburgh not Paris.' This demonstrates that even collective dilemmas as fundamental as climate change still depend upon states agreeing to work together for the common good. Even though the Biden administration swiftly rejoined the Paris Agreement in 2021, several countries, including Russia and Australia, have fallen short of the cuts in their carbon emissions which they promised.

> ### Topic link
> The extent to which the global community is effectively responding to climate change is covered in Chapter 6.

To what extent has globalisation created a global monoculture?

'Cultural homogenisation'?

It has been claimed that the spread of a global consumer culture based upon a common adulation of certain products and brands has undermined the significance of national boundaries in determining the culture of a nation-state. The resulting 'cultural homogenisation' of once diverse cultures has created a global monoculture, as the differences between cultures are ironed out. What makes a society, culture or civilisation unique is therefore lost through conformity to certain global cultural norms.

'McWorld'

Cultural globalisation is closely associated with consumerism and the global dominance of certain brands. Author and filmmaker Naomi Klein has referred to this as 'commodity fetishism', whereby we become so obsessed with materialism and brand culture that we undermine the uniqueness of our own culture.

The top five most recognisable brands in the world in 2020 were, in rank order: Apple, Google, Amazon, Microsoft and Coca-Cola, showing how American companies possess huge cultural outreach. People all over the world also define themselves through the designer label clothing they wear such as Nike, Gucci, Adidas, Louis Vuitton and Cartier. A striking example of the global appeal of shopping is that the most popular attraction for Chinese tourists in the UK after Buckingham Palace is now Bicester Shopping Village.

According to the sociologist Benjamin Barber, this has contributed to the dominance of a 'McWorld' culture, in which people all over the world crave the same sort of materialistic fulfilment, enjoy the same sort of entertainment and eat the same sort of Americanised food. In 2020, nine of the ten most successful global restaurant chains in the world, led by Subway, McDonald's and Starbucks, were American.

- In 2020, the biggest restaurant chain in the world was Subway, with almost 43,000 outlets.
- In 2020 there were almost 40,000 McDonald's in the world, employing over 200,000 people.
- The biggest restaurant chain in China is KFC, followed by McDonald's and Burger King.
- In India the dominant fast food restaurant is McDonald's followed by Starbucks.

Key terms

Cultural homogenisation The process by which those characteristics that make the cultures of nation-states different from each other are flattened out, encouraging the establishment of a more uniformly similar global culture.

Monoculture Result of cultural homogenisation, in which the similarities between the lives of people in countries across the world are greater than their differences (also relates to the terms 'Coca-Colonisation', 'McDonaldisation' and 'McWorld').

Cultural globalisation The process by which people anywhere in the world participate in the same homogenised global culture (e.g. food, clothes, entertainment, brands, products), so that our cultural differences become less striking than our cultural similarities.

The 50 most profitable films of all time have all been made in Hollywood and by far the best-selling album of all time is still Michael Jackson's *Thriller* (1982). The American *Game of Thrones* is a global phenomenon and in 2020 Netflix became the biggest entertainment company in the world, streaming to every country in the world apart from China, Ukraine, Syria and North Korea. According to its critics, the global domination of certain brands and a desire to emulate US standards of dress, food and entertainment has led to the dilution of distinct cultures. In its place has been created a bland, shallow and vulgarised faux global culture, which ultimately represents nothing of permanent value.

A global marketplace

However, cultural globalisation also has the potential to provide us with greater choice than ever before, creating a rich global diversity of opportunity rather than a 'one size fits all' experience. Therefore, it could be argued that rather than creating a monoculture, it actually creates a more globally diverse culture, as people anywhere in the world select from a global array of choices. For example:

- The *Harry Potter* books and films have won a global audience for a quintessentially British story. The porcine adventures of British icon *Peppa Pig* have a global following, especially in China where the trailer for 'Peppa Pig Celebrates Chinese New Year' (2019) went viral, gaining 1 billion views.
- Although Netflix is an American company it does not, of course, stream only American films. One of its most popular successes has been the British royal family drama *The Crown*, and it provides a huge number of foreign language films with access to a global market.
- In 2020, the South Korean film *Parasite* became the first foreign language film to win the best picture award at the Oscars.
- In 2021, the South Korean TV show *Squid Game* became Netflix's biggest debut ever. In just four weeks it gained 111 million viewers in over 80 countries.
- South Korean pop music, known as K-Pop, has become a global craze, with BTS one of the most popular bands in the world in 2020. Significantly the band is rooted in its Korean identity, indicating that global pop music is not simply Western-inspired.
- Bollywood emulates Hollywood's big budget spectacle, while adding to its distinctive Indian glamour and romance. Nollywood (Nigerian cinema) is having an increasing global impact.
- 'Scandinavian noir' fiction and Japanese manga have a world following.
- Mindfulness has achieved its massive global appeal based on Buddhist spirituality, yoga and breathing exercises.
- There are 7,000 Irish-themed pubs globally and St Patrick's Day (17 March) is celebrated with parades across the world. The biggest is in New York and in Montserrat in the Caribbean it is celebrated with a national holiday.
- In 2020, the world's most popular sports were Association Football (soccer), with a global following of 4 billion, followed by cricket with 2.5 billion.
- Real Madrid and Manchester United are two of the most popular sports teams in the world.

Walking down any high street in the UK provides further evidence of the diversity of experience that globalisation offers, with a huge number of different restaurant experiences available. One of the fastest-growing restaurant chains in the world is Nando's, a South African company with Portuguese/Mozambique influences – in 1992 it had one branch in the UK, but by 2020 there were 442. Pret a Manger trades on its continental appeal and yet it was founded in the UK in 1986. Wagamama and YO! Sushi are also British companies offering a Japanese/Asian dining experience. In short, although globalisation can encourage cultural uniformity, it can also provide a richer and more varied cultural experience than ever before. The choice is yours.

Glocalisation

A process known as 'glocalisation' has also enabled local communities to mould global brands to their own culture, which demonstrates that globalisation may be more subtle than mere 'Coca-Colonisation'. The Balti curry was developed in Birmingham and is a mixture of Indian and British–Asian influences. Chicken tikka is similarly British in origin and has frequently topped polls as the UK's favourite food. Famous brands such as McDonald's have adapted to local conditions, serving lobster burgers in Canada and vegetarian burgers to the Hindu market in India. In China, the coffee giant Starbucks has flourished by adapting to local conditions by prioritising popular drinks such as the matcha latte (green tea with frothed milk). The way in which British television programmes like *The Inbetweeners*, *The Office* and *House of Cards* have been adapted for American audiences is a further example of glocalisation.

Debate

Is globalisation another name for Americanisation?

Yes

- The US dominates the world in terms of its cultural outreach: casual American-style clothing is ubiquitous, while US festivals such as Halloween now have a global following, challenging national festivals such as Bonfire Night.
- The biggest box office successes have all been American, led by *Avengers: Endgame* (2019), *Avatar* (2009) and *Titanic* (1997).
- In 2020, nine of the ten restaurants with the biggest global revenue are all American, including Starbucks (1), McDonald's (2) and Subway (3).
- Fortune's ten most admired companies in the world in 2020 were US-led, with Apple first, followed by Amazon (2), Microsoft (3), Walt Disney (4) and Berkshire Hathaway (5).
- American websites are the most visited in the world (2020), led by YouTube (1), Facebook (2), Wikipedia (3), Twitter (4) and Amazon (5).
- According to Coca-Cola, every day, in 200 countries, 1.9 billion of its products are drunk.
- The US is the dominant global economy, representing a quarter of global GDP (US$21.44 trillion) in 2020. The free-trade principles that have dominated the global economy since the end of the Cold War are firmly rooted in the principles of the Washington Consensus.
- The World Bank, IMF and WTO all advance the interests of the Washington Consensus.
- US principles of liberal democracy were hugely influential in leading to the collapse of communist power in Russia and eastern Europe.

No

- The internet has provided new opportunities to challenge the US's cultural outreach. It provides a level playing field on which the US now competes equally with other nation-states, cultures and ideologies.
- The most watched YouTube films are not American. In 2021, South Korea's *Baby Shark Dance* had the highest number of views in history with 9.3 billion. *Masha the Bear* (based on a Russian folk tale) was the eighth with 4.5 billion.
- The most popular global sport is association football, followed by cricket.
- British 'values' have a global appeal through the worldwide popularity of television programmes *Downton Abbey*, *The Crown* and most powerfully the *Harry Potter* books and films.
- Although the US came first in terms of global soft-power influence in 2016 and 2020, its dominance is regularly challenged by France (first place, 2019, 2017) and the UK (first place, 2018).
- Rival news channels such as the BBC, RT and Al Jazeera challenge the influence of CNN.
- The carnage that resulted from the UK-American invasion of Iraq in 2003, including detention at Guantánamo Bay and the atrocities at Abu Ghraib, have undermined US global influence. Islamic fundamentalism, rather than liberal democracy, influenced the Arab Spring.
- The 'America First' policies of the Trump administration, together with its handling of the Covid-19 pandemic, may have reduced positive perceptions of the US.
- In 2000, 83% of British citizens had a favourable view of the US. By 2020 it was just 41%. In Germany the decline was even more striking: from 78% in 2000 to 26% in 2020.

→

- US global troop deployments are unparalleled, further extending the US's interests and ideals. A total of 180,000 US troops are stationed throughout the world, including 54,000 in Japan, 34,000 in Germany, 26,000 in South Korea and 4,000 in Bahrain (2020).

- China's Belt and Road Initiative is aimed at connecting Asia, Africa and Europe in order to enable China to play a dominant role in global trade. The establishment of the AIIB is designed to challenge the dominance of the World Bank in the developing world. Such ambitious projects represent a significant challenge to American economic hegemony.

Evaluation prompt: Although globalisation has historically encouraged the universalisation of American values, the changing balance of world power and the opportunities provided by the internet suggest that the US will increasingly struggle to dominate global culture.

The limits of materialism

Cultural globalisation can also create a negative backlash, which, far from contributing towards a global monoculture or encouraging tolerance and diversity, can instead reinforce ethnic and national identities, so undermining global cosmopolitanism. In that case, rather than bringing the world closer together, critics suggest that globalisation does exactly the opposite by stirring up resentment against what many regard as the vapid consumerism that the 'McWorld' culture represents.

In 1964, the left-wing philosopher Herbert Marcuse in *One-Dimensional Man* warned that an obsession with materialism diminished our humanity: 'The need for possessing, consuming, handling and constantly renewing the gadgets, devices, instruments, engines, offered to and imposed upon the people, for using these wares even at the danger of one's own destruction, has become a "biological" need.' The force of his argument has increased over time and modern critics of cultural globalisation argue that consumerism and the instant gratification of social media create a cultural void based on ultimately unfulfilling greed and narcissism. More compelling ideologies can step into this void, offering deeper and more profound cultural experiences based upon shared cultural, ethnic and religious experiences.

Globalisation can also make people feel that they have declining influence over the decisions that affect their lives. On 2 November 2001, the veteran Labour politician Tony Benn noted in his diary that because people feel that they have no control over globalisation, 'When things go wrong everyone rallies round their own tribe or religion or village or town and fights off anyone else.' This can further encourage a more insular outlook, which far from bringing people together creates greater alienation and distrust of perceived outsiders.

Activity

The Road to Somewhere

In 2017 David Goodhart published *The Road to Somewhere*, in which he argued that globalisation has created a new division in British society between those who feel that globalisation benefits them (the 'anywheres') and those who feel threatened by it (the 'somewheres'). 'Anywheres' are likely to be wealthier and better educated and so enjoy the increased opportunities that globalisation offers to work and travel across the world. 'Somewheres' have fewer skills and are more rooted in their communities and so are fearful that their jobs, culture and communities may be threatened by forces beyond their control.

1. According to Goodhart, 'somewheres' were likely to support Brexit. Why?
2. In the 2016 and 2020 US presidential elections do you think 'somewheres' were more or less likely to vote for Donald Trump? Explain your answer fully.
3. To what extent do you think that Goodhart is right in arguing that hyper-globalisation challenges rather than encourages global cosmopolitanism?

The rise of identity politics

The uncertainties which globalisation creates may help to explain the current popularity of political movements and leaders who emphasise the unique and distinctive qualities of their own culture and promise to safeguard it from alien influences.

- In Hungary, Viktor Orbán has generated huge appeal by emphasising the country's Christian heritage as a frontier state resisting Muslim advance.

- In France, Marine Le Pen and the National Rally claim to represent France's unique cultural identity.

- In the UK, the 2016 vote to leave the European Union and Boris Johnson's decisive victory in the 2019 General Election on a pledge 'to get Brexit done' suggests that many voters saw European integration as a threat to their traditional way of life.

- In the US, the popularity of Donald Trump among large swathes of the American population has been due to his forthright 'America first' policies and his claim to be protecting America's heritage from external and internal threats.

- Turkish President Recep Tayyip Erdoğan appeals to Turkey's Islamic culture and in 2020 he made the controversial decision to turn Istanbul's Hagia Sophia from a museum back into a mosque.

A clash of civilisations?

In his 1996 book *The Clash of Civilizations*, Samuel Huntington acknowledged the paradox that the popularity of Western-influenced consumer goods can actually create a negative reaction rather than a global monoculture. This is because threatened cultures can seek to reassert their own values in defiance of 'Coca-Colonisation'. We must therefore beware of assuming that just because American films, celebrities and brands are globally dominant this means that other cultures want to adapt to the same American individualist, liberal free-market consumer-driven ideals. Huntington makes his point powerfully when he notes, 'During the 1970s and 1980s Americans consumed millions of Japanese cars, TV sets, cameras and electronic gadgets without being "Japanized" and indeed while becoming considerably more antagonistic toward Japan. Only naïve arrogance can lead Westerners to assume that non-Westerners will become "Westernized" by acquiring Western goods.'

In response, civilisations may therefore seek to protect their own culture, traditions and identity through characterising their values as different from or even superior to those of the West. Indeed, the Western conviction that the right of individual self-fulfilment is universal has led to a powerful backlash.

- Although the right to determine your sexuality is acknowledged throughout most of the West, in 2021 gay sex was still illegal in 69 countries and punishable by death in 11. When Ugandan president, Yoweri Museveni, criminalised gay sex he warned Western powers that they should 'respect African societies and their values. If you don't agree just keep quiet … if we are wrong we shall find out by ourselves'.
- In Russia, there has been a resurgence of national identity during the Putin years closely associated with Slavic pride and the moral conservatism of the Orthodox Church. In 2020, Russians voted by a majority of 78% to 22% for a new constitution which restricts marriage to a man and woman and affirms Russia's roots in its Christian heritage. Urging Russians to vote for the new constitution, Putin stated

Activity

In 2019, President Putin told *Financial Times* journalists that liberalism is 'obsolete'. According to Putin, 'Traditional values are more stable and more important for millions of people than this liberal idea, which, in my opinion, is really ceasing to exist.'

1 In what ways has Russia re-embraced traditional values? Provide examples of other nation-states in which there has been a similar trend.

2 Explain why you think that this has been the case.

3 Do you agree with Putin that globalisation has failed to establish a global monoculture based on shared liberal ideals?

that 'the sovereignty of Russia is supported by our feelings of genuine patriotism … as well as respect for our history, culture, language and traditions'.

- Although liberal scholars had hoped that China's dramatically increased engagement in global free trade would lead to it adopting a more liberal and democratic form of government, the opposite seems to have been the case. The government has imposed authoritarian forms of government on Hong Kong and during his address to the 19th Party Congress in 2020, president Xi Jinping pledged that 'scientific socialism is full of vitality in twenty-first century China, and that the banner of socialism with Chinese characteristics is now flying high and proud for all to see'.

Therefore, the way in which Americanisation and materialism has contributed towards a cultural backlash should not be underestimated. Huntington especially focuses on the way in which the globalisation of these Western values might be seen as a threat to Islam, making cultural conflict between Western and Islamic civilisations a significant risk. According to Huntington, 'Muslims feel the need to return to Islamic ideas, practices and institutions to provide the compass and the motor of modernisation'.

Critics of Huntington's thesis note that he unhelpfully generalises Islam and that evidence of a fundamental clash between the West and Islam is overstated. Others argue that the nature of Islam makes it more difficult for it to accommodate western liberal, democratic and secular principles so creating the possibility of a clash of civilisational beliefs.

Recent evidence that supports a clash between Islam and the West includes:

- Some political leaders of Islamic countries have been critical of liberal values, creating a clash with the values held by most Western states. For example, Turkey's long-time president Recep Tayyip Erdoğan has criticised feminism, stating: 'our religion [Islam] has defined a position for women: motherhood.' He has also strongly criticised LGBT rights. In 2020, in an address to the nation he stated that, 'some people seek to normalise perversions that have been condemned throughout human history to poison young minds.' The return of the Taliban to power in Afghanistan has raised significant concerns about the future of Afghan women's rights.
- Some powerful militant Islamist groups, as Huntington predicted, have gained significant power in recent decades and have pitched themselves against both Western foreign policy and cultural ideas. This includes the militant groups al-Qaeda which carried out the 9/11 attacks in the United States in 2001, ISIL which has carried out numerous atrocities in the pursuit of establishing an Islamic state and Boko Haram (meaning 'Western education is forbidden') which has carried out terrorist actions in West Africa.

Recent evidence against there being a clash between Islam and the West includes:

- There are many powerful Muslim civil society activists and human rights advocates who campaign for improved women's and LGBT rights. For example, Pakistan's Nobel Peace Prize laureate Malala Yousafzai has campaigned internationally for improved access to education for women and girls. The pressure group Musawah was launched in 2020 and campaigns for women's rights within Islam based upon Muslim tradition.
- Although some Muslim states such as Iran, Saudi Arabia and Egypt are authoritarian, there are democratic Muslim states. Since 1998, Indonesia has transitioned from an authoritarian regime towards becoming the world's most

populous Muslim democracy. Tunisia and Senegal are also democracies. Non-Muslim nations can be hostile towards democracy as the rise of authoritarianism in Russia and one-party rule in China demonstrates.

- Socially conservative values are found all over the world, in many different states. Russia, which is strongly influenced by the Orthodox Church, has become increasingly antagonistic towards LGBT rights. In the United States, socially conservative elements of the Republican Party are opposed to LGBT rights and seek to reduce women's rights to abortion.

- As the political scientist Edward Said has explained in his critique of Huntington, there are so many different traditions within Islam that it is misleading and unhelpful to generalise about the faith and principles of almost two billion Muslims. Although Islamist terrorism directed against the West has achieved world-wide notoriety, the actions of such minority groups cannot be seen to represent Islam.

What is the difference between the liberal and realist approaches towards globalisation?

Liberalism and globalisation

Liberals are globalisation optimists. Given their emphasis on the importance of global cooperation, liberals see globalisation as a way of encouraging greater connectivity between states and peoples, thereby creating greater trust and understanding. According to the Dell Theory of Conflict Resolution, the way in which economic globalisation has dramatically increased global trade binds countries into the same global supply chains, preventing conflict. Political globalisation also develops cooperation between states and non-state actors over issues such as climate change, conflict resolution, nuclear non-proliferation and terrorism. Liberals therefore regard globalisation positively, since it establishes foundations for global governance in which states see greater value in cooperation than in conflict.

The advance of regionalism also challenges the primacy of the nation-state, so reducing the risk that nationalist rivalries and ethnic resentments may lead to war. A more globalised world will, liberals claim, be a safer world in which states are motivated less by egotistical principles of power maximisation than by working together to resolve collective security dilemmas. Since liberals argue that state egoism caused the wars of the twentieth century, the only way of avoiding war in the future, as well as safeguarding the future of the planet, is to embrace globalisation as a method of enhancing common humanity.

Realism and globalisation

Realists are sceptical about the extent to which globalisation can, or should, challenge the primacy of the state in global relations. Realists claim that the nation-state should act according to the interests of its citizens. In a dangerously anarchic world, attempts to pretend that we all pursue the same interests are both hopelessly idealistic and ultimately self-defeating. Therefore, attempts to put constraints on states' freedom of action and to pool sovereignty through regional or intergovernmental organisations are dangerous and undermine the absolute right of the state to determine policy itself.

Realists also doubt the extent to which liberal cooperation works. They are wary of attempts to develop universal human rights, since this can dangerously challenge Westphalian principles of state sovereignty, the bedrock of global stability. Realists further dismiss attempts to create greater regional integration, most notably in the EU, since only the nation-state can meaningfully lay claim to the loyalty of its citizens. Humanitarian attempts to intervene in the affairs of other states, although they may be guided by the best of intentions, are also likely to cause more harm than good and so, as former US secretary of state Henry Kissinger said, you may 'with a bleeding heart have to let it go'.

Realists also argue that states should advance the interests of their own citizens in global trade and so are generally less ideologically committed to free trade than liberals. The way in which the Trump administration (2017–2021) pursued protectionist trade policies represented a highly realist approach to international trade, in which his focus on protecting US workers' jobs contrasted with liberals' ideological commitment to free-trade economic globalisation.

The essentially pragmatic nature of realism is well expressed by the Victorian prime minister Lord Palmerston who noted that, 'We have no eternal allies, and we have no perpetual enemies. Our interests are eternal and perpetual, and those interests it is our duty to follow.'

> ### Synoptic link
>
> Liberalism and realism are fully covered in Chapter 1.

To what extent has globalisation transformed the world?

Hyper-globalisers

Hyper-globalisers argue that globalisation is creating a revolutionary shift in the structures of global power, which will ultimately make the nation-state obsolete. Greater economic integration, worldwide capital flows, instantaneous global communication, the growing influence of MNCs and the rise of influential non-state actors have combined to challenge the centrality of the state in international relations. So much of modern life is so inextricably connected through trade and capital flows that the nation-state can no longer determine its own future and must work within economic and financial parameters established through globalisation. As a result, hyper-globalisers infer that an increasingly 'borderless world' is being created – state borders are more permeable than ever before to goods, people, capital and ideas.

In this 'post-sovereign state' world, irresistible global trends dilute the unique characteristics of states. The end result tends towards greater global governance and potentially, at some distant point, **world government**. According to this thesis, the impact of economic globalisation has been so great that it is making the state primarily a depot through which global trade and capital flow. Academic and lawyer Philip Bobbitt has referred to the state being 'hollowed out' by globalisation, as supra-territorial interests and decisions challenge the importance of territorial integrity and nation-states' authority.

> ### Key term
>
> **World government** The concept that all political decision making becomes centralised within one supranational authority that would possess sovereign authority over citizens of the world.

Globalisation sceptics

Globalisation sceptics question the extent to which globalisation is new and whether it really has challenged the authority of the state. Sceptics point out that the world has experienced globalisation before. For example, between 1870 and 1913 dramatic advances in telegraphic communication, the size and speed of ships, Great Britain's commitment as global hegemon to advancing free-trade liberalism and the role of the Royal Navy in policing the world's sea lanes established a first wave of globalisation. A global commitment to the gold standard, the monetary system in which a country's currency or paper money has a value directly linked to gold, further increased the necessary stability to encourage overseas investment. However, although this combined to generate more global trade than ever before, it did not undermine state sovereignty. Indeed, rival nationalisms would help provoke the outbreak of the First World War in 1914.

Modern-day globalisation has also failed to create a more global community. The collapse of the Doha Round of WTO negotiations shows that sovereign nations in the developing countries are not prepared to accept that they should continue to open up their markets without reciprocal Global North arrangements for agriculture. The limited effectiveness of both the ICJ/World Court and the ICC confirms the ongoing significance of the nation-state in international relations.

The way in which the UK negotiated its departure from the European Union on the most favourable terms it could achieve in 2020 provides a good example of nation-states adopting a highly state-centric approach to international negotiations.

Transformationalists

Transformationalists acknowledge that globalisation has had a deep impact on state sovereignty. They emphasise the totality of the globalisation experience. Economic, political and cultural developments have been so profound that states have to engage with a new set of rules in an increasingly closely connected world. According to this interpretation, new stakeholders such as MNCs, IGOs and NGOs continually challenge states' sovereign authority.

However, transformationalists do not agree that globalisation signals the decline of the state. Rather, the state is continually having to adapt to the challenge globalisation presents. Membership of regional bodies, such as ASEAN and the EU, and the influence of the World Bank, the IMF and the WTO have challenged state sovereignty and yet member states still negotiate the best deal they can for their citizens. For instance, when nation-states have embarked upon regionalism, this has often been so that member states can use globalisation to their advantage by pooling their influence on the world stage.

States' sovereign authority may even be enhanced by globalisation. China's power as a nation-state has dramatically increased as a result of globalisation, making it more assertive in advancing its national interests, as its growing pressure on Hong Kong and Taiwan illustrates. The internet, as well as creating a global marketplace of ideas, has been used by states to advance their national interests, as the intense Russian nationalism of RT demonstrates.

The Covid-19 pandemic which began in 2020 is a direct result of the way in which globalisation has created greater connectivity between people all over the world through business, trade and tourism. However, the way in which governments have reacted to the spread of the virus by closing their borders and giving themselves unprecedented peacetime control over what their citizens were able to do demonstrates the ongoing importance of the nation-state in global relations.

The implications of globalisation for the nation-state and national sovereignty

The way in which globalisation has impacted state sovereignty is very controversial. Realists have generally argued that by challenging the nation-state's centrality in international relations, globalisation is dangerously destabilising. Liberals, however, argue that it creates greater prosperity and makes the resolution of global collective dilemmas easier.

In what ways has globalisation challenged the nation-state?

Economic globalisation

Since the world is so economically closely connected, states cannot insulate themselves from global financial crises such as the 2008 collapse of US bank Lehman Brothers. The huge financial influence of MNCs, such as Apple, Google and Microsoft, also means that states need to shape policy in such a way as to attract investment from MNCs. In 2003, Luiz da Silva's government of Brazil abandoned many of its most socialist commitments to stop MNCs withdrawing funds from the country. A nation's policymakers are therefore primarily concerned with creating conditions favourable for foreign investment, which significantly reduces its freedom of manoeuvre. A global consensus in favour of the guiding principles of economic liberalism further restricts governments' freedom of action since, in order to attract trade and investment, governments are forced to adopt policies of low corporate taxation and free-market reforms, sometimes at the expense of workers' rights.

Intergovernmentalism

In an increasingly interconnected world, the interests of nation-states are bound together with IGOs such as the IMF, World Bank and WTO. Nation-states have to accept the authority of these bodies even if governments perceive them to be against their national interests. Member states have to adopt WTO judgments. As lenders of last resort, both the IMF and World Bank impose conditions on recipient states that they have little choice but to accept.

UN war crimes tribunals and the establishment of the ICC have also been instrumental in developing universal standards by which nation-states should be expected to abide in relation to their citizens. Increasingly it is IGOs, rather than sovereign states, that take the lead in addressing collective dilemmas such as climate change, global crime and terrorism, and nuclear proliferation.

Regional organisations

The spread of regionalism has impacted state sovereignty. The EU provides the most advanced example of regionalism, as decisions, made by a qualified majority voting on the Council of Ministers, are legally binding to all member states. The ECB sets a common interest rate for Eurozone members and the Treaty of Lisbon provides the EU with a legal identity so that it can negotiate with sovereign states, as it has done with the signing of the Trans-Atlantic Trade and Investment Partnership (TTIP). The majority of EU members still adhere to the Schengen Agreement, which allows passport-free travel between member nations. Other regional organisations, such as Mercosur, NAFTA and ASEAN, have also imposed certain free-trade rules on their members, thereby limiting member states' sovereignty.

The internet

The increasing reach of the internet compromises states' physical borders. Access to anti-government websites and the organising power of social media contributed to the Arab Spring. The internet can also create new supranational allegiances through, for example, radicalisation, which challenges national identity. Cyber terrorism and cyber warfare further challenge the ways in which a state protects its citizens – computer hackers can now penetrate right to the heart of government, making the protection of territorial state borders irrelevant to a state's survival. Some have argued that Twitter's decision to permanently ban President Trump in 2021 provides a strong indication of the influence MNCs have over world leaders' ability to communicate.

Non-governmental organisations

Myriad NGOs are challenging the influence of the nation-state on its population as their transnational influence, which the internet facilitates, reaches across borders. NGOs include global pressure groups such as Human Rights Watch and Greenpeace, which now inform political debate across the world. Celebrities play an increasingly key role in global issues. The way in which climate change has become such a pressing global concern owes more to global opinion formers such as Greta Thunberg and David Attenborough than to the leaders of nation-states. Global foundations such as the Bill & Melinda Gates Foundation and the Clinton Foundation play a huge role in fighting poverty in the developing world, while the near total eradication of guinea-worm disease has been due to the Carter Center.

Actress Angelina Jolie is also a UN Special Envoy for Refugees

Challenges from below

Forces from within also challenge the integrity of the nation-state. Instead of nationalism declining in importance, it is striking how people still wish to define themselves according to ethnic and nationalist identities, even if these ideals threaten existing state allegiances. Kosovo's and East Timor's independence has been justified on the grounds of self-determination, while the Russian annexation of Crimea in 2014 is based upon the nationalist principle that Crimeans view themselves as Russians rather than Ukrainians. In 2014, Scotland only narrowly voted against independence and Scottish nationalism remains a powerful challenge to the continued existence of the United Kingdom. A powerful separatist movement in Catalonia favours independence from Spain, while Kurdish and Palestinian demands for the recognition of their national aspirations continue to impact policy making across the middle east.

In what ways is the nation-state still important?

The limits of liberalism

The nation-state remains the key decision maker when negotiating with other states. Although there are more opportunities for global cooperation via IGOs than ever before, nation-states choose the extent to which they will work with other countries. The UN is based on the principle of the 'sovereign equality' of all its members (Article 2). The permanent five members of the Security Council exercise their national vetoes on whether or not to engage in conflict resolution and war. Nation-states negotiated the Paris climate change agreement and its success depends upon states being prepared to fulfil the obligations which they set themselves. Meetings of the G7 conclude with communiqués of intentions, but member states retain the right of whether or not to fulfil them.

Even in the EU, the most advanced example of regionalism in the world, member states retain the right of veto on key issues that define a sovereign state, including foreign policy, defence, taxation and non-EU immigration. Article 50 of the Treaty of Lisbon also provides a mechanism by which nation-states may reclaim their sovereignty.

The Trump administration (2017–2021) approached international relations from a transactional 'America First' standpoint. Its withdrawal from the Paris Agreement, negotiation of trade deals outside the World Trade Organization and its refusal to join the Trans-Pacific Partnership illustrates how a powerful nation-state can pursue what it perceives to be its own best interests in defiance of global criticism.

Whether or not nation-states choose to cooperate with each other therefore remains at the core of global relations.

Activity

In 2019, as forest fires raged in the Amazon, President Macron of France called for an international response to the crisis since the Amazonian rainforest produces 20% of the world's oxygen. In a tweet Macron stated, 'Our house is burning. Literally.' In response Brazil's nationalist president, Jair Bolsonaro, angrily accused Macron of having a 'colonialist mindset' and warned the international community not to interfere with Brazil's sovereignty.

1 Research other examples of nation-states refusing to change their policies in response to international condemnation.
2 To what extent do you think sovereign nation-states should be made to adapt themselves to a global consensus over issues such as environmental and human rights protection?

Policy and the state

The state still retains power over most issues that determine the life of its citizens. National governments determine fiscal and tax policy and the diverse ways in which nation-states have responded to Covid-19 demonstrates how crucial they still are to their citizens' lives. The state also determines the way in which citizens are educated, and cared for in old age, while defence policy, immigration and foreign policy are decided and implemented at a national level.

The state can also police the internet. The Chinese 'firewall' is highly effective and Russia has enacted legislation that bans 'undesirable' foreign NGOs from operating in the country if they are perceived to threaten 'the foundations of the constitutional system of the Russian Federation, its defence capabilities and its national security'.

States are not, therefore, simply the depots through which foreign capital and goods pass – they remain crucial in determining the sort of lives their citizens lead.

National borders and security

Although liberals predicted that globalisation would reduce the significance of state borders and gradually replace them with supra-territorial flows of goods, capital and people, the opposite has in fact proved to be true. Terrorist atrocities since the events of 9/11 have instead made states much more determined to protect their borders. The US Department for Homeland Security was established in 2002 in order to better police US borders, and it is now the third-biggest federal employer, with 240,000 employees (2020). The Syrian refugee crisis has also called into question passport-free travel within the Schengen Agreement zone. The Covid-19 pandemic which began in 2020 has further emphasised the continued importance of borders with nation-states rigorously enforcing them in order to try to protect their citizens from the spread of the virus.

Liberal hopes that the nation-state will be hollowed out by globalisation have been further eroded by the way in which governments have given themselves unprecedented peacetime powers to limit what their citizens can do. This suggests that the role of the nation-state in determining what happens within its borders may be of enduring relevance and significance.

Attempts by asylum seekers to illegally reach the UK demonstrates the way in which nation states still forcefully guard their borders

Human rights and civil liberties

When the Cold War ended liberals hoped that this would lead to the universalisation of a human rights culture. The US's commitment to human rights had provided them with a soft-power advantage which had enabled them to triumph over the Soviet Union. Therefore, it was widely anticipated that as the sole remaining superpower, the secular/democratic values of the US would transform global attitudes towards human rights. However, rival religious and political world views have proved more resilient than Soviet communism and the nature and extent of people's rights and liberties often depend more upon religious/cultural traditions than universality.

In 1993, for example, the Bangkok Declaration provided a clear statement of 'Asian Values'. These focus more on social rights and communal values rather than just those of the individual. In most Muslim countries the moral codes of the Qur'an inform the nature of one's human rights. In Russia, the conservative values of the Orthodox Church have increasingly influenced political decision making. Indeed, the emphasis of the UDHR on individual human rights and self-fulfilment is seen in many parts of the world as encouraging a form of Western cultural imperialism.

Therefore, nation-states continue to be the main arbiters of human rights. In the US, for example, the death penalty is legal and yet it is not within the EU. In western Europe, attitudes towards homosexuality have dramatically liberalised and yet homosexuality is still illegal in a third of the world's countries.

International law

When the ICC was established, China refused to join, arguing that 'the statute is an attempt to interfere with the domestic affairs of a sovereign nation'. The US, another non-signatory, signed a number of bilateral trade agreements with other countries, obliging them not to submit US personnel to the ICC's jurisdiction. Although human rights have gained greater international coverage in recent years, nation-states still determine the extent to which they will abide by international standards of human rights and accept the international arbitration of disputes.

The judgments of the International Court of Justice (ICJ), sometimes referred to as the World Court, require states to accept them if they are to be enforced. For example, in 1992, El Salvador and Honduras agreed to accept the ICJ's settlement of a border dispute between the two countries. However, Israel has consistently ignored the ICJ's opinion that the wall separating Israel from Palestinian territories is illegal according to international law. The UK has also refused to hand back the Chagos Archipelago to Mauritius in spite of the ICJ declaring that its control is illegal (2019).

International law is therefore 'soft' law. For example, when India and Pakistan reneged on their obligations to the Treaty on the Non-Proliferation of Nuclear Weapons by announcing they had achieved nuclear defence capability, they were criticised but no international action was taken against them. In 2014, the Organization for Security and Co-operation in Europe declared that the Crimea referendum on whether it should replace Ukrainian with Russian sovereignty was illegal, and yet it still went ahead, with Russia declaring the result as binding.

Topic link

The courts and tribunals responsible for upholding international law are covered in Chapter 5.

National allegiance

Although liberals anticipated that globalisation would lessen citizens' allegiance to their nation-state, state loyalty continues to be remarkably potent. National identities still matter in determining an individual's sense of who they are. President Putin has reasserted Russia's sense of its own unique destiny, stating that 'we will be sovereign or we will dissolve in the world'. Across Europe, the dominance of pro-European parties is being challenged by populist parties like the French National Rally and Alternative for Germany. In Poland and Hungary, nationalist parties have been highly successful in appealing to powerful ethnic and religious traditions. Scottish, Palestinian and Basque nationalist movements further illustrate how important nationhood is to those who do not possess it.

State egoism

States still generally act out of sovereign self-interest rather than according to more liberal cosmopolitan values. The UN did not provide a mandate for the UK-American invasion of Iraq in 2003, and both countries ignored calls for international restraint in order to achieve their strategic objectives in the region. In 2014, Russia annexed Crimea from Ukraine in defiance of international condemnation that it had illegally infringed Ukrainian sovereignty. Defence spending by China, Russia and the US is dramatically increasing, and China is increasing its geostrategic position in the South China Sea by militarising reefs and expanding the reach of its naval manoeuvres. The main players in the Syrian civil war – Iran, Russia and Turkey – each have their own strategic objectives in the region, which have undermined attempts to achieve a political settlement acceptable to all. Examples such as these suggest that states are primarily 'power-maximisers' and that realist principles of self-interest still play the key role in determining the relationship between states.

Is globalisation a new phenomenon?

A global village?

Hyper-globalisers assume that our experience of globalisation is unique in the way in which it has established such interconnectedness between states and citizens across the world. Indeed, some liberal critics of the nation-state have even speculated that we are now living in a 'global village', in which what binds us together outweighs our differences. The internet penetrates almost everywhere in the world and global capital flows are instantaneous, creating a supra-territorial world in which state sovereignty and borders matter less than ever before.

However, it would also be misleading to suggest that states and peoples are more connected today than ever before in history. In reality, the way in which leaders such as Vladimir Putin, Xi Jinping, Narendra Modi and Recep Erdoğan deploy nationalistic rhetoric and policies to win public support indicates that nationalism is, if anything, becoming more important in global relations. This is a far cry from earlier periods of history, when where one came from was significantly less important than it is today.

Pre-twenty-first-century global imperialism

Historians can claim, with some justification, that earlier periods of history have been considerably more 'globalised' than we are today. The first age of modern globalisation lasted from 1870 to 1913, when global trade dramatically expanded

As president of Turkey, Recep Tayyip Erdoğan has set his country on an increasingly authoritarian and conservative path

and British **imperialism** guaranteed the world's sea lanes. British values, such as free trade, a meritocratic civil service, opposition to slavery and even cricket, had then a global influence arguably more profound and far-reaching than today's commercialisation and materialism. Mahatma Gandhi played a key role in ending British rule in India, but his autobiography demonstrates how deeply he had absorbed British values.

The nineteenth century was also the great age of global migration, when millions sought a new life in the US and there was extensive movement of peoples within the British Empire. So rapid was the expansion of continental railways that in 1861 France even abandoned the passport, and passport-free travel became the norm across Europe until the First World War.

In the eighteenth century, intellectuals crossed borders in a way that would be surprising even today – as well as authoring the Declaration of Independence (1776), Thomas Jefferson advised on France's Declaration of the Rights of Man (1789). Even earlier, during the medieval period, the universality of the Catholic Church created a shared concept of Christendom uniting people across Europe and providing an authority to rival that of the Crown. In the Roman period, a single language, culture and citizenship brought together peoples throughout western Europe and the near east. The Emperors Trajan and Hadrian were both born in what is now Spain and in the Acts of the Apostles (22:24–30) St Paul avoids being flogged when he declares to the authorities his Roman citizenship.

The internet: unity or disunity?

The internet has made it possible for people virtually anywhere in the world to communicate with each other in ways that would, until very recently, have been unthinkable. This globalisation of communication challenges the power of the state in determining the political allegiance and cultural preferences of its citizens. Liberals optimistically therefore hope that the internet can become a way of creating a genuinely global dialogue in which people exchange ideas and shared experiences beneath the radar of government.

For example, the use of Facebook and Twitter helped to provoke the Arab Spring, as citizens succeeded in organising themselves electronically, so undermining the authority of repressive governments. International pressure groups, such as Make Poverty History, also use the internet to coordinate 'global people power', which further illustrates how instantaneous electronic communication has the potential to create new supranational movements and allegiances.

In 2020, following the murder of George Floyd, Black Lives Matter became a dominant force on social media, forcing governments, universities, schools and businesses to re-examine how they approach issues connected with history, racism and equality. There is so much more global awareness of the need to take action on climate change because of the way in which climate change activists like Greta Thunberg have gained such an international following on the internet.

However, what liberals fail to appreciate is that there is no reason why states should not use the internet to advance their own nationalistic world view at the expense of others. RT (formerly Russia Today) illustrates how the power of the internet can be deployed to advance nationalism and ridicule Western democracies.

Key term

Imperialism Where one nation-state exerts significant military and economic influence over another, often in the pursuit of the more powerful state's national interest.

The Chinese government has successfully used the internet to advance its own nationalistic agenda, while restricting outside electronic influences through its 'firewall'.

The way, too, in which social media is more likely to create echo chambers in which one's political opinions/prejudices are reinforced rather than challenged further indicates that the internet is a long way from creating a virtual town hall in which everyone's opinions are welcomed and listened to. Any controversial post, for example, is more likely to generate vulgar abuse than stimulate informed discussion.

Debate

Is state sovereignty becoming less important?

Yes

- Global acceptance of free-market liberalism, encouraged by the Bretton Woods Institutions, restricts the economic choices that governments can take. According to Susan Strange, 'Markets are now masters of governments.'
- States now share power with non-state actors: for example, the decisions of MNCs directly impact the job prospects and living conditions of working people globally.
- The internet influences citizens and potentially creates new, supranational allegiances.
- Global opinion formers are as likely to be private individuals (Greta Thunberg) and global popular movements (Black Lives Matter) as the leaders of nation-states.
- There is pooling of sovereignty within regional organisations such as the EU, ASEAN and NAFTA/USMCA.
- Collective dilemmas such as climate change, nuclear proliferation, terrorism and international crime require intergovernmental solutions.
- States accept legal limitations on their domestic jurisdiction in the ECtHR, ICC and ICJ. According to Kofi Annan, former UN secretary-general, sovereignty must be 'responsible', suggesting that it can be forfeited by unjust acts (UN R2P, 2005).

No

- Nation-states choose whether or not to cooperate with non-state actors. Globalisation has involved many more 'stakeholders' in political debate, but nation-states retain their exclusive rights of sovereign decision making.
- Nation-states enter relationships with other nation-states in regional organisations and international treaties that limit their absolute freedom of action. However, states are free to withdraw their involvement.
- It is difficult to enforce international law or international standards of justice within nation-states. China rejects criticism of its treatment of the Uighur Muslims, while Israel continues to construct settlements in the occupied territories in defiance of UN resolutions.
- The Syrian government's human rights abuses have not triggered a response from the international community according to the principles of 'conditional sovereignty' outlined in the UN's R2P.
- State allegiance still determines the loyalty of a state's citizens – such loyalty seems to have increased rather than lessened in the face of the growing uncertainties globalisation provokes.
- In order to be successful, the Paris Agreement (2015) requires nation-states to fulfil their INDC.
- The way in which nation-states have responded to the Covid-19 pandemic by tightly controlling their borders and placing unprecedented restrictions on their citizens demonstrates the continued indispensability of the nation-state.

Evaluation prompt: This is a finely balanced debate with strong arguments on both sides. The liberal optimism that the nation-state would become just one among many global actors seems though to be less convincing now than it was at the end of the Cold War.

Has globalisation changed the world?

Yes

- According to hyper-globalisers, economic globalisation has dramatically increased global trade, lifted millions out of poverty and created the potential for greater convergence between the Global North and Global South. According to the World Bank, as a result of globalisation, more than 85% of the world's population can now hope to live to at least 60, which is double the global life expectancy of 100 years ago.
- As a result of economic globalisation, China is on course to become the world's biggest economy, challenging US economic, political and military hegemony. This represents a shift of the global balance of power eastwards towards emerging economies.
- The pace of regionalism has increased as regions work more closely together in order to take advantage of new global opportunities for trade.
- Since the world is so economically and financially interconnected, no state can avoid being impacted by global crises, such as the collapse of Lehman Brothers in 2008 or the Covid-19 pandemic (2020–).
- As a result of the internet, global capital flows are now instantaneous, interlinking economies all over the world. National borders have become more porous as goods and capital flow more freely between states, and MNCs rather than nation-states increasingly determine employment opportunities and labour rights, especially in the developing world.
- Personal laptop possession enables anyone to become an entrepreneur (Thomas Friedman has used the metaphor of 'The Rise of the Windows' to illustrate how ownership of a Windows PC/Apple Mac provides anybody, anywhere with limitless opportunities for business success).
- There are few truly national products remaining, as MNCs such as Adidas and Nike manufacture and sell across the world.
- Cultural globalisation has homogenised world culture, creating a global enthusiasm for the same brands, products and trends.
- Nation-states are working more closely together in IGOs to resolve collective dilemmas and the UN R2P has encouraged a more universal standard for human rights.
- NGOs such as Black Lives Matter and global activists such as Great Thunberg and Vanessa Nakate have added another layer to global decision making, further challenging the exclusivity of nation-states.
- The internet has facilitated the spread of alternative (religious/ethnic) allegiances, undermining national cohesion.

No

- Globalisation sceptics respond that global interconnectedness is not entirely new. The first wave of modern globalisation occurred in 1870–1913. Previous periods of history experienced remarkable degrees of integration.
- As the UK's departure from the EU and the US's renegotiation of NAFTA (USMCA) demonstrates, nation-states join regional organisations to advance their national interests.
- Nation-states remain the key players in global politics, but IGOs require states to work together if they are to be successful. The success of the Paris climate change agreement depends upon whether or not powerful nation-states like the US choose to engage with it.
- The global impact of the 1929 Wall Street Crash and even the South Sea Bubble in 1720 demonstrates that the global economy is not uniquely interconnected today.
- Citizens still identify with their nation-state – globalisation has not created a global citizenry and there has been a global rise in the popularity of populist parties emphasising an exclusive national identity.
- Realist self-interest, rather than liberal cooperation, determines nation-state policy, for example the Russian annexation of Crimea, China's restriction of self-government within Hong Kong and the UK's refusal to acknowledge the ICJ's right to adjudicate over ownership of the Chagos islands.
- Cultural globalisation has reinforced nationalist, ethnic and religious identities as a reaction against homogenisation and materialism.
- The extent of one's human rights is still determined within states and cultures – the universalisation of human rights is undermined by continued allegiance to other value-sets (Muslim, Asian, African and Russian, for example).
- Terrorist threats, migration and the Covid-19 pandemic have led to the reassertion of national control over borders.

Evaluation prompt: There is a danger that this essay could simply become a contest between hyper-globalisers and globalisation sceptics in which there is no common ground. Why not consider whether a transformationalist approach would enable you to acknowledge how globalisation has changed the world but sometimes in unexpected ways which have actually reinforced the importance of the nation-state?

What you should know

Having read this chapter you should have knowledge and understanding of the following:

→ The extent to which rumours of the death of the nation-state might have been exaggerated. In the euphoria following the end of the Cold War, remarkable advances were made in global trade and political interconnectivity, which did suggest that the authority of the nation-state was being challenged.

→ The nation-state now has to compete with many more stakeholders, and political dialogue is no longer primarily between states. Instead, states and non-state actors increasingly work together, both formally and informally.

→ The urgency with which collective dilemmas need to be resolved has further encouraged intergovernmental solutions to world problems.

→ A global acceptance of the principles of economic liberalism and the rising importance of transnational corporations has limited the socioeconomic solutions that nation-states can deploy to address domestic problems.

→ Instantaneous capital flows have encouraged the rise of supra-territorial global capitalism.

→ The internet has 'flattened out' many of the cultural differences that have made nation-states unique.

→ However, the state has actually proved much more resilient than many liberals and hyper-globalisers anticipated.

→ Nation-states remain the key players in decision making and, although they may cooperate with non-state actors, ultimate authority still lies with them.

→ Nation-states have frequently acted in defiance of international law and yet the international community has been slow to punish them. The establishment of a supranational universal standard of human rights is as distant as ever.

→ The Trump administration's protectionist policies challenged the extent to which states must act within the boundaries of free-trade liberalism.

→ The regional and global implications of Brexit for the nation-state have yet to be fully understood.

→ The internet, far from transforming the world into a global village, has encouraged the resurgence of national pride, resentments and prejudice, reinforcing rather than challenging state autonomy.

→ We should be careful of suggesting that globalisation has transformed the world, especially since history suggests that there have been earlier, possibly even more profound, periods of globalisation.

→ Modern-day globalisation is, nonetheless, in the process of changing the world, and yet rather than the nation-state succumbing to new challenges, it has adapted to them. In some ways the new challenges and uncertainties of the twentieth century have even strengthened the nation-state. As Mark Twain suggested, rumours of the death of the nation-state may indeed have been 'much exaggerated'.

Further reading

Chang, H. (2011) *23 Things They don't Tell You about Capitalism.* Penguin.

Collier, P. (2008) *The Bottom Billion.* Oxford University Press.

Frankopan, P. (2020) *The New Silk Roads.* Bloomsbury.

Friedman, T. (2007) *The World is Flat.* Penguin.

Goodhart, G. (2017) *The Road to Somewhere.* Penguin.

Haass, R. (2017) *A World in Disarray.* Penguin.

Haass, R. (2020) *The World: A Brief Introduction.* Penguin.

Jefferies, J. (2020) 'The resurgence of the nation state', *Politics Review*, Vol. 30, No. 2, November.

Norberg, J. (2020) *Open: The Story of Human Progress.* Atlantic Books.

Practice questions

Section A

1 Examine the differences which exist between hyper-globalisers and globalisation sceptics. *[12 marks]*

2 Examine the criticisms which are made of cultural and economic globalisation. *[12 marks]*

3 Examine the impact that economic globalisation has on global poverty and on the environment. *[12 marks]*

4 Examine the ways in which IGOs and NGOs contribute to international dialogue and debate. *[12 marks]*

5 Examine the ways in which the US has expanded its economic and cultural influence as a result of globalisation. *[12 marks]*

Section C

1 Evaluate the extent to which nation-states have become more or less influential in global politics since 2000. *[30 marks]*

2 Evaluate the extent to which cultural globalisation has had a more positive impact on the developing world than economic globalisation. *[30 marks]*

3 Evaluate the extent to which globalisation has decisively changed the global balance of power. *[30 marks]*

4 Evaluate the extent to which human rights are better protected as a result of globalisation. *[30 marks]*

5 Evaluate the extent to which globalisation has made it more or less difficult to resolve the challenge of climate change. *[30 marks]*

3 Global governance: political

Learning outcomes

By the end of the chapter you should understand:
- → what is meant by political global governance
- → the role and significance of the UN and its key organs
- → how effective the UN has been in achieving its objectives
- → how effective the UN Security Council is and whether it should be reformed
- → the role and significance of NATO, its current role and its strengths and weaknesses

Getting you started

On 4 March 2018, Sergei Skripal – a former Russian military intelligence officer – and his daughter Yulia Skripal collapsed on a park bench in the county town of Salisbury in southern England. Within hours, and with the pair in a critical condition in hospital, the police investigation was pointing to the use of a military nerve agent called novichok against the Skripals.

The Metropolitan Police team concluded that the nerve agent, developed by the Soviet Union in the Cold War, had been deployed onto Mr Skripal's front door from an adapted perfume bottle. This original weapon was later found by a local woman, Dawn Sturgess, who died after coming into contact with the nerve agent.

The British government quickly identified the Russian state as responsible for the attack. UK Prime Minister, Theresa May, gave a statement to the House of Commons just days later stating that 'the government has concluded that it is highly likely that Russia was responsible'. By September, the UK government identified two Russian nationals it believed to be responsible for the attacks, and shared CCTV footage of two suspects it alleged travelled from Russia to Salisbury to carry out the attacks. For its part, the Russian government strongly rejected that it was responsible and the two suspects appeared on television denying their involvement.

Believing its national interest and the wider international interest were under threat, the crisis posed an immediate challenge from the perspective of the UK. How could Russia be held accountable for its actions? How could the UK ensure that the attacks were not repeated?

The British Army deploying in Salisbury after the Sergei Skripal novichok poisoning

Might the **United Nations** be an international organisation that could help in this situation? With both the UK and Russia being permanent members of the UN Security Council, the dispute resolution forum of the UN on matters of peace and security, there was a limited amount that could be achieved, despite the US publicly backing up the UK's conclusions of Russian culpability. In a session of the UN Security Council, the UK and Russia once again set out their claims and counterclaims, with no action taken.

Might the **North Atlantic Treaty Organization (NATO)** be any more help? This alliance of like-minded states, set up as a military counterweight to the Soviet Union, was more decisive in condemning Russia for 'the first use of a nerve agent on NATO territory' and a 'reckless breach of international norms'. But NATO stressed that it remained 'committed to strong defence and dialogue with Russia'.

Within weeks, the UK, US, EU and NATO had responded substantively to the attacks by expelling Russian diplomats from embassies. The US ordered 60 Russian diplomats home and the European Union did the same for 30 diplomats based across 16 of its member states. In return, Russia responded by expelling precisely the same number of diplomats in each state.

These incidents expose the challenges of dealing with international peace and security through organisations such as the United Nations and NATO. With no prospect of – or appetite for – a world government that would be able to impose its authority on nation-states, the institutions of global political governance are all we have to rely on. How these institutions make their decisions and their effectiveness are the focus of this chapter.

Key terms

United Nations (UN) The world's principal intergovernmental organisation, founded in 1945 and comprising 193 member states. It has a wide range of responsibilities and powers (e.g. international peace and security, economic development, human rights and social progress).

North Atlantic Treaty Organization (NATO) A military alliance consisting of the US and its key allies in western Europe, with the purpose to protect western Europe from military threats from the Soviet Union.

What is global governance?

The government of a sovereign state is relatively easy to identify: it has a leader, often elected and in the form of a president or prime minister. Usually, the leader and his or her government have to follow clear rules that set out what their powers are and the limits of their power, often in the form of a constitution. If elected directly by the population, the government is usually seen as legitimate and the population accepts its actions. The legislature usually makes laws that its population must follow. Courts and a police force enforce these laws and there are clear consequences when people break them. The government proposes policies to manage the state effectively, for example public services such as health and education.

In the most stable states, these combined activities are called 'governance', whereby the state is managed effectively, resources are distributed fairly and challenges are met with decisive solutions. There is good governance, broadly following the principles set out above, and bad governance, where power may be held illegitimately and resources are scarce, or managed corruptly or incompetently (for example, in the case of failed states).

Increasingly, states have recognised the need for some form of global governance. Challenges such as the global financial crisis, international terrorism, climate change, world poverty, global pandemics, global human rights abuses and violent conflict can only be resolved by states working together. These threats affect many states and many states contribute to these threats. Only by states working together are they likely to have any impact on reducing these threats. Just as national governance seeks to exploit opportunities and manage threats experienced at the national level, global governance seeks to do exactly the same at a global level.

Why is global governance difficult?

However, attempts at global governance are much harder and less successful than national governance. This is because nation-states remain powerful and decisive actors in global politics. They are sovereign, meaning that they are usually able to take their own decisions, and it is rare for a higher authority to force states to do something against their wishes (see Chapter 1).

It is difficult to insert a layer of formal authority above nation-states because there is no recognised 'world government', in the sense of a government that nation-states accept as legitimate to act on their behalf, and which has sovereign power and the authority to act. These difficulties include the following:

- **States are the principal actors:** they make or break global governance initiatives. Nothing is agreed globally unless states agree to take action. They are the building blocks of unified action. Some states can opt out of or block agreements (for example, the Kyoto Protocol, see page 229), making these agreements meaningless or ending in failure.
- **International law is largely unenforceable:** in the case of most nation-states' laws, every citizen is required to comply and is held accountable in the courts if they break the law. By contrast, international law is often optional and requires states to actively sign up in order for the law to cover them (states can choose not to sign and ratify key treaties, such as the Rome Statute, which created the ICC). States can also change their minds and withdraw from treaties that they have signed. Customary international law (see page 11) is law

that is so widely accepted that it applies to states regardless of whether they have signed up to it or not. However, the same difficulties arise if powerful or rogue states simply ignore attempts by, for example, international courts to hold them to account.

- **Lack of international enforcement:** even if states have signed up to international law, there are few means of international enforcement (for example, international or regional human rights courts) that can hold states accountable and force them to change their behaviour.

How far states are willing, or able, to participate in global governance is linked to the different types of power that they have and the way that they use their power (see Chapter 7).

Rogue states: these states, particularly those in which there is an illegitimate government that is exceeding its powers (such as North Korea), often have no desire to be part of, and therefore influenced and persuaded by, any systems of global governance.

Failed states: these states are not fully in control of their internal governance (such as Somalia). They are rarely effective participants in global governance, as they cannot yet hold authority over their own populations. Insurgent groups, such as Boko Haram in Nigeria or ISIL in Iraq and Syria, often take over regions within failed states, meaning that the government does not exercise full control over all of its territory. The term 'fragile states' is perhaps more commonly used now to describe these states.

Powerful states: these states can pick and choose which global agreements they are part of and simply ignore international pressure (as seen in the example of Russia's actions in Ukraine, but also the refusal of the US to sign climate change agreements such as the Kyoto Protocol).

Since no single, authoritative world government exists, states work within global institutions or intergovernmental organisations (IGOs) and negotiate treaties between two or more states so that they can reach agreements on issues of shared importance. Sometimes, this is easier than trying to reach bigger agreements that include a wider range of states.

Non-governmental organisations are increasingly important in global governance initiatives, but the work of global governance is primarily conducted between nation-states, either within IGOs or working together in more informal, ad hoc discussions.

> ### Key term
>
> **Non-governmental organisations (NGOs)** Not-for-profit organisations that are independent from states and IGOs, and are engaged in a wide range of activities. They are usually funded by donations but some are primarily volunteer-run.

Table 3.1 Types of global governance

Type of global governance	Why is it needed?	Examples
Political global governance (Chapter 3)	Political global governance covers all forms of collective decision making between states. When states come together to make decisions on matters of peace and security, human rights or climate change, they are doing so within political institutions or processes. In this way, environmental, judicial and economic global governance are all subsets of political global governance.	This chapter focuses on the key IGO, the UN, and its most powerful decision-making body, the UNSC. NATO is also a key example of global political governance as a collective security alliance.
Economic global governance (Chapter 4)	Economic global governance is needed to help states trade with each other more easily and to resolve economic crises that have an impact on multiple states. It can also help with states' economic and human development, supporting international objectives in the Sustainable Development Goals.	A number of key economic IGOs, such as the International Monetary Fund (IMF), the World Trade Organization (WTO) and the World Bank, have been established to help both rich and poor states with their economic development.

Type of global governance	Why is it needed?	Examples
Human rights global governance (Chapter 5)	Since the UN Universal Declaration of Human Rights (UDHR) was agreed in 1948, human rights have been thought of as universal and having global relevance, irrespective of national borders and different cultures. Human rights global governance has made various attempts to agree global human rights laws and establish courts and tribunals to hold states and others abusing human rights to account. The principal aim is to ensure that states cannot hide behind national sovereignty and abuse human rights without punishment.	There are a number of international human rights laws (such as the covenants and conventions) which have now put the aspirations of the UDHR into international law. Courts such as the International Criminal Court (ICC) and the European Court of Human Rights enforce many of these laws.
Environmental global governance (Chapter 6)	Global warming and climate change are increasingly recognised as global responsibilities requiring urgent action. Global conferences and agreements have attempted to take action to reduce the harmful effects that states have on the global commons (see page 207). It is perhaps the most obvious example of a challenge that cannot be resolved by states acting alone and one in which all states (developed and developing alike, where there is a key clash on which states bear the greatest responsibility) must take action.	Global action to tackle environmental degradation is primarily driven through international summits such as the Copenhagen and Paris summits of 2009 and 2015. States sometimes sign international agreements, such as the Paris Agreement, when they commit to taking joint action.

Types of global governance

There are four main types of global governance (see also Table 3.1):

1   Political (examined fully in this chapter)
2   Economic (Chapter 4)
3   Human rights (Chapter 5)
4   Environmental (Chapter 6)

Political global governance

There are three main ways in which states can work together in political global governance, each of which we will examine in this chapter. Which of these approaches is used, in any particular context, depends on the nature of the issue and the motivations of the states involved in tackling the issue.

1   **Intergovernmental organisations (IGOs):** these organisations – principally the UN – provide a permanent and formal rules-based framework in which states can negotiate and form agreements. Most IGOs are intergovernmental in the sense that nation-states work together to make agreements by consent. It is only in regional organisations (principally the EU, see Chapter 8) that supranational powers are to be found, which is where an IGO can force states to do things that not every member state may agree with.
2   **International treaties:** a means of creating international law more flexibly on specific issues, either within or independent of IGOs, and between two (bilateral treaties) or more (multilateral treaties) states. This is useful for a smaller number of states working on an issue of specific concern to them only or on which they are all in agreement and motivated to act.
3   **Ad hoc meetings:** states can meet in informal meetings and undertake negotiations and agreements on a more ad hoc basis.

Each of these methods of political global governance carries a number of different features and functions, which states can use to their advantage. However, sometimes states can also suffer from the methods' disadvantages (see Table 3.2).

Table 3.2 Advantages and disadvantages of possible approaches to global political governance

Approach and examples	Advantages	Disadvantages
IGOs (e.g. the UN (page 83), NATO (page 114))	A permanent forum for debate and negotiation, in which long-term projects can be pursued (such as the Sustainable Development Goals (SDGs)) and long-term relationships built. An authoritative and legitimate actor in global politics, based on clear rules and international law (for example, the founding UN Charter). Good for smaller countries, if all countries have an equal voice (such as in the UN General Assembly (UNGA)). Membership itself can be made dependent on states becoming part of key agreements (for example, all UN member states must sign and ratify the UDHR).	Can become gridlocked, particularly if powerful states are given veto powers (for example, the veto power of the five UNSC permanent members). Less meaningful for smaller countries if they have no clear powers and are out-muscled by more powerful states. Effectiveness is dependent on the collective determination of an IGO's member states. If this, collectively, becomes weak, the IGO becomes weak (for example, declining defence spending of NATO countries). States are likely to find ways of limiting the IGO's power if they feel it threatens state sovereignty.
International treaties (e.g. the Treaty on the Non-Proliferation of Nuclear Weapons (NPT) (page 114), the North Atlantic Treaty (page 114))	Allows like-minded states to create binding international law on any issue in which they have a common interest. Making agreements outside IGOs, states can sometimes be more flexible and responsive rather than acting only with a consensus or majority.	States can choose not to sign and ratify treaties, meaning that they are not covered by them and creating inconsistency. For example, key states that have acquired nuclear weapons either did not sign or withdrew from the NPT. Even when states have signed treaties, their cooperation largely remains a choice and it can be difficult to force states to comply with treaty obligations.
Informal meetings/ negotiations/ agreements (e.g. the 2015 Paris Agreement (page 233))	Allows states to respond very quickly to crises and form agendas with maximum freedom. For example, the London Group of Twenty (G20) Summit in 2009 quickly developed an agenda designed to tackle the global financial crisis.	Sometimes seen as less legitimate, or even illegal in international law (for example, the US-led invasion of Iraq in 2003). Decisions or agreements are not binding in international law, and are therefore even less enforceable. States are at liberty to make their own independent choices and protect their sovereignty, making blockages more likely.

The United Nations

Former US ambassador to the UN Henry Cabot Lodge stated that:

> This organization is created to prevent you from going to hell. It isn't created to take you to heaven.

The UN is the world's most comprehensive and powerful IGO. It has more member states and it carries out a wider range of activities in more places across the world than any other IGO. Since it was founded in 1945, it has become a highly respected international organisation, seen as legitimate in its own right and a source of legitimacy for other actions and actors in global politics. For example, for a newly independent state, becoming a member of the UN is an important confirmation of statehood and the UN Security Council's decisions in respect of military action are widely accepted to be legitimate.

The UN has its central headquarters in New York and has a global presence in offices and regional headquarters across the world. Its objectives range across a wide

The UN Headquarters in New York

number of responsibilities, including tackling global conflict, reducing poverty and upholding human rights. It is the most important institution and forum for global political governance that exists in modern global politics.

However, the UN is not without its critics. Some analysts argue that it is powerless to deal with international crises effectively. For example, some say that the US's foreign policy during the War on Terror sidelined the UN and rendered it powerless, while others say it has turned a blind eye to recent atrocities in Syria and was ineffective in preventing or limiting the Covid-19 pandemic.

This section will examine the UN's founding objectives and its relevance today, and how the major organs of the UN – including the UN Security Council – work. It will also evaluate how effective the UN really is at dealing with the major challenges of conflict, human rights and global poverty.

How and why was the UN founded?

Signed just months after the end of the Second World War, the language of the UN Charter – the UN's founding document and constitution – is heavy with the regret and determination of a war-weary world to create a more stable future (see Box 3.1).

Box 3.1

Preamble to the UN Charter

The UN Charter was signed on 26 June 1945 in San Francisco, US, at the conclusion of the UN Conference on International Organization. It came into force on 24 October 1945.

We, the peoples of the United Nations, determined ...

... to save succeeding generations from the scourge of war, which twice in our lifetime has brought untold sorrow to mankind;

... to reaffirm faith in fundamental human rights, in the dignity and worth of the human person, in the equal rights of men and women from countries large and small;

... to establish conditions under which justice ... and international law can be maintained;

... to promote social progress and better standards of life in larger freedom.

... have agreed to the present Charter of the United Nations and do hereby establish an international organization to be known as the United Nations.

The UN Charter's Preamble demonstrates the key priorities of world leaders in 1945. The Second World War had caused huge human and economic destruction and suffering across the world. In 1945, there was a united global desire to create an international organisation aimed at preventing future conflict and human rights abuses similar to those seen during the war. There was also an urgent need to coordinate efforts to rebuild shattered economies and infrastructure destroyed by war.

After the First World War, several nation-states created the League of Nations (1920–46), which had similar objectives to prevent another global conflict. The outbreak of the Second World War confirmed that the League of Nations had utterly failed. The League had, in fact, consisted of only a limited number of nations, with nothing like the universal membership of today's UN. Major powers had joined and left (Germany and Japan left in 1933), failed to join (the US) or were expelled (the USSR, in 1939). The League of Nations' replacement needed to make sure that major powers stayed the course in order to solve challenges collectively, rather than leaving at the first sign of challenge to state sovereignty. Above all, it needed its members to stick together, and take effective action to deal with major international crises.

The UN Charter

To form the UN, member states agreed and then signed the UN Charter, the UN's constitution. The charter is the multilateral treaty that sets out UN powers within international law and outlines how the UN works and carries out its key functions. It also sets out member states' rights within the UN, the powers of its organs (see page 87) and the relationships between the various organs. The founding objectives in Chapter 1 of the charter were, and remain, as follows:

- To maintain international peace and security and 'to take effective collective measures for the prevention and removal of threats to peace'.
- To maintain friendly relations among nations.
- To promote and encourage respect for fundamental human rights.
- To uphold respect for international law.
- To promote social progress and better standards of life.

Other key parts of the UN Charter include Chapters VI and VII, which are often referred to in UNSC decisions and resolutions.

- **Chapter VI:** sets out the UN's powers to resolve disputes between nation-states using peaceful means. This can include negotiation and peace talks.
- **Chapter VII:** sets out the UN's powers to resolve disputes between nation-states and, increasingly, non-state actors using the military force of its member states. A UNSC Resolution (see page 3) that invokes (that is to say, makes use of for legal purposes) Chapter VII will legitimise the use of member state force. Chapter VII also includes Article 51, which allows states to use force in self-defence. Article 42 is the clause that specifically allows for military action if peaceful means have not been successful.

Current challenges

The UN's role has expanded considerably from its founding purpose to focus on a number of specific challenges or threats.

Climate change

The UN has taken more action to reduce harm to the environment, conscious that the global commons (see page 205) requires collective action to be adequately protected. The UN's key task has been to get a majority of member states to agree on the existence and impact of climate change and to take meaningful action to prevent further harm to the environment.

The UN organises key international summits within the UN Framework Convention on Climate Change (UNFCCC, see page 221) and set up the Intergovernmental Panel on Climate Change to ensure that the political process was supported by the most comprehensive and informed scientific research. A series of annual international environmental summits has taken place under UN leadership, leading to some important agreements such as the Kyoto Protocol (signed in 1997) and the Paris Agreement (signed in 2016).

> **Topic link**
>
> The UN's role in environmental global governance is explored in Chapter 6.

Human rights

The UN has overseen the drafting and agreement of a succession of international human rights laws, starting with a non-binding, aspirational Universal Declaration to binding covenants and conventions covering specific types of human rights (such as the Covenant on Civil and Political Rights signed in 1966) and protecting specific groups of people (such as the Convention on the Rights of the Child signed in 1989). The UN's Human Rights Council is an elected body of member states which monitors individual states' human rights records and puts pressure on states to rectify breaches of human rights. Short of the UN Security Council agreeing humanitarian intervention in another state, the UN is mostly reliant on trying to persuade states to improve their human rights compliance by soft power.

Topic link

The UN's role in human rights global governance is explored in Chapter 5.

Limiting the spread of nuclear weapons

Since the 1960s, the UN has also developed a leading role in limiting the spread, or proliferation, of nuclear weapons and other weapons of mass destruction. The Treaty on the Non-Proliferation of Nuclear Weapons (NPT, see page 113) was opened for willing states to sign in 1968. The UN provided a vital forum for a treaty to be signed in which some states agreed not to acquire nuclear weapons and states that were already nuclear powers pledged not to share the means of producing nuclear weapons. Although four UN member states have not signed the treaty (and it is not a requirement of UN membership to sign it), the UN played a key leadership role. The UNGA has a dedicated Disarmament Commission (UNDC) and within the UN Secretariat, the UN Office for Disarmament Affairs takes a lead. The UN's impact on nuclear issues is explored further on page 114.

Peace and security

UN peacekeeping activities have expanded hugely in scope and number during the organisation's lifetime (see page 106). Any UN peacekeeping operations need to be approved by the UN Security Council, which became more active on matters of peace and security after the Cold War ended in 1991. Before this, gridlock between the US and the Soviet Union made decision making in the UNSC difficult. The 1990s saw the biggest increase in UN-approved military humanitarian intervention, including in Somalia (1992), Rwanda (1994) and Bosnia (1995), though success was mixed. In the War on Terror period since 2001, and as the global distribution of power has become more multipolar (see page 263), it has become harder once again for the UN to exert its authority (for example, in respect of the conflicts in Ukraine and Syria since 2011).

Promoting sustainable development

The UN has also expanded its role in promoting sustainable development and reducing global poverty. The Millennium Development Goals (MDGs, see page 153), agreed at the UN's Millennium Summit in 2000, represented a huge increase in focus and scope for the organisation's development efforts. The UN continued this focus by reshaping the MDGs into the Sustainable Development Goals (SDGs) when the MDGs reached their agreed endpoint in 2015. This is a good example of the UN expanding its work beyond the objectives that it originally set itself.

Topic link

The UN's role in economic global governance and reducing poverty is explored in Chapter 4.

Key UN organs

The UN's main headquarters is in New York. The main deliberative bodies of the UN, including the UNGA and the UNSC, are based and have their meetings there. Other major UN offices are in Geneva, The Hague (the ICJ), Milan, Nairobi and Vienna.

The UN is notorious for its complex structure and the relationships between its many agencies, secretariats, councils, assemblies and courts (see Figure 3.1). The second UN secretary-general, Dag Hammarskjöld, lamented in 1955 that people thought of the UN as a 'weird Picasso abstraction', so complicated was its organisational structure.

There are six main institutions, known as 'organs', of the UN, each of which has specific functions and powers (see Table 3.3). The most powerful organ is the UN Security Council.

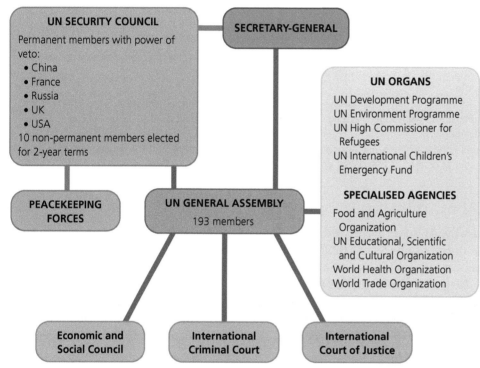

Figure 3.1 The UN's main institutions and organs

Table 3.3 The UN and its principal organs

Principal organ	Function and related bodies
UN Secretariat	The UN's 'civil service', or bureaucracy, led by the UN secretary-general.
	Staffed by UN officials from across the world.
	Includes branches such as the Department for Peacekeeping Operations (DPKO) and the Office for the Coordination of Humanitarian Affairs (OCHA), which organises humanitarian responses to natural disasters.
UN Security Council (UNSC)	The UN's executive committee, responsible for peace and security, and for passing binding resolutions under Chapters 6 and 7 of the UN Charter. It does not involve itself in matters beyond peace and security, such as climate change.
	Its five permanent members (China, France, Russia, the UK, the US) have veto powers and can block any proposed resolutions with which they disagree.
	It has a further ten non-permanent members chosen by regional quotas, who serve 2-year terms.

Principal organ	Function and related bodies
UN General Assembly	The UNGA can be thought of as the UN's parliament. Every member state can participate in debates and is represented equally, with one vote per state.
	Its annual meeting is held at the UN Headquarters in New York each September. It allows world leaders to address the UN and there are often votes on major issues (such as the 2012 vote on Palestine's observer status membership of the UN).
International Court of Justice	The ICJ makes judgments mainly on territorial disputes between states and not on human rights matters (the ICJ should not be confused with the ICC (see page 52)). The ICJ is not a criminal court.
	There are 15 judges at the court, which is based in The Hague. The court can only hear cases brought to it by states and by UN organs and agencies (individuals and NGOs, for example, cannot be considered).
UN Economic and Social Council (ECOSOC)	Responsible for economic security and development, and human rights.
	ECOSOC is made up of 54 member states, elected by the UNGA for 3-year terms.
	It allows member states to pass non-binding resolutions in its areas of policy responsibility and to direct the work of many UN programmes and funds such as the World Health Organization (WHO) and the UN International Children's Emergency Fund (UNICEF).
UN Trusteeship Council	Includes all five members of the UNSC. It was set up to oversee the decolonisation process with the goal of ensuring all trust territories successfully gained secure independence with stable governments.
	Currently its role is redundant, however it served a crucial purpose in the post Second World War era. Its operations were suspended in 1994 after the last remaining trust territory (Palau) gained independence.
	The Council is headed by Anne Guegen and also has a vice president; it meets on occasion as per her request or that of the UNSC or UNGA.

UN membership

Initially, 51 states signed the UN Charter and became the founding members of the organisation. As of 2022, the UN has 193 member states. The most recent full member of the UN was South Sudan, which gained independence from Sudan in 2011 and joined the UN in the same year. The UN's membership increased dramatically in the 1950s and 1960s, as many former colonies achieved independence. All undisputed nation-states in the world are UN member states. Indeed, there is a direct link between being recognised as an independent nation-state and becoming a UN member state.

Where a state's sovereignty is not internationally recognised, it may be given non-member observer status if it is agreed by a vote of the UN General Assembly. Palestine, whose independence is still disputed, has been given non-member observer status (the Vatican is the only other). This allows its voice to be heard at the UNGA, but stops short of giving it full recognition as an independent state or allowing it voting rights.

The UN was founded on the basis that all member states would be equal, regardless of their size or power (see Chapter 2). The UN Charter states that the UN will operate on the basis of the 'sovereign equality of all of its members'. From the beginnings of the UN and its Charter, it was recognised that the UN would respect state sovereignty and the independence of states. Chapter 1 of the charter states that the UN 'should not intervene in matters which are essentially within the domestic jurisdiction of any state'. This was an early indication that the UN would focus its activities only on those issues that required a unified, global approach and not interfere with anything best left for states to deal with independently. The UN is therefore dependent on states consenting to the activities it proposes – nothing is forced on states (except in rare circumstances, with UNSC authorisation).

While the UN Charter commits to treating all member states equally, regardless of power or size, the same charter gave additional powers to the five permanent members (frequently abbreviated to the P5) of the UNSC, making them in effect more powerful than other member states in some areas. These additional powers are explored in greater detail later in the chapter.

The UN Secretariat and secretary-general

The UN Secretariat is the UN's civil service or administrative body, overseeing the work of the entire UN and its subsidiary bodies and agencies. It has tens of thousands of staff across the world, under the overall leadership of the UN secretary-general at the headquarters in New York. The secretary-general's role includes the following:

- Acting as the UN's public spokesperson. Former secretary-general Kofi Annan spoke of the need for the UN to have 'someone with a status that governments would recognise, someone with authority to speak to humanity as a whole. Who could that be, if not the secretary-general of the United Nations?' The UN secretary-general can be useful in cajoling states to act in the international interest, particularly when states might be either not minded to act or too slow in reaching agreements (for example on climate change).
- Leading the UN Secretariat and setting the UN agenda, to be approved by consensus with the member states in the UNGA. Once decisions and resolutions have been passed by member states, the various organs and institutions of the UN then are tasked with the administration of these policies, for example organising the UN Development Programme's work in support of the Sustainable Development Goals.

Table 3.4 UN secretaries-general

Period in office	Secretary-general	Nationality
1946–52	Trygve Lie	Norway
1953–61	Dag Hammarskjöld	Sweden
1961–71	U Thant	Myanmar (Burma)
1972–81	Kurt Waldheim	Austria
1982–91	Javier Pérez de Cuéllar	Peru
1992–96	Boutros Boutros-Ghali	Egypt
1997–2006	Kofi Annan	Ghana
2007–16	Ban Ki-moon	Republic of Korea (South Korea)
2017–	António Guterres	Portugal

The UNGA appoints the secretary-general on the recommendation of the Security Council, for a 5-year term (see Table 3.4). The secretary-general is expected to represent the interests of the UN and not any single nation-state or group of nation-states. In reality, the secretary-general's powers are limited, but the role usually carries considerable persuasive or soft power (see page 247), enhanced through being seen as neutral and defending the UN's founding values. Both Hammarskjöld and Annan were awarded the Nobel Peace Prize for their UN leadership. Of course, this does not prevent the public statements of the secretary-general from sometimes being ignored, particularly if the UNSC does not back those statements (significant power in the UN resides in the decisions of the UNSC and the consent of the UNGA).

However, some secretaries-general have used the role to set a decisive agenda for the UN. For example, Kofi Annan led the Millennium Summit and Report, which culminated in the agreement of the MDGs. The same report also adopted the suggestion of a doctrine known as the Responsibility to Protect (R2P), which recognised the need to legitimise external intervention when states abuse human rights. Previously, Secretary-General Dag Hammarskjöld was the driving force in creating the UN peacekeeping forces, famous for their blue helmets or berets.

The secretary-general's power also depends on the prevailing geopolitics of the time. During the Cold War, secretaries-general found it difficult to project a distinctive agenda during the bipolar standoff between the Soviet Union and the US. After the 9/11 terror attacks, Secretary-General Kofi Annan attempted in vain to persuade the US, motivated to protect its perception of its national interest, to pursue its interests through the UN. Annan expressed his regret that the 2003 invasion of Iraq was launched unilaterally, without a specific UNSC Resolution, declaring the military action illegal and contrary to the UN Charter.

The UN Security Council

The UNSC is the UN's executive committee and is responsible for maintaining international peace and security. It is the most powerful branch of the UN, with powers to:

- issue binding resolutions in international law, by which all UN member states must abide
- issue economic sanctions and call upon other UN member states to adopt them
- authorise military action, ranging from humanitarian intervention to no-fly zones
- decide whether new member states should be recognised by the UN General Assembly.

The UNSC is the supreme decision-making body for dealing with international crises. It is comprised of five permanent members and ten elected, non-permanent members. The UN Charter grants special powers to its permanent members, such as the right to veto UNSC Resolutions, preventing them from being agreed and taking effect.

The UNSC in session at the UN Headquarters in New York

The UNSC's streamlined membership is designed to make it an active and decisive body on international security matters. The larger membership of the League of Nations, with powerful states and less powerful states seen as equals, had led to the powerful states leaving in order to protect their national interests. The UNSC allows the possibility of joint action where there is agreement but also allows the most powerful states the right to veto and protect their national interests. Its effectiveness is, therefore, dependent on what its members, particularly its permanent members, are able to agree.

Membership

The UNSC is made up of five permanent members: China, France, Russia, the UK and the US. The permanent members were the most powerful states when the UN was founded, including the victors of the Second World War. There are also ten non-permanent members, which the UNGA elects for 2-year terms (see Table 3.5).

The permanent members have the right to veto any resolution with which they disagree. Non-permanent members have no veto power.

Some states have served as non-permanent members more frequently than others. For example, Japan and Brazil have respectively served 11 and 12 terms on the Security Council. This reflects a willingness for the UN General Assembly to re-elect powerful non-permanent members. There are many states, often smaller and less powerful states, that have never served as non-permanent members.

Functions and powers

Table 3.5 UNSC permanent and non-permanent membership, 2021

Permanent members	Non-permanent members
France	Regional allocation, overlapping
China	Africa: three seats
Russia	Western Europe and Oceania, Asia, Latin America and the
UK	Caribbean: two seats each
US	India, Ireland, Kenya, Mexico, Norway (until end of 2022)
	Albania, Brazil, Gabon, Ghana and the United Arab Emirates (until end of 2023)

Some have called the UNSC the most powerful body in international politics, owing to the powers it has. Its resolutions create binding international law and other states are legally required to comply with them. It is the only part of the UN that can authorise military action against other states.

UN Security Council resolutions can ultimately authorise whatever action the members decide is necessary to support the founding objectives of the UN 'to maintain international peace and security' and 'to develop friendly relations among nations'. A resolution is passed if:

- there is no veto from a permanent member
- there are nine votes in favour from permanent and non-permanent members.

Most typically, the UN Security Council has a range of options available, in increasing order of severity:

- setting up a process of peace talks, with the authority of the UN
- requiring a ceasefire to enable humanitarian assistance to be provided or talks to take place

- economic sanctions – for example, freezing the financial assets of key individuals or companies
- authorising a UN peacekeeping mission or other military action (this might be relatively small in scale, such as observers to monitor the conflict, or large in scale, such as a full peacekeeping force with the authority to use force to protect civilians).

The UNSC should be thought of as a forum for negotiation and discussion, where states group together to propose resolutions and to agree the wording and the action that the Council wishes to take. The non-permanent members are often sidelined by the permanent members (especially the US, France and UK) in the drafting of resolutions. If seven non-permanent members vote against a resolution, it will not pass, even if all five permanent members vote in favour (the so-called 'sixth veto', but to date this has never occurred).

The veto: vital safeguard or cause of paralysis?

It is possible to criticise the veto for giving too much power to the permanent members, making the UN Security Council sometimes ineffective when important resolutions are blocked. Surely, it cannot be right that one powerful state has the right to block a resolution that might help resolve a conflict. However, it is important to consider why the permanent members were given veto power.

Firstly, if enough permanent members felt that they could not stop decisions and resolutions that went against their national interest, they might choose to leave the forum altogether. Powerful states would be unlikely to accept a situation in which they could be outvoted on matters as important to powerful states as peace and security. This would result in considerable instability if the major powers refused to participate in such a forum at all and no permanent forum therefore existed. So, the veto power was given to the most powerful states to keep them within the UN system.

Secondly, there is the idea that it is in the international interest for action only to be taken when the most powerful states agree. This is known as 'great power unanimity'. Imagine if, with no veto power, Russia and China could be outvoted by the US, France and the UK (or vice versa) and resolutions launching military action were readily passed without all of the major powers agreeing. This could potentially lead to a series of resolutions being passed that actively brought the major powers into conflict with each another. It is perhaps better to have a system in which national interest is being defended using a veto than permanent members feeling they needed to retaliate with military action or sanctions to block a decision by other members of the Security Council.

Consequently, the design of the UN Security Council recognises that some states are (or were) more powerful than others. The more powerful states needed to have their superiority recognised and for decisions on peace and security matters to be taken in a smaller group, where these states could defend their interests using the veto. The veto therefore recognises the importance of powerful countries remaining within the UN. States may also abstain if they do not agree with a UNSC Resolution but do not feel strongly enough to veto.

Whether or not and how often the permanent members use their veto depends on how powerful they are, and on the balance of power in the UNSC itself, at any time:

- Russia is the most frequent user of the veto – it has used the veto more than 100 times since 1945. It also used the veto more times than any other state during the Cold War period.

- The US is the second most frequent user of the veto. It also vetoed frequently during the Cold War period, although it vetoed less frequently than the Soviet Union during the Cold War as it was less isolated in the UNSC.
- The Cold War saw the Soviet Union and the US frequently use the veto, reflecting the bipolarity of the world order in which both nation-states were equally powerful and intent on challenging each other.
- After the Cold War, the US became the most frequent user of the veto as it became the dominant power in a unipolar world order. A defeated former Soviet Union, now the Russian Federation, did not veto as much as it had during the Cold War.
- Since 2001, a more multipolar world order has frequently seen Russia use the veto and, for the first time, China has been increasingly willing to veto. This has been especially problematic in the UN's response to the conflict in Syria, where disagreements between Russia and France, the UK and the US have seen frequent vetoes of resolutions on both sides.
- France and the UK have not vetoed since 1989. This arguably reflects the fact that, as less powerful permanent member states, they recognise that it is better to abstain on issues that they disagree with rather than veto and raise further questions about the legitimacy of their permanent membership.

Often just as important as the permanent members' use of the veto are the occasions when a resolution was not put to a vote because it was known in advance that a permanent member intended to use its veto. For example, in 2003, France and Russia made it clear that they would veto a UK/US-led resolution seeking final authorisation for the military invasion of Iraq. The UK and the US knew that their resolution would be vetoed and that there was a fundamental difference of opinion since France and Russia believed that Iraq should be given more time to comply with UN weapons inspections. Therefore, they abandoned their resolution and instead took military action without UNSC approval and with the UNSC powerless to stop it.

The UNSC is especially weak, indeed powerless, when a permanent member misbehaves or decides to take unilateral action in defiance of the UNSC (for example, the US-led invasion of Iraq in 2003 and Russian forces' annexation of Crimea in 2014). Similarly, in a Security Council meeting in 2018, the UK directly accused Russia of using a nerve agent against civilians in UK territory in Salisbury earlier that year. Clearly, there was no prospect of the UNSC issuing a resolution against Russia, and the UK successfully encouraged its allies (including the US) to issue sanctions independently and without UNSC backing.

There have been several high-profile examples of resolutions vetoed, with permanent members voting against to protect their allies or national interest and suggesting that the UNSC is often gridlocked on important matters.

- In 2020, Russia and China vetoed three resolutions calling for improved humanitarian assistance to Syria and demanding that all parties comply with international law.
- In 2018, the US vetoed a resolution that condemned Israel's use of force against Palestinian civilians.
- In 2017, the US vetoed a resolution calling on states to refrain from recognising Jerusalem as the capital of Israel (as the US had recently done).
- In 2015, Russia vetoed a resolution calling for an international criminal tribunal to investigate those responsible for crimes connected with downing Malaysian Airlines flight MH17 over Ukraine in 2014.

UN Security Council achievements

Despite the focus on the veto, it is important to consider the actions that the UNSC has successfully agreed and achieved. Against the many examples of gridlock by permanent members' use of the veto, the UNSC has been remarkably active and is capable of acting decisively when there is agreement among its permanent members.

The UNSC has passed many significant resolutions in its lifetime (see Table 3.6). It has authorised peacekeeping forces across the world in more than 70 operations since 1948. This is perhaps the most impressive achievement of the UN Security Council, authorising a range of peacekeeping missions including:

- UN military observers tasked with monitoring the actions of parties in a conflict. This helps to discourage parties from fighting each other or escalating tensions. It helps the Security Council to understand, should conflict resume, which parties have been responsible for escalating conflict. There has been a UN observer mission in Israel and Palestine since 1948, the UN's longest peacekeeping operation.
- In more unstable countries, such as South Sudan, there have been UNSC authorised peacekeeping missions involving a mixture of military troops, civilian experts and police officers from UN member states.
- The UN has authorised many important humanitarian interventions (see Chapter 5) including those in Libya (2011), the former Yugoslavia (from 1992) and East Timor (1999–2005).

Topic link

The effectiveness of UN-led humanitarian intervention is explored further in Chapter 5.

Beyond peacekeeping, the UNSC has taken the following types of action in recent years:

- **Peace talks:** the UNSC has passed resolutions setting up a process of talks between key parties in the Syrian conflict since 2015. As of 2021, these had not led to any ceasefire or conclusion to the conflict.
- **Sanctions:** the UNSC authorised sanctions against Iran from 2005 until 2015 and, more recently, strengthened sanctions against North Korea. It has also issued sanctions against violent non-state actors, including ISIL and al-Qaeda.
- **Ceasefire:** UNSC resolutions called for a ceasefire in Libya and set up a UN support mission which helped to secure the signing of a ceasefire agreement in 2020 between the key parties.

A further UNSC success story is that the permanent members have all remained within the UN system and have – without any interruption – maintained the UNSC as a forum for negotiation and diplomacy since 1945. This record contrasts with the League of Nations' failures, where the most powerful states felt that the only way to protect their national interests was to leave the organisation altogether.

Table 3.6 Significant UNSC Resolutions

Date	UNSC Resolution	Effect
22 November 1967	242	The UNSC calls on Israel to withdraw from territory that it occupied in the Six Day War, including the Gaza Strip, Golan Heights and West Bank. Israel has not complied with this resolution and has occupied the territory since 1967.
8 November 2002	1441	The UNSC unanimously gives Iraq and its leader Saddam Hussein a 'final opportunity with its disarmament obligations', stating that the country was in material breach of previous UNSC ceasefire resolutions. It warns of 'serious consequences' in the event of future violations. The UK and US governments claimed that this authorised the 2003 invasion of Iraq. Many experts in international law – including the UN Secretary-General Kofi Annan – disagreed.

Date	UNSC Resolution	Effect
31 July 2006	1696	Concerned that Iran is developing nuclear weapons, the resolution demands that Iran 'suspend all enrichment-related and reprocessing activities, including research and development'. The resolution threatened economic sanctions would follow if Iran did not comply within a month. When Iran did not comply, four successive UNSC resolutions between 2006 and 2010 imposed various, increasingly tough, economic sanctions on Iran.
17 March 2011	1973	The UNSC demands a ceasefire in Libya and agrees 'all necessary means short of foreign occupation' for the protection of civilians. It also establishes a no-fly zone. China and Russia abstain. NATO then begins an air campaign that includes bombing key Libyan government targets.
27 September 2013	2118	The UNSC requires Syria to disarm itself of chemical weapons, establishing a process removing chemical weapons overseen by the Organisation for the Prohibition of Chemical Weapons (OPCW). This did not prevent Syria from developing further improvised 'barrel bomb' chemical weapons and using them against civilians.

Debate

Does the veto prevent the UNSC from getting anything done?

Yes

- Permanent members are too powerful and are able to veto anything that threatens their national interests and prevent action from being taken – the UNSC has been powerless to act meaningfully on Syria, for example.
- Powerful permanent members can misbehave and veto any action against them (for example, Russia's actions in Crimea in 2014).
- The UNSC is powerless to stop powerful countries from acting alone (or unilaterally) to pursue their interests (for example, the US-led invasion of Iraq in 2003).

No

- The UNSC achieves a lot, passing many resolutions successfully.
- Under its Chapter VI powers, it has authorised over 70 peacekeeping missions around the world since 1948. Under its Chapter VII powers, it has authorised military action (most recently in Libya in 2011) and has imposed successful sanctions on regimes posing a risk to international security.
- The veto supports the idea of 'great power unanimity', meaning the UNSC can only take actions with the agreement of the major powers of the P5. This reduces the likelihood that the UN will take action that will bring the P5 themselves into conflict.

Evaluation tip: clearly, the veto does not prevent the UNSC from getting *anything* done. One could further evaluate whether the UNSC is able to act on the most serious issues.

Arguments for reform

Many criticise membership of the UNSC as outdated, saying that it represented the most powerful states at its creation in 1945, but not the major powers of today. While it can still be argued that China, Russia and the US are major world powers, whether France and the UK still deserve great power status and the veto rights that come with it is debatable. British and French membership is still largely linked to their status as nuclear weapons states, their power at the end of the Second World War and their subsequently high-profile roles in international diplomacy.

There have been calls for newly risen, and some long-established, powers to be included as permanent members. Brazil, Germany, India and Japan – all of which are much more powerful than they were in 1945 – have been the most widely suggested new permanent members. There have also been calls for an African state, such as Nigeria or South Africa, to gain permanent membership – the continents of Africa and South America are currently entirely unrepresented.

These changes would require amendments to the UN Charter, for which changes would need a two-thirds majority of the UNGA with none of the permanent members voting against. The current permanent members would therefore be able to prevent any new permanent members that were not to their liking or if they feared these new members would diminish their own influence. Even agreeing on potential new permanent members is fraught with difficulty. Pakistan would be likely to oppose a permanent membership for India. Choosing which of Africa's main economic powers, perhaps Nigeria or South Africa, gets membership is not an obvious or easy choice.

Options for reform include:

- adding new permanent members with veto power
- adding new permanent members that do not have veto power (this was proposed by Germany, Japan, Brazil and India in 2005)
- removing veto power from some or all of the current permanent members
- increasing the number of non-permanent members, or having them serve longer terms than the current non-permanent members (the number of non-permanent members was successfully increased from six to ten in 1965).

Debate

Should the UNSC be reformed?

Yes

- France and the UK are no longer significant world powers and should either be replaced or supplemented with other powers that have emerged since 1945.
- The UNSC's composition does not represent the current distribution of global power. This is especially glaring in not taking into account newly emerged powers such as Brazil, Germany, India and Japan.
- More non-permanent or permanent members without veto power could be a compromise that would allow for greater representation without giving new members too much power. Adding more powerful states as permanent 'non-veto' members and continuing to require a two-thirds majority would reduce the power of the P5.
- The UNSC was already successfully reformed in 1965, when the number of non-permanent members increased from six to ten.

No

- The current permanent members would be likely to be a significant obstacle to reform, as they would all need to agree to any change to the UN Charter in the UN General Assembly. This makes any removal of permanent members impossible.
- Agreeing on new members to be put to the UN General Assembly as part of any amendment to the UN Charter would be fraught with difficulty. Pakistan would likely oppose India's membership, seeing this as a direct threat to its interests. The amount of non-permanent members was reformed in 1965, allowing for greater representation.
- More states having veto power would further increase the likelihood of resolutions being vetoed and, therefore, the UNSC being unable to act. Even with only two states, Russia and the US, active users of the veto (see Figure 3.2), the UNSC is often in stalemate.
- Measures such as abolishing the veto altogether, or otherwise restricting the ability of the major powers to protect their national interests, could see the UN return to the problems of the League of Nations, where the major powers withdrew because they had no facility to defend their national interests.

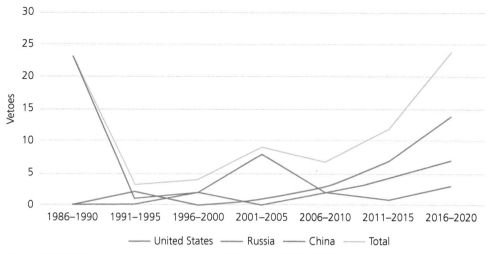

Figure 3.2 **UNSC permanent members' use of the veto, 1986–2020**

Military power

The UN does not have a military force of its own. The UN Charter attempted to set up a Military Staff Committee that would take charge of planning military operations. However, the UNSC permanent members did not provide the military forces needed to set up an independent military contingent. This partly reflected nervousness and the fractured nature of the Cold War period. However, it was also clear that the permanent members did not wish to divert and dilute their own military resources to a UN force.

Consequently, the UNSC has had to rely on organisations such as NATO and the African Union (AU) to carry out military operations on its behalf. The African Union Mission in Somalia (AMISOM) has operated under a UNSC Resolution, and is funded and supported by the UN Department for Peacekeeping Operations. The UNSC authorised military action in Libya in 2011, but NATO carried out the action.

Table 3.7 **Strengths and weaknesses of the UNSC**

Strengths	Weaknesses
'Great power unanimity' ensures that nothing is agreed that would de-stabilise relations between the major powers.	Undermined by outdated and exclusive membership, with the non-permanent members sidelined.
Streamlined, exclusive membership ensures that decisions can be (and are) taken.	Frequently in gridlock as permanent members increasingly using veto power and acting in national, not global, interest.

Activity

When looking at the work of the UN Security Council, it is interesting to consider the full range of its meetings, not just the resolutions that are successfully passed. Have a look at the meetings of the UNSC in a particular year, using this link:

www.un.org/press/en/content/security-council/meetings-coverage

1 Are the global issues that it has discussed the ones you would expect?
2 Which issues have been discussed by the UNSC but *did not* result in a UNSC resolution? Why do you think this is?
3 Which issues have been discussed by the UNSC and *did* result in a UNSC resolution? Why do you think this is?

The UN General Assembly

Often called the UN's parliament, the UN General Assembly (UNGA) is the UN forum in which all 193 member states have an equal voice and vote (see Figure 3.3). It is the only UN organ in which every member state has a permanent representative. NGOs are often allowed to attend and address UNGA meetings, further widening the accessibility and inclusivity of the UNGA as a forum for debate.

The UNGA's main occasion is its annual meeting, held every September at the UN Headquarters in New York at the UNGA's debating chamber. This equality of representation is notable for allowing countries to have a voice regardless of their size or power, but it does mean that the UNGA is relatively weak in its powers. Unlike those of the UNSC, its resolutions are not binding and carry no force in international law. Member states can therefore ignore these resolutions, meaning they carry mostly symbolic status. The UNGA also has no authoritative voice on matters of international security, which are largely left to the UNSC to deal with alone.

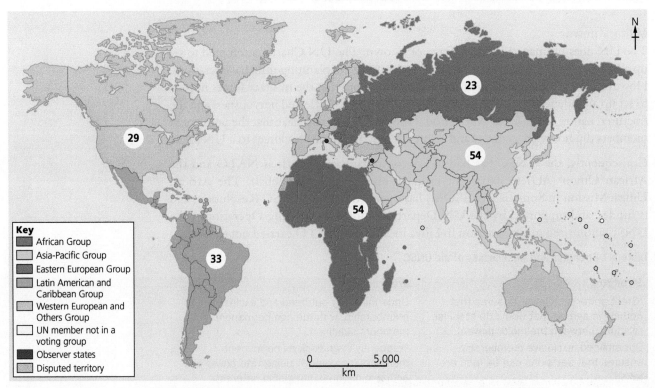

Key
- African Group
- Asia-Pacific Group
- Eastern European Group
- Latin American and Caribbean Group
- Western European and Others Group
- UN member not in a voting group
- Observer states
- Disputed territory

Figure 3.3 Division of the UNGA – numbers in circles show the number of states in that UNGA division

Functions and powers

The UNGA's primary functions include:

- electing UNSC non-permanent members, and members of ECOSOC
- appointing the secretary-general based on the UNSC's recommendation
- considering and debating reports from ECOSOC and the ICJ
- approving the UN's budget
- electing judges to the ICJ.

Decision making in the UNGA can be challenging and time-consuming, given that every member state can take part in debates. UNGA decisions on resolutions relating to peace and security, admission of new members and the UN budget need a two-thirds majority, making it difficult to reach consensus on the most controversial issues.

However, the UNGA can take decisive action. Its most enduring achievement was the UN's UDHR, signed in 1948. The UDHR remains the foundational and guiding global human rights framework, and it has influenced subsequent international and domestic human rights law. More recently, in 2000, the UNGA approved the Millennium Declaration, which agreed a unified set of global economic and human development targets, the Millennium Development Goals (MDGs). The UNGA agreed the successor to the MDGs, the Sustainable Development Goals (SDGs), in September 2015. The SDGs set out a new series of targets for development that will run until 2030 (see Box 3.2, which sets out further aspects of the 2016 UNGA agenda).

More controversial decisions are also not beyond the powers of the UNGA. Palestine was granted non-member observer status in 2012, despite powerful and vocal opposition from Israel and the US, which both voted against the resolution (138 states voted in favour, 41 abstained, including the UK, and nine voted against). This recognition of Palestine at the UN subsequently allowed it to successfully become the 123rd signatory to the Rome Statute, whereupon it formally joined the ICC. This meant that, for the first time, it was within ICC powers to investigate Israeli security forces in Palestinian territory for alleged war crimes.

The decisions taken by the UN General Assembly have been increasingly successful in pushing forward the UN's development work. This is partly due to the expanding membership of the Assembly since the 1960s, with a majority now from African and Asian states. Before this, when the UN's membership was smaller, the US and its allies could count on a two-thirds majority (the NATO members enjoyed this in the early decades of the UN). This accounts for the General Assembly's major achievement of the last few decades, in agreeing the Millennium and Sustainable Development Goals.

Box 3.2

Extracts from the Agenda of the UN General Assembly, September 2021

The UNGA Agenda is categorised into nine main sections for discussion, some of which, from the 2021 Agenda, are included below.
- International peace and security:
  - the situation in Afghanistan
  - the situation in the occupied territories of Ukraine
  - the situation in the middle East
  - peacebuilding and sustaining peace
  - report by the UNSC
- Economic growth and sustainable development:
  - report by ECOSOC
  - improving global road safety
  - tackling malaria in developing countries, particularly in Africa
  - building a better world through sport and the Olympic ideal
- Human rights:
  - report by the Human Rights Council
  - elimination of racism, racial discrimination, xenophobia and related intolerance

→

- Humanitarian and disaster relief assistance:
  - strengthening of the coordination of emergency humanitarian assistance of the UN
  - assistance to the Palestinian people
- Justice and international law:
  - report by the ICJ
  - report by the ICC
  - oceans and law of the sea
- Disarmament:
  - reduction of military budgets
  - prevention of an arms race in outer space
- Organisational and administrative matters:
  - report of the secretary-general
  - appointment of the UN secretary-general
  - election of the five non-permanent members of the UNSC

Case study

The UN General Assembly as an influencer?

The UN General Assembly, while less powerful than the UN Security Council, has the power of increased legitimacy through its full membership. This has enabled it to take some important decisions, even if the more powerful states do not always have to comply with these decisions.

2000 – The Millennium Declaration: this special declaration was agreed by the UNGA at a special Millennium Summit in 2000 and reaffirmed the UN member states to the principles of the UN Charter. It agreed the UN's Millennium Development Goals which revitalised the international development agenda behind a series of eight goals towards which all states, IGOs and NGOs would work in a more coordinated effort.

2005 – Responsibility to Protect (known as 'R2P', see page 27): the principle that states have a responsibility to protect their own civilians and those in other states from human rights abuses was agreed by the General Assembly in 2005. This was the result of years of political pressure in the General Assembly, with UN Secretary-General Kofi Annan putting forward the idea regularly as part of his interactions with the Assembly. While not binding and certainly not ensuring that states always comply with these principles, the UNGA agreeing a resolution on R2P has given the concept considerable legitimacy and authority.

2017 – Syria: with the UN Security Council unable to condemn the Syrian government for human rights abuses, the UN General Assembly passed a resolution condemning the use of chemical weapons and calling on all parties to protect civilians. Although not as powerful as a UNSC Resolution, the UNGA resolution went further than the UNSC was prepared to go in condemning the Syrian government and other actors in the conflict. It served as a statement of the strength of international opinion from the wider membership of the UN.

Activity

Across the world, many students take part in Model United Nations (MUN), a simulation of the UN's debates and procedures. This provides an excellent way of understanding the UN's processes and how individual states make their views known and shape cooperative policies on issues of importance to them. Many MUN conferences replicate the UNGA's sub-committees, which then propose ideas for the entire UNGA to vote on.

→

1 Research how UNGA Resolutions are written here: **http://bestdelegate.com/model-un-made-easy-how-to-write-a-resolution**

2 Working in groups, write your own UN Resolution on an issue in global politics that you care about.

3 As a class, you could come up with your own agenda of different issues to be discussed and then debate them together, using this resource as a guide: **http://bestdelegate.com/how-to-debate-resolutions**

Committees

The UNGA committees (see Table 3.10) are a means of streamlining the work of the Assembly into specific, focused committees. The committees have much smaller membership and put forward proposals for resolutions to be voted on, and therefore adopted by, the full UNGA. During the course of a year, each committee will submit as many as 60 draft resolutions for the UNGA to consider. The committees are an important means for states to call for action on specific issues and apply pressure on other actors in global politics.

The Human Rights Council is another subsidiary body of the UNGA and elects 47 member states to 3-year terms to promote and monitor states' compliance with international human rights laws (such as the Covenants on Political and Civil Rights and on Economic and Social Rights). The Human Rights Council has been criticised for including prominent states which themselves are responsible for human rights abuses, with Human Rights Watch accusing it of being 'a jury that includes murderers ... who are determined to stymie investigation of their crimes'.

Table 3.8 Strengths and weaknesses of the UN General Assembly

Strengths	Weaknesses
Includes all member states, each with one vote (equality).	Agenda can be too full and decision making too slow/impossible to agree as reaching two-thirds majority on important matters is difficult.
Resolutions can have symbolic power, especially when the UNSC is unable to agree. Its resolutions legitimise the work of the UN.	
	Lacks authority, resolutions are non-binding. Dominance of less powerful states puts it at odds with agenda of more powerful states.
Covers wide range of issues and has had a big impact on development agenda.	
Supervises other committees (e.g. ECOSOC).	Subordinate to the UN Security Council on matters of peace and security.

The Economic and Social Council

ECOSOC is one of the principal organs of the UN and is responsible for economic security and development across the UN's member states. It is made up of 54 member states, elected by the General Assembly for 3-year terms.

It has several key functions, all of which relate to issues of economic and social development:

- to act as a forum for debate
- to agree specific policies that can be implemented by other UN agencies (such as the World Health Organization)
- to lead on international development goals set out in the Millennium Development Goals (2000–2015) and the Sustainable Development Goals (2015–2030).

ECOSOC provides an opportunity for a smaller number of states to share responsibility for social and economic policy. Doing so in a smaller forum than the UN General Assembly enables greater efficiency and focus. ECOSOC has 14 subsidiary bodies, which include well-known UN agencies and funds that are allocated large amounts of the UN's budget to carry out their work (see Table 3.9).

It passes resolutions which are drafted by member states in a similar way to the UNGA and UNSC, which require a simple majority to pass but are not binding on member states. The initiation of the Millennium Development Goals by the UN General Assembly in 2000, creating a clear set of development targets, gave even greater focus to ECOSOC's work and, with it, significant responsibility to ECOSOC for overseeing progress towards targets in the MDGs and the renewed Sustainable Development Goals (SDGs) from 2015. For example, ECOSOC manages a specific forum which monitors progress towards the SDGs and meets annually.

ECOSOC's specialised agencies have the power to set their own agenda and some, for example the IMF, are highly influential players on the world stage. The leaders of these agencies, for example the IMF's Kristalina Georgieva, speak with real independence and authority. Its programmes and funds also bear huge responsibility for delivering much of what the UNGA pledges to do. For example, the UNDP (UN Development Programme) has led all the UN's work on human and economic development across the world, with a large budget of over US$5 billion.

Table 3.9 ECOSOC: major specialised agencies and funds

Specialised agencies	Programmes and funds
Specialised agencies have their own budgets, leadership and organising assemblies made up of a small number of member states. They include: • the UN Educational, Scientific and Cultural Organization (UNESCO) • the World Bank (see page 28) • the IMF (see page 28).	ECOSOC directly administers and manages programmes and funds while UNGA supervises them. They are less autonomous than the specialised agencies, and include: • the WHO • the UN Development Programme (UNDP) • the World Food Programme (WFP)

Table 3.10 UNGA committees and their functions

Committee	Functions and key decisions
Disarmament and International Security Committee	Considers all disarmament and international security matters, including matters ranging from preventing the proliferation of nuclear weapons to the illegal small arms trade. The committee reports to the UNGA, which can vote on ideas the committee discusses. For example, an UNGA Resolution was passed in 2010 pressing for a nuclear weapons-free zone in the middle east.
Economic and Financial Committee	Considers issues relating to economic development, including international trade and poverty reduction. For example, during the Covid-19 pandemic in 2020, the committee was analysing the impact on the progress of the Sustainable Development Goals and passed resolutions on the impact of the crisis on migrants. This is an excellent example of the specifics that the sub-committees can get into, ensuring that the UN system hears the interests of a very specific group of states.
Social, Humanitarian and Cultural Committee	Debates specific areas of human rights concern, such as the rights of women and refugees. The committee can call for action relating to specific human rights abuses in specific countries. For example, in 2020 it put forward resolutions to the General Assembly condemning abuses in Syria, Myanmar and Iran.

Case study

ECOSOC and its role in the Covid-19 pandemic

During the Covid-19 global pandemic beginning in 2020, ECOSOC became an important forum for discussion and agreeing policy action of its various agencies.

- **Impact on the Sustainable Development Goals:** a key focus for ECOSOC's discussions was to evaluate how progress towards the SDGs was being affected by the global pandemic. Looking ahead to the economic recovery, ECOSOC identified the risk that states might neglect sustainable development when devising their economic plans. ECOSOC warned that the pandemic might reverse decades of development progress.
- **Vaccines:** the World Health Organization, as one of ECOSOC's UN agencies, was participating in an international effort to improve access to Covid-19 vaccines

worldwide. In partnership with the European Union and the G20, the COVAX programme included encouraging wealthier states to donate vaccine doses to the programme to ensure more equal access to the vaccine. It also coordinated projects to help improve tests for the virus, improve and share knowledge on treatment and carry out research to help individual countries identify blockages in their health systems.

- **Education:** Another of ECOSOC's UN agencies focused on the educational impact of the pandemic, estimating that in the first year of the pandemic schools for as many as 168 million children had been closed for a full year. It also worked to coordinate international procurement of Covid-19 vaccines as part of the COVAX programme. Its global 'good will' ambassadors, including former England footballer David Beckham, led public information campaigns encouraging people to get vaccinated.

Table 3.11 Strengths and weaknesses of ECOSOC

Strengths	Weaknesses
• Oversees a wide range of other impactful UN bodies, including the World Health Organization and the IMF. • The SDGs and the MDGs have given a very clear focus to the work of ECOSOC, with greater ability to monitor progress and agree future action.	• There is some overlap and confusion between the roles of ECOSOC and the UN General Assembly. • ECOSOC's role in respect of human rights is merely one of monitoring and it does not have enough powers to force states to change their behaviour.

Activity

ECOSOC is responsible for a significant amount of the UN's activities, especially in economic development and human rights, through its various UN agencies and funds. Use the websites for the organisations below to write your own summary of the work of the UN bodies below, focusing on a) current projects and b) impact.

1 The World Health Organization: WHO | World Health Organization
2 United Nations Children's Fund (UNICEF): UNICEF

The International Court of Justice

The ICJ is the principal judicial organ of the UN. Based in the Peace Palace at The Hague, in the Netherlands, it has two key functions:

1 To settle legal disputes between member states.
2 To give advisory opinions on legal questions submitted by authorised agencies.

The ICJ is based in the Peace Palace at The Hague

It is sometimes assumed that the ICJ makes rulings on human rights matters, but it is not a criminal court. It does not have the powers to investigate, for example, crimes against humanity and this is largely left to the International Criminal Court and the international criminal tribunals (see page 51). It mostly focuses on disputes over territory and breaches of other international laws or treaties that states have signed.

The court has 15 judges, all of whom the UNGA elects for 9-year terms and are independent, rather than representing their home state. Unusually for a legal process, the court does not have automatic authority to hear cases between states — instead both sides must agree that the court has jurisdiction (or the legitimate legal authority to make a ruling) on the matter. This has allowed states simply to declare that they do not recognise the court's authority in respect of cases that are not to their liking.

States will be subject to the ICJ's rulings if:

- they make a special agreement with one or more other states to submit a case on which they disagree to the ICJ
- they sign a treaty specifying that any disputes relating to that treaty will be resolved by the ICJ (over 300 international treaties do so)
- they sign a 'unilateral declaration' accepting the ICJ's authority in any dispute that might arise in the future (only 72 states have done so).

Topic link

The effectiveness of international courts and tribunals in upholding human rights is explored in Chapter 4.

The ICJ has successfully made rulings on contentious cases and carries out an important role in arbitrating between states that are in dispute with each other. For example, in 2004, it ruled that the security fence Israel constructed around the Palestinian West Bank, in territory that a UNSC Resolution continues to call for Israel to withdraw from, was illegal under international law. However, Israel chose to ignore this ruling and continued to build the barrier, stating that it was vital to its internal security.

In theory, ICJ rulings are binding on UN member states. If they do not comply, the UN Charter allows for the matter to be referred to the UNSC for enforcement. However, again action is entirely dependent on the UNSC issuing a resolution forcing states to comply.

Case study

The UK and Chagos Islands dispute

In 2019, the International Court of Justice ruled that the UK's claims of sovereignty over the Chagos Islands in the Indian Ocean were unlawful. When Mauritius gained independence from the UK in 1968, the UK kept territorial control of the islands and later leased one of the islands, Diego Garcia, to the US to run as a military base. Over a thousand islanders were deported from the islands to Mauritius. The airbase was an important strategic asset to US and UK air forces during the conflicts in Afghanistan and Iraq.

The ICJ case had been prompted two years earlier, when the UN General Assembly passed a resolution calling for the court to issue an 'advisory opinion' on the UK's claims on the Chagos Islands. An advisory opinion is a judgment made by the ICJ in response to a recommendation from one of the UN's organs, such as the General Assembly.

In response to the judgment, the UK government said it had 'no doubt as to our sovereignty over the British Indian Ocean Territory, which has been under continuous British sovereignty since 1814. Mauritius has never held sovereignty and the UK does not recognise its claim'. The UN General Assembly issued a further (non-binding) resolution setting the UK a deadline for withdrawing from the Chagos Islands. As of 2022, the Chagos Islands remain under UK control.

Table 3.12 **Strengths and weaknesses of the International Court of Justice**

Strengths	Weaknesses
• With and without the consent of states, the ICJ is still able to make important judgments which carry authority and many states see the ICJ as a useful mediator in disputes. • Many international treaties specify that the ICJ is the designated means of resolving disputes for the agreements they set out.	• States effectively give their permission to be subject to the court's decisions; this is not automatic. • Enforcement of rulings is dependent on the UNSC, but this is rare. The UNGA can merely apply pressure with non-binding resolutions. • Rulings, therefore, can easily be ignored.

How effective is the UN?

Evaluating the effectiveness of the UN in its key areas of responsibility – resolving conflict, reducing poverty, safeguarding the environment (see page 85) and upholding human rights (see page 86) – is not a simple matter. The UN works in every country in the world, with huge budgets devoted to thousands of individual projects, and it has been working to these objectives across many decades (see Figure 3.4). The UN is not responsible for everything, good or bad, that happens in the world. There are many events and factors in global politics that are outside the UN's control, but its founding objectives are clear that it intends to be a force for good and to encourage states to make progress on issues such as peace and security, economic and social development, human rights and the environment.

Points to bear in mind when evaluating the effectiveness of the UN include the following:

- Who is responsible for its successes and failures – the organisation and institutions themselves or the member states (particularly its most powerful members)?
- What can be defined as 'effectiveness'? This is a subjective term. If the UN organises peace talks but the peace talks do not succeed, is that a failure? Could the peace talks have been organised without the UN's influence? Is the success of peace talks only judged on whether or not they succeed in the ultimate goal of ending conflict, or do they serve a more subtle and meaningful purpose?
- From a realist perspective, if states are the most authoritative and powerful actors in global politics, is it reasonable to expect the UN to be more effective and decisive?

To come to a fair evaluation of its effectiveness, we cannot consider all that the UN has tried to do in its history. Instead, we can look at some key moments, crises and ideas where the UN might have been expected to be effective.

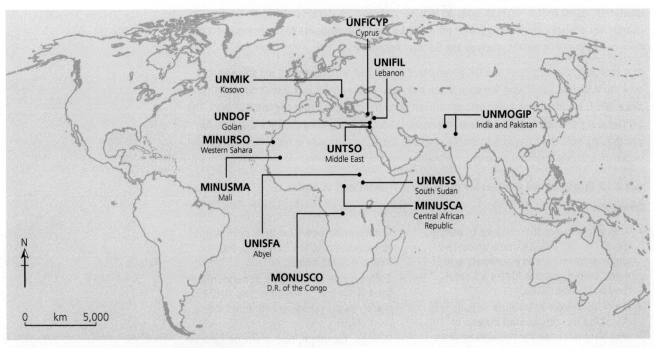

Figure 3.4 UN peacekeeping operations in 2021

Maintaining international peace and security

One of the central objectives of the UN when it was founded in 1945 was to maintain international peace and security and 'to take effective collective measures for the prevention and removal of threats to peace'.

Clearly, the UN has not managed to prevent conflict altogether, and it would be unreasonable to expect it to have done so. In any case, the founding objectives are more nuanced and realistic, committing the UN to removing 'threats to peace'. What influence has the UN had in some of the major threats to peace and security that have emerged since 1945? To evaluate, it is helpful to divide the post-1945 period into several key periods. These divisions are also a useful way of thinking about key periods in the balance of power in global politics.

The Cold War (1945–91)

A military standoff between the Soviet Union and the US dominated the early decades of the UN, from 1945 until the fall of the Berlin Wall in 1989 and the collapse of the Soviet Union in 1991. The UN – in particular, the Security Council – was powerless to influence the conflict, given that two UNSC permanent members were, in effect, at war with each other.

More influential during this period was NATO, which created a specific security alliance for the US and its western European allies, like-minded states that felt a shared threat.

The NPT was also influential during this period in preventing a major spread of nuclear weapons beyond the Soviet Union and the US. However, the Cold War did not prevent the UN from agreeing to send peacekeepers to conflicts, for example in Africa, which the two countries felt did not affect their core security interests.

Post-Cold War: instability in Africa and Europe (1991–2001)

The Cold War's aftermath saw the collapse of the Soviet Union and of Russian power. Fifteen new and independent states split from Moscow's control. With the US now the predominant world power (hegemon) and Russia less inclined to oppose its former enemy in the UNSC, there was the prospect of the UN being more decisive and activist. However, the UN's limitations became apparent in a series of high-profile peacekeeping failures during this period:

- In 1992, UN peacekeepers in Somalia were unable to defend themselves against a rebel attack and were forced to retreat. US troops attempted to rescue the situation by fighting back against the militias with disastrous results, as portrayed in the 2001 film *Black Hawk Down*.
- In 1994, UN peacekeepers in Rwanda were powerless to stop a genocide from taking place in front of them. The UN had not given the peacekeepers permission to intervene with force against the tribal fighters. Between half a million and a million civilians lost their lives.
- Peacekeeping operations in Bosnia (1992–95) failed to prevent Serb forces from executing 8,000 Bosnian Muslims in Srebrenica, when Serbian forces overran a UN-declared 'safe haven'.

The War on Terror (2001–09)

On 11 September 2001, the US suffered devastating terrorist attacks in New York and Washington that killed 2,977 people and destroyed the twin towers of the World Trade Center. It was quickly established that the al-Qaeda terrorist network, under the leadership of Osama bin Laden, was responsible for the attacks. The Taliban government in Afghanistan had allowed al-Qaeda to plan the attacks from bases in the country and, within months, the US government launched military action to remove the Taliban from power and pursue al-Qaeda. President George W. Bush framed his foreign policy as a global 'War on Terror' and identified other key threats, including in Iraq.

The UN was largely sidelined during the so-called War on Terror as a decade emerged where the US was relentlessly focused on protecting its national interest. While a UNSC Resolution authorised and created the International Security Assistance Force (ISAF) in Afghanistan and the UN was heavily involved in reconstruction and development work in Afghanistan throughout the conflict, ISAF was under US, not UN, military command.

Within 18 months of the 9/11 attacks, the US was engaged in further military conflict in Iraq, this time without UN involvement or authorisation. The US and UK claimed that there was a regional and international threat from weapons of mass destruction (WMD) in Iraq and had grown impatient with a UN programme of inspections. Attempts to secure a UNSC Resolution authorising military action failed, as France and Russia urged for inspections to be given more time. The US and UK (with a small number of other countries) invaded in March 2003 and remained engaged in combat operations until 2011. UN Secretary-General Kofi Annan later condemned the Iraq War as being:

> illegal and not in conformity with the UN Charter ... I think that in the end everybody is concluding that it is best to work together with allies and through the UN to deal with those issues.

Once again, the UN's various humanitarian and development agencies were involved in reconstruction efforts in Iraq but the decade was marked by unilateral action by UNSC permanent members. Russia, for example, also became more involved in military action in both Chechyna and Georgia (2008).

Post-War on Terror: the Arab Spring (2010–12) and the present

During this period, the US government under President Barack Obama stopped using the term 'War on Terror' and began to focus on withdrawing US troops from conflicts in Afghanistan and Iraq.

In late 2010, a series of popular uprisings in the middle east and north Africa region saw several regimes toppled from power. In Syria, the uprisings were met with aggressive government resistance and sparked one of the deadliest conflicts of the century, with over 500,000 killed and more than 6 million refugees. The UN has been powerless in the face of a determined Syrian government under President Bashar al-Assad. In 2015, Russia decided to intervene unilaterally, without UN consent, with controversial military action in support of the Assad regime. The US and its allies were initially reluctant to intervene, partly due to scepticism and war-weariness at home. Eventually France, the UK and the US began air strikes against so-called ISIL in Iraq and Syria, at the request of the Iraqi government and once ISIL carried out terrorist attacks in mainland Europe.

The only meaningful UNSC action during this period was the resolution to disarm Syria of its chemical weapons. Even still, human rights observers reported that Syrian government forces were using barrel bombs with chlorine gas against rebel forces. Indeed, in April 2017, a suspected government forces chemical attack took place on the Syrian town of Khan Shaykhun, killing at least 74 people, including many children, and injuring around 550.

Another key challenge of the period since 9/11 has been the emergence of non-state actor threats from terrorist groups such as al-Qaeda and ISIL. The UN was established to deal principally with security threats from nation-states and has found it harder, if not impossible, to counter non-state actor threats.

We can see, therefore, that during periods where there are major threats to international security, such as the Cold War or the so-called War on Terror, the major powers have tended to prioritise their own national interests. During these periods, the effect of protecting that national interest has been that the UN has at best been overlooked and at worst deliberately bypassed.

Another means of assessing the UN's effectiveness in peace and security is to consider the distribution or balance of power in global politics at various points. Especially relevant in terms of the behaviour of the UNSC permanent members, this plays a major part in determining whether the UN has been able to act or not. The balance of power becomes more obvious the more that major powers see a particular issue as affecting their core national interests.

The UNSC has, however, been able to agree action in states and regions where the permanent members do not have a clear national strategic interest at stake (see Box 3.3). Most UN peacekeeping operations have been in Africa and states of less geopolitical importance to the major world powers.

Topic link

The impact of the distribution of power in global politics is explored in Chapter 7.

Box 3.3

What factors are required for success in peacekeeping operations?

The following factors all contribute to success in UN peacekeeping operations. There must be:
- genuine commitment to a political process from all parties in working towards peace (there must be a peace to keep)
- clear, credible and achievable mandates, with matching personnel, logistical and financial resources
- unity of purpose within the UNSC, with active support to UN operations in the field
- host-country commitment to unhindered UN operations and freedom of movement
- supportive engagement from neighbouring countries and regional actors
- an integrated UN approach, effective coordination with other actors on the ground and good communication with host-country authorities and population
- the utmost sensitivity towards the local population and upholding the highest standards of professionalism and good conduct (peacekeepers must avoid becoming part of the problem)

Source: UN Department for Peacekeeping Operations

Case study

Rwanda and Srebrenica: failures of UN peacekeeping?

The UN peacekeeping missions in Rwanda (1994) and Bosnia (1995) have been much criticised for failing to prevent two major genocides. In Rwanda in April 1994, the Hutu majority government attacked the Tutsi minority, killing as many as 1 million in just over 100 days. In Srebrenica, Bosnia, in July 1995, Serbian forces killed 8,000 Bosnian Muslims in just over 10 days. In both cases, UN peacekeepers were present. How, then, did these atrocities happen?

Rwanda

- A 1999 inquiry concluded that not enough was done to respond to indications that a genocide was likely to happen.

- 2,500 UN peacekeepers were withdrawn after ten Belgian peacekeepers were killed earlier in the conflict.

Bosnia

- Bosnian Muslims had surrendered their weapons to UN peacekeepers days before the massacre took place. Serbian forces exploited this. The UN peacekeepers refused a request from the Bosnian Muslims to have their weapons returned.
- Srebrenica was a UN-declared 'safe zone', but Serbian forces ignored this. They overwhelmed UN peacekeepers, who did not have sufficient resources to defend themselves so they stood aside.

Table 3.13 Power distribution and its impact on the UN's effectiveness

Period	Nature of power distribution	Impact on the UN and its effectiveness
1945–89	Bipolarity (two major powers opposed to each other)	It is difficult, even impossible, for the UN to act if permanent UNSC member states are at war or disagreeing with each other. In these circumstances, the use of the veto becomes so frequent or likely that many issues are simply dealt with outside the UN system.
1989–2001	Unipolarity (a single hegemon)	There is the potential for the UN to be very active on the issues that the single major power (in this period, the US) favours. Less powerful states may be disinclined to use their veto power.
2001–present	Multipolarity (many world powers competing with each other)	Arguably, this is the current balance of power in global politics, with a resurgent Russia increasingly challenging Western power and the emergence of powerful non-state actor threats (al-Qaeda and ISIL). UNSC agreement has once again been difficult on major issues, with both China and Russia increasingly wielding their veto power.

Debate

Has the UN been effective in maintaining international peace and security?

Yes

- The UNSC has been extremely active, approving peacekeeping operations, military intervention and sanctions across the world.
- Nuclear proliferation has been controlled and few new nuclear weapons states have emerged.
- The UN is limited in what it can do by what its member states agree. The UN is not always unable to act, it merely has to operate within the constraints of what its most powerful members perceive as their national interest.
- The UN has so far succeeded where the League of Nations failed in preventing another world war. Inter-state war has decreased considerably since the UN was founded and democracy has spread.

No

- The UN has struggled to respond to security threats from non-state actors, including al-Qaeda. The UN was largely sidelined during the early stages of the War on Terror.
- UN peacekeepers have seen tragic failures in Somalia, Rwanda and Bosnia. Unless there is peace already in place, UN peacekeepers are unable to have a positive impact.
- Civil wars have increased, even while inter-state war has decreased. The UN has been less able to respond to internal conflict, as it was designed to deal with inter-state conflict.

⚙ Evaluation tip: The UN has largely achieved what its most powerful member states (especially the P5) have been willing to agree, but no more. This is unsurprising, given how much power and responsibility these states are given in the UN Charter.

Other challenges – human rights, environment, poverty

Other chapters examine in more detail the effectiveness of the UN's activities in the challenges of human rights (Chapter 5), the environment (Chapter 6) and poverty (Chapter 4). However, to understand the impact and scope of the UN's work as a whole, it is useful to consider these together.

Table 3.14 The UN: major agreements and institutions by policy area

Policy area	Major agreements	Major institutions
Human rights	The UN has been the forum in which major international human rights laws have been negotiated and agreed, including the Covenants on Political and Civil Rights and Economic and Social Rights, as well as numerous conventions protecting specific groups (e.g. children, migrant workers).	The UN Human Rights Council is a sub-body of ECOSOC and is responsible for monitoring compliance with international human rights laws. However, it can only issue reports and name and shame countries, rather than taking binding action.
Environment	The UN organised the 1992 Rio Earth Summit and oversees the UN Framework Convention on Climate Change, which is the basis for all international summits on climate change. The Paris Agreement in 2015 was negotiated by way of a UN summit.	The Intergovernmental Panel on Climate Change is a UN body, which gathers authoritative scientific research on climate change to help inform member states and push them towards taking appropriate action.
Poverty	UNGA agreed the Millennium Development Goals and the Sustainable Development Goals in 2000 and 2015.	There are a huge number of UN agencies working on the SDGs including the UN Development Programme, the World Health Organization and UNICEF. ECOSOC annually reviews the progress towards achieving the SDGs.

Treaties

International organisations such as the UN are not the only way in which states try to tackle shared threats and opportunities. Treaties have been used since medieval times to allow states to come to formal, tailored agreements with other states, usually allowing major powers to come to peace settlements or agreements. One of the most notable treaties in studies of modern global politics is the Treaty of Westphalia, signed in 1648 at the end of the Thirty Years' War (see Chapter 2). The treaty marks the beginning of the modern idea of the sovereign nation-state, with respect for internal and external sovereignty being key principles of the treaty.

In modern global politics, treaties are frequently the legal basis on which IGOs are founded (for example, the UN Charter and the Treaty of Rome, which founded the European Community, now the EU). States frequently come together to agree treaties on specific issues, such as arms control, international justice, climate change or free trade. They offer a flexible means of agreeing action on any matter between two or more like-minded states. Treaties between two states are known as bilateral treaties, and those between many states are multilateral treaties.

Are treaties an effective means of global governance?

Treaties can be very targeted and aimed at specific issues. There are many examples of successful international treaties (see Table 3.15).

Treaties are a useful tool in modern global politics for the following reasons:

- They allow states to form agreements on any issue, ranging from the environment to world health.
- They are targeted and specific, unlike IGOs, which may cover a range of policy areas and competencies. This is attractive to states that wish to retain more control over their sovereignty, as they essentially get to pick and choose the international agreements that suit their particular interests.
- They represent formal international law, increasing (but not guaranteeing) the likelihood of enforcement and accountability.

Table 3.15 Successful international treaties

Treaty	Function	Effectiveness
Treaty of Rome (1957) (political governance)	Founded the European Community (EC), later the EU	Six countries signed the founding treaty and the EC has since become the EU, with 28 member states (although the UK decided in 2016 to become the first EU member state to leave the union).
ASEAN Free Trade Area agreement (1992) (economic governance)	Founded the ASEAN Free Trade Area, which has now become the regional trading bloc known as the Association of Southeast Asian Nations (ASEAN)	ASEAN has rapidly moved towards creating a free market, reducing tariffs on imports and exports.
Kyoto Protocol (1997) (environmental governance)	Committed its state parties to reduce emissions	Major polluting states did not sign up, notably the US.
Rome Statute (1998) (human rights governance)	Created the ICC, signed and ratified by 121 states (although it is not signed and ratified by three of the permanent five members – China, Russia and the US)	The ICC has successfully convicted eight individuals, however there is criticism that its conviction rate is too low. Non-participation of the most powerful states undermines its legitimacy.

A weakness of treaties is that states can choose whether or not to sign and ratify them. For example, three out of the five UNSC permanent members (China, Russia and the US) have not ratified the Rome Statute (the treaty that established the ICC). The fact that the most significant military powers in the world have been able to opt out of a major treaty represents a serious weakness.

Similarly, while the NPT (see page 113) is the most widely signed arms control treaty in the world, key states have opted not to sign it, or have signed and then later withdrawn from the treaty (North Korea), or have developed nuclear weapons (India, Israel, North Korea and Pakistan). However, it should not be taken for granted that the 190 states that signed the treaty made a conscious decision in international law to agree not to pursue their own nuclear weapons programmes. Clearly, a state could simply withdraw from the treaty and develop nuclear weapons, but the overwhelming majority of states have stayed within a powerful collective and mutually assuring framework.

Case study

The Treaty on the Non-Proliferation of Nuclear Weapons

The Treaty (known as the NPT) came into force in 1970 and is the world's most widely signed arms control treaty, with 190 signatories. It was agreed and is monitored under the auspices of the UN.

The five permanent members of the UNSC all have nuclear weapons and have signed and ratified the NPT. This confirms in international law that they are nuclear weapons states and commits them to not sharing nuclear technology except for peaceful purposes (such as nuclear power) and, ultimately, disarmament. These states are:
- the US (since 1945)
- Russia (since 1949)
- the UK (since 1952)
- France (since 1960)
- China (since 1964)

Three states possess nuclear weapons and have not signed the NPT:
- India (since 1974)
- Pakistan (estimated to be since the mid-1980s)
- North Korea (since approximately 2006, when it carried out the first official test)

Israel is widely suspected, but not confirmed, to have had nuclear weapons since perhaps the early 1960s.

Only India, Israel, North Korea, Pakistan and South Sudan (which shows no ambition to become a nuclear weapons state, but rather is a newly independent state) are not currently part of the treaty, which has two categories of states signed up to it.
- **Nuclear weapons states:** those committed to nuclear disarmament and to not sharing skills and technology that could help other states to possess nuclear weapons.
- **Non-nuclear weapons states:** those committed to not developing nuclear weapons of their own.

One of the NPT's successes is that, apart from North Korea, no state has successfully developed nuclear weapons since the mid-1980s. Non-nuclear weapons states that signed the treaty have, therefore, kept to their promise. One former nuclear weapons state, South Africa, successfully gave up its nuclear weapons entirely when it signed the treaty and disarmed itself.

Of course, states that have wanted to develop nuclear weapons, and then avoid commitments to disarming themselves, have simply chosen not to sign the treaty or be bound by its regulations. None of India, Israel or Pakistan is likely to sign the treaty and commit to nuclear disarmament. North Korea withdrew from the treaty in 2003 (the only state ever to do so) and 3 years later tested its first nuclear weapon, showing that states can quickly opt out and develop nuclear weapons.

The North Atlantic Treaty Organization

One of the most significant treaties of the post-Second World War era has been the North Atlantic Treaty, signed in 1949, which founded NATO. The North Atlantic Treaty is a collective military security agreement that was signed at the start of the Cold War, with the aim of protecting its members from the threat of military (especially nuclear) attack from the Soviet Union and the Warsaw Pact countries. The alliance also had wider political objectives of keeping its members politically aligned with the US and not succumbing to the communism of the Warsaw Pact and ensuring that West Germany developed the military resources and capability to be defended without developing once again into a threat to western Europe.

NATO is therefore an example of a collective security alliance. In order to prevent the spread of the Soviet Union into western Europe, and recognising that the Second World War had both economically and militarily weakened these countries which were potentially unable to defend themselves, NATO created a formal alliance backed up in international law by a treaty.

The key principle of NATO is Article 5 of the Treaty, which states that an attack on one member state shall be regarded as an attack on all member states. When Article 5 is triggered, it means that there is a collective military response from NATO member states. It provides a guarantee and a deterrent for non-NATO states to attack even the smallest of NATO states, knowing that NATO would come to that state's aid. In fact, NATO has only used Article 5 once, when NATO allies indicated their support for the US after the 9/11 terror attacks.

While Article 5 has only ever been invoked in support of its most powerful member state, one of NATO's founding objectives was to protect smaller states (particularly those in western Europe and bordering the Soviet Union). Being part of NATO, a formal military alliance with many nation-states, makes smaller states more powerful than they would be alone. In reality, the US has always been the dominant military power within NATO, and NATO membership can also be seen as an alliance with the US.

The NATO headquarters are located in Brussels, Belgium. NATO has a civilian secretary-general (currently former Norwegian prime minister Jens Stoltenberg), who acts as the organisation's chief executive and main spokesperson. There are 30 members (see Figure 3.5).

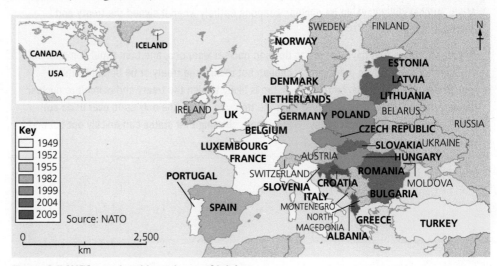

Key
- 1949
- 1952
- 1955
- 1982
- 1999
- 2004
- 2009

Source: NATO

0 ———— 2,500
km

Figure 3.5 NATO membership and year of joining

Changing role

Since the end of the Cold War, some have questioned the continuing relevance of NATO. President Donald Trump regularly complained that the US was contributing too much to NATO's budget and that other NATO member states were not contributing enough. The US still accounts for more than two-thirds of the defence spending of all NATO allies, reflecting its far larger military power and historic influence. France, Germany and the UK account for half of NATO members' defence spending of the non-US NATO allies. This makes NATO members very reliant on a small number of powerful states, though this is perhaps the very point of a collective security alliance.

In 2006, NATO members agreed a 'guideline' that states should spend a minimum of 2% of GDP on defence. The number of states meeting this guideline has increased in recent years. As recently as 2015, only five states were meeting this commitment. In 2020, NATO confirmed that 10 states met this commitment (US, Greece, Estonia, UK, Poland, Latvia, Lithuania, Romania, France and Norway). Perhaps some of the pressure from the US under President Trump, including the fear that the US might withdraw from NATO, had an impact. Alternatively, the perception of a returning threat from Russia might account for increased defence spending in Baltic states bordering Russia.

While the Cold War may have ended, those arguing for a continuing role for NATO point to Russia's incursion into Ukraine in 2014 as evidence of renewed Russian power and its desire to recapture territory lost after the fall of the Soviet Union. Former Soviet states and now EU and NATO member states Latvia, Lithuania and Estonia all have borders with Russia. In 2014, NATO expanded its Response Force from 13,000 to 40,000 troops, creating a new 'spearhead force' of 5,000 troops, and established new headquarters in its member states in the Baltic and eastern European regions. NATO hailed this as 'the largest reinforcement of collective defence since the end of the Cold War'.

NATO and Russia established in 2002 the NATO–Russia Council designed to allow dialogue between the two powers. This channel of communication was formally suspended in 2014, following the annexation of Crimea from Ukraine by Russia, though NATO and Russia remain engaged in informal, ad hoc dialogue. From a Russian perspective, the expanding membership of NATO and its highly active role in international affairs since the end of the Cold War has caused considerable concern. In 2016, President Vladimir Putin highlighted NATO specifically as a key national security threat to the Russian Federation. Putin pointed to the 'intensification of military activities, further expansion of the alliance and moving military infrastructure closer to Russia's borders' as evidence of the perceived threat. In 2018, Putin criticised NATO for trying to expand its membership to Ukraine and Georgia, urging NATO to 'think about the possible consequences of such an irresponsible policy'.

NATO–Russia relations have been growing in tension in recent years. For its part, NATO has identified 'proactive military activities near NATO's borders; aggressive military posture; and the nerve agent attack in the UK in 2018, which was a clear breach of international norms'. The tensions are a relevant example of the so-called security dilemma in global politics. The security dilemma reflects the fact that when one world power feels a threat from another, it increases its security defences, which in turn leads to the other power feeling a growing threat and increasing its own security defences accordingly. In the Cold War, this was seen most powerfully through the nuclear arms race between the Soviet Union and the US.

Military operations since the Cold War

Despite being founded with the objective of countering the threat from the Soviet Union at the end of the Second World War, NATO's first offensive military operations did not take place until 1995. Humanitarian concerns primarily motivated two operations in the 1990s, both in former Yugoslavia:

- In 1995, Operation Deliberate Force included air strikes against the Bosnian Serb army, which had carried out massacres in so-called UN safe zones, including in Srebrenica, where in July 1995 Bosnian Serb forces killed some 8,000 Bosnian Muslims. A UNSC Resolution had authorised this military operation, making this a good example of the UNSC using the forces of another international organisation (NATO) to carry out its objectives.
- In 1999, NATO launched nearly 80 days of air strikes in Kosovo, in former Yugoslavia. Operation Allied Force was primarily a humanitarian mission to protect Kosovar Albanians from the armed forces of the Federal Yugoslav Republic and its leader Slobodan Miloševic. This operation was not backed by a UN Security Council Resolution, with Russia opposed and condemning the campaign as a breach of international law.

It is important to note that NATO's first military operations came in a theatre of conflict and with objectives very different from those initially intended. Neither of these two campaigns in former Yugoslavia was carried out to protect a fellow NATO member state, as the collective security alliance intended. In the immediate aftermath of the Cold War, NATO focused on humanitarian crises within Europe and was able to do so both with and without the support of Russia.

NATO conducts anti-piracy operations off the coast of Somalia

Since NATO invoked Article 5 in 2001, the organisation's operations have further expanded beyond their original geographical space, moving beyond Europe to the middle east and south Asia. Military operations in Afghanistan (2001–21) were conducted under NATO's leadership. Similarly, the military no-fly zone and subsequent campaign of air strikes against Colonel Muammar Gaddafi's regime in Libya in 2011 was a NATO-led operation.

NATO has also conducted counter-piracy operations in the Indian Ocean off the coast of Somalia, in order to protect international shipping lanes. These operations confirm that NATO is now a military alliance with its widest range of deployments, and indeed NATO has to some extent rebranded itself, by leaning towards a more humanitarian role in order to remain relevant. With a resurgent Russia, NATO is also rediscovering and redefining its role as a collective security alliance to counter Russian aggression.

Case study

NATO under pressure?

In 2019, HM Queen Elizabeth hosted a reception at Buckingham Palace to mark NATO's 70th anniversary. But recently, NATO has been coming under pressure from various sources.

- **A sceptical US president:** NATO summits under President Trump were tense occasions. In 2018, Trump highlighted concerns about NATO's European members' reliance on Russian energy supplies, claiming that Germany was 'totally controlled by Russia'. At the 2017 NATO leaders' summit, he laid bare the divisions in the alliance and openly called for NATO members to increase their defence spending and to 'contribute their fair share'. Former National Security Adviser to Trump, John Bolton, claimed that Trump had even considered withdrawing from NATO in 2018.
- **Growing Russian power:** The annexation of Crimea in 2014 has led to some analysts concluding that there is a 'new Cold War' between Russia and the West. NATO continues to fear further Russian military activity on the border between Russia and Ukraine.
- **Tensions with Turkey:** NATO allies expressed concern when member state, Turkey, purchased a $2.5 billion air defence system from Russia in 2019. The US went further, with President Trump issuing sanctions against its NATO ally. These sanctions were not lifted when President Biden took over in 2021.
- **Afghanistan:** NATO's longest military deployment has been of questionable success. President Joe Biden began withdrawing the last of NATO's troops in 2021, two decades after NATO had begun military action in support of the US global 'War on Terror'.

Activity

Review the interactive map showing NATO's military operations at this link:
www.nato.int/cps/en/natohq/topics_52060.htm.

1 Where is NATO currently deployed?
2 What current threats is NATO focused on?

Table 3.16 Strengths and weaknesses of NATO

Strengths	Weaknesses
• A collective security agreement between allies (compare with the UNSC), with the capacity to act and to agree. • Vital protection for smaller and weaker states, especially those bordering Russia, creating a strong deterrent and balance of power in western Europe. • An organised, collective military force which is at a constant state of readiness is useful in a world of declining national defence budgets and is backed by the world's pre-eminent military superpower.	• Reliant on US military and economic power, with the risk that European states become over-reliant on the US. • The security dilemma (see page 115) might suggest that NATO's growing role post-Cold War has once again rekindled tensions between Russia and the West. • Unity in NATO might be seen to be fragmenting, with high-profile tensions between the US and Turkey and between the US and western European allies under Trump.

Debate

Are economic global governance institutions more successful in achieving their objectives than political global governance institutions?

Yes

- There are more incentives for engaging in economic global governance and more shared interests, for example in keeping tariffs low and helping states that would otherwise put global economic stability at risk.
- There are more economic global governance institutions that work in partnership with each other, with clearly defined responsibilities, for example the Bretton Woods Institutions working in partnership with the G7 and G20 and with other development banks and the focus given by the MDGs and SDGs.
- Political global governance institutions are increasingly gridlocked and are not inclusive (the UN Security Council) or they are just made up of like-minded allies working to resolve their own narrow interests (NATO).

No

- Political global governance institutions have more power to achieve their objectives, notably using hard power (UNSC and NATO) of military action and peacekeeping.
- Political institutions that are based on smaller groups of allies can be more effective in deciding and achieving their objectives than organisations such as the World Trade Organization that act by consensus.
- In global economic governance, there are increasing tensions, for example trade wars between major powers and the splits evident in both the G7 and G20. The latter also suffer from a lack of legitimacy and do not have a budget to engage in long-term work, so they are subordinate to the UN.

Evaluation tip: All global governance institutions are only as effective as states want them to be, so judging which of the two it is most commonly in states' interests to support will be key to your answer.

Further reading

Andrews Sayle, T. (2019) *Enduring Alliance: A History of NATO and the Post-War Global Order.* Cornell University Press.

Hanhimäki, J. M. (2015) *The United Nations: A Very Short Introduction.* Oxford University Press.

Ki-moon, B. (2021) *Resolved: Uniting Nations in a Divided World.* Columbia University Press.

Murphy, R. (2015) 'Is the UN Security Council fit for purpose?', *Politics Review Online*, Vol. 24, No. 4, April.

What you should know

Having read this chapter you should have knowledge and understanding of the following:

→ Global governance is the process by which states and intergovernmental organisations try to bring order and security to global politics. It does not try to create a world government, as this is not possible. Instead, states try to create state-led institutions and laws that allow them to solve shared problems and seize international opportunities that are in their national interest.

→ The UN was founded to maintain global peace and security, improve economic development and advance human rights. Its role has since expanded to include preventing environmental degradation and increased responsibilities for UN peacekeepers.

→ One of the most powerful bodies in international relations is the UN Security Council (UNSC). Its permanent members have a powerful right to veto proposed resolutions. Sometimes this results in stalemate. Nevertheless, the UNSC has still had a considerable impact, even if it cannot always resolve crises in which its permanent members wish to block action.

→ The North Atlantic Treaty Organization was founded to act as a collective security alliance against the Soviet Union. It has since expanded both its membership and the scope of its operations. Today, it is more actively involved in combating global threats outside Europe, and has led offensive operations in Afghanistan and Libya. Its military stance against Russia is more defensive and is intended to act as a deterrent.

→ Global political governance depends, ultimately, on states' agreement. States use intergovernmental organisations and sign treaties primarily to pursue their own national interest. Sometimes, national interest and international interest are the same. This is when global governance efforts are most successful.

Practice questions

Section A

1 Examine the main criticisms that can be made of the UN Security Council and NATO.   *[12 marks]*
2 Examine the key weaknesses of the UN General Assembly and ECOSOC.   *[12 marks]*
3 Examine the main factors which account for the changing priorities of the UN and NATO.   *[12 marks]*

Section C

1 Evaluate the extent to which the United Nations has been successful in achieving its founding objectives.   *[30 marks]*
2 Evaluate the extent to which the UN is effective in responding to the challenges of a globalised and interconnected world.   *[30 marks]*
3 Evaluate the extent to which NATO is more powerful and effective than the UN in addressing conflict and global stability.   *[30 marks]*

Global governance: economic

Learning outcomes

By the end of the chapter you should understand:
- → the role and significance of key economic intergovernmental organisations including the World Bank, the International Monetary Fund and the World Trade Organization
- → the role and significance of the Group of Seven and the Group of Twenty in economic global governance
- → the criticisms of economic global governance institutions
- → how economic global governance deals with the issue of poverty
- → the economic theories which explain how countries develop and why there is inequality between countries

Getting you started

A global economy out of control?

There have been two major economic shocks in the first two decades of the twenty-first century. First, the global financial crisis of 2008, which began in the US but the effects were felt across the world. Second, the Covid-19 global pandemic had a devastating effect on economies when huge parts of states' normal economic activity were paused or diminished as a result of months of lockdown.

The global financial crisis of 2008 was the worst economic downturn since the Great Depression

Both crises demanded an international response. When such a response is needed, it is the international institutions of economic global governance – created at the Bretton Woods conference in 1944 to plot a route out of the economic turmoil of the Second World War – that our global political system turns to. The International Monetary Fund, the World Bank, the World Trade Organization, and the informal forums of the G7 and G20.

An additional challenge with the Covid-19 global pandemic was that global governance institutions could not meet physically and continue their work with the normal interactions and summits that we have become used to. International travel itself went into lockdown.

Economic global governance responded more quickly and effectively to the global financial crisis of 2008, by agreeing public spending to bail out banks and resuscitate global markets, than it did for the global pandemic. But in many ways, crisis though it was, the impact was not as widespread and targeted solutions were possible and affordable.

With Covid-19, the economic impact will be played out over many years, perhaps even decades. Few countries were able to escape shutting down significant parts of their normal economic life, meaning that a targeted response from economic global governance has been harder and therefore much more piecemeal – with institutions needed to spread limited funds fairly across a wide range of suffering economies.

Economic global governance is probably – compared with political, human rights and environmental – the form of global governance in which countries have the least choice as to whether they get involved. Participating in international trade, for example, is hardly optional. Any state that chose not to participate would risk economic isolation and would be economically left behind. But even without these two major crises, the challenges for the traditional, US-led international institutions have been very real.

The continuing rise of China and the widening Global North make the global economy increasingly multipolar and one in which the Bretton Woods organisations are struggling for influence. The US and China have, over recent years, engaged in trade wars with each other and economic tensions have been running high. Significant progress has been made in reducing poverty, but our global economy remains one where inequality is widening and many countries remain in relationships with more powerful states that have echoes of colonialism, where one nation-state exerts overwhelming economic and political control over another.

Can economic global governance be a force for good in resolving tensions between states even as each country strives to maximise its wealth and economic power?

What is economic global governance and why is it needed?

In an interdependent world, states need to work together on economic matters as well as political matters. Globalisation has quickened this process. International trade has increased as communications and transport have created better links between states. The number of states involved in international trade has also increased. The impact, both positive and negative, of individual states' economic fortunes is increasingly felt in other states.

Key terms

International Monetary Fund (IMF) Established following the Bretton Woods Conference in 1944. It aims to encourage global financial stability by providing loans to countries facing economic crises and by providing technical advice to its 190 member states.

World Bank Established at the Bretton Woods Conference in 1944. It focuses on long-term development and provides grants and conditional loans to developing countries.

Currency The money in circulation within a nation-state or region. For example, the British Pound Sterling is the national currency of the UK.

Group of Twenty (G20) An international forum comprised of the leaders of the 19 wealthiest countries in the world and the EU. Unlike the G7, it includes countries from both the developed and the developing world.

Colonialism Where one nation-state exerts economic and political domination and control over another, usually by gaining full or partial control over territory.

The Bretton Woods Conference

The need for more effective economic global governance was first seen close to the end of the Second World War at the Bretton Woods Conference, held in the US in 1944. The 44 nations of the Second World War Allies met in a remote mountain resort in New Hampshire, to consider how the world's financial systems and trade could be managed in peacetime. Many of today's global economic governance institutions were founded at the conference, including the IMF and the World Bank.

There was also agreement among the Allies that economic pressures had played a part in the rise of fascism in Germany, where the Nazi Party had mobilised a domestic financial crisis as a rallying issue. Just as the world had turned to the League of Nations and then the UN for political global governance, so economists of the Allied nations began to think about how greater international order could be brought to the global economic order.

The aims of the Bretton Woods Conference were to:

- create an agreed system of rules for international economic matters, including world trade
- stabilise world currencies and reduce wide fluctuations in the value of currencies
- prevent a repeat of the Great Depression that occurred in the 1930s
- bolster capitalism against the rise of communism as a competing economic model in the Soviet Union.

The Bretton Woods Conference created the following economic global governance IGOs and arrangements.

- **The IMF (1944):** established the US dollar as the basis against which all other states' currencies would be valued, thereby stabilising world currencies from major fluctuations in their value.
- **The International Bank for Reconstruction and Development (1944):** later known as the World Bank. Its aim is to provide a pool of investment for middle-income states.
- **The General Agreement on Tariffs and Trade (GATT) (1947):** later known as the **World Trade Organization (WTO)**. It is an international forum in which states can make trade deals and international rules on trade.

Collectively, these institutions and the principles on which they were founded (free trade) are known as the Bretton Woods System. This refers to the forums and institutions of global economic governance that states have put in place to manage the global economy. All three of these founding institutions still exist today, although they have been modified and their roles have developed considerably.

In more recent decades, global cooperation on economic governance has focused on the following:

- **Poverty/development:** the value of international coordination through the UN and other forums has progressed considerably. Developed states have increased spending on development. The Millennium Development Goals (MDGs) and Sustainable Development Goals (SDGs), agreed in 2000 and 2015 respectively (see page 153), represent the most coordinated effort of IGOs and states to work towards common development targets.

(see page 153)

> **Key term**
>
> **World Trade Organization (WTO)** Established in 1995 and the successor to the GATT (1947). It has a membership of 164 states and is designed to facilitate free trade by encouraging global trade deals and resolving trade disputes between member states.

- **Free trade:** there has been an increase in multilateral free-trade agreements, most notably the Single Market of the EU but also NAFTA which has now been replaced with the USMCA. The Trans-Pacific Partnership (TPP), agreed in 2016, established a free-trade agreement between most countries of the Pacific Rim, although President Trump's unilateral withdrawal of the US from the deal in 2017 led to other Pacific states agreeing the Progressive Agreement for Trans-Pacific Partnership without the US.
- **Single currency:** the economic debate in the EU in the 1990s focused on developing a single currency, the euro. The euro came into circulation in 2002 and is now the currency of 19 of the 27 EU member states. While most economic global governance in global politics is entirely intergovernmental in nature, the Eurozone countries have agreed to strict economic rules and given up significant freedom to make economic decisions nationally (such as setting their own interest rates) to supranational institutions, notably the ECB.
- **Forums:** there is a need for a forum for discussion and decision making to enable states to resolve international economic crises. The global financial crisis of 2008 posed a particular challenge for key economic IGOs, notably the IMF. In response to the crisis, the IMF dramatically increased the loans it makes to bail out failing economies.

Economic global governance involves many of the same actors as other forms of global governance.

- **IGOs:** principally the World Bank, the IMF and the UN (including the UN Development Programme (UNDP)).
- **Informal intergovernmental forums:** such as the Group of Seven (G7) and the G20, which include the world's most industrialised states and the biggest global economic powers.
- **Multinational corporations (MNCs):** privately owned companies that operate in more than one state.
- **Multilateral forums:** such as the World Economic Forum (WEF), which provides an opportunity for world leaders, IGOs, business leaders, NGOs and economists to discuss the challenges facing the global economy.

> **Key term**
>
> **Group of Seven (G7)** An intergovernmental forum comprising the leaders of seven highly industrialised countries.

The International Monetary Fund

The IMF was one of the key global economic governance institutions agreed in 1944 at the Bretton Woods Conference. It became fully operational in 1947 and its headquarters are in Washington, DC.

Role

When the IMF was founded, its main role was to encourage stability in world exchange rates. During the Great Depression in the 1930s, many currencies had been devalued, causing great uncertainty and ultimately deep economic recession. The IMF oversaw a system of fixed exchange rates, linked to the US dollar, which in turn was fixed to the price of gold. This system brought much increased stability and prevented unsettling fluctuations in currency value. States and traders in the international financial system knew how much currency was worth and could make investments with a greater degree of stability, rather than being buffeted by variations in the value of a currency.

The IMF arose from the Bretton Woods Conference held at the Mount Washington Hotel in 1944

The fixed exchange rate system broke apart in 1971, when US president Richard Nixon abandoned the fixed link between the value of the US dollar and gold. The decision reflected the US's desire to have greater flexibility over its monetary policy and the value of its currency, faced with high inflation and unemployment.

With the collapse of the IMF's founding purpose, from the 1970s onwards its role changed to the one it retains today (see Table 4.1):

- The IMF provides economic stability by giving financial support or loans to states that are suffering, or are likely to suffer, from debt crises (when a state is unable to repay loans that it owes to financial institutions such as the IMF or private banks). This has predominantly seen the IMF focusing on the developing world, but it has also made loans to developed countries. In 1976, the UK borrowed US$3.9 billion from the IMF as it struggled to deal with a deep financial crisis. More recently, Greece, Portugal and Spain have received IMF loans in order to help save their economies from bankruptcy.
- It monitors the economic outlook of both the world economy and individual member countries, including forecasting and commenting on potential threats and weaknesses.
- It advises member countries on how best to manage their economies, particularly less developed member countries in which technical economic expertise may be lacking.

Table 4.1 IMF functions

Functions	How it does this
Surveillance and monitoring	Reviews country policies and national, regional and global economic and financial developments through a formal system known as surveillance. The IMF advises its 190 member states, encouraging policies that foster economic stability, reduce vulnerability to economic and financial crises, and raise living standards.
Lending	A member country may request IMF financial assistance if it suffers or is likely to suffer a debt crisis – that is, if it lacks or potentially lacks sufficient financing on affordable terms to meet its net international payments (e.g. imports, external debt redemptions).
Capacity building	IMF experts provide training to member states to help them manage their economy more effectively. For example, experts on tax collection may advise a state that is not taxing its population adequately how to implement a fair and effective taxation system. It has established Regional Training Centres in Africa to help build expertise in Sub-Saharan African states.

Structure

The IMF has 190 member states, therefore including the majority of the world's states. Aside from very small states such as Monaco, only North Korea is not a member country.

A managing director leads the IMF. Since 2019, this is the Hungarian former Vice-President of the European Commission, Kristalina Georgieva. The IMF makes frequent interventions and commentary on the global economy as a whole and the economic fortunes of IMF member countries. It publishes an annual report on the world economic outlook and works to identify risks in the economic and financial policies of its member states.

During the 2016 referendum on the UK's membership of the EU, the IMF and its then managing director, Christine Lagarde, provoked criticism from the 'Leave' campaign by publishing a report a week before the referendum that predicted Brexit would lead to increased inflation and reduce the UK's GDP by 5.5%, pushing the UK into recession. Critics argued that this was unnecessary interference in a decision that should have been left to the British people. On the other hand, some argue that the IMF acts as a useful additional source of economic advice and forecasting to help states and their populations make informed decisions and to avoid collateral economic shocks. After all, there is no other organisation above nation-state level that carries out this function on such a global scale.

Resources

The main source of the IMF's financial resources is payments made to the fund by its member countries. These so-called quotas broadly reflect members' relative positions and wealth in the world economy. The IMF increased the amount of funds available for lending to its member countries in 2008 in response to the global financial crisis, with member states asked to pay more in their quotas. Box 4.1 gives an indication of the funds available to the IMF and where it has focused most of its lending.

Some have criticised the IMF for being undemocratic, as voting power is weighted according to how much states contribute financially in the quota. This means that the most economically powerful states pay the most to the IMF and in return are allocated more power over decision making. A counter argument is that it is legitimate that those states that contribute the most have influence over how their contributions are allocated. Less economically powerful and less developed states argue that this leads to the powerful states dominating the goals, terms and conditions of the IMF's lending.

Box 4.1

IMF resources and current loans (2021)

In its 2020 Annual Report, the IMF had the following commitments and sources of income:
- $165 billion of lending to 83 countries, including $16 billion to low income countries.
- The majority of IMF loans went to Western hemisphere countries including Chile, Colombia and Mexico, with Sub-Saharan Africa the next biggest region including loans to Ethiopia and Nigeria.
- The US was the largest contributor to the IMF, accounting for 17% of member states' contributions. China provided the next largest share of contributions, at 6%.

Response to crises

A key role of the IMF is to respond to financial crises that impact one, and often many, states. The key aim is to try to keep afloat the economies that are suffering the most, and to prevent them collapsing or getting into so much debt that they are unable to pay it back. The other key aim in an interdependent global economy is to prevent a financial crisis from spreading to other countries.

Apart from the global financial crisis of 2008, the IMF has assisted with three major recent financial crises:

1 The Asian financial crisis (1997)
2 Emergency lending to Brazil (1998) and Argentina (2000)
3 The Eurozone crisis (from 2008 onwards)

Structural adjustment programmes

When the IMF makes a loan to a member country that is in need, it is often conditional. Specifically, the state must undergo economic reforms to overcome the problems that led it to request help in the first place. Historically, these were called 'structural adjustment programmes' and specified a range of macro-economic reforms that states would have to implement to receive an IMF loan.

For example, this might include:

- cutting public spending and raising taxes, to eliminate the **budget deficit**
- selling government-owned assets to private ownership, known as privatisation
- increasing the amount of taxes that the state collects to help it pay for its own public services
- reducing public sector wages or state pensions.

Although the IMF no longer uses the term '**structural adjustment programmes**', it does still make its loans conditional on proposing economic reforms and regularly monitors progress. For example, before the IMF loaned to Argentina in 2019, the government set out plans to increase taxes on wealth and create a new independent body to review the government's budget and make forecasts. This was part of a package of proposals, with deadlines, on which future disbursement of IMF funds was conditional.

A criticism of making loans conditional and demanding structural adjustment is that they make excessive demands on states, and that this infringes on state sovereignty, often imposing a neoliberal model of economic policy along the lines of the Washington Consensus (see page 36). On a more basic level, sovereignty is impacted because a state's economic policy is no longer decided independently but negotiated and monitored by the IMF.

Key terms

Budget deficit When a state spends more than it raises in revenue (for example, through tax revenue), it is said to be running a budget deficit.

Structural adjustment programme (SAP) A programme of economic reform usually following a neoliberal agenda, including government spending cuts and privatisation, which is imposed on a state as a condition of it receiving an IMF loan.

Table 4.2 Examples of IMF conditionality

Member country	Conditions proposed	Impacts
Argentina	Before receiving the largest loan in the IMF's history of over $56 billion, Argentina was required to put forward a plan to increase taxes, cut public spending and create an independent watchdog for budget responsibility.	Argentina's government continued to raise taxes but in 2019 defaulted on its debt for the ninth time in its history. The value of Argentina's currency stabilised against the dollar. It owes billions of dollars to the IMF and international lenders and the Covid-19 pandemic has further reduced economic growth.
Pakistan	With debts of over $100 billion owed to international lenders, Pakistan agreed another 3 years of IMF loans amounting to $6 billion. Pakistan was required to make further tax reforms.	Negotiations have been ongoing between Pakistan and the IMF over tax reform for over a decade and the amount raised in taxes has been steadily rising in the last decade.

In defence of structural adjustment, it is argued that states that have got themselves into financial difficulty should not be given unconditional loans and should have an incentive to prevent recurring economic difficulty that might impact the global economy.

Frequently, the IMF does not act alone in helping states with emergency loans. In the case of the Greek sovereign debt crisis (see page 313), the IMF worked in partnership with the ECB and the European Commission to agree a joint loan package. This three-way partnership, dubbed the 'Troika', required negotiation and agreement between the three institutions on the amount and conditions of the loans.

The Greek government has faced fierce protests in response to its handling of the country's economic crisis

Activity

Imagine that you have been asked to review the conditions on which IMF loans are based. List the conditions you might want to impose on states in order to agree loans. Which conditions are reasonable and unreasonable to make? Can you think of any alternatives to conditions?

Specific criticisms of SAPs include the following:

- Economic reforms, such as privatisation, see an increase in corporate profits that are not necessarily shared with wider society.
- Some developing countries see increased prosperity but also an increase in inequality and child poverty, suggesting that the programmes disproportionately benefit the richest.
- Tax rises can sometimes hit the poorest the hardest, particularly indirect taxation such as a sales tax, which poor people cannot avoid if they are going to continue to buy goods.
- With many of the poorest working in subsistence activities or the informal sector (such as family-based farming for survival), reform of the formal sector of the economy (such as registered, profit-making companies) has little impact on improving their lives.
- Opening markets to foreign investors clearly aids in boosting foreign direct investment (FDI), but can also expose fragile economies to the effects of foreign economic crises.
- There is a fundamental clash with state sovereignty, particularly if an SAP is at odds with the policies that a democratic government has been elected to implement.

Case study

The IMF and the Greek debt crisis

Greece has been a major recipient of IMF loans. The country had accumulated large debts in the international financial markets due to high public spending and low GDP growth. As the world banking system froze in response to the global financial crisis, heavily indebted Greece was unable to make repayments and defaulted on its debts.

The so-called Troika of the ECB, the European Commission and the IMF decided that the impact of the Greek debt crisis could spread within the euro currency zone and a rescue package was needed. In 2010, the first package of 110 billion euros to Greece was approved.

In return, the Troika demanded that Greece implement austerity measures to reduce public spending and privatise expensive state-owned assets. The Troika negotiated a 50% reduction (a so-called haircut) on the amount Greece owed to private banks.

By 2014, with two bailouts, a deepening economic recession and rising unemployment, the anti-austerity party Syriza won a snap general election. This pitched a legitimately and democratically elected party rejecting austerity measures against the Troika, which was demanding the measures as its condition for keeping the Greek economy afloat. It prompted attempts to renegotiate the conditions, and represented a unique clash between political and economic IGOs and state sovereignty.

When renegotiations between the Syriza government and the Troika broke down, Prime Minister Alexis Tsipras called a referendum, asking the Greek people directly whether they supported the conditions of the bailout package. They overwhelmingly rejected the package by 61% to 39%.

In 2015, Greece failed to make a payment to the IMF, the first developed country ever to do so. Banks closed as fears grew that Greece would leave the Eurozone (so-called Grexit) and cash machines were limited to withdrawals of 60 euros per day. Ultimately, the imperative of preventing 'Grexit' prevailed, with a new bailout deal agreed later in 2015 to keep the Greek economy afloat.

Activity

Are the interventions that the IMF made in Argentina and Pakistan an unjustifiable interference in state independence and sovereignty? Debate the arguments for and against.

Debate

Is the IMF a force for good in the world economy?

Force for good

- The IMF gives loans to states and helps to reduce their likelihood of falling into economic recession.
- It helps to prevent economic difficulties in one state from spreading to others.
- Pooling of funds as a fundamental liberal idea for many states to contribute to helping those in need is a good thing, providing a clear framework for states to help each other.
- It provides an independent monitor of state economies, helping states to identify threats and opportunities.
- It helps to encourage states to reform their economies to an economic model that has delivered considerable economic growth in most developed states.

Not a force for good

- The IMF forces states to comply with conditionality in a way that interferes with sovereignty. It relentlessly promotes a neoliberal, Western-dominated economic model.
- SAPs do not benefit the poorest, but boost corporate profits and serve the interests of developed states.
- It failed to predict and prevent the global financial crisis in 2008 by failing to challenge reckless lending and inadequate regulation of global financial institutions.
- It was unable to prevent the spread of the global financial crisis.

The World Bank

The World Bank was founded at the Bretton Woods Conference in 1944. Its headquarters are in Washington, DC. The founding objectives of the World Bank were, as the name suggests, to act as a source of loans for reconstruction and development projects in countries lacking financial capital. The immediate priority in the aftermath of the Second World War was to help with rebuilding key infrastructure such as roads and electricity. Eventually, the World Bank moved from emergency reconstruction to longer-term development needs and to the developing world outside Europe.

In the 1980s, it used SAPs focused on wider macro-economic reform as part of its conditions for lending (see page 37). However, with the poorest countries it has now moved its focus away from providing loans to giving grants for specific projects. For loans to middle-income countries, conditionality is not always required.

There are two key institutions within the World Bank.

1 **The International Bank for Reconstruction and Development:** is responsible for providing loans to help meet middle-income countries' development needs. For example, the World Bank has provided the State Bank of India with a loan of over $700 million to develop solar energy projects. Some loans come with conditions which are monitored in partnership with the IMF.
2 **The International Development Association:** provides loans to the poorest countries (only those below a certain level of GDP per capita). These loans tend to have very low rates of interest and sometimes no interest at all.

Since the creation of the Millennium Development Goals and the Sustainable Development Goals, its projects have worked in support of this wider UN human and sustainable development agenda and focus predominantly on medium to long-term projects rather than emergency assistance. For example:

- It provides loans, technical and financial assistance to support reconstruction and development. The World Bank deploys around $50 billion in various types of financial assistance each year and has supported over 12,000 projects worldwide since it was founded.

- It has a growing emphasis on reducing poverty, linked strongly to the MDGs and now to the Sustainable Development Goals (SDGs). The overarching goal of the World Bank is to end poverty within a generation and boost shared prosperity.
- It funds specific medium to long-term development projects (see Table 4.3).
- It provides technical assistance to states, with this advice focusing on human and social development (in contrast to the IMF, where the technical assistance is focused on economic growth and management of public finances).
- It carries out analytical work on development matters, which is made freely available to states and NGOs working on development, adding to global research on the factors that aid and impede development.

Table 4.3 Examples of World Bank projects

Objective	Country	Project
Water and sanitation	India	The World Bank has provided $3.4 billion to improve access to clean drinking water and sanitation. This has been a long-term project in place since 2000 and the bank estimates that it has helped about 36 million people.
Reconstruction in Afghanistan	Afghanistan	Since 2002, the World Bank has invested over $4.7 billion for development and reconstruction in Afghanistan. This has been mostly through grants (over $4 billion) and no-interest loans, and the Afghanistan government has also part-funded many projects.

The World Bank Executive Board agrees new loans, programmes, budgets and priorities. These decisions are then put to a member vote. There are 189 World Bank member states and membership of both the World Bank and IMF is linked (states must first be a member of the IMF before being accepted to the World Bank).

As with the IMF, voting power is weighted according to the amount that states contribute to the World Bank. The US carries 16% of the voting power. No other state has more than 5% voting power.

The US has traditionally dominated the World Bank as its largest shareholder – every president since its creation has been a US citizen and is nominated by the US. In 2019, President Donald Trump nominated his Treasury Under Secretary and former investment banker, David Malpass, as the current president of the World Bank.

Case study

The rise of other development banks

Since the creation of the World Bank, several other development banks have been set up. One of the most significant is the AIIB, which launched in 2016. It operates on a similar membership basis to the World Bank and its 103 members include China, India, Russia, Canada and the United Kingdom. The US is not a member. It has a similar weighting of voting power as the World Bank and China holds the most votes with nearly 300,000 compared with India second with nearly 86,000 votes.

The creation of the Bank adds to the funds available for global development, though for the US it reduces the power that it has over where global development funds are directed. There was some diplomatic pressure exerted on the UK by the US against the UK becoming a member as part of Prime Minister David Cameron's policy of engaging positively with China on economic links. The Bank focuses on projects that it judges will be of economic benefit to Asia and it mostly gives loans (unlike the grants issued by the World Bank). Separately, the New Development Bank was established by Brazil, South Africa, China, India and Russia in 2015, with each country holding an equal share and voting power.

Since the World Bank's focus has changed towards human and sustainable development, it has achieved considerable success in its aim of reducing world poverty:

- It is recognised as a base for the world's foremost experts in development economics, working across the world, who offer technical advice and assistance to projects to ensure they are delivered effectively, and acts as an accessible 'think tank' on development best practice.
- It has acted as a source of finance to many states as they sought to develop, such as South Korea which received nearly $15 billion from the World Bank and now itself is a leading donor to poorer states. It has also moved increasingly away from conditional loans to grants and has become less demanding on economic reform.

However, the World Bank does have its weaknesses:

- There are now many competing development banks such as the Asia Infrastructure and Investment Bank (AIIB) set up by China and the New Development Bank (set up by Brazil, Russia, India, China and South Africa). This means that the World Bank is becoming less powerful, though part of the reason that other development banks have been set up has been to create other less-US dominated sources of finance.
- Historically, it has been criticised with the IMF for structural adjustment programmes that pushed a neoliberal reform agenda on states too aggressively. The resulting 'shock therapy' in economies across the world (Argentina and Russia, for example) has been criticised as undemocratic and an attempt to impose a US-centric economic model on states too quickly and arguably in the global interest as opposed to the recipient states' interests.

Distinguish between

The IMF and the World Bank

The IMF

- The IMF emphasises global and national economic growth.
- It assists state governments with loans, often to enable them to pay their debts to private banks. Unlike the World Bank, it focuses mostly on emergency assistance (for example, in a debt crisis).
- It provides states with technical assistance on how to more effectively manage their economies as a whole (macroeconomic focus).

The World Bank

- The World Bank emphasises ending extreme poverty and focuses on sustainable development.
- It provides grants to state governments for specific long-term development projects. Many projects are funded through direct grants, rather than loans.
- It provides technical assistance to states on specific development needs, including health and education.

International trade

The desire for states to trade with each other has existed for centuries. At certain points in history, international trade was carried out by force. States aimed to conquer other territories in order to gain their resources or strategic positions on key transport links. In the eighteenth and nineteenth centuries, Great Britain and other powerful states often went to war, colonising entire empires of territory in order to maximise their economic output and control of strategic resources and territory. It was not until the late nineteenth century that states began to negotiate formal free-trade deals with each other in an attempt to bring order to international trade.

In the twentieth century, a clash of economic ideology between free-market capitalism and the communist model dominated. The capitalist world organised its trade by creating the General Agreement on Tariffs and Trade (later the WTO) to agree international rules of trade. With the collapse of the Soviet Union in 1989, capitalism seemed to have won the battle of economic ideas. The post-war period saw a new enthusiasm for free-trade agreements between states. Economic integration was deepest in western Europe, with the creation of the European Economic Community (EEC) and the Single Market.

In an interdependent world, states have therefore moved from challenging each other for economic power through force to making the most of their economic power and trading opportunities peacefully, through international agreements.

Today's economic global governance arrangements concerning world trade therefore push states to work together in a more liberal and cooperative manner. This should not be surprising, since the reality of international trade forces all but the most isolationist of states to work together because it is in their economic interest to do so. States may choose a particularly liberal approach, such as that demonstrated by EU states, which have given up significant sovereignty over matters of trade. Or they may choose a more protectionist approach, by entering into agreements but also trying to protect their own interests, via tariffs or restrictions, against competition from elsewhere in the global market.

The World Trade Organization

There was a recognition at the Bretton Woods Conference in 1944 that an international organisation needed to be created to reduce obstacles to international trade, and in 1947 the General Agreement on Tariffs and Trade (GATT) was signed by 23 founding nations. The aim of this international treaty was to agree a set of international trade rules where tariffs on goods would be reduced and more states joined the treaty in successive rounds of negotiations.

By 1995, the GATT had been signed by over 100 states and had reduced tariffs on goods amounting to approximately $300 billion of world trade. With the steady spread of economic globalisation, what was needed now was a specific and permanent institution with dispute resolution forums. The previous agreements made under the GATT remain the basis for the international trade rules of the WTO. Work continues to remove more barriers to trade, through further rounds of negotiation.

Based in Geneva, the WTO's primary goal is to reduce barriers on trade in both goods and services, which includes:

- reducing and removing tariffs imposed by states on imports from other states to agreed levels (for example, under WTO rules there is a 10% tariff levied on imported cars)
- quotas (or limits) on the amount of imports of particular goods from other states.

The WTO is not the only means by which states can reduce tariff barriers – states are free to enter into agreements with one or more other states. For example, the European Union and the United Kingdom do not trade with each other on WTO rules but have a specific free-trade agreement signed in December 2020 (the EU–UK Trade and Co-operation Agreement). However, the European Union and Australia do not have a specific trade agreement with each other and therefore trade under WTO rules. For WTO member states without specific free-trade agreements, this is the default position if no other agreement is in place.

What the WTO does offer is the opportunity to put together extremely comprehensive trade agreements that will involve nearly all international trade.

The WTO also:

- checks that states are following trade agreements
- helps to resolve trade disputes between states, in order to avoid states from engaging in unilateral trade wars with each other.
- produces research on global trade and economic policy.

The WTO has 164 member countries, fewer than both the IMF and the World Bank. The member states account for 97% of world trade. It can take years to go through the process of joining the WTO – Algeria applied to join in 1987 and still has not become a full member. States currently applying to join include Iraq, Libya, Somalia and Sudan, and the most recent new member was Afghanistan, which joined in 2016. The EU is a member of the WTO and its member states are also members in their own right, but EU member states have to act together as a unified bloc of states.

Membership of the WTO involves both:

- rights, such as the right to export to other countries and to expect WTO rules to be followed fairly on these exports, and
- obligations, such as the need to limit tariffs on imports and to follow rules on, for example, intellectual property rights, state subsidies and 'dumping' (where exports are sold below the price they would normally be sold in the state of origin).

The highest decision-making body of the WTO is the Ministerial Conference, which meets every 2 years. Decisions are made by consensus and are binding, so every member has to agree to a trade deal or there is no trade deal. The need for consensus can make decision making in the WTO very slow.

The WTO operates on six key principles:

1 **Non-discrimination:** states should treat their trading partners equally and fairly (though exceptions allow states to form free-trade agreements with each other). They should not discriminate between their own and foreign products once tariffs have been paid.
2 **More open:** there is commitment to free trade and to progressively lowering tariff and non-tariff barriers, such as import bans or quotas where the amount of imports is restricted.
3 **Predictable and transparent:** states should not raise trade barriers without warning or arbitrarily. A predictable system of international trade helps with stability and job creation and allows for steady competition and lower prices.
4 **More competitive:** states should not interfere in order to give themselves an unfair competitive edge, for example by subsidising exports that would otherwise be uncompetitive or unsustainable or 'dumping' goods at prices below their market value.

5 **More benefits for less developed countries:** allows scope for less developed countries to catch up and transition to becoming full participants in international trade.

6 **Protection of the environment:** environmental protection must be respected both nationally and internationally.

WTO rules

At its simplest, the WTO is a set of rules that its members agree to abide by. The founding rules of the WTO, agreed in the original GATT in 1947, still stand today and have been added to in subsequent years through specific negotiating 'rounds'. Every member must agree for the round to be successful. There have been nine negotiating rounds, some of which have taken many years to agree, the most recent being in 2001 (see Table 4.4). The WTO has not been able to agree a new set of rules since then.

Table 4.4 Examples of GATT and WTO rounds of agreement

Agreement	Rules included and scope
General Agreement on Tariffs and Trade (GATT), 1947	45,000 tariff removals were agreed, which still stand today and impacted US$10 billion worth of international trade.
Kennedy Round, 1962–67	Expanded the removal of tariff barriers worth US$40 billion. For the first time, this negotiating round dealt with an issue not related to tariffs – that of states 'dumping' products cheaply in other states to dominate the market in that state.
Uruguay Round, 1986–94	The longest successfully concluded negotiating round of the WTO. This was also the WTO's largest trade agreement, as 123 countries were involved. The WTO was formally created in this round. There was a particular focus on reducing agricultural subsidies, although the EU's system of agricultural subsidies, the Common Agricultural Policy (CAP), was largely unaffected.
Doha Round, 2001–date	The WTO's most recent negotiating round has been ongoing since 2001 and is effectively defunct. A so-called Development Round, it was intended to make progress in widening free trade with developing countries. The talks are in gridlock due to disagreements over further reductions in agricultural subsidies, which developed states are defending in the face of a perceived threat from cheaper agricultural imports. The Organisation for Economic Co-operation and Development (OECD) has estimated that the agricultural subsidies give an unfair advantage worth US$300 billion annually. The US in particular has been criticised for not challenging its powerful farming lobby.

Criticisms and gridlock: the Doha Development Round

In 2001, the WTO began a new round of negotiations aimed at improving developing countries' access to global markets, particularly for agricultural products. This was intended to reduce government subsidies on exports that boost prices and domestic subsidies that go directly to farmers. Agriculture is a particularly important sector for developing countries and for some represents nearly a quarter of their GDP.

Among the specific proposals of the Doha Development Round were reductions in government agricultural subsidies of up to 75% and 66% for the EU and the US respectively. There has been resistance from both developed and developing states to the proposals in the Doha Round, with developed states seeking to defend their interests and developing states rejecting compromises they judge to be against their interests.

The failure of the Doha Round to reach agreement has raised criticism of the WTO's effectiveness. Critics say that the powerful nations, including the EU and the US, are blocking less developed nations and attempting to preserve the status quo for protectionist reasons. In recent decades, this has led the WTO to become gridlocked (since the WTO was created in 1994, it has successfully agreed only one major international trade deal).

Negotiations in the Doha Round have agreed improvements to customs procedures which have reduced costs, but reductions on agricultural subsidies remain a sticking point. Although the WTO agreed in 2015 to cut export subsidies, these changes will not come into force until 2023. The Doha Round was effectively abandoned without agreement in 2015. Until new WTO efforts are made, states must resort to negotiating with as many other states as possible, in order to agree further liberalisation of tariff barriers.

The failure of Doha also highlights that the WTO is unable to make decisions quickly, its Ministerial Conferences are too infrequent and the need for consensus among all members further slows decision making. The difficulties in reaching agreement at the WTO might be seen as the reason for states seeking to agree trade deals outside of its forums, such as the Comprehensive and Progressive Agreement for Trans-Pacific Partnership. It also reflects the fact that states are better able to make agreements that meet their interests within a smaller group of states with shared interests.

Case study

A return to trade wars?

A key role of the WTO is to resolve trade disputes between states and to reduce the risk that states will take matters into their own hands, engaging in 'tit for tat' trade wars. There is evidence that, in recent years, the WTO has been powerless to avoid increasing tensions between major powers, especially the US and China.

The key disputes between the US and China revolve around accusations of unfair competition with state-owned and supported industries in China and stealing intellectual property from US companies. Between 2018 and 2019, the Trump administration imposed tariffs on $550 billion worth of goods and China retaliated with tariffs worth $185 billion. President Trump argued that the WTO was not doing enough to ensure China followed its rules. In 2020, the WTO ruled that US tariffs on China were against international trade agreements. It was not possible for the US to appeal the ruling as the WTO's appeals panel was no longer functioning as member states had failed to agree on appointing new judges.

Table 4.5 Key problems and successes of the WTO

Key problems of the WTO	Key successes of the WTO
Consensus decision making is slow	Has reduced the cost of international trade by successively reducing tariffs
Frequently sidelined by states forming their own agreements or engaging in retaliatory measures	Has expanded a single set of trade rules to 164 member states
Economically powerful states hold considerable bargaining power over less powerful states	Increased predictability and order in world trade, with a dispute resolution forum

Box 4.2

The World Economic Forum

The WEF is an annual conference of world leaders, business leaders, IGOs, NGOs and economists held in Davos, Switzerland each January. The forum allows all of these actors to contribute to setting the agenda for world economic issues. World leaders, for example, give key speeches setting out their government's policies. The 2020 summit focused on climate change and took steps to offset the carbon emissions of the many world leaders flying to the summit.

Some criticise the Davos get-together of the great and the good of the world economy as elitist and out of touch. It does not have a set agenda and is more a forum for discussion than formal agreement. It is also seen as almost a celebration of the capitalist economic model, although China has nevertheless been attending since 1979.

The Group of Seven (G7)

The G7 is an informal forum that was founded in 1975 after a successful ad hoc gathering in Paris of the finance ministers of the world's six wealthiest economies (France, Italy, Japan, the UK, the US and West Germany, the Group of Six). There is no formal application or criteria for membership – it can invite and expel whom it likes. Canada became the seventh member in 1976. In 1997, Russia was invited to join and decided to accept (forming the G8) but was temporarily suspended in 2014 in response to its annexation of Crimea (see Box 4.3).

Box 4.3

G7 members

The current members of the G7 include:

- Canada
- France
- Germany
- Italy
- Japan
- UK
- US

Russia joined in 1998, but was suspended in 2014. Representatives for the EU also attend.

The G7 does not include all of the world's major economic powers, with China a notable absentee. The group's membership has always been intended to be made up of like-minded states sharing similar values and international outlook. Russia's suspension in 2014 reflects the group's refusal to tolerate a member diverging from its values. The Council on Foreign Relations has described the G7 as a 'steering group for the West'. The group now meets annually to monitor and address developments in the world economy.

Informal forums like the G7 (and the G20, see page 140) are different from IGOs because of the following:

- The G7 has no formal rules. The UN, by contrast, has the UN Charter, which clearly sets out its purpose and processes.
- It can invite any states, IGOs or NGOs to its meetings.
- It can choose to remove any of its members from meetings, if the presidency state has not invited them to the meetings. In this sense, it has a flexible membership of like-minded allies.
- It has no budget or supporting secretariat, unlike IGOs such as the UN or IMF. If its members want to take action that costs money, the individual member states pay for it (or not).
- The decisions it takes are not binding and rely on the individual will of the participating states to deliver on the commitments they have made.
- There are no defined objectives. This allows it enormous flexibility in tackling any issues that matter to the presidency state and its members.
- It is primarily a forum for world leaders to interact at an annual summit. Between the summits, the G7 drives little organised activity.

The G7 presidency rotates among members, with the presidency state hosting and organising the annual summit. Russia held the G7 presidency in 2014 but the meeting was cancelled due to the other members' opposition to Russia's annexation of Crimea. The UK hosted a meeting of the G7 in Cornwall in 2021 (see Table 4.6).

The meetings usually take place outside the capital city of the presidency country, often allowing the leaders to take advantage of a more informal and relaxed setting. During the UK presidency in 2021, members met at the remote Carbis Bay in Cornwall. In 2012, US president Barack Obama hosted the G8 at Camp David, the president's country retreat.

Table 4.6 Agenda and outcomes of the 2021 G7 meeting (held in the UK)

Agenda item	Outcome
Covid-19 pandemic response	Committed 1 billion vaccine doses between the summit and mid-2022, with the G7 states having previously provided 2 billion doses since the start of the pandemic.
Covid-19 economic recovery	Committed to a 'tax system that is fair across the world' including a global minimum corporation tax of 15%, with the aim of bringing G20 states into this commitment.
Climate change	Reaffirmed commitment to limiting global temperature rises to 1.5°C. G7 states also committed to net zero carbon emissions by no later than 2050, halving collective emissions over the two decades to 2030.
Democracy and the rule of law	In a sign of its focus on shared values, the G7 reaffirmed its commitment to harnessing 'the power of democracy, freedom, equality, the rule of law and respect for human rights'. The G7 pledged $2.75 billion over 5 years to the Global Partnership for Education.

The UK hosted a meeting of the G7 in Carbis Bay, Cornwall, in 2021

Performance and impact

The first observation about the G7 is that its impact on state sovereignty is very negligible. However, this also means that the extent to which its decisions are delivered or enforceable is similarly weak.

Significant G7/G8 decisions include the following:

- **2002:** the G7 becomes the G8. This was the first meeting of the G8, having been expanded to include Russia. Russia is invited to host a G8 summit for the first time.
- **2006:** Russia hosts its first G8 summit in St Petersburg. Before the summit, other G8 leaders were critical of Russia's record on human rights and Russia responded by criticising Western 'colonialist rhetoric'. Energy security, including increasing dependence of other G8 members on Russian energy supplies, was a key focus of the summit. Early discussions were also held regarding Russia's membership of the WTO, which was completed in 2012.
- **2007:** the Gleneagles Summit during the UK presidency – G8 leaders agreed to major debt cancellation to heavily indebted poor countries.

Criticism and pressure for reform

There are criticisms of the G7:

- Its membership reflects an outdated vision of the world's economic powers. The world's second (soon to be largest) economic power, China, is excluded. Rising powers such as Brazil and India are also not included.
- The G7 became painfully divided during the presidency of Donald Trump (see case study). An organisation of like-minded allies became a very public demonstration of a clash of world outlook between the US and its traditional allies, which undermined the unity and cohesive vision and image that the G7 arguably exists to project. Some commentators labelled the group as the 'G6+1'.
- It is made up of a group of states that (normally) agree with each other. Expelling Russia in 2014 confirms this. There was no attempt to use the G8 as a means of negotiating or persuading Russia to pursue a different course, but rather as a means of punishment.
- The scope for the G7 to achieve major breakthroughs is limited. The issues of the moment tend to dominate summits. The Covid-19 pandemic and the fair distribution of vaccines, for example, dominated the UK's hosting of the G7 in 2021. There is a sense that the G7 responds to events, rather than shapes them.
- The G7's flexibility and informal approach makes it difficult to hold its members to account for commitments made at the summits.

Arguments for reform suggest that the G7 should widen its membership to include other significant emerging and established economic powers. Attempts have been made to broaden the G7 by including the so-called Outreach Five, consisting of Brazil, China, India, Mexico and South Africa. However, these attempts have been devalued by the existence of the G20, which already exists as a wider group and has become more powerful, taking a much more significant role in international efforts to address the global financial crisis, for example.

In defence of the G7, it is argued that a narrower group of like-minded states is better able to come to agreement and make decisions in a way that would not be possible in the G20.

Debate

What are the strengths and weaknesses of the G7 compared with IGOs?

Strengths

- For realists, the G7 has little impact on state sovereignty. The forum never forces states to do things that they do not agree with.
- Informality allows its members to focus on any issue of importance and to respond to the major issues of the moment.
- A smaller number of member states prevents gridlock in decision making. By contrast, the WTO has a far larger membership but has been unable to agree a new trade deal for its members since 2001.

Weaknesses

- The G7 meets less frequently, so it acts in bursts rather than consistently.
- It is a forum for like-minded allies, rather than for active problem solving and resolving differences of opinion.
- It is a forum for the richest and most powerful states to preserve their own interests.
- It no longer reflects the states that are the most economically powerful.
- There is little accountability – for example, there is no checking that states deliver on the commitments they have made.

Case study

A divided G7?

Divisions between the G7 burst into the open at a particularly divisive summit in Quebec in 2018. The agenda comprised of a series of topics on which President Donald Trump and the other G7 leaders were not in agreement: climate change (with the US threatening to withdraw from the Paris accord), international trade (with 'tit for tat' tariffs between the US and the EU and Canada respectively), Iran (with the US having withdrawn from the so-called Iran nuclear deal agreed by the permanent members of the UN Security Council plus Germany) and the response to Russia after the novichok poisonings in Salisbury earlier that year.

The US president left the summit early and withdrew his support for the summit's traditional closing statement which summarises the topics that G7 leaders have discussed and on which its members pledge to act. This was the first time in the history of the group that a member had not been willing to give its support to the closing statement. The disagreement centred on US tariffs of 25% on steel and 10% on aluminium, to which the EU and Canada responded with retaliatory tariffs. Trump argued that 'the US has been taken advantage of for decades … the piggy bank that everyone keeps robbing'.

This highlights that how effective and meaningful the G7 is depends on how unified its member states are and that is weakened when one or more member states no longer buy into its shared values.

Activity

Imagine that the leaders of the G7 and G20 have tasked you with modernising both forums to suit today's global politics.

How would you redesign the forums? Would you keep both the G7 and G20 or merge them into a new organisation? How would that organisation be set up and what would its objectives be? Think about which states you would want to include and how you resolve any current weaknesses (such as exclusive membership) but not lose some of the strengths (such as responsiveness to crises).

The Group of Twenty (G20)

The G20 was created in 1999 as a means of expanding the G7 to include a wider group of industrialised states and emerging economic powers. The stated objective of the G20 when it was founded was for it to be:

> an informal forum that promotes open and constructive discussion between industrial and emerging-market countries on key issues related to global economic stability

Like the G7, the G20 began principally as a meeting of the states' finance ministers and heads of national central banks. By the time of the 2008 global financial crisis, it had become the key annual forum for world leaders to meet and discuss global economic policy.

Distinguish between

The G7 and the G20

The G7

- The North American (US/Canada) and western European nations dominate the G7, making it outdated.
- It is an alliance of like-minded states, which has the power to expel those it disagrees with.

The G20

- The G20 has wider membership, reflecting a broader range of economic powers, both established and emerging.
- It is broader geographically, including African, Asian and South American countries.
- It is better at and more relevant when dealing with major economic crises, such as the 2008 global financial crisis.

Whereas the G7 can be criticised as being a narrow alliance of the oldest and most established economic powers, the G20 includes many emerging economic powers and a more geographically diverse range of states.

China, for example, is a key member of the G20 but is not a member of the G7, despite many economists predicting that its economy will overtake the US's as the largest in the world in the next decade. The so-called BRIC countries (Brazil, Russia, India and China), which have been experiencing rapid economic growth since the early 2000s, are included in the G20. A mixture of rising and established economies from South America (Argentina), southeast Asia (Indonesia), the middle east (Saudi Arabia) and Africa (South Africa) are included.

Key features of the G20 include the following:

- Its membership represents both established and emerging economies which, together, account for almost two-thirds of the world population, more than four-fifths of gross world product and three-quarters of world trade.
- The G20 also has the key economic IGOs attending all of its meetings (see Table 4.7). All of the Bretton Woods Institutions attend, along with the UN and the EU. This is very different to the G7, where the EU is the only IGO in attendance.
- Meetings usually take place annually, with a rotating presidency, as is the case for the G7. The presidency state has considerable power over which additional states or other international organisations it invites and the agenda for that year's summit.
- The agenda for G20 meetings has become increasingly broad, extending beyond purely economic matters. Climate change and global terrorism, for example, have featured on recent agendas.

Table 4.7 Attendance at the 2020 G20 summit in Riyadh, Saudi Arabia

G20 member states	Permanent guest invitees	Additionally invited to this summit
Argentina	African Union	Jordan
Australia	ASEAN	Singapore
Brazil	EU, represented by the ECB and the European Commission	Switzerland
Canada		United Arab Emirates (representing the Gulf Cooperation Council)
China	Financial Stability Board	
EU (see next column)	International Labour Organisation	
France		
Germany	IMF	
India	New Partnership for African Development (part of the AU)	
Indonesia		
Italy		
Japan	OECD	
Mexico	Spain	
Russia	UN	
Saudi Arabia	World Bank	
South Africa	WTO	
South Korea		
Turkey		
UK		
US		

Some see the G20 as becoming a more influential actor in economic global governance than the G7. During the global financial crisis of 2008 it was the G20, rather than the G7, that led the response to the crisis of the world's most powerful economic states (see page 144).

The following factors have made the G20 the more effective informal forum:

- The G20 is a balance between traditional, historic economic powers (such as France, the UK and the US), newly emerged economic powers (such as China, Brazil and India) and emerging economic powers (such as Argentina and Indonesia). This makes the G20 more effective, as it is neither too exclusive (a weakness of the G7) nor too comprehensive (a weakness of the WTO) to be able to make decisions.
- The membership also includes more states that do not always agree with each other. This enables the G20 to be more of a forum for dispute resolution and problem solving than the G7, whose members usually agree with each other on most matters and has suspended a member (Russia, in 2014) with which the majority did not agree. The G20 is a forum for influencing climate change, where newly emerging economies, such as India, have very different views from more established economies. It can be argued that this makes the G20 more useful. For example, in 2019 it was at a G20 summit that Presidents Trump and Xi agreed to resume trade talks and de-escalate their trade war (in 2020, the US and China signed a 'phase one' trade agreement to take action to resolve trade grievances).
- The G20's inclusion of and partnership with the major Bretton Woods economic IGOs has significant benefits. It provides the most powerful world economies with a dedicated means of influencing these IGOs and coordinating action on economic matters between them and states. The G20 also brings in key regional organisations and other international actors such as the UN, EU and ASEAN and is therefore less state-centric than the G7, recognising that states work in partnership with IGOs.
- The widening of the G20 agenda to include non-economic matters provides another international forum for dispute resolution and influencing. It also provides world leaders from a more diverse range of states (than, for example, the UN Security Council) with a dedicated forum in which to build personal relationships and, occasionally, to make joint statements on issues ranging from the plight of refugees to global terrorism, which can set the global agenda.
- The G20 has taken decisive action on both economic and non-economic matters. It played a central role in agreeing that states would inject significant amounts of government money into banks to ensure they did not collapse and could lend to each other again during the global financial crisis. It has also taken action to ensure that the wealthiest states and IGOs work together, in order to prevent and more tightly regulate those bank accounts funding terrorists.

The G20, however, is not without its critics, who state the following:

- Its meetings have often been a focal point for anti-capitalist protests and it has been criticised for prioritising the needs of its member states and defending the interests of global capitalism. These protests were particularly significant in the early 2000s. Protesters regularly targeted summits for large-scale demonstrations, including violent protests in London during the 2009 summit.

- While its diversity is a strength, divisions in the G20 – particularly clashes between the US and its allies and Russia and China – have become more tense in recent years. Some also criticise the G20 as just a slightly less exclusive, but still exclusive, version of the G7 with no transparent criteria for membership.
- G20 summits conclude with a communiqué (see Box 4.4) agreed by each state in attendance. There is sometimes criticism that G20 outcomes are 'watered down' or 'lowest common denominator' – in other words, they are the most that each state present could agree upon rather than necessarily the most decisive agreement. Furthermore, there is criticism that states cannot be held accountable for the decisions or actions they agree at G20 summits.

Box 4.4

Summary of final communiqué from the 2020 G20 Summit

The summary of the final communiqué from the 2020 G20 Summit, held in Riyadh, Saudi Arabia, included:

- a commitment to taking immediate and exceptional measures to tackle the Covid-19 pandemic
- supporting research into vaccines, diagnostics and therapeutics
- improving global pandemic preparedness
- accelerating efforts to end poverty and reduce inequalities

---

The global financial crisis – a failure of global economic governance?

In 2008, a deep recession in the US brought about a worldwide economic downturn, the worst since the Great Depression in the 1930s. Banks providing ever-greater mortgages without sufficient proof they could be repaid caused the 'great recession'. Having over-lent, some banks started running out of money. House prices began to fall, and there was a loss of consumer confidence, resulting in a global downturn in trade.

This 2008 global financial crisis was exactly the kind of situation that IGOs, such as the IMF and the World Bank, had been founded to deal with. An economic crisis had spread beyond any single nation-state and it required the collective action of many states to bring the world economy back from the brink. Exactly how well did these IGOs respond and could they have done more to prevent the financial crisis in the first place?

One of the key causes of the financial crisis was a lack of strict regulations in the global financial system. Many economists concluded that banks were able to take too many risks, lending large amounts that borrowers eventually could not pay back. Both states and the world's economic IGOs had shown no desire for a global effort to tackle this lack of regulation. Indeed, there was general agreement that minimal regulation was to the benefit of the world economy.

The IMF admitted that it had failed to see the global financial crisis coming. It did not predict the risks that dangerous levels of lending in the US posed. In fact, until April 2007, the IMF was forecasting that 'world growth would continue to be strong'. Many have since criticised the IMF's monitoring of the global financial system's health as being too reliant on states' self-assessment of their own financial position. Monitoring – or surveillance, as the IMF calls it – is a key part of its role.

Economists have also blamed a global imbalance between states in the world economy. For example, China held a large currency surplus and its financial institutions were able to lend easily to the US, which was running a large deficit. This imbalance ultimately led to large amounts of lending and created an economic bubble in which house prices rose quickly. When house prices fell, mortgage holders could not pay back loans that had become more valuable than their homes, creating the so-called credit crunch.

Could economic global governance have prevented the 2008 economic crisis?

Could economic global governance have done anything to prevent this situation? A combination of global agreement and enthusiasm among states for such an economic model and a lack of any forecasting that this economic model might risk a global economic downturn makes this unlikely. The global imbalance also created a complex interdependence between a Chinese economy with an enormous capacity to lend and a US economy with an enormous need for loans.

Did global economic governance do any better once the crisis hit? Informal forums, including the G20, provided an essential means by which the world's most economically powerful states could discuss measures to tackle the crisis. The London G20 summit in 2009 saw states take important decisions to inject capital into their banking systems in order to prevent the collapse of the entire global banking system. This was arguably the most important action taken to resolve the crisis, as it provided protection to banks that were regarded as 'too important to fail'. Most states took this action themselves. For example, the UK government decided to place one failing private bank, the Royal Bank of Scotland, under state ownership. The US took the same measure to save the banks Fannie Mae and Freddie Mac. Both bailouts cost the national governments billions.

The IMF mobilised its funds to lend up to US$700 billion to states that were most affected by the downturn, including Greece, Portugal and Spain. It also required states to donate more to IMF funds, to act as a 'firewall' to prevent future crises from spreading. Belatedly, the IMF also supported tougher regulation of the banking sector, which many states agreed to. The World Bank tripled its lending, primarily to middle-income states, in order to prevent prolonged economic recession spreading further in the global economy.

The global financial crisis was a crucial test for global economic governance. The IMF and the World Bank played a significant role in resolving the financial crisis but, ultimately, nation-states played a larger role in bailing out failing banks and reforming their own systems of financial regulation. The crisis demonstrates the complex network of actors involved in economic global governance and the impact that an economic shock in one state can have globally.

Activity

Look at the responses to the global financial crisis by economic global governance institutions.

1   What were the most successful parts of the global response to the financial crisis?

2   Do you think that economic global governance could have done more to respond to the crisis? What might this have involved?

Poverty and development

A key role for economic global governance is addressing the challenge of world poverty and global inequality. Much of the economic global governance examined so far in this chapter has considered how states can develop their economies, put rules in place to bring order to the global financial system and trade with each other more effectively. This section deals with how states and IGOs work at a global level to reduce poverty. It also considers whether inequality between countries is being reduced or whether globalisation drives global inequality.

The focus on human poverty is not a new concept within the field of economic global governance. One of the UN's founding objectives was to reduce poverty and promote economic development. We have seen that the World Bank and the IMF have a key role to play in reducing poverty.

There are several aspects to understand:

- what poverty is and how it is measured
- the nature of global inequality and the existence of a North–South divide
- key theories of economic development and the effectiveness of different approaches to resolving poverty.

Topic link

The role of the United Nations is explored further in Chapter 3.

What is poverty?

At its simplest, poverty is when human beings lack the things that they need in order to live a secure, stable and fulfilling life. This covers two central issues:

1 **Income poverty:** not earning an income at all or earning an income that is not sufficient for living safely.
2 **Lack of social needs:** for example, access to shelter, healthcare, education or human rights.

There is clearly a wide range of differences between incomes and the standard of living of people in poverty across the world – poverty in the UK has very different characteristics to poverty in Sub-Saharan Africa.

In order to understand poverty in a global context, the UN provides several measures of poverty:

1 **Extreme poverty:** a person earns less than US$1.90 per day. The UN currently estimates that over 700 million people are living in extreme poverty and 80% live in South Asia and sub-Saharan Africa.
2 **Relative poverty:** this puts the poverty that people are experiencing into context by comparing it with other people who live in the same society or state. It judges whether people have the minimum income needed to access the average standard of living that people in that country enjoy. This is frequently based around those who live in households that earn below 60% of the middle or median income typical in that state.
3 **Multi-dimensional poverty:** this moves beyond income and considers indicators of standard of living, such as access to drinking water, sanitation and electricity as well as the health and education indicators of child mortality, nutrition, years of schooling and school attendance. An important measure of this is the UN's Human Development Index (HDI).

Reducing world poverty was the first and main objective of both the Millennium Development Goals and the Sustainable Development Goals. The percentage of the world population living in extreme poverty declined rapidly between 2010 and 2015, dropping from 15.7% to 10%. However, the UN has reported that this rate of reduction slowed between 2015 and 2020, reducing only to around 8%. The impact of the Covid-19 global pandemic was expected to result in an additional 77 million people living in extreme poverty and further slow the reduction – the first rise in global poverty since 1998 and putting progress back to 2017 levels of extreme poverty.

What is development?

Having defined poverty, it is important to understand what the term 'development' means. This is the idea that societies can improve socially and economically and, by doing so, reduce poverty and improve standards of living.

Case study

Human rights and development

There is a link between human rights and economic global governance given the increasing amount of attention given in development work to building human rights and democracy. Indian economist Amartya Sen has argued in *Development as Freedom* (1999) that 'development requires the removal of major sources of unfreedom: poverty as well as tyranny, poor economic opportunities as well as systematic social deprivation, neglect of public facilities as well as intolerance or repressive states'.

As a result, the UN Development Programme and many NGOs focus on building the rule of law, access to justice and women's rights among other aspects of human rights. The Sustainable Development Goals also expanded into this area, with 'peace, justice and strong institutions' one of the new goals introduced in 2015. Working to help refugees and those displaced by conflict is a particularly important priority, with the UN estimating that 68.5 million people have had to leave their homes because of human rights violations. Another major concern for economic global governance is the extent to which states continue to prioritise international trade with challenging individual states over their human rights records and whether, for example, the World Trade Organization could do more to promote workers' rights.

There is no single agreed definition of development. There are different views because people disagree on which priorities within development are the most important.

Table 4.8 Orthodox and alternative views of development

'Orthodox' view of development	'Alternative' views of development
The 'orthodox' view of development sees it purely in terms of advancing economic growth, with an economy that is productive and generates revenue. Critics of this definition suggest that it fails to consider the share of wealth across society. For example, the richest may be getting even richer and the economy can be booming, but large sections of the population remain in poverty. The key measure of economic growth is GDP.	Alternative views of development have emerged since the 1980s and focus on human development and wellbeing. This goes beyond economic growth and considers a broader range of factors including life expectancy, education and income. The Human Development Index (HDI) and Multi-dimensional Poverty Index (MPI) are the key measures of this type of development.
This view of development is related to neoliberalism and classical and neo-classical development theory (see page 149). It has been particularly favoured by the IMF in its structural adjustment programmes and by the idea that there will be a 'trickle down' in improving economic development as a result of international trade.	Amartya Sen took this further and argued that democracy and human rights are an important part of human development. Sen argued that people are most likely to lift themselves out of poverty when they are empowered to do so.
This view also focuses on 'modernisation', which is normally seen through the prism of encouraging industrial development.	Sustainable development (see page 86) is now the primary focus of all UN development work and the Sustainable Development Goals that it is working on with partner organisations and member states until 2030. This is the idea that the development needs of today cannot put at risk the development needs of tomorrow, for example degrading the environment to the extent that it can no longer provide for the next generation.

Distinguish between

Realism and liberalism: economic development

Realism

- States should focus on their own economic development first and spend government money on the needs of their own populations.
- States only help other states to develop if this helps to protect or advance their own interests (for example, the US invests most aid assistance in Afghanistan).
- Aid is likely to make the recipient nations dependent on funds and skills from other states.
- Debt relief encourages states to continue to mismanage their economic resources.

Liberalism

- Developed states have a responsibility to help less developed states. It is in the global interest for less developed states to be helped.
- IGOs have a key role to play in coordinating the efforts of the international community, for example through the MDGs.
- Aid can be used to empower developing states, for example through microfinance initiatives.
- Debt relief gives states the opportunity to invest in their own development, rather than repaying loans.

Global inequality and the North–South divide

This idea of a divide between the Global North and Global South (**the North–South Divide**) is a means of identifying and observing the inequality of wealth that exists in the global economy. It is not a theory about what causes this inequality, which will be examined later.

The idea gained prominence after the former chancellor of West Germany Willy Brandt published a report in 1980. In it, he devised the Brandt Line, which divides predominantly North America, Europe, Russia and Australasia into a developed 'Global North', with Africa, South America and South Asia the less developed 'Global South'. The result is a rough approximation of the North and the South on an economic divide, not a geographically straight line.

Many of these differences between the Global North and Global South remain valid more than 40 years later. For example:

- MNCs based in the Global North are seen to be exploiting states in the Global South for natural resources and cheap labour. The profits were returned to and benefited the North, rather than being shared with the South. States in the Global North had used colonialism as a means of dominating states in the Global South and even after de-colonisation were continuing to exert overwhelming economic and political power.
- States in the Global South that have rapidly industrialised and grown their economies still suffer from considerable poverty and income inequality, with India the most notable example. By the time the MDGs concluded in 2015, Sub-Saharan Africa lagged significantly behind the rest of the world on most measures of development (see page 146).
- States in the North created the Bretton Woods Institutions for their own benefit and they continue to dominate the decision making of, for example, the WTO and the IMF. Solutions proposed by the IMF to help economies in the Global South are based on a neoliberal economic model that was created by, and serves the interests of, the Global North. Wealthier states in the North continue to have more decision-making power over IMF loans and the conditions attached. The

Key term

North–South divide Term coined in the Brandt Report on overseas development in 1980. It is a political rather than a geographical term and contrasts the developed, industrialised world (Global North) with the developing, agricultural world (Global South).

Topic link

The impact of globalisation on poverty is explored in Chapter 2.

failure of the Doha Development Round at the WTO shows that international trade is still not a level playing field.

- A lack of industrialisation and reliance on agriculture exports were not creating wealth for the South. Many Global South countries and their exports were not yet part of global free-trade agreements, such as the WTO. This meant there was not a level playing field for the countries in the South and protectionism in the Global North (for example, agricultural subsidies) was making market access difficult.

However, there is increasing evidence that some (by no means all) states in the Global South are managing to close the gap with the Global North and that the idea is outdated.

- Many states in the Global South have successfully industrialised. These include the so-called newly industrialising countries (NICs), such as Brazil, India, South Africa and Malaysia.
- China, officially in the Global South according to the Brandt Line, has seen a dramatic increase in its economic growth and is set to become the world's largest economy by around 2028. Far from being a continuing member of the Global South, it has itself become an investor in states in the South (predominantly in Sub-Saharan Africa), through its Belt and Road Initiative.
- Sustainable development is a huge challenge as states in the Global South attempt to catch up with the North, while ensuring they do not harm the environment. The South is particularly vulnerable to the effects of climate change from extreme weather, rising sea levels and impact on food production. The World Bank estimated that high-income states in the Global North had been responsible for two-thirds of the carbon dioxide released into the atmosphere since 1850. However, in 2005, China became the world's largest emitter of greenhouse gases. Brazil and India were respectively in fifth and eighth place.
- There is some evidence of more inclusion of states in the Global South in economic global governance and this has improved greatly in terms of increased membership of the WTO and inclusion in the G20. Countries in the South are also increasingly forming alliances within IGOs, such as the BASIC group in climate change talks (see page 231).

(see page 231)

Activity

Look at the evidence for and against there being a North-South divide.

1. What have been the biggest changes to the divide that Brandt identified?
2. Is there a more accurate way of describing and mapping global inequality in today's global politics?

Case study

Failed and fragile states

There is a complex link between poverty and conflict, with conflict causing poverty and poverty often itself a contributing factor in causing conflict. Somalia is an example of a failed/fragile state that has been in a state of conflict since the early 1990s and has been receiving help from the United Nations and from the African Union, which first sent a peacekeeping force in 2006 to stabilise the country.

The UN estimates that 12.3 million people in Somalia (out of a total population of around 15.5 million) are 'chronically or acutely vulnerable' and the country suffers from food insecurity, a violent insurgency involving the militant Islamist group Al-Shabaab and severe environmental pressures with two devastating droughts in 2011 and 2017. 260,000 people are estimated to have died due to drought between 2010 and 2012 alone.

The response needed from economic global governance institutions is therefore urgent and challenging. The IMF and the World Bank have agreed a series of economic reforms in Somalia that put the country on a pathway to reducing its foreign debt from $5 billion to around $500 million. Meanwhile, resolving poverty depends on improving the security situation and with African Union peacekeepers' withdrawal in 2021, the task of securing the state was handed over to the fragile Somali federal government.

What causes and can resolve poverty?

When we consider what causes and can resolve poverty, there are many competing theories and different schools of thought. These all focus on the economic systems and approaches that their proponents believe are most likely to create prosperity and also seek to explain what holds back economic development and deepens inequality between states.

The following theories will be considered:

- **World systems theory and dependency theory:** these are structural theories in the sense that they look at the overall system and structures of the global economy, rather than merely what happens in individual states.
- **Neoliberalism and classical and neo-classical development theory:** these theories focus on the idea that economies should be as free as possible from government intervention. If this happens, the market will naturally smooth out any problems or inequalities.

World systems theory and dependency theory

World systems theory and dependency theory are closely linked to each other. These theories are 'structural' because they look at the overall structures and systems of the global economy rather than what happens purely in individual countries. Importantly, these theories seek to explain how colonialism (and neocolonialism, the continuation of exploitative power relationships even after major powers had given up their colonial empires) and the global capitalist system are responsible for locking less developed states in a permanent state of 'underdevelopment'.

These theories have links with the Marxist critique of capitalism that you have studied in socialism. They are in direct opposition to the views of neoliberals, who defend the capitalist global model as best suited to delivering prosperity and reducing poverty (see page 36).

Dependency theory sees some of the same structural problems with capitalism at an international level as those identified by Marxists and neo-Marxists at the domestic level.

- Workers in poorer states are exploited by an elite both within their state and internationally that is focused on keeping workers in low pay to maximise their profits, which are not shared. These elites own the means of production (for example, the factories and mines) resulting in systemic inequalities of wealth which will always exist if capitalism exists.
- Colonial powers, through their empires, embedded a system of colonialism in which powerful states aimed to subordinate other populations to maximise their political and economic power. Economic activity in colonised states has the sole purpose of making the colonising power more powerful and richer. The dependency this generates is particularly stark because colonised states are not politically sovereign and the underdevelopment puts these states at a long-term economic disadvantage.
- The system of colonialism has persisted in other forms even after colonised states have gained independence, with an imbalance of power continuing to trap states in a relationship that is subordinate to and dependent on major economic powers. This neocolonialism, for dependency theorists, is evident in many areas. This includes the reliance of poorer states on foreign investment; exploitative extraction of natural resources with profits not shared and skills not developed; and large amounts of debt owed through borrowing.

> ## Key term
>
> **Dependency theory** The idea that resources flow from a 'periphery' of poor and underdeveloped states to a 'core' of wealthy states, enriching the latter at the expense of the former.
>
> **Neocolonialism** Where a nation-state exerts strong economic or political influence over another, often but not limited to nation-states that had previously been colonised.

World systems theory was proposed by the US economist Immanuel Wallerstein, in his 1974 book *The Modern World System*. He identified similar relationships of dependency in the global economy and argued that global capitalism creates three groups of states which work in a hierarchy that restricts the development of poorer states, making them dependent on richer states. Where Wallerstein differs from other dependency theorists is in his argument that this world system is restrictive rather than prohibitive – it is possible (but very difficult) for states to move between the groups.

The three groups of states in this world system are shown in Table 4.9.

Table 4.9 World systems theory – state examples

Group	Example
Core states: many of these are based in the global North. They are highly industrialised economies, in which multinational corporations are based, and dominate both domestically and globally, paying high wages and producing a wide range of manufactured goods. These countries' populations are internationally mobile, well-educated and highly skilled.	**US:** large multinational corporations such as the oil company Exxon Mobil are based in the US and it extracts and refines oil from states in the periphery such as Angola where it has a 20% market share. Profits are shared among international shareholders and reinvested into the company; and in turn Angola becomes highly dependent on and vulnerable to international oil prices.
Periphery states: these states are poor and underdeveloped. Many of these are based in the global South. They are yet to industrialise, but typically possess natural resources that the core states need. Because they lack well-developed industries or manufacturing of their own, they have a surplus of, for example, natural resources that they have little capacity to use but which, by contrast, the core countries often need more and more of.	**Democratic Republic of Congo (DRC):** one of the poorest countries in the world. It ranks 175th out of 188 countries in the HDI. The mineral coltan is extracted using cheap and sometimes child labour from mines in the DRC and exported to core countries. Coltan is a key component in making smartphones, an industry which has seen foreign-owned MNCs, including Apple and Samsung, become some of the world's richest companies. DRC remains stuck in a low-wage, low-technology economy that is reliant on the poorly paid investment of foreign MNCs.
Semi-periphery states: these states fall somewhere between the previous two definitions and it is possible for periphery states to join the semi-periphery states. This involves becoming more industrialised and developing a more powerful position over states in the periphery while still being dominated by the core states.	**Brazil, South Africa:** come into the category of newly industrialising countries (NICs). There is a debate as to whether the best route to breaking out of dependency is by engaging in free trade or protectionism (for example, subsidising exports to boost prices and restricting imports with high tariffs). Increasingly, the WTO and the IMF are pushing states towards free trade.

Neoliberalism and classical and neo-classical development theory

While dependency theory and world systems theory identify global capitalism as a problem, neoliberalism sees global capitalism as the preferred and best model of economic development. There are two closely related ideas.

- **Classical development theory (or classical liberalism):** this links to the original ideas of the economist and philosopher Adam Smith (1723–1790), who argued that the market could and should regulate itself free from outside intervention by the state. He believed that stepping back and adopting a 'laissez-faire' approach was the best means of ensuring fair prices and wages. Smith also argued that the best way to develop the economy was to focus on increasing production and making this as efficient as possible, with the idea of a 'division of labour'.

- **Neoliberalism and neo-classical development theory:** these both link to the New Right ideas studied in conservatism and the main beliefs of classical liberals. These ideas became so widespread that they are also known as the Washington Consensus, given the extent to which it has been adopted by the likes of the IMF, WTO and World Bank. It emerged as a dominant economic ideology in the 1980s, most famously advocated by US President Ronald Reagan and British prime minister Margaret Thatcher, who sought to reassert and reapply the classical liberal economic model in a modern setting.

The key elements of neoliberalism include:

- keeping government spending low
- tax reform (keeping personal and corporate taxes low)
- minimal rules for financial markets, known as deregulation (setting the market free to innovate and take risks)
- private ownership of companies (including the privatisation, or sale, of state-owned industries, such as electricity, gas, airlines)
- openness to foreign direct investment
- free trade.

Box 4.5

John Maynard Keynes

Neoliberalism has become so embedded in the economic policies of countries in the Global North that it might be assumed that it has always been the dominant model. However, an alternative model which promoted strong government investment in the economy to stimulate growth and demand (as opposed to the non-interventionist approach of classical and neoliberalism) was put forward by the British economist John Maynard Keynes (1883-1946) and became known as Keynesianism.

Keynes represented the UK at the Bretton Woods Conference in 1944 and argued that the state could play a positive role as investing in infrastructure would create jobs and stimulate demand by way of a 'multiplier effect' (investment creates jobs, which boosts consumer spending, which boosts demand and creates jobs in other parts of the economy).

British economist John Maynard Keynes

There is plenty of evidence of the influence that neoliberalism has had on the global economy. Its key beliefs have become almost a checklist for the conditions that the IMF demands of states in its structural adjustment programmes. States around the world adopted a lighter touch approach to the regulation of their economies, by keeping government rules and restrictions on businesses and individuals as minimal as possible.

The two major global crises of this century – the global financial crisis of 2008 and the Covid-19 pandemic of 2020 – reopened familiar arguments about whether neoliberalism had benefited economic development and what the role of the state should be in responding to major crises.

Activity

1 What policy proposals would you suggest that a) states b) economic IGOs carry out to reduced the North South divide?

2 What policy proposals would you suggest that a) states b) economic IGOs carry out to reduced the effects of dependency theory?

Table 4.10 Opposing viewpoints on neoliberalism

In defence of neoliberalism	In criticism of neoliberalism
Free trade and removal of tariff and non-tariff barriers has allowed more states to access global markets. Keeping taxes low gives individuals more choice over how they spend and invest their money, including setting up new businesses. If public spending is high, then taxes will need to rise or the state will need to borrow money (or both). This can result in the state running a high budget deficit which, in the global financial crisis of 2008, led to some states being unable to service their debts. This led to Greece, Ireland, Portugal and Spain resorting to loans from the IMF and European Central Bank.	Neoliberalism has seen inequality rise both within states and between states. The state needs to intervene to stimulate growth and to ensure a fairer distribution of income and wealth – the 'invisible hand' does not work. Lack of regulation in the banking sector contributed to the 2008 global financial crisis which then required costly state intervention to bail out banks that were 'too big to fail'. Austerity was then needed to pay for this intervention. Keeping public spending low can lead to under-investment in key public services, such as healthcare (making the response to the global pandemic less effective) or education (the lack of which widens inequality).

Debate

Has economic global governance helped to reduce global poverty?

Yes

- The MDGs and the SDGs have made significant progress, with extreme poverty falling by half and most progress made since the MDGs were launched.
- Economic global governance activity to reduce poverty is now very well coordinated, with very clear division of responsibility and many IGOs and NGOs working to the same objectives.
- The North–South divide has been reducing, showing that dependency theory is no longer inevitable and newly emerging economies (such as the BRICS) demonstrate that it is possible for countries to plug into the global economy.

No

- The MDGs and the SDGs have made progress, but this has been inconsistent, with sub-Saharan Africa lagging behind and global inequality widening.
- The Bretton Woods Institutions still do not do enough to make global trade more accessible and the conditionality of loans from the IMF has often had a detrimental effect on economies.
- There continues to be a North–South divide and dependency theory continues to keep some states underdeveloped.

Evaluation tip: Try to link this answer back to dependency theory and the existence of a North–South divide. Is there evidence that economic global governance provides a means of alleviating poverty or does it entrench inequality between states?

Role of global civil society and non-state actors

While much of the focus of economic global governance lies with the Bretton Woods Institutions, there is a far wider range of actors involved.

- **The United Nations:** through the Millennium Development Goals and the Sustainable Development Goals, the UN has a significant impact in setting the global development agenda and coordinating funding.
- **NGOs:** this includes a huge range of organisations including Oxfam and Médecins Sans Frontières which are independent of state governments and international organisations. Some operate globally, while many other smaller NGOs operate in individual countries or communities. NGOs are considered part of global civil society, which includes all groups that are non-governmental and non-profit, including community groups and charitable organisations.

- **Multinational corporations:** this is a complicated actor to analyse within economic global governance. While there is the capacity for positive action (for example, from creating jobs and tax revenue to charitable corporate social responsibility projects and donations), we need to consider the considerable power and influence that MNCs hold – with many wealthier and more powerful than states.

The United Nations

A discussion of economic global governance would not be complete without considering the role of the UN and its many agencies. There are too many agencies of the UN involved in development and alleviating poverty to give a full list, but they are well established and have considerable global impact. For example, the United Nations International Children's Emergency Fund (UNICEF) works in 190 countries on development projects to provide clean water, food, education and emergency support for children; and the UNDP is the UN's lead agency for implementing the Sustainable Development Goals.

Agreed in 2015, the Sustainable Development Goals (SDGs) were the successor to the Millennium Development Goals (MDGs) that were introduced in 2000. Before the MDGs, international development work lacked cohesiveness and many UN agencies and NGOs were working towards different development targets. The MDGs were the first internationally agreed set of collective goals.

The MDGs helped states to coordinate their efforts, ensuring that duplication of effort was kept to a minimum. They also provided a useful set of guidance to developing states themselves on how they should prioritise development activities.

MDG successes

The MDGs achieved a number of significant successes:

- Extreme poverty was reduced by half, falling from 1.9 billion people in 1990 to 836 million in 2015. The UN reported that most progress had been made since 2000.
- There was an increase in primary school enrolment, from 83% in 2000 to 91% in 2015. The proportion of girls in school also increased.
- Child mortality was reduced by more than half, from 90 to 43 deaths per 1,000 live births between 1990 and 2015.
- Maternal health improved, with mortality declining by 45% worldwide since 1990. A particularly dramatic decrease of 64% was seen in southern Asia.

There were several notes of caution alongside the apparent success of the MDGs:

- Economic development and rapid growth in China have been responsible for most of the success in eradicating extreme poverty. Progress elsewhere has been less marked.
- The target of halving the number of people suffering from hunger was missed.
- Former UN Secretary-General Ban Ki-moon acknowledged that global inequality remained a significant issue.
- The private sector was not given enough of a role in the implementation of the MDGs. This is a gap that has been addressed in the SDGs.

The MDGs were successful in producing an increase in the number of children attending primary schools

The Sustainable Development Goals

The key aim of sustainable development is that the development needs of today must not risk the development needs of tomorrow. The SDGs have the same lifespan as the MDGs (a 15-year period lasting until 2030).

The SDGs introduced new goals on the environment, including action on climate change, clean water and more sustainable management of ecosystems. In addition, there is reference to political freedom as a key goal for the first time, through the inclusion of peace, justice and strong institutions. This responds to one criticism of the MDGs, that they did not refer to conflict, and makes developing peace and security one of the major factors to tackle in reducing underdevelopment and poverty (SDG 16).

The SDGs retained many of the MDGs where progress had been made but where there was still more to do. For example, the SDGs retain the commitment to end poverty.

Non-governmental organisations (NGOs)

The most striking aspect of NGOs' contribution to development is the sheer number of organisations and their rapid growth over recent decades. The number of NGOs worldwide is measured in millions and nearly 5,000 have special consultative status at the UN, meaning they can attend meetings of the Economic and Social Council and influence UN policy making.

NGOs carry out an extremely wide range of work, from campaigning and advocacy (for example, Human Rights Watch) to humanitarian assistance (for example, the International Committee of the Red Cross) to long-term development work in specific communities in areas as diverse as education, health and climate change (for example, Save the Children).

Funding for NGOs comes from a variety of sources, including donations from private individuals. They also often bid for funding from national governments and international organisations such as the UN. Receiving money from national governments does not tend to harm the neutrality on which NGOs pride themselves, though funding will often be linked to specific projects that are designed in partnership with their donors.

The advantage of NGOs is that they vastly expand the range of actors involved in development work beyond IGOs and nation-states and are a hugely valuable source of expertise and additional capacity. Smaller NGOs that operate at a local level and are based in specific countries and communities can also build local skills and expertise, reducing dependency on international aid agencies.

Table 4.11 NGOs: examples of resources and impact

NGO and its resources	Impact and focus
International Committee of the Red Cross (ICRC): based in 100 countries with 18,800 staff, and an annual expenditure of approximately $2 billion.	The ICRC focuses on humanitarian assistance in conflict, particularly in Syria, South Sudan and Iraq. It has provided medical care, distributed food and helped displaced people.
Save the Children: based in the UK and operating in over 100 countries worldwide. In 2019 it spent £271 million on its projects. It received £73 million from private individuals and £131 million from the EU, the UN and the UK government.	Save the Children focuses on education, food and medicine for vulnerable children. It has worked in sub-Saharan Africa to alleviate child malnutrition and has supported girls' education. In the UK, it provided emergency grants to vulnerable children during the Covid-19 pandemic.

Multinational corporations

These are an important non-state actor in global economic governance. Clearly, multinational corporations create jobs and tax revenue that keep unemployment low and provide necessary funding for public spending. For neoliberals, they should be as free as possible from state intervention to enable them to grow and innovate naturally within a free market. For dependency theorists, MNCs are part of the global capitalist model that locks individuals in a state of underdevelopment.

Many MNCs have wealth and influence that far exceeds some states. This gives MNCs considerable bargaining power over states and can sometimes force states to change their economic policy to attract foreign inward investment (for example, by keeping taxes on business low and regulation minimal). A key problem has been ensuring that MNCs are not able to exploit their globalised nature by avoiding paying tax in the states in which they operate. The Organisation for Economic Cooperation and Development (OECD) estimates that between $100 and 250 billion annually is lost in tax revenue globally due to MNCs avoiding paying corporate taxes, sometimes entirely legally. The G7 and G20 have attempted to take action to reduce tax loopholes but with limited success.

At the same time, MNCs are also increasingly understanding the benefit to society (and to their public image) of investing in corporate social responsibility projects. For example, Apple's operations in India have invested in a number of renewable energy projects and in education and disaster relief management. Some states have passed legislation which requires companies to allocate a certain amount of their profits to corporate social responsibility projects.

Activity

Research the work of two NGOs. Try to find one that is most involved in campaigning (such as on human rights) and one that is most involved with humanitarian assistance.

1 What projects have they recently been involved with?
2 How do you think this work helps with economic global governance?

The Millennium and Sustainable Development Goals

The MDGs

- The first global attempt to agree and implement a coordinated set of world development targets.
- Eight goals, focused primarily on human development.

The SDGs

- Agreed by the UN in 2015 to replace the MDGs.
- The 17 SDGs took the MDGs forward, keeping some of the MDGs but adding new goals including tackling climate change and a focus on political development, with the inclusion of goals to promote peace, justice and strong institutions.

Further reading

Collier, P. (2019) *The Future of Capitalism.* Penguin.

Conway, E. (2015) *The Summit: Bretton Woods, 1944: J. M. Keynes and the Reshaping of the Global Economy.* Pegasus.

Murphy, R. (2018) 'Has global economic governance dealt with poverty?', *Politics Review*, Vol. 27, No. 3, February.

Raworth, K. (2018) *Doughnut Economics: Seven Ways to Think Like a 21st Century Economist.* Random House.

What you should know

Having read this chapter you should have knowledge and understanding of the following:

→ Global economic governance efforts began with the Bretton Woods Conference in 1944. Since then, the IMF, World Bank and WTO have been the principal means of coordinating efforts to bring about global economic development, promote free trade and reduce poverty.

→ The WTO at one time worked effectively to reduce trade barriers and protectionism. As it has grown larger, it has become more difficult to find global agreement on further extending global free trade.

→ The IMF provides an essential safety net for states when they get into economic difficulty. States are working together to ensure that they limit the wider negative impact of states' economic difficulties. The IMF has sometimes been criticised for demanding that states comply with its recommendations in return for loans, creating a clash with state sovereignty.

→ There is still a divide between the richest and the poorest states. Global inequality between states and within states is rising. World systems theory argues that the richest states are trapping the poorer states in a cycle of dependency, which prevents poorer states from catching up.

Practice questions

Section A

1 Examine the main criticisms that can be made of the International Monetary Fund and the World Bank. [12 marks]
2 Examine the factors that contribute to dependency theory and the North–South divide. [12 marks]
3 Examine the criticisms that have been made of the World Trade Organization and the G7. [12 marks]

Section C

1 Evaluate the extent to which economic global governance is failing when it is needed most. [30 marks]
2 Evaluate the extent to which economic global governance is effective in dealing with issues of poverty. [30 marks]
3 Evaluate the extent to which economic global governance institutions are in need of reform. [30 marks]

5 Global governance: human rights

Learning outcomes

By the end of the chapter you should understand:

→ the significance for the development of human rights of the Charter of the United Nations, the United Nations Declaration of Human Rights and the European Declaration of Human Rights

→ different interpretations of human rights and why it is difficult to establish a universal standard of human rights

→ the reasons why international human rights law is difficult to enforce

→ how to evaluate the success of the International Court of Justice (or World Court), various United Nations tribunals, the European Court of Human Rights and the International Criminal Court

→ how to refer directly to a number of specific cases associated with these courts and tribunals

→ why humanitarian interventionism increased during the 1990s

→ why the UN Responsibility to Protect was introduced and its significance

→ how to compare and contrast a number of humanitarian interventions, and those factors that contribute to their comparative success and failure

→ why humanitarian interventions take place in some circumstances but not in others

Getting you started

On 2 October 2018, the journalist Jamal Khashoggi visited the Saudi Arabian consulate in Istanbul to arrange his marriage documentation. An investigative reporter with strong anti-authoritarian and pro-democratic views, Khashoggi was highly critical of political repression and religious intolerance in the Arab world and had recently condemned Saudi Arabia's military intervention in Yemen. When Khashoggi failed to reappear from the embassy, an investigation was launched, the Saudi government eventually admitted that he was murdered by 'rogue operatives' soon after entering the building. The Office of the High Commissioner for Human Rights, however, put the blame squarely on the Saudi Arabian government, accusing it of the 'premeditated extra-judicial execution' of Khashoggi. Some sources, including the CIA, have even suggested that the Saudi Arabian crown prince, Mohammed bin Salman, may have ordered the killing.

In 2019, as international condemnation grew, Saudi Arabia tried a number of people for the crime. However, the trial took place behind closed doors and the names of those convicted were not released. According to the UN's Special Rapporteur Agnès Callamard, the Saudi trial represented 'the antithesis of justice'. In 2020, Turkey then began its own trial of 20 Saudi officials whom it believed were involved in the killing. However, the trial took place without the accused being present since Saudi Arabia, as a sovereign nation-state, was not prepared to cooperate in the proceedings.

The conflict involved in bringing those who murdered Khashoggi to justice encapsulates why it is so difficult to establish an international standard of human rights protection. Although Khashoggi, at the time of his murder, was working for *The Washington Post*, the Trump administration was unwilling to pursue justice. Indeed, according to the veteran journalist Bob Woodward, Trump openly boasted to him that he 'saved' Mohammed bin Salman's 'ass' by persuading 'Congress to leave him alone'. After all, too great a criticism of Saudi Arabia risked hugely important economic ties and so Trump jokingly told Woodward that he had persuaded Congress to 'back down' by telling them, 'Let them trade with Russia instead. Let them buy a thousand planes from Russia instead of the United States. Fellas, you've got to be smart.'

However, Trump's position was not unique. Neither China nor Russia criticised Saudi Arabia over the murder, while even Turkey's strong stand against Saudi Arabia might not be quite as selfless as it might appear. After all, the two are major strategic rivals, bidding for leadership in the middle east, and Turkey is always keen to discredit its rival. Boris Johnson has cultivated strong links with Mohammed bin Salman and in 2020 the British government resumed arms sales to the kingdom in spite of widespread concern from human rights groups that these could be used against civilian targets in Yemen.

The way, therefore, in which nation-states' foreign policy is still so often guided by realist self-interest constantly challenges human rights. Equally, the way in which Saudi Arabia has used its sovereign independence from outside interference to keep the details of what happened a closely guarded secret further undermines the potential for an international standard of justice.

However, in 2020, Saudi Arabia failed in its bid to be re-elected to its seat on the UN's Human Rights Council as it saw its support dramatically fall away on the UN General Assembly. Even more concerning for the kingdom, during his presidential campaign, Joe Biden issued a stern rebuke to Saudi Arabia on the anniversary of Khashoggi's murder stating that he would 'reassess our relationship with the kingdom … and make sure America does not check its values at the door to sell arms or buy oil'. International pressure groups such as Amnesty International and Human Rights Watch, as well as human rights activists such as Khashoggi's fiancée, Hatice Cengiz, continue to pressure the kingdom on its human rights record.

The extent to which human rights can and should direct the affairs of nations remains one of the most contentious and fought-over debates in international relations. It could be seen as encapsulating the core differences between a realist and liberal approach to international relations. This chapter will investigate those ways in which human rights can be, and are being, protected, as well as why horrific crimes, such as the murder of Khashoggi, can still be so difficult to punish.

Key term

International law The rules that govern relations between states. States generally accept the binding authority of international law, since it provides a framework for cooperation between states and guards against the dangers of global anarchy. However, there is no supranational authority that can force obedience.

Human rights and international law

The origins and development of international law

International law has helped govern international relations since the rise of the nation-state from the seventeenth century onwards. For most of modern history, international law been founded on the way in which states react to each other. Adherence to international law is also based upon the principle of reciprocity. In other words, if you obey an international agreement, it is more likely that another state will see a reciprocal interest in obeying it as well. This is why during the Second World War the European powers did not use poison gas against each other. Pragmatic considerations of self-interest governed this decision – moral considerations did not enter into it at all.

Today, most countries abide by the terms of the Treaty on the Non-Proliferation of Nuclear Weapons (1968) and so do not seek to acquire nuclear weapons. Their reasoning generally derives not from any moral revulsion towards nuclear weapons, but from the belief that if they disobey the treaty, others will follow suit, making the world much more dangerous and so undermining global security.

The Nuremberg Trials, 1945–46

Westphalian principles of state sovereignty have traditionally enshrined the concept that human rights are relative. This means that the government under which one lives determines the nature and extent of one's rights. These principles derive from the Hobbesian belief that the rulers of a nation state must be obeyed irrespective of whether they act morally. However, following the Second World War, the Nuremberg Trials, in which leading Nazis were tried as war criminals for 'crimes against humanity' and 'waging aggressive warfare', demonstrated what could happen if a government acted in defiance of all moral principles. In such circumstances, the realist defence that the actions of a national government were outside the prerogative of the international community seemed inadequate. The way in which the Nazi state had persecuted many of its own citizens, waged war and committed acts of mass genocide suggested that nation-states could not be allowed to act with impunity. Instead, there must be a higher natural law according to which the actions of nation states ought to be judged. If the international community did not learn lessons from these horrors, they would be repeated. As the US chief prosecutor Robert Jackson put it in his opening address at the trial:

> The wrongs which we seek to condemn and punish have been so calculated, so malignant, and so devastating, that civilisation cannot tolerate their being ignored, because it cannot survive their being repeated.

The crimes exposed at Nuremberg made the development of a human rights-based approach to international law an urgent concern. No longer was international law simply a way in which states achieved just enough global stability to survive. Instead, it would have to take into account human rights as well as states' self-interest. In order to achieve this, nation-states would need to come together to establish international institutions of justice and global standards of moral behaviour. Only by doing this could they create a world of peace and justice and contain the aggressive impulses of nation-states. According to the Spanish-American philosopher George Santayana, 'Those who cannot remember the past are condemned to repeat it.' This dictum had particular meaning for those who met at San Francisco in 1945 to establish the UN.

The crimes exposed at Nuremberg made the development of a human rights-based approach to international law an urgent concern

The Charter of the United Nations, 1945

The Charter of the United Nations was drafted in San Francisco during the closing months of the Second World War and in October 1945 the UN was formally established. Given that the two world wars had caused suffering on a global scale, the charter sought to 'banish the scourge of war, which twice in our lifetime had brought untold sorrow to mankind'. It would do this by establishing the UN as the international forum in which disputes would be settled, development encouraged and human rights affirmed. As President Harry Truman put it, when he addressed delegates at the closing session of the UN conference:

> If we had had this charter a few years ago and, above all, the will to use it, millions now dead would be alive. If we should falter in the future in our will to use it, millions now living will surely die.

The Universal Declaration of Human Rights, 1948

In 1948, the UN drew up the UDHR, which established the absolute civil, political and social freedoms that all humans enjoy. The UDHR is based upon 'the inherent dignity' and 'the equal and inalienable rights of all members of the human family'. According to Eleanor Roosevelt, who chaired the committee that drew up the document, 'the declaration may well become the international Magna Carta for all men everywhere'. Indeed, it is often regarded as one of the most influential political statements of all time.

The UDHR has also provided the basis for the International Covenant on Civil and Political Rights (1966) and the International Covenant on Economic, Social and Cultural Rights (1966), both of which entered into force in 1976 and codified the rights of the UDHR. Taken together, these three documents comprise the International Bill of Human Rights and act as a constant reminder that there are international standards of moral behaviour that states should aspire to and to which they can be held accountable.

International Human Rights Timeline

- **1948:** The United Nations General Assembly adopted the Universal Declaration of Human Rights as well as the Genocide Convention. Over the years, the General Assembly has recognised several covenants which have further expanded the meaning and scope of international human rights law.
- **1951:** Refugee Convention, which recognises and protects the rights of refugees.
- **1966:** Economic, Social and Cultural Rights Covenant. This expands the Universal Declaration of Human Rights to recognise social and economic rights including education, employment and healthcare.
- **1966:** Civil and Political Rights Covenant. This confirmed several rights such as the right to a fair trial and freedom of association and religion.
- **1979:** Discrimination against Women Convention. Nation-states must actively end discrimination against women in order to achieve full equality between the sexes.
- **1984:** Convention on Torture. Nation-states cannot engage in torture.
- **1989:** Children's Convention. As a result of their vulnerability, the rights of the child fully recognised.
- **1989:** Indigenous People's Convention. Since indigenous people's cultures are especially at risk from globalisation their right to their own culture and identity was recognised.
- **1990:** Convention on Migrant Workers. Another highly vulnerable group had their rights given legal status.
- **2006:** Convention on Persons with Disabilities. People with disabilities must be provided with the same rights as any other human being.

United Nations High Commissioner for Human Rights, 1993

The end of the Cold War provided human rights with a new centrality in international relations. In 1993, at the World Conference on Human Rights, the position of UN High Commissioner for Human Rights was established. The commissioner's responsibility is to promote adherence to human rights and expose their violation.

Although lacking in coercive power, the position is important since it carries great moral authority. Since 2018, the former president of Chile, Michelle Bachelet, has held this role. On Human Rights Day in 2019, she reminded her audience that,

> A world with diminished human rights is a world that is stepping backwards into a darker past, when the powerful could prey on the powerless with little or no moral or legal restraint.

Activity

LGBT rights

In terms of contemporary human rights protection, there is a strong case to suggest that LGBT rights are the most pressing human right which still needs to be recognised. Almost a third of the world's nation-states criminalise homosexual acts and even in countries where they are legal, institutionalised prejudice is still widely accepted.

1 Can the LGBT community claim any protection in international human rights law?
2 Why has it proved so difficult to recognise LGBT rights as an international human right?
3 To what extent has globalisation helped to advance LGBT rights?

Topic link

Chapter 3 analyses the work of the United Nations in trying to achieve a more rules-based system of international relations in greater detail.

The role of non-governmental organisations

Growing numbers of NGOs have also highlighted human rights abuses. These include:

- Amnesty International
- Human Rights Watch
- Save the Children.

These global pressure groups use the internet to its full potential, ensuring instantaneous coverage of humanitarian crises. This puts new pressure on the international community to pay attention to abuses. Human Rights Watch, for example, publishes its annual World Report, which catalogues nation-states' records on human rights. In 2020, it focused particularly on the way in which China's increasingly blatant disregard for human rights 'poses an existential threat to the international human rights system'.

In 2021, Human Rights Watch also demanded an immediate investigation into the way pro-Trump supporters had been able to storm Congress. In particular, it demanded that Trump be held to account for his 'reckless campaign' to 'undermine democratic process and the rule of law since his electoral defeat', as well as why the police response to Black Lives Matter demonstrations in 2020 had been significantly more aggressive.

How successfully do judicial institutions enforce human rights?

The International Court of Justice

Sometimes referred to as the World Court, the **International Court of Justice (ICJ)** is the judicial agency of the UN and permanently sits in The Hague, the Netherlands. It was established by the Charter of the United Nations in 1945 and is designed to settle disputes between the UN's member states.

> **Key term**
>
> **International Court of Justice (ICJ)** The UN's primary judicial branch established by the UN Charter in 1945. Sometimes known as the World Court.

The scales of justice: the ICJ is the primary judicial branch of the UN

What is the purpose of the International Court of Justice?

The ICJ's 15 judges represent the 'main forms of civilization and the principal legal systems of the world'. It settles legal disputes submitted to it by states and provides advisory opinions on legal questions submitted to it by international branches, agencies and the UN General Assembly. The ICJ therefore attempts to enforce the rule of law in international disputes in order to create a more stable and peaceful world.

Article 94 of the UN Charter lays down that all members of the UN should 'comply with the decision of the Court in any case to which it is a party'. If a state does not comply with an ICJ judgment, the other party may approach the UN Security Council (UNSC) to enforce the judgment.

In what ways has the International Court of Justice been successful?

Liberals regard the ICJ as a vital way of establishing a more rules-based approach to international affairs. Rather than resorting to war, cases can be submitted to the ICJ for arbitration. The ICJ possesses great moral authority and nation-states can be unwilling to question its ruling. It has been successful in resolving a number of disputes:

- In 1988, the American warship USS *Vincennes* shot down an Iranian airliner over the Straits of Hormuz. 290 people were killed because the American missile cruiser had mistakenly identified it as a fighter jet. Iran brought a case against the US at the ICJ and although the US refused to accept liability, it did express 'deep regret' for shooting down the airliner and paid US$61.8 million in compensation to the victims' families.
- In 1992, the ICJ settled a complicated border dispute between El Salvador and Honduras.
- In 2002, the ICJ settled a dispute between Nigeria and Cameroon over the ownership of an oil-rich peninsula.
- In 2012, the ICJ decided that Senegal must put the former president of Chad, Hissène Habré, on trial for crimes against humanity and torture. Habré had sought refuge in Senegal but, as a result of the judgment, Senegal put him on trial. In 2016, he was found guilty of the killing of 40,000 people and was sentenced to life imprisonment.
- In 2019, India brought a case against Pakistan at the ICJ. According to India, Pakistan was breaking international law by not allowing consular access to Kulbhushan Jadhav, an Indian naval officer, convicted in Pakistan of spying. India won the case when Pakistan agreed that, 'As a responsible state, Pakistan will grant consular access to Commander Kulbushan Jadhav according to Pakistani laws.'

Why has the International Court of Justice not been more successful?

Although the ICJ is supposed to operate as a World Court, resolving issues between states before they become armed struggles, its effectiveness is severely limited. Realist national interest still frequently influences the behaviour of states. Consequently, as 'power-maximisers', states will often put their sovereign interest above that of international law, so challenging the authority of the court.

ICJ influence is therefore undermined because:

- its liberal principles conflict with realist state egoism
- it cannot initiate cases and can only try cases that are presented to it
- states are able to choose whether or not to be subject to the decisions of the court by signing an optional clause, which accepts in advance that they will be subject

to the court's ruling (in 2021, just 74 of the 193 members of the ICJ had signed this optional clause)
- although the UNSC is supposed to enforce ICJ rulings, the veto-wielding permanent five members would be unlikely to do this – this is because the only effective way of ensuring compliance would be coercive action but, according to Chapter VII of the UN Charter, this can only be undertaken when international peace and security are threatened.

As a result of these limitations there have been a number of cases when the ICJ has delivered judgments that the corresponding state has ignored. In such circumstances, it has been almost impossible to hold that state accountable for its actions:

- In 1980, Iran refused to acknowledge ICJ sovereignty when the US brought a case against it for seizing the US embassy in Tehran in 1979.
- In 1984, the Sandinista government of Nicaragua brought a case against the US for aiding the Contra rebels by mining Nicaraguan harbours. Although the ICJ found in favour of Nicaragua, the US refused to accept the judgment, arguing that its actions were helping states like El Salvador that were 'threatened' by Nicaraguan-backed communist rebels and were therefore 'entirely consistent with international law'.
- In 2020, the ICJ ordered the government of Myanmar to take all necessary measures to stop genocide against the remaining Rohingya Muslims still in the country. In response, Myanmar's then leader, Aung San Suu Kyi, stated that the issue was an 'internal armed conflict' which Myanmar would deal with itself without outside interference.
- Advisory opinions are even more difficult to put into action and depend upon the willing compliance of a state. For example, when the UNGA asked for advice on the wall that Israel was building to separate it from the Palestinian territories, the ICJ declared the structure 'illegal'. The then-Israeli prime minister, Ariel Sharon, condemned the ruling as 'one-sided and politically motivated' and made clear that 'the state of Israel absolutely rejects the ruling [of the court]'.
- In 2010, the ICJ delivered the advisory opinion that Kosovo had been legitimately able to declare independence from Serbia in 2008. The decision was welcomed by those states that recognise Kosovo's independence, but unsurprisingly it was ignored by Serbia and its key supporter Russia.

Activity

In 1968, the UK granted Mauritius independence. As part of the deal, Mauritius had to cede the Chagos Islands to the UK (see the case study in Chapter 3). The British government then evicted thousands of Chagossians and allowed the Americans to open a military base at Diego Garcia. In 2019, the ICJ stated that the UK's possession of the Chagos Islands was 'illegal' and that they should be returned to Mauritius 'as rapidly as possible'. The UN General Assembly then voted 116/6 that the islands should be returned to Mauritius. The UK has, however, refused to comply, claiming that the Chagos Archipelago will only be returned 'when it is no longer required for defence purposes'.

1   In what ways has the British government followed a realist approach in this dispute?
2   Why do you think the UK has been prepared to risk global condemnation by not cooperating with the ICJ?
3   To what extent do you think nation-states should always obey international law even if it conflicts with their national and strategic best interests?

Topic link

A further discussion of the way in which realism influences global relations can be found in Chapter 1.

United Nations special tribunals

In the 1990s, there was growing concern about the way in which the international community should react to genocide, war crimes and crimes against humanity occurring in Rwanda, Sierra Leone and the former Yugoslavia. The UN also worked with the Cambodian government to try the surviving perpetrators of the country's 1970s genocide.

As a result, the UNSC authorised the establishment of four UN war crimes tribunals. These represented a major advance in the development of international law, since an international panel of judges would judge crimes that had happened within states. The tribunals would also have the authority to try heads of state for crimes against humanity and set a precedent for the establishment of the ICC in 2002.

The aims of the UN tribunals were to:

- punish and bring to justice those guilty of human rights abuses (retribution)
- develop the liberal principle of a global community that will no longer tolerate nation-states deliberately abusing the rights of its citizens
- establish the legal principle that the international community can try heads of government for crimes committed within their country
- make public the extent and horror of crimes of genocide, war and crimes against humanity so that they will not be repeated.

Former Yugoslavia

The International Criminal Tribunal for the Former Yugoslavia was instituted in 1993. It was the first international court set up since the Nuremberg Trials to try individuals accused of war crimes. Its aim was to 'spear-head the shift from impunity to accountability', since without the influence of the tribunal it is very unlikely that the Balkan states would have been willing or able to prosecute those accused of human rights violations. Its supporters noted a number of successes:

- The court claims to have 'brought justice for thousands of victims and given them a voice', and so advanced the cause of a rules-based standard of international justice.
- By the time it closed in 2017, the court had convicted and sentenced 90 war criminals, ranging from low-ranking soldiers to senior figures in the military and political leaders. Radovan Karadžic, the former president of the Bosnian Serb Republic, was sentenced to 40 years in prison for the Srebrenica Massacre. In 2019, when he appealed the sentence it was increased to life. The last case the court tried was that of the Bosnian Serb general Ratko Mladic, who was sentenced to life imprisonment for war crimes and acts of genocide.
- Like Nuremberg, the cases before the tribunal have made public the atrocities committed so it is now much more difficult to deny them. The trial, for example, of the Bosnian Serb leaders Ratko Mladic and Radovan Karadžic uncovered vast amounts of evidence relating to the 1995 Srebrenica Massacre.

Cambodia

The Cambodia Tribunal is a national court that was established in conjunction with the UN in 1997. It has both Cambodian and international judges and has tried the surviving members of the murderous Khmer Rouge government (1975–79), which was responsible for the deaths of 2 million people. The court has handed out three life imprisonment sentences, to:

- Nuon Chea, Khmer Rouge chief political ideologist
- Kaing Guek Eav, head of the S21 mass killing centre
- Khieu Samphan, the former head of state.

As well as punishing the guilty, the tribunal has engaged many young Cambodians in a better understanding of what happened in their country during the 1970s – in the first trial involving multiple Khmer Rouge leaders, almost 100,000 people attended the hearings in the capital Phnom Penh. The court also offers internships to Cambodian and international lawyers so that they can develop their understanding of international law and genocide.

Rwanda

The International Criminal Tribunal for Rwanda investigating the Rwandan genocide, in which 800,000 Tutsis were murdered, opened its first case in 1997. The tribunal convicted 61 individuals of complicity in the genocide, including former prime minister Jean Kambanda, who became the first head of government to be convicted on charges of genocide. Significantly, the tribunal developed international law by establishing the precedent that rape could be used as a way of perpetrating genocide and that the media could be held legally accountable for encouraging genocide.

The International Criminal Tribunal into the Rwandan genocide led to former prime minister Jean Kambanda being the first head of government to be convicted on charges of genocide

Case study

Justice delayed

Almost certainly the least well-known defendant at the 1945–46 Nuremberg war crimes tribunal was the journalist Hans Fritzsche. As the former head of German radio during the Third Reich, Fritzsche was accused of inciting genocide. According to the US chief prosecutor, Robert Jackson, Fritzsche 'by manipulation of the truth goaded German public opinion into frenzied support of the regime and anesthetized the independent judgment of the population so that they did without question their masters' bidding'. Fritzsche was acquitted.

In 2003, however, the Rwanda Tribunal handed out long prison sentences to three Hutus convicted of using the radio and press to encourage genocide. According to the court, Hassan Ngeze, Jean-Bosco Barayagwiza and Ferdinand Nahimana 'without a firearm, machete or any physical weapon ... caused the deaths of thousands of innocent civilians'. Given growing concerns that the online media can be used for hate purposes and to discriminate, this ruling provides an important new precedent in international law.

Activity

Read the case study and answer the following questions:

1 What other new precedents in international law have UN tribunals and the ICC established?
2 What do you think have been the other main successes of the UN tribunals and the ICC?
3 To what extent do you think that the UN tribunals and the ICC have fulfilled the aims of their founders?

Sierra Leone

In 2002, the UN established the Special Court for Sierra Leone to try those who had committed atrocities during the country's 10-year civil war. During the 1990s, Liberian president Charles Taylor had supported opposition groups in their attempts to gain control of the country's diamond mines. In the resulting carnage, the Revolutionary United Front and allied criminal gangs, such as the West Side Boys, murdered or hacked off the limbs of their victims. By 1999, when the British intervened to end the violence, 50,000 had already died.

In 2012, the tribunal sentenced Taylor to 50 years' imprisonment for complicity in the civil war's atrocities, the first head of state to be convicted of war crimes. According to prosecutor Brenda J. Hollis, the conviction of Taylor was so important because it 'reinforces the new reality, that heads of state will be held to account for war crimes and other international crimes' and that 'No person, no matter how powerful, is above the law.' The tribunal has also imprisoned 14 others, including Issa Sesay, the commander of the Revolutionary United Front, who was sentenced to 52 years in prison.

The limitations of international tribunals

At the end of the Second World War, the Nuremberg and Tokyo **international tribunals**, which tried those accused of war crimes, were accused by some of delivering 'victors' justice'. The US, for example, sat in judgment on Japanese war criminals and yet the Americans could themselves have been accused of war crimes for the destruction of Hiroshima and Nagasaki with nuclear bombs. Soviet judges also represented a regime that was responsible for mass murder, while the British destruction of Dresden, Germany in March 1945, which led to the deaths of thousands of civilian refugees, may well have been a war crime.

Key term

International tribunals
UN-mandated international criminal tribunals established to prosecute those responsible for crimes against humanity, war crimes and acts of genocide.

Activity

In 2003, Robert S. McNamara, Secretary of State for Defence under President Kennedy and President Johnson, was interviewed about his controversial career in Errol Morris' documentary 'Fog of War'. In a poignant moment McNamara accepted that as a young officer during the Second World War he had been a key figure in the decision to fire-bomb Japan which killed in one night alone 100,000 civilians in Tokyo. According to McNamara, he had been acting as a 'war criminal' but was never held accountable for his actions since 'What makes it immoral if you lose but not immoral if you win?'

In 2003, President George W. Bush ironically responded to criticism that his policy in Iraq was contrary to international law: 'International law? I'd better call my lawyer. He didn't bring that up to me.'

1   Research other examples of powerful nation-states not taking responsibility for alleged war crimes and crimes against humanity.

2   Using these two quotations and your own knowledge, to what extent do you think that international human rights law is undermined by the ability of powerful nation-states to avoid the consequences of their actions?

The same criticism has been made of more recent tribunals.

- Mary Robinson, then-UN High Commissioner for Human Rights, has criticised NATO air bombing of Serbia during the Kosovo War in 1999. According to Robinson, the civilian loss of life invalidated claims that this was a **humanitarian intervention** and NATO could even be held accountable for inflicting war crimes. Both Human Rights Watch and Amnesty International have condemned as a war crime the deliberate bombing of the headquarters of Serb Radio/Television, which killed 16 civilian workers. However, NATO has never been held responsible for the military actions it carried out in Serbia. This may suggest that there are some grounds for allegations of 'victors' justice'.

- The UN tribunal investigating the Rwandan genocide has also been criticised for only having convicted Hutus. The Tutsi Rwandan Patriotic Front, which now forms the country's government, also committed atrocities during this period. The court never investigated these crimes, leading to accusations that the tribunal has endorsed the official 'narrative' of the war.

- The trial of Charles Taylor of Liberia was held in The Hague and he has been subsequently imprisoned in the UK. Western powers also funded the tribunal's operation, and so critics claim that the court has helped to reinforce **neocolonial** stereotypes that Africa cannot deliver justice itself.

The effectiveness of international tribunals has also been undermined by the circumstances in which they are established and the extent to which nation-states are prepared to cooperate in their establishment:

- Unlike other heads of government, former Iraqi leader Saddam Hussein was not tried by an international court. Instead, the US declared that his countrymen could try him in Iraq. Critics of the trial's legitimacy claim that this demonstrates how powerful countries can manipulate international law – by being tried in Iraq, Saddam would be liable to the death penalty, which international UN tribunals cannot deliver. Such a partisan approach to global justice challenges the whole rationale of criminal tribunals. If they are only set up in certain circumstances, maybe they do simply represent victors' justice?

Key term

Humanitarian intervention Based upon the liberal principle that as members of a global community, all states should strive to protect human life through intervention in another sovereign state, if that state is unwilling to resolve a conflict or unable to cope with a natural catastrophe.

Neocolonialism Where a nation-state exerts strong economic or political influence over another, often but not limited to nation-states that had previously been colonised.

- In 2015, Russia vetoed the establishment of a UN tribunal into the shooting down of Malaysian Flight 17 over Ukraine. Russia was widely condemned for being the only member of the UNSC to exercise the veto. The former US envoy to the UN Samantha Power criticised Russia for 'callously disregarding the public outcry in the grieving nations'. However, Russia felt that the court would not serve in its interests and so was able to resist its establishment.

The International Criminal Court

What is the purpose of the International Criminal Court?

During the 1990s, the euphoria that greeted the end of the Cold War soon gave way to horror and disbelief that mass murder, ethnic cleansing and even genocide could claim so many lives in nationalist, ethnic and tribal conflicts. Determined UN secretaries-general Boutros Boutros-Ghali and Kofi Annan put their moral weight behind the creation of an international criminal court. UN special tribunals had set a precedent for the development of human rights-based international law. However, an international criminal court would sit in permanent session as a constant reminder to the global community of the permanence, impartiality and reach of international justice.

In 1998, the Rome Statute established the **International Criminal Court (ICC)** as 'a court of last resort'. It would try individuals, including heads of state, accused of genocide, crimes against humanity and war crimes when national governments were unprepared or unable to do this themselves. In 2002, the ICC was established at The Hague to try 'the most serious crimes of concern to the international community'. A total of 124 states (2021) have ratified the Rome Statute and so accept the ICC's jurisdiction.

> **Key term**
>
> **International Criminal Court (ICC)** IGO and international tribunal that sits in The Hague. The ICC has the jurisdiction to prosecute individuals for the international crimes of genocide, war and crimes against humanity.

In what ways has the International Criminal Court been successful?

From 2003 to 2021 the ICC had two determined chief prosecutors: Luis Moreno-Ocampo and Fatou Bensouda who significantly raised the global standing of the court. In 2021, the British barrister, Karim Khan, became the ICC's third chief prosecutor.

By 2021, the ICC had secured eight convictions including:

- 2012: Thomas Lubanga Dyilo, a Congolese warlord, was sentenced to 14 years for human rights abuses, including recruiting child soldiers. He was released in 2020.
- 2014: Germain Katanga, another Congolese warlord, was sentenced to 12 years for atrocities committed during Congo's civil war.
- 2016: Ahmad al-Mahdi, a militant Islamist, was sentenced to nine years for destroying historic sites and artefacts sites in Mali. The verdict has been important in developing the concept of 'cultural terrorism' in international law.
- The ICC has expanded its investigations significantly beyond Africa, launching investigations into alleged human rights violations by allied forces in Afghanistan (2020) and the Israeli Defence Force on the West Bank and the Gaza Strip (2019).
- In 2020, the Sudanese government agreed that its former president, Omar al-Bashir, should face ICC charges of war crimes, crimes against humanity and genocide in Darfur. Although Omar al-Bashir was indicted in 2009, his government refused to acknowledge the legitimacy of the court to try him. However, when he was overthrown in 2019, the new Sudanese government agreed to cooperate with the ICC.

Why has the International Criminal Court not been more successful?

Although the ICC was supposed to initiate a new approach to global justice based upon the centrality of human rights, it soon became obvious that sovereign state self-interest would undermine its liberal intentions:

- China, Russia and the US (the three most powerful members of the UNSC) do not accept the ICC's jurisdiction over their internal sovereign affairs. The US has signed a number of bilateral agreements with other states in which they are required not to cooperate with the court in handing over US citizens to its jurisdiction. India also does not recognise the ICC's authority, meaning that 70% of the world's population is outside the jurisdiction of the court.
- The unwillingness of a significant number of nation-states to accept limits on their sovereignty significantly undermines the ICC's scope and authority. In 2021, just 123 states had ratified the Rome Statute which means that they fully accept its jurisdiction within their borders.
- The ICC undertakes to investigate cases presented to it by nation-states or by the UNSC, although the ICC's chief prosecutor can also take the initiative in launching investigations. However, the court has no coercive power of its own and if nation-states are unprepared to cooperate with it, there is little it can do.
- The ICC indicted Kenyan president Uhuru Kenyatta for the killing of over 1,000 people following the country's disputed 2007 election. Lack of cooperation by the Kenyan government forced the ICC to drop its prosecution. President Kenyatta subsequently claimed that its attempt to prosecute him had been 'blatantly biased' and that the court was simply the 'toy of declining imperialist powers'.
- Since its establishment, the ICC has only indicted and convicted Africans. This has raised complaints that it is institutionally prejudiced. Consequently, the African Union (AU) has urged its members not to cooperate with the ICC and in 2017 Burundi became the first country to withdraw from the ICC.
- A further blow to the ICC's authority came in 2016 when President Putin withdrew his signature from the Rome Statute over the court's criticism of the Russian annexation of Crimea. Russia had not ratified the Rome Statute and so was not subject to ICC authority, but the decision nonetheless further undermined the Court's authority. The Russian Foreign Ministry's criticism of the ICC for being 'one-sided and inefficient' is therefore another sign that the goodwill it needs to flourish is in increasingly short supply.
- In 2019, the Philippines withdrew from the ICC following its decision to investigate the enormous numbers of killings associated with president Duterte's war on drugs. Like a number of other leaders Duterte accused the court of bias against the developing world and stated, 'I am only responsible to the Filipino. Filipinos will judge.'

Topic link

The problems that international judicial institutions face in seeking to establish a global standard of accountability are associated with all the key elements of global politics: the importance of state sovereignty, the tension between realism and liberalism, and the importance of power in determining outcomes.

Is the International Criminal Court effective?

No

- The ICC interferes with state sovereignty. Nation-states have the responsibility to protect their citizens. The international community has no mandate to intervene within states and the court therefore lacks legitimacy.
- Article 2 of the UN Charter lays down the principle of 'sovereign equality' of all member states and 'that nothing contained in the present Charter shall authorie the United Nations to intervene in matters which are essentially in the domestic jurisdiction of any state'.
- The withdrawal of the Philippines from the court as a result of the ICC's investigation into its government's war on drugs demonstrates that to be effective it requires the cooperation of member states.
- Its authority is undermined by the refusal of three members of the UNSC (China, Russia and the US) to accept its jurisdiction. With so many powerful countries absent, the ICC only provides 'partial' justice and cannot claim to provide international justice.
- By 2021, the ICC had only secured eight convictions (one of which, Jean-Pierre Bemba's, was overturned on appeal). Critics thus claim that the ICC is costly, very slow moving and has achieved little.
- So far, the only people to have been indicted by the court are Africans. Given the global extent of human rights abuses, this indicates an inbuilt bias against Africa. This is why Burundi has withdrawn from the court.

Yes

- Since the ICC is in permanent session, unlike ad hoc tribunals, it provides a constant standard of international justice to which governments should aspire.
- By convicting human rights abusers before an international court, it establishes precedents for the development of international human rights-based law. This includes the crime of cultural terrorism, for example.
- By delivering retribution and punishment within countries, future human rights abuses may be deterred, as war criminals realise they cannot hide from justice behind borders.
- It has recorded and made public evidence of atrocities, so making subsequent 'denial' more difficult.
- It is able to provide justice in cases where nation-states might not be able to, either because of prejudice or lack of governance.

⚙ Evaluation prompt: After twenty years, the liberal ambitions of the ICC seem to have been stalled by the realist self-interest of nation-states more concerned with protecting their sovereignty than with advancing a global standard of legal accountability.

The European Court of Human Rights

What is the purpose of the European Court of Human Rights?

In 1949, the Council of Europe (not to be confused with the EU) was established. It is responsible for promoting human rights and the rule of law in Europe, and in 1950 it drafted the European Convention on Human Rights (ECHR). In the wake of the devastation of the Second World War, the ECHR sought to define those rights that all European citizens could claim. This would protect the rights of individuals from possible persecution and so help to contribute to peace in Europe.

The European Court of Human Rights (ECtHR) was established in 1959. The court sits in Strasbourg, France and has 47 judges, one for each member of the European Council. European states and individuals can apply to the court in cases where they feel that human rights have been abused.

In what ways has the European Court of Human Rights been successful?

The ECtHR possesses great moral authority and its decisions carry great weight. Compliance with its judgments is therefore generally very high, although some member states have proved much more compliant than others.

The number of cases on which the ECtHR is asked to deliver verdicts has dramatically increased in recent years and in high-profile cases it has significantly advanced human rights law. The following cases all date from the same year and show that, although the court finds it difficult to enforce its judgments, it is continually encouraging nation-states to prioritise and protect human rights.

- *Beizaras and Levickas v Lithuania* (2020): When two gay men posted a picture of them kissing on Facebook this unleashed a storm of criticism against them in Lithuania, much of it very violent. The authorities, however, decided not to launch an investigation since the couple's actions were so 'eccentric' that they were bound to generate hostility, 'as the majority of Lithuanian society very much appreciated traditional family values'. According to the ECtHR, by failing to prosecute, Lithuania had shared in this discriminatory mindset and so was in defiance of Article 14 (freedom from discrimination).
- *Buturuga v Romania* (2020): Ms Buturuga's claims that she had suffered significant and continued domestic violence from her husband and that he had accessed her private electronic communications was dismissed in the Romanian courts as insufficiently serious for a prosecution. In its judgment, the ECtHR stated that Romania had failed to recognise Ms Buturuga's right not be subject to torture, inhumane or degrading treatment (Article 3) and her right to privacy (Article 8).
- In 2020, the Azerbaijan Supreme Court quashed the 2014 conviction of the opposition politician, Ilgar Mammadov, after the ECtHR had declared that his conviction was based solely on his criticism of the government.

The ECtHR's supporters argue that it provides all European states with a moral code to emulate and, by its judgments, is continually holding European nation-states accountable for their observance of human rights.

Why has the European Court of Human Rights not been more successful?
As with other international courts, state sovereignty weakens the ECtHR's authority. If sovereign states ignore the rulings of the court, it has no coercive power. Therefore, states may be prepared to risk criticism of the court if it means that they can still act according to their perceived national interest:

- In the Sejdic-Finci case (2009) the ECtHR ruled that the constitution of Bosnia-Herzegovina was discriminatory because it restricted election to public office to Croats, Bosniaks and Serbs, so excluding Jews and Roma. As of 2021, Bosnia-Herzegovina is still in defiance of Article 14 of the European Convention of Human Rights which forbids discrimination.
- In 2017, the ECtHR stated that the conviction of Russian opposition leader, Alexei Navalny, for money laundering and fraud was 'arbitrary and unfair'. Russia has, however, ignored this ruling and in 2021 Navalny's suspended prison sentence was changed to a prison sentence in spite of condemnation by the US and the European Union.
- In 2020, the Council of Europe expressed 'profound concern' that the UK government had not complied with ECtHR judgments that it should reopen cases involving killings carried out by the security services in Northern Ireland.
- In 2021, in two separate judgments the ECtHR declared that Russia had committed war crimes during its war with Georgia in 2008 and that its annexation of Crimea in 2014 was illegal. Moscow has however ignored both judgments.

According to Nils Muižnieks, the former Council of Europe's Commissioner for Human Rights, 'Our work is based on cooperation and good faith. When you don't have that, it's very difficult to have an impact ... It's worrying. People have forgotten why the system was created, and that it's a game that everyone has to play by the rules or it all falls apart.'

Conclusion

Although they have achieved some successes and have also developed the principle that the international community can try crimes committed within states, international courts and tribunals do still find it difficult to enforce a universal standard of human rights due to a lack of:

- universal human rights hard law (anarchic world order)
- global jurisdiction to which all states are equally accountable
- enforcement tools.

Human rights and state sovereignty

The clash between human rights and state sovereignty neatly illustrates the conflict between the realist and liberal approaches to international relations. For realists, the state determines the extent of the human rights that one may claim. Conversely, for liberals, human rights are universal and derive from our shared humanity rather than from the nation-state in which we are born or choose to live.

Why is it so difficult to enforce an international standard of human rights?

State sovereignty

The cosmopolitan values of **universal human rights** conflict with the theory of state sovereignty. According to the principle of external sovereignty, states are independent and autonomous, and so determine the legality of everything that happens within their borders. Article 2 of the UN Charter confirms the 'sovereign equality' of all nation-states, and UNGA Resolution 2131 (1965) acknowledges that, 'no state has the right to intervene, directly or indirectly, for any reason whatsoever, in the internal or external affairs of another state'.

As a result, the claims of international law, such as the UDHR, merely represent soft law. This is because nation-states remain sovereign over their internal affairs and can choose whether to accept outside jurisdiction in cases affecting their citizens. The lack of a supranational authority to which all states are equally accountable therefore undermines the potential for enforcing an international standard of human rights:

> **Key term**
>
> **Universal human rights**
> Rights to which people are entitled because they are human, regardless of race, nationality, sex or religion. They are fundamental, universal, indivisible and non-negotiable, since they define the fundamental freedoms that lie at the core of humanity.

- The UK government has refused to comply with the ICJ's judgment that it should hand the Chagos Islands to Mauritius.
- A UNSC resolution censured Israel in 2016 for its policy of building settlements in the occupied territories. However, Israel's prime minister, Benjamin Netanyahu, immediately responded that, as a sovereign state, his country would continue constructing settlements.
- Saudi Arabia has also been criticised for human rights violations. In 2015, the blogger Raif Badawi was sentenced to 1,000 lashes and 10 years in jail for 'insulting Islam'. Saudi Arabia also legally equates terrorism with atheism, while

abandoning Islam for another religion is a capital offence (apostasy). When challenged on BBC's *Newsnight*, the Saudi Arabian ambassador to the United Nations, Abdallah Al Mouallimi, responded that, 'We believe that we are holding ourselves to the highest standards. If that doesn't please someone here or there that's their problem not ours'.

- At their first meeting at Geneva in 2021, President Biden was critical of the Russian government's imprisonment of the political activist, Alexei Navalny. Putin, however, refused to discuss the issue, claiming that it was purely a domestic matter.

Activity

The internet and human rights

The internet provides extraordinary opportunities for the state to intervene within the lives of its citizens. In China, for example, since 2021 children under 18 are restricted to gaming for three hours a week, only at the weekend.

1 Research other ways in which nation states can electronically intervene within the lives of their citizens and even compel them to act in a certain way.
2 How might governments justify such actions?
3 Does international human rights law provide any meaningful protection from excessive government surveillance?

Activity

Article 18 of the UDHR and Article 9 of the ECHR both state that:

> Everyone has the right to freedom of thought, conscience and religion; this right includes freedom to change his religion or belief, and freedom, either alone or in community with others and in public or private, to manifest his religion or belief in teaching, practice, worship and observance.

However:

In Saudi Arabia, those who abandon Islam are deemed to have committed the crime of apostasy. According to Saudi Arabia's penal code, this is punishable by death.

In France, Muslim women who fully veil their face and bodies in public can be fined since this is in conflict with France's powerful secular tradition (laïcité). Belgium goes further and imposes a prison sentence of up to seven days for infringing the ban.

1 Why do you think that 'freedom of thought, conscience and religion' is so controversial in terms of international human rights law?
2 Research other examples of nation-states which are in defiance of the UDHR and the ECHR over these freedoms.
3 If states act in defiance of these principles is there anything that the international community can do to enforce them?

Topic link

The importance of state sovereignty in global politics is fully discussed in Chapter 1 and Chapter 2.

Different cultural traditions

In spite of the UDHR, there is no one standard of international human rights. Western powers have generally been influenced by the principles of the Enlightenment, which emphasised the importance of the individual's right to self-expression. It is therefore claimed that the concept of human rights is too euro-centric and does not take into account the competing claims of very different cultural traditions.

Cultural relativists argue that each culture determines the rights that its people enjoy, and that the concept of a universal standard of human rights is an example of Western cultural imperialism. The West may no longer possess territorial empires, but it still seeks moral empire through the transmission of its values via the UDHR and the ICC. As Edward W. Said put it in his 1978 book *Orientalism*:

> What is right for one society may not be right for other societies, a position that suggests that the outside world should respect the choices made by individual nation-states.

The following are examples of competing claims of different cultural traditions:

- The 1993 Bangkok Declaration of Asian governments rejects the West's focus on the rights of individuals and instead focuses on communal rights that we all owe to society. It is this emphasis on the community that many states, such as China, use to justify the death penalty.
- In the West, for most people LGBT rights are self-evident and yet in large parts of the developing world, which is generally more socially conservative, homosexuality is a crime. In 69 countries, primarily in Africa and Asia, same-sex sexual activity is illegal and in 11 countries it is punishable by death (2021). In 2015, when president Obama urged Kenyans to respect LGBT rights, Kenyan president Kenyatta was unequivocal, 'I repeatedly say that for Kenyans today the issue of gay rights is really a non-issue.'
- In Russia, the conservative principles of the Orthodox Church are reflected in the government's unwillingness to treat homosexuality and heterosexuality as equally legitimate. Furthermore, the members of the pop group Pussy Riot were prosecuted for 'offending public morals by their sexually explicit actions' within an Orthodox Church. President Putin has said that individualism and moral relativity lead to decadence and depravity, and he deplores the deteriorating 'moral values and ethical norms' of the West. For Putin, Russia now stands as a bastion of 'family values' against a West that, as a result of the decline of Christianity, accepts 'the equality of good and evil'.
- In many Muslim countries, standards of human rights are determined by the 'higher law' of Islam. Iran, for example, is an Islamic theocracy in which the Qur'an is the ultimate authority in determining the meaning of the law. Saudi Arabia bases its legal system on a literalist Wahhabi interpretation of the Qur'an, which sets it at odds with many of the UDHR's Enlightenment principles. On issues such as freedom of belief and gender equality, the West has been highly critical of Saudi Arabia's legal position. In response its leaders state its values are superior to those of the West, since they are divinely ordained.

In large parts of the developing world, which is generally more socially conservative, homosexual acts are illegal

Activity

Read the case study and answer the following questions.

1 Why do you think the US State Department reacted so differently to these two shocking events?
2 Research more examples of 'double standards' influencing the attitude of the US to human rights abuses committed by other nation-states.
3 If a universal standard of human rights is selectively deployed do you think that this makes it ultimately meaningless?

Activity

Read the case study and answer the following questions.

1 Imagine this is a debate. Put forward the case for Saudi Arabia.
2 Then put forward the case for Canada.
3 To what extent do you agree that different nation-states' laws and cultural traditions should always be respected in global politics?

Case study

Middle Eastern human rights abuses

In 2019, the US State Department expressed outrage that Iran had executed two teenagers, Mehdi Sohrabifar and Amin Sedaghat, after they were convicted of rape. According to the State Department, the reports were appalling but sadly 'consistent with Iran's egregious overall human rights record'. Amnesty International further noted that the trial was unfair and that the boys were flogged before they were executed.

In the same year, Saudi Arabia beheaded 37 people on the same day for what were dubbed terrorist-related offences. Human rights activists dispute the charge and note that three of those executed were under the age of 18 when they were sentenced and that the authorities have been accused of securing a number of confessions through torture. One of the bodies was subsequently publicly crucified. However, on this occasion, there was no response from the US State Department, leading to this tweet from the Iranian Foreign Minister, Mohammad Javad Zarif: 'After a wink at the dismembering of a journalist [Jamal Khashoggi], not a whisper from the Trump administration when Saudi Arabia beheads 37 men in one day – even crucifying one two days after Easter.'

Case study

Speaking up for human rights

In 2018, Canada publicly called for the release of human rights activists being held in Saudi Arabia. These included several female activists including Samar Badawi, the sister of Raif Badawi who was sentenced to ten years in prison and a thousand lashes for 'insulting Islam'. In response, Saudi Arabia furiously condemned Canada's 'blatant interference in the kingdom's domestic affairs' and expelled Canada's ambassador as well as freezing all new trade links. Prime Minister Trudeau responded that he would not be stopped from standing up for 'Canadian values and human rights'. Canada's stance was widely condemned in the Arab world and gained such little positive support among Western powers that the influential Saudi women's rights activist Manal al-Sharif tweeted, 'Thank you, Canada for speaking up. When are we going to hear from the US, the UK and the EU about these arrests?'

Powerful states are unaccountable for their actions

If an international standard of human rights law is going to exist, all states would need to be held equally accountable before that law. If international law, like domestic law, is to be legitimate, it must treat all states in the same way. This principle is undermined because powerful states often ignore international law if it is against their national interests:

- The War on Terror demonstrates how the US has been prepared to infringe human rights in order to achieve its goals of defeating terrorism. When a US senate enquiry stated that the CIA utilised 'abhorrent techniques' such as waterboarding in the War on Terror, former vice-president Dick Cheney responded, 'I think what needed to be done was done. I think we were perfectly justified in doing it. And I'd do it again in a minute.'
- The US's use of extraordinary rendition whereby terrorist suspects were transferred to states such as Pakistan and Egypt, where they could be more harshly interrogated, further highlights the way in which the unaccountability of powerful states undermines the principle that human rights can be universally applied.
- On the inauguration of President Biden in 2021, the United Nations urged the new administration to shut the detention camp at Guantánamo Bay, which

still holds 40 prisoners, most of whom have still not been charged with any offence.

- In 2019, India provided an amnesty for non-Muslim illegal immigrants which provides them with the opportunity to claim citizenship. By discriminating against Muslims in this way this undermines India's claim to be a secular state.
- In Pakistan, the Ahmadis (a religious minority that considers itself Muslim but which Pakistan does not recognise as such) are legally forbidden from 'indirectly nor directly posing as a Muslim'.
- Saudi Arabia has been accused of targeting civilians during its military intervention in Yemen. According to Human Rights Watch the Saudi-led coalition has 'conducted numerous, indiscriminate and disproportionate airstrikes killing thousands of civilians and hitting civilian structures in violation of the laws of war'. Such criticisms did not though stop Saudi Arabia from hosting the G20 in 2020.

These examples demonstrate that the censures of the international community do not concern powerful and influential states. Since leaders are unlikely to be held accountable for their actions, they are able to act with impunity. For human rights to be effectively protected, all states would have to be equally accountable before the law. The way in which powerful states can put their own interests before those of international standards of human rights therefore creates the sort of double standards that undermine the potential for global human rights. As the philosopher and political activist Noam Chomsky once put it, 'For the powerful, crimes are those that others commit.'

Debate

Are human rights effectively protected in the modern world?

No

- International human rights law is soft law. Westphalian principles of state sovereignty undermine liberal principles of human rights observance.
- Nation-states are unprepared to sacrifice their realist self-interest to liberal cosmopolitanism.
- Powerful states, including China, Russia and the US, do not accept the ICC's authority, while state sovereignty limits ECtHR jurisdiction.
- In order to be effective the ICC requires member states to cooperate with it, but this is often not the case.
- Different cultural traditions challenge the principle of a universal standard of human rights.
- Emerging powers like China are less committed to human rights protection than Western powers and as China's global influence increases so it will become more difficult to enforce a global standard of human rights protection.

Yes

- The establishment of international courts, such as the ECtHR and the ICC, shows willingness to protect human rights through legal methods.
- UN criminal tribunals (Cambodia, former Yugoslavia, Rwanda and Sierra Leone) have been set up to bring to justice those who have committed crimes against humanity.
- Leading war criminals, such as Radovan Karadžic and Charles Taylor, have been convicted for terrible crimes.
- These courts have developed the principle that heads of government may be held accountable for war crimes, and have set new precedents in an international setting, such as including rape as a way of perpetrating genocide.
- The 2005 UN Responsibility to Protect (R2P) and the establishment of the principle that state sovereignty is 'provisional' present the message that states that abuse their own citizens forfeit their sovereignty, giving the UN a 'responsibility' to intervene.
- The internet has made human rights abuses more globally known. States, as well as MNCs, are now more likely to be held accountable for their actions.
- NGOs, such as Amnesty International and Human Rights Watch, work to highlight abuses. MNCs are increasingly concerned to demonstrate corporate social responsibility.

Evaluation prompt: The post-Cold War optimism that human rights protection would become a priority in global relations has now been replaced with the sobering realisation that there is declining political momentum to establish such a liberal world order.

Why did humanitarian intervention increase during the 1990s?

Human intervention is based upon the liberal principle that as members of a global community, all states should strive to protect human life. If sovereign states cannot do this, either because they are deliberately perpetrating mass murder or are unable to cope with the enormity of a natural catastrophe, the international community should intervene to restore order and save lives. Therefore, humanitarian intervention is instigated by the altruistic principle of 'saving strangers' rather than geostrategic considerations of self-interest.

The end of the Cold War

The end of the Cold War was greeted with such optimism that it generated huge international support for liberal principles of global governance and international justice. 'People power' played an important role in the collapse of communism in eastern Europe and the Soviet Union, placing people at the centre of political debate in a way not seen during the Cold War.

In the early 1990s, the future therefore appeared to be one of greater global cooperation, as states increasingly embraced common values. This led President George H. W. Bush to speak of a 'New World Order' based on a global community working together to resolve the problems it jointly faced.

The First Gulf War (1991)

This new, more positive world order was illustrated in 1991 when states cooperated to expel Iraqi forces from Kuwait. This seemed to suggest that the global community was prepared to live up to UN ideals and punish what George H. W. Bush termed the 'naked aggression' of Saddam Hussein. However, Bush was not prepared to topple Saddam because this would be going beyond the UN mandate and, consequently, be in defiance of international law.

However, when Saddam went on to brutally suppress Kurdish uprisings in northern Iraq, this was too much for the UNSC. Its speedy passage of UN Resolution 688, condemning Saddam Hussein's retribution against Kurdish rebels, provided France, the UK and the US with the authority to establish 'no-fly zones' within Iraqi borders. This signalled that the state would no longer be all-powerful if it sought to persecute its own people. Significantly, the intervention was code-named 'Operation Provide Comfort', indicating the way in which morality, rather than strategic self-interest, was used to justify action.

Somalia (1992–93)

Operation Provide Comfort was not a one-off. In December 1992, in one of his last acts as president, George H. W. Bush committed 28,000 US troops to Somalia, a state that had disintegrated into anarchy and in which over a million were threatened with starvation. When General Colin Powell, then Chairman of the Joint Chiefs of Staff, asked Bush what the US's objective was, he stated it was 'to end the starvation'. Then, in his broadcast to the nation, he declared that the US would 'answer the call' and 'get the food through'.

Such humanitarianism was easier to achieve in the 1990s since, following the collapse of the Soviet Union, the US was the sole global superpower. If the US was prepared to act according to moral principles in the development of a New World Order, it appeared that a more liberal world order could indeed be established.

The lessons of Bosnia and Rwanda

The civil war that erupted upon the break-up of the Yugoslav Federation severely tested the principle of humanitarian intervention. President Bill Clinton (1993-2001) was wary of involving the US in such a complicated and bloody conflict. The EU was similarly paralysed by indecision and unwilling to take sides. The UN sent peacekeepers into the warzone but, as the UN Secretary-General Boutros Boutros-Ghali put it, they were being expected to keep the peace 'when there was no peace to keep'.

As a result of this lack of resolve, the killings multiplied. In the biggest mass murder in Europe since the end of the Second World War, Bosnian Serbs murdered 7,000 Bosnian Muslim men and boys when they overran the UN safe haven of Srebrenica. This coincided with developments in satellite broadcasting, which made the killings 'instantaneous news', further highlighting the moral consequences of a failure to intervene.

The Rwandan genocide took place from April to June 1994. As many as 800,000 Rwandans may have been killed in the bloodbath out of a population of 6.3 million (1993). The tiny UN force in Rwanda did not have either the manpower or the mandate to take decisive action. When, at last, the UNSC did agree to send reinforcements, the killing was mostly over. As the scale of this tragedy became known, so the failure of the international community to intervene was widely condemned.

Clearly, if humanitarian intervention were to work in the future, it would require full military involvement, acceptance that there would be risks and casualties, and an absolute commitment to success. According to Samantha Power, the former US ambassador to the United Nations, a great part of the problem is that the US has not been prepared to provide a sufficient moral lead, 'We speak loudly but carry no stick at all.'

NATO's intervention in Bosnia (1995)

By 1995, the extent of suffering in Bosnia at last persuaded NATO to intervene in the civil war. Bosnian Serb artillery attacks on Sarajevo, including a particularly bloody attack on a busy civilian marketplace, together with the Srebrenica Massacre, proved to be the final straw.

Since its establishment in 1949, NATO's purpose had been to deter Soviet aggression. However, with the Cold War over and a humanitarian disaster occurring on the EU border, NATO leaders agreed to deploy troops and air power to its 'near abroad'. It launched Operation Deliberate Force against the Bosnian Serbs, who were soon pushed back by the overwhelming military power that NATO could deploy. In December 1995, all sides agreed to the Dayton Peace Accords. To ensure compliance, NATO deployed 60,000 troops in Bosnia, with a robust mandate to disarm rival military factions, rebuild Bosnia and try to restore trust between the rival ethnic and religious groups in the region.

Nation-building in Bosnia

The commitment NATO made to rebuilding Bosnia after the civil war demonstrated that, if it was to work, humanitarian intervention would have to involve nation-building. It was not enough to stop the fighting – peacekeeping forces would need to step in to create the conditions necessary for lasting peace. In 2002–06, former Liberal Democrat leader Paddy Ashdown served as International High Representative for Bosnia and Herzegovina. He had many practical successes during his time as High Representative, but some criticised the intervention as neocolonialism. However, if it was imperialism, it was a very benign form, designed to establish the conditions necessary for the rebuilding of Bosnia.

Case study

The moral force of Mr Gladstone

During 1876, a nationalist revolt broke out in Bulgaria (then part of the Ottoman Empire). Turkish forces crushed the rebels with extreme severity – poorly disciplined irregular forces were responsible for atrocities against the civilian population and, in Philippopolis alone, it is estimated that 15,000 people were murdered. The Conservative government of Benjamin Disraeli ignored these atrocities. Its main foreign policy objective was to prevent the expansion of the Russian Empire, and that meant bolstering the Turkish Empire as a counterweight. Issues of morality simply did not play a part in the British government's grand diplomatic strategy.

Disraeli's great political opponent and leader of the Liberal Party, William Gladstone, was at that time contemplating retiring from politics. But the events in Bulgaria galvanised him into action. For Gladstone, politics was inseparable from moral considerations, and Britain could not stand idly by in the knowledge that such atrocities were taking place. In 1876, he swiftly wrote *The Bulgarian Horrors and the Question of the East*, in which he reminded the public of the moral responsibility of government to place human life above self-interest. The pamphlet quickly sold 200,000 copies and established Gladstone as the moral voice of Victorian Britain.

The battle-lines were therefore drawn between the realist pragmatism of Disraeli, who quipped that of all the Bulgarian atrocities Gladstone's prose style was the worst, and the liberal idealism of Gladstone, who demanded that 'the Turks now carry away their abuses in the only possible manner, namely by carrying off themselves'. Eventually, at the Congress of Berlin in 1878, Disraeli helped negotiate a settlement that prevented a general European war. It did little to protect the rights of Bulgarians, but it did allow him to proclaim 'peace with honour'. However, Gladstone's moral legacy has arguably had even greater impact. A silver wreath still hangs in the Gladstone Library, which was laid on his tomb 'from the grateful Bulgarian nation', and his dictum that 'nothing that is morally wrong can be politically right' has influenced politicians from Woodrow Wilson to Tony Blair.

Activity

Read the case study and answer the following questions.
1 How do the responses of Gladstone and Disraeli to the Bulgarian Horrors demonstrate the differences between a liberal and a realist approach to global relations?
2 In what ways did Tony Blair take a Gladstonian approach to crises in Kosovo (1999) and Sierra Leone (2000)?
3 What did the Catholic writer G. K. Chesterton mean when he suggested that the greatest threat to peace and stability is when 'virtue runs amok'?
4 To what extent do you think that foreign policy should be based upon moral considerations? Use as many examples of modern humanitarian intervention as you can to justify your arguments.

Tony Blair and the principle of the international community

In 1997, Labour leader Tony Blair became UK prime minister. The most devoutly Christian prime minister since Gladstone, Blair shared his predecessor's conviction that politics and morality are inseparable. Foreign policy must, as his first foreign secretary Robin Cook put it, be 'ethical' and so Blair would use his international stature to encourage the international community to live up to the idealism of a more liberal global cosmopolitanism. Under Blair's government, respect for human rights would inform British foreign policy just as much as geostrategic self-interest.

Kosovo (1999)

In 1999, conflict in the Balkans once again gained international attention. This time the violence was within Serbia. Kosovar Albanians wanted to separate from Serbia and establish an independent state. In response, the Serbian president, Slobodan Milošević, launched a major military offensive in order to crush the separatist movement. To many in the West this seemed to herald yet more 'ethnic cleansing' in the region and Tony Blair, remembering how long it had taken to end the war in Bosnia, was among those most eager to push for military intervention. In March, NATO began an aerial bombardment against Serbia. In April, Blair flew to Washington, DC to persuade President Clinton that NATO might need to prepare for a full-scale land invasion.

Eventually, the threat of a NATO ground offensive forced Milošević to hand over Kosovo to NATO administration, although it would legally remain a part of Serbia. Subsequently, Kosovo Force (KFOR) took over the responsibilities of re-establishing the infrastructure, disarming rival groups, resettling refugees and preventing acts of revenge.

In some ways, Kosovo represents the high point of humanitarian intervention. During the conflict, Blair was unequivocal on his assertion that NATO had intervened to protect our 'fellow human beings' and that it was 'simply the right thing to do'. In his Chicago speech in April 1999, he reinforced these commitments in what later became known as the 'Blair Doctrine', in which he stated that 'acts of genocide can never be a purely internal matter'. At the dawn of the new millennium, it really did seem as though a new empire of the good was under creation: if nation-states chose to make war against their own people, they would have to face the consequences.

Activity

Read the case study and answer the following questions.
1. What was the context in which Blair made this speech?
2. Do you think that his justification is idealistic or pragmatic?
3. In what ways does Blair develop a new approach to global human rights protection in this speech?
4. How convincing do you find his arguments? Support your arguments with examples of the results of humanitarian intervention and non-intervention.

Case study

On 22 April 1999, Prime Minister Tony Blair made a speech in Chicago, offering the international community a set of criteria for deciding when and how to intervene militarily in the affairs of another country where the threat was not to the outside world, but to a domestic population. These proposals came to be known as the 'Blair Doctrine'.

According to Blair, in the end, values and interests merge. If we can establish and spread the values of liberty, the rule of law, human rights and an open society then that is in our national interests. The spread of our values makes us safer. As John Kennedy put it, 'Freedom is indivisible and when one man is enslaved who is free?' Non-interference has long been considered an important principle of international order. And it is not one we would want to jettison too readily ... But the principle of non-interference must be qualified in important respects. Acts of genocide can never be a purely internal matter. When oppression produces massive flows of refugees which unsettle neighbouring countries then they can properly be described as 'threats to international peace and security'.

The Clinton Doctrine (1999)

When President Clinton announced that when mass human rights violations were taking place, the US should be prepared to intervene, liberals were further emboldened to believe that the new millennium would usher in a more humanitarian approach to foreign policy. Like Tony Blair, Clinton further accepted that 'Genocide is in and of itself a national interest where we should act' and that the US had a responsibility to promote human rights and democracy. This was not only morally right, but a world governed according to these principles would be safer and more secure for US interests. Possibly, too, his assertions were fuelled by guilt: in the early years of his presidency, Clinton had ignored the Rwandan genocide. His foreign policy legacy would therefore be to challenge Westphalian principles of state sovereignty by emphasising the universality of human rights.

The United Nations Responsibility to Protect (2005)

As UN secretary-general, Kofi Annan was keen to refine the extent to which a state could act in defiance of the moral precepts of the international community. In the wake of the Kosovo intervention in 1999, Annan argued, like Blair and Clinton, that states could now no longer claim absolute authority over their citizens. Instead, a state's sovereignty was 'conditional' upon its ability to protect its citizens' human rights. This represented a dramatic assault on Westphalian principles, since it suggested that state sovereignty involved responsibilities as well as rights.

The International Commission on Intervention and State Sovereignty was established in 2000 and coined the term 'responsibility to protect'. According to this principle, the state has a 'responsibility' to protect its citizens from harm. If it fails in this duty, that 'responsibility' passes to the international community. In a global political commitment, all UN members voted to endorse the Responsibility to Protect (R2P) at the UN World Summit in 2005, in order to prevent genocide, war crimes, ethnic cleansing and crimes against humanity. Where such atrocities occur, the UNSC should be prepared to authorise humanitarian intervention.

The concept of 'responsible sovereignty' established a new onus on both nation-states and the global community to ensure that people could live without fear of violent persecution within their own countries.

Synoptic link

The liberal basis to a human rights focused approach to international relations is fully covered in Chapter 1.

Activity

According to UN R2P, the responsibility to protect gives the world community the right to intervene in the case of national authorities manifestly failing to protect their populations from genocide, war crimes, ethnic cleansing and crimes against humanity.

The liberal cosmopolitan principles of the UN R2P therefore present the international community with the right to intervene in states to protect the human rights of their citizens.
1   What is the justification for this principle?
2   Since its publication in 2005 there have been several occasions when the R2P would have mandated action within states, and yet nothing has happened. Why do you think this has been the case?

Why have some humanitarian interventions been more successful than others?

Successful interventions

The Balkans (1992–1995)

The fact that UN peacekeepers were not mandated to take offensive military action undermined initial UN involvement in the conflict in former Yugoslavia. Peacekeepers were operating in a war zone, but without the means even to defend themselves. For example, Srebrenica fell when lightly armed UN Dutch peacekeepers handed over control of the enclave to superior Bosnian Serb forces.

However, when NATO launched Operation Deliberate Force in 1995, it established conditions for a lasting peace. Subdued by air power, the Bosnian Serbs agreed to a peace deal at Dayton, Ohio. As part of the settlement, NATO forces were deployed to rebuild Bosnia. The operation's success was due to the fact that, at its peak, 60,000 troops were deployed, often in a policing role. Furthermore, a UN mandate confirmed NATO's operational legitimacy when it established and assigned a UN High Representative to ensure good and impartial governance in the region. The commitment to nation-building demonstrated in Bosnia established a model for rebuilding the foundations of a civil society.

This model of active nation-building was followed in Kosovo. When Serb forces evacuated, NATO troops quickly replaced them. Once again, a new civilian administration was established and as many as 50,000 troops were deployed in order to provide the necessary conditions for the restoration of peace and stability. As in Bosnia, NATO troops were actively involved in a wide variety of military and non-military roles, ranging from disarming militias to safely accompanying children to school. This demonstrated that active participation in a nation's reconstruction is vital if it is to be successful.

East Timor (1999–2001)

Indonesia annexed East Timor, a former Portuguese colony, in 1975. The cultural heritage of East Timor was very distinct from Indonesia and large parts of the mostly Catholic population demanded independence. Following years of separatist resistance, in 1999 the Indonesian government reluctantly agreed to allow East Timor an independence referendum. Those in favour of independence won 78% of the vote. This provoked a violent backlash by pro-Indonesian militias backed by the government in Jakarta.

During the resulting violence, half a million East Timorese were driven from their homes, threatening a refugee crisis. Australian prime minister John Howard swiftly declared that, as the largest regional power and the one most likely to be affected by a refugee catastrophe, Australia would lead any UN force deployed to keep the peace. Meanwhile, President Clinton put significant economic pressure on Indonesia to allow a UN peacemaking force into the country. As a result of such concerted international pressure, UN Resolution 1264 authorised a multinational force, led by Australia, to enter East Timor, with a robust mandate to defeat and disarm militias. Once stability had been restored, in 2001, elections were held for East Timor's constituent assembly, which approved a constitution. On 20 May 2003, East Timor formally gained independence.

Without UN intervention, East Timor's early attempts at democracy could have quickly descended into extreme violence

Sierra Leone (2000)

During the 1990s, Sierra Leone endured a particularly brutal civil war. The Revolutionary United Front (RUF), led by Foday Sankoh, was responsible for numerous atrocities, including mutilation, and was backed by Charles Taylor,

President of Liberia, in return for 'blood diamonds'. In May 2000, as the RUF advanced on the capital, Freetown, the Blair government sent a military force to help evacuate foreign nationals. Having quickly achieved this, elite British troops began to engage in highly mobile operations against the RUF and allied militia, such as the West Side Boys. What were, in effect, criminal gangs were no match for British troops' superior training and equipment. Consequently, the Sierra Leone government was able to successfully crush the rebels.

Having turned the tide, British troops remained to train and advise Sierra Leone's armed forces and, in 2001, the RUF agreed to disarm. In 2003, as a result of international pressure and condemnation, Taylor stood down as president and went into exile. In 2006, the UN's Special Court for Sierra Leone charged Taylor with 11 counts of war crimes and he was sentenced to 50 years in prison.

Côte d'Ivoire (2011)

In 2011, President Laurent Gbagbo of Côte d'Ivoire refused to accept defeat in the general election. This provoked a political crisis, which pushed the country towards civil war. The UNSC mandated the destruction of Gbagbo's military capability and France, the former colonial power, militarily intervened with both air and ground forces.

The legitimacy of the intervention was never in doubt, especially since UN observers were unequivocal that Gbagbo had lost the election. Furthermore, as with Sierra Leone, Côte d'Ivoire is relatively compact and, being on the west coast of Africa, was readily accessible to French intervention. Gbagbo's remaining supporters were mostly armed gangs whose only loyalty was to the president. When Gbagbo was arrested and the legitimate government took office, favourable conditions for peace and stability were created.

Unsuccessful interventions

Somalia (1992–93)

President George H. W. Bush deployed US troops in Somalia with the best possible humanitarian intentions. However, troops soon found themselves in a quagmire, unable to distinguish between rival clans, militias and civilians. Lacking a legitimate government to defend, the US military was unable to successfully cooperate with forces within Somalia. US troops were quickly seen as an alien occupying force.

The US people also quickly forgot the initial humanitarian justification for intervention, especially after grisly footage of the aftermath of the Battle of Mogadishu was broadcast on national television. Lacking public support for continued US involvement and with no end in sight to the fighting, President Clinton withdrew all US forces from Somalia by 1994. To achieve its objectives, a humanitarian intervention therefore needs to have both a realistic chance of success and the political will to be carried through to completion. In Somalia, neither proved to be the case.

Afghanistan (2001–2021)

Although Western intervention in Afghanistan after 9/11 was primarily launched to eliminate the terrorist threat from al-Qaeda, it also had a humanitarian dimension. Even before 9/11, there had been widespread international condemnation of the

Taliban's brutal rule, which involved extensive human rights abuses. By establishing the conditions for a liberal democracy in Afghanistan, foreign intervention would make the world safer from terrorism, end the violation of female rights and create a more tolerant and inclusive society.

However, such high-minded idealism was unsuited to a country as culturally remote from the West as Afghanistan. Even though NATO made a huge military commitment, as the US had found in Vietnam, it was one thing establishing a temporary presence in a village or town, but quite another ensuring its long-term security. Fundamental Islamism, especially in the majority Pashtun areas of southern and eastern Afghanistan, was also far more resonant in local conditions than liberal attempts to encourage gender equality and human rights. Equally, it was extremely difficult for Western forces to understand the significance of ethnic, tribal and family alliances and tensions. This undermined attempts to build trust within communities.

In October 1963, when he handed office to Alec Douglas-Home, former UK prime minister Harold Macmillan is alleged to have advised him, 'My dear boy, as long as you don't invade Afghanistan you'll be absolutely fine.' Unfortunately, post-9/11 intervention in Afghanistan was simply too ambitious in its aims. John Reid, Tony Blair's defence secretary, had optimistically said that he would be happy for British forces to leave Helmand province without firing a shot. Like Blair, he had fatally ignored the master of realpolitik Otto von Bismarck's guiding dictum that 'politics is the art of the possible'. In August 2021, the abject failure of intervention was demonstrated when the Taliban entered Kabul as Western embassies and the airport were besieged by desperate Afghans terrified of what might happen to them under the Taliban. Such scenes, so reminiscent of the fall of Saigon in 1975, could hardly have provided a worse twenty year commemoration of 9/11.

Iraq (2003–)

Iraq, like Afghanistan, was a post-9/11 liberal intervention designed to stabilise the region and reduce threats to the international community. By overthrowing Saddam Hussein and replacing his brutal dictatorship with a liberal democracy, regional and global stability would be encouraged, and the Iraqis' human rights would be protected.

Unfortunately, although Saddam Hussein was quickly overthrown, almost no attention was paid to post-war reconstruction. The Bush administration had an optimistic faith that, once Saddam was removed, Iraq would move towards democracy with minimum outside interference. Indeed, the US secretary of defence, Donald Rumsfeld, was determined that the US should only have a 'light footprint' in post-war Iraq. This would not only save money, lives and resources but would prevent accusations of American imperialism. President George W. Bush himself told his National Security Council that, 'we don't do police work'.

In consequence, chaos quickly ensued. By disbanding the Iraqi army and dismissing the government and civil service, the US encouraged the disintegration of law and order. Sunni Muslims, whose interests had been most closely associated with Saddam, launched an insurgency. This, in turn, provoked widespread killing and brutal arrest and interrogation by occupying forces, who were too few to provide real security and yet numerous enough to exacerbate anti-Western hatred. The subsequent spread and horrifying brutality of ISIL was a direct result of this failure to achieve nation-building in post-war Iraq.

In spite of the liberation of Iraqi territory from ISIL in 2019, by 2021 there were still almost two million internally displaced Iraqis. A ISIL suicide bomb attack in Baghdad in January 2021 which killed 32 people shows just how much progress Iraq still needs to make towards a lasting peace.

Libya (2011)

In 2011, an uprising against the regime of President Gaddafi broke out in Libya. Civil war quickly ensued and, as government troops moved on the rebel stronghold of Benghazi, Gaddafi announced on radio: 'We are coming tonight. There won't be any mercy.'

As the bloodshed increased, UN Security Resolutions 1970 and 1973 authorised that 'all necessary measures' be taken to protect Libyan civilians. NATO took on responsibility for enforcing these resolutions and focused on destroying Gaddafi's air force and artillery. Deprived of air support and heavy weapons, Libyan government forces were pushed back. Gaddafi was killed and the Libyan National Transitional Council took control of the country. NATO Secretary-General Anders Fogh Rasmussen called the operation 'one of the most successful in NATO history' when he announced that the organisation was withdrawing its forces from Libya 'because our military job is now done'.

However, lessons learned in Iraq were not transferred to Libya. Although Rasmussen expressed confidence that Libyans could now control their own destiny without any further outside involvement, in reality the country was a mess of competing ethnic and clan rivalries, previously held together by Gaddafi's brute force. Lacking any history of liberal democracy, centralised government broke down, as armed gangs seized control of large parts of the country and terrorists extended their influence in the power vacuum.

In 2020, with France and Russia backing the self-proclaimed General Khalifa Hafta's Libyan Arab Armed Forces (LAAF) against the Turkish-supported Government of National Accord (GNA) it became even clearer just how unstable and ungovernable Libya had become as a result of military intervention. According to Human Rights Watch both the LAAF and the GNA have been responsible for appalling human rights abuses.

Relative success

Darfur (2007–21)

Darfur, western Sudan, has a black Muslim population that claims independence from Sudan. As separatist demands grew, the government sent in Arab militia, known as Janjaweed, who pillaged and murdered throughout the region. As early as 2004, US Secretary of State Colin Powell told the Senate Foreign Relations Committee that this systematic policy of violence against Darfuris amounted to 'genocide'. It is estimated that 300,000 people have died during the conflict and 2.5 million have been made homeless.

Demonstrating that it had yet to learn lessons from the Rwandan genocide, the UNSC dithered over whether the atrocities amounted to 'genocide' or 'war crimes'. China, in particular, was wary of condemning Sudan for genocide, since it had significant economic interest in the country.

Eventually, in 2007, when most of the killing had already taken place, Sudan's president, Omar al-Bashir, agreed to allow a UN/AU peacekeeping mission

(UNAMID) into Darfur. At its peak, UNAMID had 24,000 personnel in the field, but Darfur's size, remoteness and lack of basic infrastructure made its work extremely difficult. The UN also had to balance respect for Sudan's sovereignty with its commitment to protecting Darfuris from government-backed militias. However, the presence of UNAMID did provide more security than there would otherwise have been, especially in its protection of refugee camps. As UNAMID prepared to leave in 2021, many Darfuris were fearful that their security would now be in the hands of the Sudanese government.

Debate

Has the changing balance of world power undermined the likelihood of humanitarian interventions?

Yes

- Western powers have been most likely to launch humanitarian interventions. As their geostrategic influence declines so they will lack the confidence to launch humanitarian interventions.
- Emerging powers such as China, India and Russia have a Westphalian approach to state sovereignty and so are less likely to favour humanitarian interventions within a nation-state.
- The growing self-confidence of China and Russia on the UN Security Council makes it more likely that they will use their influence to oppose proposals for humanitarian interventions.
- Emerging powers are more likely to actively oppose Western humanitarian interventions as examples of outdated neocolonialism.

No

- The US still possesses overwhelming global military outreach and so could still launch a humanitarian intervention if it chose.
- The Biden administration is more favourable to a human rights-focused foreign policy than the Trump administration, suggesting that the US may still be prepared to provide global leadership for humanitarian intervention.
- The way in which the West's failure to intervene in Syria has led to a decline in its influence in the region may encourage a more assertive approach to humanitarian intervention in the future.
- The European Union is an emerging power and is committed to human rights protection in its near abroad.

⚙ Evaluation prompt: The way in which you respond to this question is likely to be informed by the extent to which the Biden administration (2021–) is prepared to provide renewed American leadership in global human rights-enforcement.

Topic link

Chapter 7 covers the way in which the global balance of power is changing.

What factors determine whether or not a humanitarian intervention is successful?

Feasibility

Although humanitarian interventions are motivated by the principle of 'saving strangers', they also need to have achievable objectives. Some crises may be so intractable and open-ended that, as Henry Kissinger put it, you 'may with a bleeding heart have to let it go':

- By the time the US intervened in Somalia, it was already a failed state and US forces were quickly dragged into clan fighting, which they did not understand.
- Tribal warfare in the Democratic Republic of the Congo (DRC) may have caused the deaths of 6 million people since the late 1990s. However, the DRC

is the size of western Europe, and the intricacies of tribal conflict are difficult for outsiders to comprehend. To try to resolve such conflicts may require a level of military commitment and nuanced local understanding that is realistically impossible to achieve.

- The logistical difficulties of imposing a Western-influenced democracy on a country as vast, inaccessible and culturally conservative as Afghanistan were never fully appreciated.
- The attempt by Russian forces to occupy such an alien country as Afghanistan in 1979 also ended in complete disaster. In such a country, NATO-led nation-building was never very likely to be successful and the Trump administration's decision to come to terms with the Taliban in 2020 is understandable.
- The intervention in Kosovo had a much stronger chance of success. NATO commanders estimated that Serb resistance against overwhelming air power could not last long, especially because, in 1999, Serbia could not rely upon support from a still-weakened Russia. Once Serbia agreed to withdraw its forces from Kosovo, large numbers of NATO troops were ready to be deployed in a nation-building operation under the authority of the UN.
- The British intervention in Sierra Leone also stood a good chance of success. Sierra Leone is easily accessible by both air and sea and is relatively small. The main threat to stability was from armed gangs, and there was a legitimate government to protect. In such circumstances, a targeted British response was able to quickly achieve its objectives.
- Côte d'Ivoire represented a similar scenario. Like Sierra Leone, it lies on the west African coast and so was easily accessible to the French military. Gbagbo's power basis was declining, the illegitimacy of his government was widely acknowledged and there was a rival government in waiting.

It is therefore very important that outsiders do not rush into interventions on the principle that 'something must be done'. Instead, there must be a cool and calm analysis of 'cost–benefit'. How likely is it that an intervention will achieve its objectives? How long will it take? What will the likely loss of life be? This may seem harsh, but ill-thought-out interventions have proven to stir up yet more violence by bringing another player to the field. Furthermore, new military and humanitarian equipment is introduced into conflict, which can too easily fall into the wrong hands, financing yet more fighting (this represented a serious problem during initial UN involvement in Bosnia). Governments therefore seriously need to consider a number of factors before taking action, or intervention can lead to catastrophic consequences.

A robust mandate and commitment to success

If an intervention is not mandated to exercise sufficient force, this will undermine its potential for success. If a military solution to a problem is going to be attempted, it is therefore vital that no half measures are taken and that the intervening powers are fully committed to success.

In 1957, Winston Churchill reflected that if he had been prime minister instead of Anthony Eden, he would never have intervened in Egypt to take over the Suez Canal. But if he had, he would not have left until he had secured total victory. It is this sort of mindset that is necessary if military success is to be achieved.

Other such failures of will include the following:

- UN peacekeeping operations in Bosnia in the early 1990s were hampered by restrictions on the offensive military action they were able to take. Unable to act proactively, forces could not repel aggression. Too often they seemed passive in the face of aggression, such as when UN peacekeepers surrendered the 'safe haven' of Srebrenica to Bosnian Serb forces, resulting in the massacre of 7,000 men and boys.

- In Rwanda, UN peacekeepers were only mandated to 'monitor' the situation. As a result, the tiny force was able to protect only a small number of Tutsis within the capital city, Kigali. Elsewhere, Hutu killing squads were able to act with absolute impunity.

- In both Afghanistan and Iraq the escalating loss of life for such little obvious progress led to massive military disengagement as the American public tired of such unprofitable wars. During the Obama administration, the US commitment to Afghanistan was scaled down from a peak of 100,000 personnel to just 8,400 by 2017. By 2020, President Trump had reduced the number of US troops in Iraq to only 5,000 with 4,000 in Afghanistan. Although the Biden administration optimistically put their faith in the Afghan army, the subsequent collapse of resistance to the Taliban in 2021 was hardly surprising.

- However, in East Timor an Australian-led UN force was able to operate under much more robust terms of engagement. Trained in counter-insurgency and prepared to engage in aggressive police actions against criminal gangs, it was able to establish the conditions necessary for free elections.

- In Bosnia in 1995, NATO was able to take offensive military action, which led to the signing of the Dayton Peace Accords. In 1999, NATO bombed Serbia when it was accused of ethnic cleansing in Kosovo. Initially, it seemed as though Serbia would not back down, but Tony Blair took the lead in unequivocally stating that NATO would do all that was necessary to achieve its humanitarian objectives.

Following twenty years of failed nation-building, western powers abandoned Afghanistan to the Taliban in 2021 in a hurried evacuation

A commitment to nation-building

If a humanitarian intervention is launched without a commitment to nation-building, it is unlikely to be successful. States that have been under the control of brutal dictators or those that have descended into anarchy will not possess the necessary political heritage or viable organs of government to ensure stability and the rule of law. If intervention takes place, it must be done with the proviso that without a subsequent commitment to nation-building, it may do more harm than good.

For example:

- In Bosnia and Kosovo, UN protectorates were established, which encouraged a return to political stability. The way in which NATO troops then took on a policing role in the Balkans further enabled normal life to resume – in Kosovo, there was one peacekeeper for every 48 people. However, in Afghanistan, there was one peacekeeper for every 5,000. Since large parts of the country were so inaccessible to patrols, it was impossible for them to engage in meaningful reconstruction.
- In East Timor, UN forces adopted an assertive policing role, which crushed the criminal gangs and militias that had threatened anarchy once Indonesian troops had withdrawn.
- The absence of NATO nation-building in Libya allowed the country to descend into anarchy. Western leaders like David Cameron and former French president Nicolas Sarkozy were too ready to take the credit for overthrowing President Gaddafi and saving Benghazi, without giving sufficient thought to what happened next. This was a massive mistake. Gaddafi had ruled Libya since 1969 and the country lacked any history of pluralist democracy. Freed from his ruthless dictatorship, Libyans lacked the necessary democratic traditions and tools to craft their own future.
- In Somalia, US troops, who had not been trained in principles of police work, were soon engulfed by the anarchic conditions they encountered. Unable to distinguish between rival clans and lacking a legitimate government to work with, there was no formal strategy for success and so, in 1994, President Clinton ordered their withdrawal.
- In Iraq, US forces only gradually appreciated the importance of attempting to nation-build and in the early stages of the occupation their lack of appreciation of Iraqi culture made it easy for them to be portrayed as an alien influence, so fuelling the insurgency.

At the time of the 2003 invasion of Iraq, the US secretary of state, Colin Powell, referred to the 'Pottery Barn' analogy. In this analogy, if you are driving along a US highway you may occasionally see a Pottery Barn (a US upscale home furnishings store) selling wares. The sign on the door may say 'If you break it, you own it.' This, according to Powell, is also true of interventions in another state. Once you do it, you 'own' that state. You can only properly withdraw once you have given it a newer and brighter future.

A legitimate government

The existence of a legitimate government can be vital to the success of interventionism. In the 1960s and 1970s the US-supported government of South Vietnam was brutal and corrupt. Its lack of moral legitimacy, therefore, significantly undermined US attempts to prop it up and in 1975, communists achieved the reunification of Vietnam.

In the 1950s, the British in Malaya were far better able to repel communist insurgency. The Malayan government was generally popular and the communist insurgents were mostly Chinese and therefore 'outsiders'.

The relative legitimacy of the government you seek to support can, therefore, help to define the success or failure of an intervention:

- In Libya, NATO forces withdrew before a new government was established, encouraging the slide into anarchy.
- Afghanistan and Iraq both had elected governments, but many questioned their legitimacy and their influence was often confined to loyalist areas.
- However, when the British intervened in Sierra Leone and the French in Côte d'Ivoire, these were not failing states. Instead, the British intervened on behalf of a popular and legitimate government and the French on behalf of Alassane Ouattara, who was both nationally and internationally recognised as the victor in the 2010 presidential election.

Conclusion

The circumstances of every humanitarian intervention are different and there is, unfortunately, no golden rule for success. In Afghanistan, NATO troops did try to engage in nation-building and police work. However, the huge difference in cultural traditions, and the inaccessibility and remoteness of so much of the country, made success impossible. In Somalia, there was a large troop commitment, but conditions were so anarchic that it could not stabilise the country. Rwanda was small enough for a speedy military intervention to have stopped the gangs that were killing their neighbours. However, the UNSC lacked the political will to take action in such a remote and little-known part of central Africa.

There are, however, certain questions that should be asked to determine whether or not a humanitarian intervention is likely to succeed. If all of these questions can be answered with a 'yes', intervention may be justified. However, if any produces a 'no', the likelihood of success may be too limited to merit action.

1 Are the objectives likely to be achievable?
2 Is there international, or at least regional, support for the intervention?
3 Will the likely number of casualties be acceptable?
4 Can sufficient military force be deployed to achieve success?
5 Is there a long-term commitment to subsequent nation-building?

Why has humanitarian intervention been selective?

Legitimacy

Those who launch interventions in the affairs of other states need to be acutely aware of the importance of being able to claim legitimacy for their actions. This is vital if international and regional support is going to be forthcoming, and will be especially important if the intervention is likely to be costly in terms of lives.

- In 1995, NATO mandated the military intervention in Bosnia. The legitimacy of the action was vital in forcing the Bosnian Serbs to accept defeat and agree to peace negotiations at Dayton, Ohio. In 1999, the bombing campaign in Serbia was also a legitimate action and so helped to persuade President Milošević to withdraw his forces from Kosovo.
- In 1999, the UN oversaw the referendum over East Timor's independence from Indonesia. When violence continued, the UNSC unanimously authorised an

Australian-led multinational force to intervene, using 'all necessary measures' to restore order.

● In 2011, the NATO intervention against President Gaddafi could claim legitimacy, since UN Resolution 1973 had demanded 'an immediate ceasefire in Libya, including an end to the current attacks against civilians, which it said might constitute crimes against humanity'. NATO could claim that it was fulfilling the terms of the resolution by intervening on the side of the rebels.

● In 2013, the AU endorsed the French intervention in Mali, providing it with legitimacy. Subsequently, AU forces have cooperated with the French in trying to stabilise the country and defeat terrorism.

If, however, there is doubt over the legality of action, the case for intervention is dramatically undermined. The support of other countries will be less forthcoming and the public less likely to endure losses if the action is legally uncertain. It may even be possible that illegitimacy would provoke military and economic counter-measures:

● Although the Syrian government of President Assad is accused of having committed grave human rights violations, it still claims legitimacy and in 2020 parties loyal to Assad won 177 out of 250 seats in the Syrian parliament. Although such figures are unlikely to be a true reflection of Syrian attitudes, there is no doubt that Assad does have widespread support in parts of his country, in addition to which Russia, China and Iran recognise the legitimacy of his government. In such circumstances, the legal, practical and long-term implications of Western intervention are so uncertain that inaction is preferable.

● In 2020 Myanmar was ordered by the ICJ to protect its Rohingya Muslims from genocide. The ICC has also launched an investigation into the plight of the Rohingyas. However, Myanmar, both before and after the military coup, refuses to accept that it has pursued genocidal policies. Backed by its powerful neighbour China on the UN security council, it is difficult to see how outside forces will practically be able to protect the Rohingyas from further persecution.

In spite of widespread evidence of human rights abuses, Russian and Iranian support has helped to maintain President Assad in power in Syria

Leadership

The leadership of powerful opinion-forming states is vital in determining whether or not intervention occurs. If a world leader is prepared to take the initiative, it is more likely that an international consensus for action can be established. Failing that, regional or individual action may still be taken if the government is convinced that there is an overwhelming moral or strategic case for intervention:

- In 1991, overwhelming evidence that Saddam Hussein was committing war crimes against the Kurds provoked the British, French and Americans to establish safe havens within northern Iraq. The UK prime minister, John Major, put forward the proposal to the UNSC, stating, with characteristic understatement, that, 'I think Saddam Hussein would be very ill-advised to attack a safe haven under United Nations protection.'
- In 1992, George H. W. Bush used his presidential authority to intervene in Somalia in response to harrowing images of starvation. Having already lost the 1992 election to Bill Clinton, Bush was determined to use his remaining time in office to 'save thousands of innocents'. He was conscious, too, that as the world's last remaining superpower, the US would have to take a lead 'as a catalyst for broader involvement of the community of nations'.
- In 1999, Tony Blair deployed his popularity and charisma to persuade NATO and EU leaders that they should intervene in Kosovo. When he received the Charlemagne Prize for European Achievement for his work in Northern Ireland, he utilised the moral authority with which this endowed him to make the case for war. Commenting on President Milošević's actions in Kosovo, Blair told his audience, 'He was determined to wipe a people from the face of his country. We are determined to stop him – and we will.'
- In 2013, France sent troops to Mali to stop 'an assault by terrorist elements coming from the north whose brutality and fanaticism is known across the world'. As a former French colony, Mali has a strong connection with France and France is acutely aware that its geo-strategic interests in the region would be disrupted by a rebel takeover of the government.

However, if there is a lack of global leadership, it will be difficult to mobilise either national or international support for intervention. The good intentions of some leaders can be thwarted by the intransigence of others on the UNSC, and if powerful states are not prepared to take action, humanitarian disasters can be quickly sidelined:

- In 1994, President Clinton, having withdrawn US forces from the quagmire of Somalia, was unprepared to take a leadership role when mass killing began in Rwanda. French president François Mitterrand was also slow to take action. For 20 years French diplomacy in central Africa had been to provide support to the pro-French Hutu government against the Tutsi Rwandan Patriotic Front, which they perceived as being pro-British. Even as the genocide was occurring, it was difficult to change this mindset.
- In 2013, before Russia militarily engaged in Syria, it did seem as though the West might launch air strikes against the Assad regime after it was accused of using chemical weapons, which are banned by international law. However, the British parliament rejected Prime Minister David Cameron's calls for a military intervention, which discouraged president Obama from reacting. The momentum was lost and the West did nothing.
- The Trump administration's (2017–21) ideology of 'America First' made it temperamentally unsuited to engage in idealistic humanitarian interventions in

which there was no obvious cost benefit to the US. In 2021, the US secretary of state Anthony Blinken said at his senate nomination hearing that the Biden administration 'wanted to place democracy and human rights back at the centre of American foreign policy'. However, the withdrawal of US forces from Afghanistan just eight months later suggests that US encouragement of human rights will stop far short of military intervention.

Public interest: the 'CNN factor'

If the media succeeds in sufficiently shocking the public, it may create the irresistible impulse that 'something must be done'. Equally, if the media pays insufficient attention to a crisis, politicians may lack the public impulse to get involved. However, media influence can be a double-edged sword. It was shocking images of starvation that provoked President George H. W. Bush to intervene in Somalia, but within a year, horrifying images of dead US servicemen being dragged naked through the streets of Mogadishu persuaded President Bill Clinton to withdraw US troops.

In what has become known as 'the CNN factor', the media has influenced other outcomes:

- In 1999, ethnic cleansing in Kosovo generated a great deal of media coverage, especially in the EU – the events were worryingly reminiscent of the conditions that had allowed the Srebrenica Massacre to take place. There was, therefore, significant public pressure for action.
- On the other hand, the media has focused less on atrocities occurring in the DRC and Myanmar, and so politicians have not faced the same pressure to take action.

National self-interest

Strategic considerations can determine whether or not a nation is prepared to take the initiative in pressing for action. A humanitarian disaster that impacts a state's own security will be especially pressing. If, however, the emergency is in a distant land and outside a state's sphere of influence, it may be safer to ignore it, especially if intervention could upset the regional, or even global, balance of power. As Henry Kissinger pointed out, a purely altruistic approach to international diplomacy would be disastrous, since would it really be wise to support human rights activists campaigning for the overthrow of a close ally?

Strategic considerations have played a significant role in several recent crises:

- During the Kosovo crisis, one of the most powerful arguments that politicians, like Tony Blair, could use was that if the West did not intervene, the conflict might spread throughout the Balkans, potentially threatening the peace and stability of the EU itself.
- In 2000, Australian Prime Minister John Howard committed Australian troops to leading the UN intervention in East Timor because the developing refugee crisis would have soon threatened northern Australia.
- Neo-conservatives (those politicians with an aggressively liberal interventionist approach to global affairs) within the George W. Bush administration, such as Donald Rumsfeld and Dick Cheney, regarded the 9/11 terror attacks as an opportunity to advance US interests in the middle east by making Iraq part of an 'Axis of Evil', which had to be defeated as part of the War on Terror.
- Since 2013, the French military has, at the request of the Malian government, been combating an Islamist insurgency in the country. Both the Islamist insurgents and

Mali's military have been accused of committing human rights abuses. However, France has kept a military presence in Mali in order to stop it from becoming ungovernable and a refuge for terrorists who could then threaten Europe. As President Macron has put it, 'France isn't there with neocolonial, imperialist aims or with economic goals. We're there for the collective security of the region and ours'.

If, on the other hand, the conflict – however bloody – does not directly affect the interests of the great powers or intervention is likely to provoke a clash on the UN security council then action is much less likely.

- The civil war in the DRC pose no threat to global stability, and so there is much less incentive to become more fully involved.
- The Saudi Arabian-led military intervention in Yemen against the Houthi rebels has resulted in large number of civilian casualties mostly from air strikes. However, Yemen is within Saudi Arabia's regional zone of influence and her close relations with Western powers, Russia and China would makes a humanitarian intervention in the conflict very difficult to achieve.
- In Syria, the West has been unwilling to challenge President Assad. Attempts to overthrow him could provoke conflict with Russia and, were Assad to be removed, there is no certainty that the terrorist threat to the West would be reduced. It might even be increased. In such circumstances, the most sensible policy has so far been to steer clear of unnecessary risks.

Likelihood of success

Before intervening in the internal affairs of another state, any government will have to weigh up the likely consequences of action or inaction. One may want to intervene in a crisis but how likely is it that an intervention will save lives? Governments need to make tough decisions based upon a realistic assessment of numbers of troops required to get the job done, the international, or at least regional, support base for intervention and the risk of potentially widening the conflict. Based upon these considerations, one can see why action was taken in:

- East Timor (1999)
- Sierra Leone (2000)
- Côte d'Ivoire (2011)
- Libya (2011)
- Mali (2013)

Equally, one can appreciate why, scarred by Afghanistan and Iraq, Western powers have been much less prepared to involve themselves in other protracted conflicts, where the chance of achieving realistic success is much less. Such failures to intervene effectively include:

- DRC
- Syria
- Myanmar
- Yemen.

Does Western hypocrisy undermine the principle of humanitarian intervention?

The US promotes its commitment to being a 'beacon' of human rights in a world in which ruthless rulers can too often trample upon the rights of their people.

During the Cold War, President Ronald Reagan brilliantly articulated this concept of 'American exceptionalism', contrasting the liberties of Americans with the repression that existed under communism. So effective was Reagan that he helped to undermine the alternative 'narrative' of communism, which contributed to the collapse of communism in eastern Europe.

However, in *The Clash of Civilizations*, Samuel Huntington noted that 'hypocrisy and double standards are the price of universalist pretensions'. Therefore, although powerful countries like the US claim the moral high ground, the decisions that their governments take are much more pragmatic. Human rights abuses are condemned in some parts of the world but not in others. President Franklin D. Roosevelt was once asked how the US could condone the abuses being carried out by Nicaraguan president Anastasio Somoza García, to which he, allegedly, replied: 'He's a bitch, but he's our son of a bitch.'

Case study

China and the Uighur Muslims

An estimated 11 million Uighur Muslims live in Xinjiang province. The Chinese government regards them as a threat to the People's Republic. In 2017, Uighur Muslims were forbidden from growing long beards and Uighur women from wearing veils. Since 2017, at least one million Uighur Muslims have also been interned in detention camps in Xinjiang province. Having denied the existence of these camps, the Chinese government now accepts that they are being used for 're-education' purposes.

In 2019, 22, mostly Western, countries wrote to the UN Human Rights Council expressing their deep concern about what was happening to the Uighur Muslims. Days later, 37 other countries wrote to the UN Human Rights Council stating their support for China's 'remarkable achievements in the field of human rights'.

In 2021, Antony Blinken, President Biden's secretary of state, stated that 'The forcing of men, women and children into concentration camps; trying to, in effect, re-educate them to be adherents to the ideology of the Chinese Communist Party, all of that speaks to an effort to commit genocide.' When reports of systematic rape in detention camps reached the West, the US state department went further stating that, 'these atrocities shock the conscience and must be met with serious consequences'.

Activity

Read the case study and answer the following questions.
1 Research the current situation of the Uighur Muslims.
2 How convincing is China's defence that this is an internal issue of the People's Republic which has nothing to do with the international community?
3 Is there anything realistic that liberal internationalists can do to improve the plight of the Uighur Muslims?

Double standards

Accusations of double standards can be made about liberal interventionism. Too often when a humanitarian intervention takes place, it masks self-interest. Critics of interventionism argue that Western democracies have carefully selected those interventions that are most likely to be to their strategic and economic advantage:

- During the 1990s, interventions in Bosnia and Kosovo undermined Serbia, which is a long-time Slavic and Orthodox ally of Russia. Critics claim that by challenging Serbian influence in the region, it could be replaced with the economic and political influence of the EU.

- By intervening in Afghanistan in 2001, the US was primarily concerned with destroying al-Qaeda. If 9/11 had not occurred, it is highly unlikely that Western powers would have intervened in Afghanistan, even though the Taliban's human rights abuses were already widely known.
- Geostrategic interests motivated the 2003 invasion of Iraq. Following his invasion of Kuwait in August 1990, Saddam Hussein was perceived to be a threat to regional stability and so it was to the US and its allies' advantage to replace him with a government that was more conducive to Western economic and political interests. In the 1980s, during the Iran/Iraq War, however, the US had economically supported Saddam because he was then perceived to be a bulwark against the greater threat of Iran. Indeed, one of the worst atrocities the Saddam regime committed occurred in 1988, when his forces launched a chemical gas attack on the Kurdish town of Halabja, killing up to 5,000 people. At this point Saddam still enjoyed US support. He only irrevocably lost it when he invaded Kuwait in 1990, fatally misjudging the US reaction.

Elsewhere in the world, many other governments have been free to commit war crimes, ethnic cleansing, mass killings and possibly even genocide without being held accountable for their actions. Critics of humanitarian intervention argue that by ignoring such crimes, the moral basis of humanitarian intervention is fatally undermined:

- As a member of the UNSC and the world's largest nuclear weapons power, Russia has, unsurprisingly, not been held accountable for its actions. For example, Russia's repression of Chechen separatism in the 1990s may have caused the deaths of thousands of civilians. Prior to its assault on the Chechen capital, Grozny, in 1999–2000, the Russian military announced that 'persons who stay in the city will be considered terrorists and bandits and will be destroyed by artillery and aviation. There will be no further negotiations.' The city was then razed, making it, according to the UN, the most destroyed city on Earth.
- In 2020, a UN report also held Russia accountable for 'indiscriminate attacks in civilian areas' in Syria. Save the Children has also condemned the Syrian government's use of cluster bombs, which are banned by international law. However, given Russia's global influence, it is hard to see under what circumstances the West will hold either Russia or its ally Syria fully accountable for their actions.
- Turkey has also been accused of committing crimes against humanity against the Kurds in Idlib, a province of Syria which it invaded in 2018. However, as a member of NATO and a powerful geostrategic influence in the region, Turkey has been able to ignore any international criticism.

It would be naïve to suggest that geostrategic interests do not influence intervention. Equally, it would be cynical to suggest that they are simply a cover for the self-interest of powerful states. US intervention in Somalia, although flawed, was carried out with the best of intentions. Intervention in Sierra Leone did nothing to advance UK interests, and appalling human rights violations were taking place in the Balkans during the 1990s.

Of course, there have also been many occasions when appalling crimes have been ignored. The Rwandan genocide, mass killing in Darfur, the brutal land nationalisation programme in Zimbabwe and ongoing tribal warfare in the DRC have all attracted too little global condemnation. Human rights abuses by Russia in Chechnya and, according to Human Rights Watch, now in Syria have also gone unpunished. There is considerable concern over how China treats its ethnic and religious minorities.

However, international politics is the study of the world as it is, rather than how we would like it to be. The West may not always like what China and Russia do, but there is no way that military action is going to make them change their ways. Indeed, a US intervention against Russian and Syrian forces during the bombing of Eastern Aleppo could have had incalculable consequences for world peace. The US itself is hardly blameless – as Guantánamo Bay and waterboarding prove – when it comes to human rights violations. Terrible things occur in countries across the world, but if the government claims legitimacy would a Western intervention really make things better? Might it actually make things considerably worse and, given recent failures, would there be the necessary public support for a costly and bloody intervention with no obvious end in sight?

It would be glib to suggest that double standards wholly compromise humanitarian intervention – politicians are rarely either totally selfish or fully altruistic. This means that some horrendous crimes will be ignored, but that is not to say that others will go unpunished. As former UK foreign secretary Douglas Hurd put it, 'We should do good where we can, but not pretend that we can do good everywhere.' In other words, an ethical foreign policy will always be open to the charge of hypocrisy. That, however, is hardly a sufficient reason to totally abandon the principle.

Debate

Does the responsibility to protect outweigh state sovereignty?

Yes

- Liberals argue that there is a 'moral responsibility' to 'save strangers'. If nation-states commit atrocities against their own people, the international community should intervene to save lives.
- State sovereignty is 'conditional' – it brings with it rights but also responsibilities. A state that engages in widespread killing of its own citizens has, therefore, forfeited its sovereignty. The acknowledgement of this principle will, therefore, encourage 'responsible' sovereignty.
- If nation-states are free to abuse their own people, this encourages other would-be despots to act with impunity, leading to further violence.
- Failures to intervene have allowed appalling, but also avoidable, losses of life to occur (e.g. Darfur, Libya, Rwanda, Syria).
- Regional and global stability are threatened if mass murder and human rights abuses are not punished. The migrant crisis caused by the Syrian civil war has threatened European stability. By not intervening in Libya and by withdrawing forces from Iraq, we have created the conditions for the rise of terrorism.

No

- Westphalian principles of state sovereignty provide the foundations for global stability. Realists argue that the only justification for military action against another state is self-defence.
- According to offensive realists, states are 'power-maximisers' and, therefore, humanitarian intervention can be used as an excuse to advance strategic self-interest.
- Russia justified its war with Georgia in 2008 on the grounds that it was abusing the rights of people in the province of South Ossetia. Claims that the ethnic Russians' rights are being 'abused' could subsequently be used by Russia to justify intervening in neighbouring states for geostrategic advantage.
- The way in which humanitarian intervention can be used as a pretext for strategic self-interest could risk regional and even global war. Western intervention against President Assad would risk provoking war with his ally, Russia.
- States do not have the 'right' to risk the lives of their own citizens in conflicts that do not concern themselves.

- Enlightened self-interest can, therefore, inform humanitarian intervention. By not punishing evildoers, wickedness is legitimised and crises may then spill over, threatening the peace of other regions.
- Destabilising potential of 'zones of conflict' can only be reduced if military action is promptly taken to stop humanitarian crises spiralling out of control, engulfing a region and threatening further conflict. The French intervention in Mali is designed to protect human rights, but also to stop terrorism from spreading through north Africa, so threatening Europe.

- Humanitarian missions can raise false expectations and make the situation worse. In Somalia and Bosnia, warring factions often hijacked UN aid convoys, and post-Gaddafi Libya is ungovernable. Western intervention in Iraq has increased the terrorist threat in the middle east.
- The principle of humanitarian intervention is undermined by being selective. The justification for interventions in Bosnia and Kosovo is therefore undermined by failures to act in Rwanda, Syria or Myanmar.

Evaluation prompt: How you respond to this question will tell a lot about whether you are a liberal or a realist in global relations. Think, too, about the extent to which nation-states should be prepared to take risks in order to achieve a global standard of human rights protection.

The migrant crisis demonstrates the ongoing clash between liberal good intentions and the realist self-interest of nation states

Case study

New Wars

During the 1990s, partly in response to the Balkans conflict, the political scientist Mary Kaldor developed her 'New War' thesis. According to Kaldor, wars between states were becoming less likely. However, wars within failed or failing states would become more prevalent, with civilians finding themselves increasingly on the front line as armed militias and paramilitaries struggled for control.

→

In this sort of new environment, the traditional role of the military would have to change – no longer would military forces primarily be deployed to win battles, but troops should also be trained for police work in unstable political environments. In order to achieve successful nation-building, soldiers would have to deploy great sensitivity and restraint in highly charged environments – the excessive use of force, xenophobia, cultural arrogance or partisanship could be as devastating as losing a battle. Military intervention could no longer solely be used to defeat an adversary and secure a peace treaty. Instead, initial military engagements would become the precursor to a potentially long drawn-out occupation based on achieving an inclusive settlement.

The US has, however, been slow to adapt to these principles. In the aftermath of the Iraq War, former US defence secretary Donald Rumsfeld cautioned that 'we don't do nation-building'. The subsequent rounding up of suspects in Iraq, while failing to distinguish between combatants and civilians, and deploying soldiers in full combat gear seemed to confirm this. This has consequently created huge resentment, which has contributed to the rise of the militant group ISIL. Similarly, in Afghanistan, so great was the gap in cultural understanding between the occupying Western forces and the Afghans that it often proved impossible to establish a meaningful dialogue between the two. The difficulty, too, in providing security in such a massive country with limited military forces and no knowledge of tribal and ethnic loyalties has further undermined the potential for success.

Activity

Read the case study and answer the following questions.

1. Research intervening powers' military capability and tactics in Afghanistan, Bosnia, East Timor, Iraq, Kosovo, Sierra Leone, Libya and Mali.
2. How did they impact the success or failure of the mission?
3. Do you agree that without a commitment to nation-building humanitarian interventions are best avoided? Explain your answer fully.

What you should know

Having read this chapter you should have knowledge and understanding of the following:

→ Diverse cultural traditions possess very different approaches to the nature of human rights. We therefore need to be careful not to refer to 'human rights' as though everyone shares the same understanding of what we mean.
→ Asian and Muslim interpretations of human rights differ considerably from Western interpretations, and it is important not to presuppose that one standard of human rights is necessarily superior to another.
→ There are certain basic standards of human rights that all cultures can accept, for example the Four Freedoms, to which the Universal Declaration of Human Rights gives formal expression. However, for most of the Cold War, superpower rivalry curtailed their influence.
→ The concept of 'human rights' as a guide to foreign policy became more significant at the end of the Cold War. Liberals hoped this new period of calm would, at last, enable the UN to live up to the idealistic claims of its charter.
→ Adherence to the guiding principles of the UDHR, it was hoped, would achieve a new centrality in global affairs. George H. W. Bush's declaration of a 'New World Order' seemed to herald a brighter future. Tony Blair, Bill Clinton and Kofi Annan all imagined a world in which global standards of justice would outlaw crimes against humanity, genocide and ethnic cleansing.

→ Interventions in the Balkans, East Timor and Sierra Leone seemed to provide a template for a more stable and morally focused world order. The establishment of UN tribunals, the opening of the ICC and the publication of the Responsibility to Protect indicated that if governments chose to act in defiance of international moral standards, they would now be held accountable for their actions.
→ History, however, has not turned out as we expected. The bold hope of liberals, that there is such a thing as a global community, motivated by the same respect for human rights, soon proved to be hopelessly optimistic.
→ Russia's regaining of international self-confidence and China's growing assertiveness on the UN Security Council have further challenged the liberal dream of shared values and international cooperation. The disastrous failure to rebuild Libya after Gaddafi's downfall and the West's impotence in the face of the mounting Syrian death toll further demonstrate that the liberal impulse that Tony Blair had so memorably voiced is being challenged in this new, more realist world order.
→ Even during the optimism of the 1990s, the US pulled out of Somalia and stood by as Rwanda slid into the abyss, and in the early 2000s provided little leadership over Darfur. Failures to achieve US objectives in Afghanistan and Iraq further discredited interventionism in the White House.
→ Russia's regaining of international self-confidence and China's growing assertiveness on the UN Security Council

→

have further challenged the liberal dream of shared values and international cooperation. The disastrous failure to rebuild Libya after Gaddafi's downfall and the West's impotence in the face of the mounting Syrian death toll further demonstrate that the liberal impulse that Tony Blair had so memorably voiced is being challenged in this new, more realist world order.

→ By 2021, the ICC had achieved only eight convictions, one of which was overturned on appeal. Rather than expanding its remit, its future looks bleak, as Burundi and The Philippines withdrew from the jurisdiction of the court. This is not to say that human rights and humanitarian intervention are now only of historical interest. Interventionism has saved many lives and international courts and tribunals have punished a number of perpetrators of wicked crimes.

→ The work of the ICC and the European Court of Human Rights will continue and states will keep on weighing up the consequences of intervention in humanitarian disasters.

→ We can be certain that the questions raised in this chapter will remain fundamental to our understanding of global politics, and that the way in which they are answered will continue to surprise us.

Further reading

Human Rights Watch: **www.hrw.org**
Hurd, D. & Young, E. (2011) *Choose Your Weapons*. Weidenfeld & Nicolson.
Jefferies, J. (2019) 'The complexities of human rights', *Politics Review*, Vol. 29, September.
Power, S. (2009) *Chasing the Flame*. Penguin.
Power, S. (2010) *A Problem from Hell: America and the Age of Genocide*. Flamingo.
Sands, P. (2016) *East West Street*. Weidenfeld and Nicolson.
Weiss, T. (2016) *Humanitarian Intervention* (3rd edition). Polity Press.

Practice questions

Section A

1 Examine why cultural differences and state sovereignty make it difficult to establish a universal standard of human rights. *[12 marks]*

2 Examine the main criticisms of the International Court of Justice (ICJ/World Court) and the International Criminal Court (ICC). *[12 marks]*

3 Examine the main successes and failures of UN tribunals in encouraging a universal standard of human rights. *[12 marks]*

4 Examine why some humanitarian interventions are successful and some humanitarian interventions are unsuccessful. *[12 marks]*

5 Examine why Western powers have generally favoured the principle of humanitarian intervention more than non-Western powers. *[12 marks]*

Section C

1 Evaluate the extent to which the enforcement of an international standard of human rights protection has been made more or less effective by globalisation. *[30 marks]*

2 Evaluate the extent to which NGOs have done more than the International Criminal Court to encourage greater international respect for human rights protection. *[30 marks]*

3 Evaluate the extent which the rise of emerging powers is making attempts to establish a universal standard of human rights impossible. *[30 marks]*

4 Evaluate the extent to which the success of a humanitarian intervention depends most upon international support. *[30 marks]*

5 Evaluate the extent which humanitarian interventions in sovereign states have done more to advance human rights than the work of United Nations aid agencies. *[30 marks]*

6 Global governance: environmental

Learning outcomes

By the end of the chapter you should understand:

→ the environmental challenges facing the global commons, including the threat and potential impact of climate change

→ how to evaluate the effectiveness of environmental global governance in attempting to protect the global commons (through the United Nations Framework Convention on Climate Change and the Intergovernmental Panel on Climate Change)

→ how to evaluate different views on how to tackle environmental issues, and the obstacles to international cooperation and agreement

→ how to evaluate the strengths and weaknesses of major international agreements on climate change, including the obstacles to international cooperation and agreement

→ the role and significance of global civil society and non-state actors in addressing and resolving global environmental challenges

Getting you started

Climate emergency. These words entered the *Oxford English Dictionary* in 2019 and saw their use increase by 10,000% in that year alone. The UK Parliament declared a climate emergency without even needing to count MPs' votes. Thousands of pupils left their classrooms in over a hundred countries, going on strike in protest at their leaders' lack of action. And a 15-year-old Swedish girl, Greta Thunberg, sailed across the Atlantic to address the United Nations, pleading with countries to do more.

The extent of the challenge and degradation to our natural environment is growing fast – and faster than the global political response can keep up with. Addressing the UN Security Council in 2021 – the first time that the body normally reserved for peace and conflict issues had discussed the environment – Sir David Attenborough said that it was already too late to stop climate change. 'If we continue on our current path,' he said, 'we will face the collapse of everything that gives us our security: food production, access to fresh water, habitable ambient temperature, and ocean food chains.'

The United Nations has warned that the global average temperature has reached 1.1°C above the pre-industrial period, with UN scientists urging countries to limit global temperature rises to below 1.5°C. The window of opportunity for meaningful action is closing rapidly.

International summits and agreements have raised much hope in recent years, with the Paris Agreement seeing the largest number of countries pledging to cut emissions. But there is a recurring problem of the global governance efforts being slow and limited in their ambitions and not tough enough given the scale of the challenge. Campaign groups such as Greenpeace and Extinction Rebellion have grown in influence but are still, ultimately, unable to secure decisive action from the UK government.

Climate change is the ultimate collective action problem. It is not caused by one state alone, it does not impact one state alone and it cannot be solved by one state alone. This chapter explains the international attempts to tackle climate change at a global level: first, to agree the extent and existence of a problem and, second, to tackle it fairly and effectively.

Why is there a need for environmental global governance?

Global governance is the process by which nation-states cooperate with each other and with non-state actors in order to try to resolve collective dilemmas. As with any area of global governance, it is necessary to understand why a global governance response to environmental challenges is required and the range of issues involved. What environmental challenges does the world face that impact many states and cannot be solved by one state alone?

- **Climate change:** how to limit global temperature rises and reduce the impacts, including extreme weather events and rising sea levels.
- **Deforestation:** reducing the destruction of forests which, if destroyed, add to carbon emissions and, if preserved, can help to mitigate carbon emissions by absorbing carbon dioxide and releasing oxygen.
- **Protecting the marine environment:** there is a need to reduce pollution in our seas, from plastics to oil drilling and spills, as well as preventing over-fishing.
- **Global energy:** as a planet, there is a need to transition to renewable energy sources and reduce reliance on fossil fuels (especially coal).
- **Protecting biodiversity:** preserving the variety of plant, bacteria and animal life across the globe, ensuring the long-term survival of endangered species.

Environmental challenges are perhaps unique as a collective action problem, in that:

- every state contributes in some way, small or large, to the causes of these challenges
- every state is affected in some way, small or large, by these challenges
- every state can have an impact, small or large, in solving these challenges
- many of the resources and environments that require protection (for example, the oceans or atmosphere) are not governed by one state alone, and therefore need global governance to bring organisation and authority to these challenges

This is different to other collective action problems, such as global terrorism or the international drug trade, which may pose a large threat to some states but little or no threat to others. All states are affected in some way by environmental challenges. The widespread impact of industrialisation has seen to this, with all developed and most developing states contributing to global pollution.

To tackle environmental challenges effectively, states need to agree to international standards and laws that govern how they develop and limit their impact on the environment. If no attempts were made to make international laws to protect the environment, states would be left to their own good or bad intentions.

In addition, much of the harm caused to the environment is a result of activities aimed to generate economic development (for example, coal-fired power stations providing the energy for factories, which in turn create national wealth and prosperity). Genuinely collective action – with all states making the necessary choices and investments – is needed to reassure states that they are not disadvantaging themselves by acting alone to reduce their impact on the environment.

Just as universal human rights are of little value internationally if states do not agree to international law, so international efforts to protect the environment are likely to be fruitless without effective environmental global governance. In an essentially anarchical society (see page 6), the same difficulties of forcing states to take action come into play:

- States need a framework within which they can agree that there is a problem and how serious that problem is. With respect to the environment, this has been especially important in terms of agreeing that climate change does exist, in the face of temptation for some states to deny its existence (see page 209). It requires independent scientific advice, which provides a collective view that all states can equally trust.
- States need forums to discuss the solutions that could make a difference, to resolve disputes over how to act and to seek agreement on areas of common ground. States will not accept a higher authority forcing decisions or laws upon them, so discussion and negotiation are essential. Dedicated forums and summits, such as the 2015 Paris Summit, are required to enable states to focus on environmental issues in sufficient detail.
- States need international laws and treaties to be agreed so that they can be confident that other states (and non-state actors) are taking action and are held accountable for the promises they have made. This enables states to legitimise their actions and for this to be, potentially, meaningful.

Protecting the global commons

Clearly, if one state chooses to pollute the environment, this will have an impact both within and beyond its borders. Pollutants will most affect a state's immediate neighbours, but they may also have a global impact, certainly when combined with the pollution of other states. For example, China and the US combined account for 40% of the world's carbon emissions. Some scientists have attributed pollution in China as the cause of intensifying storms over the Pacific Ocean, which have impacted weather systems in North America.

This principle of a shared global environment that can be both harmed and protected by states' individual and collective actions is known as the **global commons**. It refers to the natural environment that is shared between nation-states. The UN defines the global commons as 'resources or areas that lie outside the political reach of any one nation-state'. This includes the following:

- **The high seas:** the world's oceans are increasingly vulnerable to the impact of waste and chemical pollution from both state and non-state actors. British Petroleum's (BP) Deepwater Horizon oil spill in 2010 was the world's worst oil disaster and caused widespread environmental damage to the Gulf of Mexico, affecting 176,000 square kilometres of ocean. Up to 12 million tonnes of plastic waste reach the world's oceans each year. Some estimates suggest that by 2050, the plastic in the ocean could weigh more than the fish that reside there.
- **The atmosphere:** environmental global governance has focused on the atmosphere since the early 1990s, when the impact of greenhouse gases on accelerating climate change gained prominence. Former UN secretary-general Ban Ki-moon called climate change the 'major, overriding environmental

Topic link

The power of nation states and the difficulty in forcing them to commit to global governance initiatives is explored in Chapters 1 and 2.

Key term

Global commons The global resources and environment that are shared among nation-states, as no government or sovereign state owns them. These include the atmosphere, oceans, polar regions and outer space.

issue of our time'. Industrial pollution from the burning of fossil fuels remains the major cause of air pollution, but emissions from aeroplanes, car exhausts and household fuel cooking also make a significant contribution. The UN Environment Programme (UNEP) highlights both the short-term impact (with 6.5 million deaths each year from air pollution) and long-term impact (changing weather patterns threatening food production and rising sea levels) of this issue.

- **The polar regions:** both the Arctic and Antarctic have huge economic potential in terms of minerals and gas resources. Both are also key indicators for scientists of the effects of climate change. In 1959, 12 states signed the Antarctic Treaty, which protects Antarctica as a region for scientific research only, and bans military activity or resource extraction. Protection of the Arctic regions is less clear, however. Oil and gas production in the Arctic is on the increase, with Russia relying on the region for nearly 20% of its supplies. The US Department of Energy estimates that 13% of the world's undiscovered oil reserves and 30% of undiscovered gas reserves are under the Arctic.

- **Outer space:** with many international actors now owning active space stations and satellites, outer space has become increasingly crowded. In 2013, the US space agency NASA estimated that there were as much as 6,000 tonnes of human-generated space debris orbiting the Earth (for example, pieces of defunct satellites or spacecraft). There is no international law governing this shared space.

Certain Arctic sea regions and passages are under dispute

There are several international laws designed to protect the global commons:

- **The UN Convention on the Law of the Sea (UNCLOS):** includes laws that prevent the pollution of seas, as well as setting out the limits of states' territorial waters. UNCLOS makes it clear that states have a responsibility to prevent pollution of their own territorial waters that would, in turn, pollute international waters.
- **The Antarctic Treaty System:** sets out various environmental protections for the region, including dedicating Antarctica solely to scientific research.
- **The UN Framework Convention on Climate Change (UNFCCC):** established a process through which international treaties have been agreed to protect the atmosphere (see page 221).

The tragedy of the commons

It is easy to agree on and identify examples of pollution of, for example, the atmosphere or the oceans, which have a harmful impact on our shared environment. It is also easy, in principle, to identify that resources such as the oceans, atmosphere, polar regions and space are beyond the authority of any single nation-state and therefore are shared between states. What is harder, in global politics, is for states to avoid competing over these supposedly shared resources, or to prevent states from harming these shared resources in the pursuit of their own national interest.

The challenge of protecting the global commons is known as the **tragedy of the commons**. At the most pessimistic analysis, the global commons is doomed to remain something that states harm and compete for through their own self-interest, rather than protect and nurture as shared goals.

This theory was first put forward by American ecologist Garrett Hardin in his 1968 essay 'The Tragedy of the Commons'. He brought the paradox to life by imagining the story of a pasture open to any farmer to graze their herd. Every farmer would want to keep as many cattle as possible on the pasture. Every farmer would calculate that increasing the number of their cattle by just one would add to their own financial return, but would be unlikely on its own to reduce or harm the resources available. However, if every farmer makes the same calculation, the tragedy emerges in which resources become inevitably depleted as more and more cattle are added to the pasture. As a result, the immediate gain to the farmers sets them on a path to fatally damaged and insufficient resources which will run out.

In global politics, the tragedy of the commons can be seen in several ways:

- States are competing for economic power and resources, and this extends to natural resources. States are not acting in isolation from each other. A state governed on realist lines will not want to slow its economic development by switching from easily exploited fossil fuels to less immediately available renewable energy which needs new investment to put in place.
- States act with realist motivations in efforts to seek to protect and maximise their own national interest. This might mean that a state will refuse to sign up to international emissions targets if it believes that doing so will be expensive or make its national economic output uncompetitive.
- Individual states only tend to see and take responsibility for their own actions, rather than those taken collectively. Avoiding the tragedy of the commons requires awareness of the collective impacts of many states, which can only be highlighted and coordinated through international organisations and non-governmental organisations.
- Realist-minded states have greater motivation to satisfy their own national interest and population, as opposed to the international interest and community.
- Rapid population growth, with the UN estimating that the world's population will grow by 2 billion in the next 30 years, only exacerbates the challenges of the tragedy of the commons.

The tragedy of the commons suggests that states' national interests and international environmental interests rarely align with one another. There are, however, increasing signs that things are changing, since sometimes what is harmful at an international level is also harmful at a national level:

- The impacts of high levels of pollution are felt most significantly at the local and national level. In India and China, air pollution accounts for around 1 million

> ## Key term
>
> **Tragedy of the commons**
> The challenge that, in a system of global politics dominated by selfish national interest and competition for economic power and natural resources, states will be motivated to use and even harm the global commons to advance their own interests, rather than working together to protect these shared resources and environments.

deaths per year in each country. The immediate impacts of air pollution have become a national and local issue, with protests increasingly seen in many states.

● In recent climate change agreements, there have been efforts to ensure that states at different levels of development take equal steps on the road to change. For example, the 2015 Paris climate change agreement outlined that developing states would receive financial assistance to help them move towards using cleaner sources of energy.

● There is increasing acceptance that climate change brings with it a risk of natural disasters, such as flooding or drought, which have an immediate impact on human security and food production. India is particularly vulnerable to the impacts of climate change and, in 2016, it agreed to ratify the Paris Agreement.

Extremely high levels of pollution in Chinese cities were a key factor in the country accepting international climate change agreements

What is climate change?

Environmental global governance has focused in recent decades on reducing the harmful impact of human activity and pollution in the Earth's atmosphere. In the 1980s, scientists established that the Earth's greenhouse gases (the natural gases that keep the Earth warm to enable it to sustain life) were increasing rapidly to harmful levels, and by as much as 35%. This increase in greenhouse gases would see a dangerous rise in global temperatures, warming the planet excessively. This is known as climate change or global warming.

Scientists have gradually concluded with increasingly convincing evidence that human activity has caused the increase in greenhouse gases. The key changes have been growing emissions of carbon dioxide (responsible for approximately 63% of global warming) and methane (responsible for approximately 19% of global warming and more powerful in their warming effect than carbon dioxide). Carbon emissions are caused by the increased burning of fossil fuels, such as oil and coal, as well as deforestation leading to fewer trees absorbing carbon dioxide from the atmosphere. Methane emissions are caused predominantly through agriculture in grazing cattle and flooded rice fields.

The Intergovernmental Panel on Climate Change (see page 223) estimates that global temperatures have risen by 1°C compared with pre-industrial levels. The IPCC assessment is that temperatures will continue to rise by approximately 0.1°C to 0.3°C every decade. Beyond these global averages, it is estimated that some regions have seen higher and faster temperature rises.

There has been growing agreement among world leaders as to the existence of climate change, and that it poses a threat to human society at both national and global levels. By 2016, the world's top three 'super-polluters' (China, India and the US) had all signed the Paris Agreement, even if they had not yet ratified it (see page 233). However, early in his presidency Donald Trump confirmed that the US would withdraw from the Paris Agreement, which had been signed by President Obama. This was quickly reversed by President Biden as one of his first presidential executive orders on the day of his inauguration.

The harmful effects of climate change include the following:

- Rising sea levels could see some nation-states disappear entirely (which has led to small island states in the Atlantic, Indian and Pacific oceans forming their own IGO – the Alliance of Small Island States – to make their case), and states and cities with vulnerable coastlines come under threat. Analysis by the UN suggests that sea levels could rise by as much as 60cm by the end of this century.
- There could be an increase in global poverty and a decrease in global food security, caused by drought and lack of predictability of agricultural production. There is also an increased risk of natural disasters occurring with greater frequency and impact. The impact of natural disasters in poor countries has been estimated as 20–30 times larger than in industrialised countries. The UN reported that, so far this century, extreme weather events had claimed 1.2 million lives and caused economic losses of nearly $3 trillion.
- UN Secretary-General António Guterres has made the link between climate change and conflict, with 70% of the most climate vulnerable countries also among the most politically and economically fragile. There is scope for conflict to worsen with increased poverty and conflict over scarce resources such as food and water. The scope for heightened tensions between India and Pakistan over Himalayan water supplies for their rapidly expanding populations is a particularly worrying potential flashpoint.

What can be done to reduce climate change?

The solutions to climate change are focused on three related areas.

1 **Bringing individual countries' emissions to 'net zero'.** The global debate is steadily moving away from merely reducing carbon emissions to more ambitious proposals to de-carbonise. While carbon emissions will not be eliminated entirely in this scenario, a 'net zero' pledge is one where emissions produced (for example, through polluting factories or air travel) will all be both reduced and removed

from the atmosphere (through 'carbon sinks', such as through planting trees which absorb carbon and release oxygen, making the net effect of combining this with reducing deforestation an especially important route to net zero). The focus of the UN is now on persuading more and more countries to pledge to become 'net zero' by 2050, which the UK and European Union have promised to do.

2 **Investing in cleaner, renewable energy sources.** In order to reduce carbon emissions, countries and individuals will need to move away from energy sources that rely on fossil fuels, such as coal, oil and gas. Although the rate of growth in reliance on fossil fuels for energy has been slowing, approximately 60% of the world's electricity comes from non-renewable sources (coal and gas). The percentage of world energy coming from renewable sources is slowly increasing and in 2021 was around 28%. Alongside these changes, global sales of electric vehicles have been increasing and some countries have set a target date for phasing out the sale of new fossil fuel reliant vehicles.

3 **Improving international cooperation and monitoring, including help for developing countries.** There remains much work to be done to persuade countries to make more ambitious pledges and to tighten the processes for monitoring these pledges.

As with any area of global governance, it is important to consider the full range of actors, other than nation-states, that can play a part in the solutions and have a role to play in tackling climate change.

What is the role of global civil society and non-state actors?

Global civil society plays a significant role in global environmental governance, although lacking the power and ability to act that states possess. Global civil society amounts to the actions of individuals and actors who are not themselves part of national or sub-national governments. Examples are campaign groups and prominent academics or celebrities such as Sir David Attenborough and Greta Thunberg. There are similarities between these actors and the pressure groups studied in UK politics, the difference being that here we are examining individuals and organisations that have global reach and impact.

Table 6.1 An evaluation of some important global civil society campaigns

Global civil society actor	Actions	Impact
Extinction Rebellion – international pressure group	Founded in 2018, Extinction Rebellion focuses on direct, often disruptive, action such as staging 'sit-ins' in city centres. Extinction Rebellion has a deliberate strategy to 'go beyond politics', calling for independent citizen assemblies to guide government action.	Extinction Rebellion has generated significant media coverage and public attention and grown to global prominence very rapidly. Its campaign for a different style of citizen-led politics has support but breaking down the traditional methods of democratic politics is a work in progress.
Greenpeace – international NGO	Established since 1969, Greenpeace combines direct action with participation in the UN system, as it has been given consultative status within ECOSOC. This allows it to present its arguments at UN meetings.	Greenpeace raises around £8 million per year from private donations. It is able to take direct action through its ships (for example, dropping a 'boulder barrier' off the UK coastline in 2021) and its campaigns have achieved success (for example, lobbying India to put forward its first Clean Air Action Plan).

→

Global civil society actor	Actions	Impact
World Wide Fund for Nature – international non-governmental organisation	Focusing on nature conservation and biodiversity, the WWF was founded in 1961. It focuses on influencing governments through advocacy and awareness-raising with prominent celebrities, rather than direct action (for example, partnering with the Duke of Cambridge and Sir David Attenborough).	Campaigns against whaling in the Antarctic have seen the number of blue whales increase in recent years and humpback whales returning to close to pre-whaling numbers. Wildlife law enforcement work and campaigning has seen positive signs of illegal poaching reducing in many African countries.
Sir David Attenborough – international celebrity advocate	The documentary 'A Life On Our Planet' was released in 2020 on Netflix. Other documentaries such as the 'Planet Earth' series have highlighted climate change and vulnerability of various species. Attenborough has addressed several UN climate change summits along with other prominent activists such as Greta Thunberg.	Reaching a global audience through Netflix, the documentaries have been watched by millions, raising awareness with many who might not normally engage with pressure groups or NGOs. Addressing UN climate change summits helps to bring a wider audience to these summits.

Overall, global civil society campaigns and non-governmental organisations carry significant advantages over individual state governments – but have some limitations as well.

Table 6.2 Advantages and disadvantages of global civil society and NGOs

Advantages of global civil society and NGOs	Disadvantages of global civil society and NGOs
They have the ability to attract significant funding in order to carry out projects that governments are unable or unwilling to do.	They lack the ability to take large-scale strategic decisions. Only national governments can take the decision, for example, to commence widespread de-carbonisation.
They are able to attract and utilise prominent celebrity activists to raise awareness, in a way that governments or politicians are unable or unwilling to do.	Some direct action tactics have been criticised for distracting from the messages of the campaign itself.
The tragedy of the commons requires there to be powerful campaign groups, independent of state interests, that are prepared to make the arguments and persuade states to take more action.	Successful campaigns depend on persuading a very wide range of actors to change their behaviours, from national governments to city mayors to individuals and households.

There are, of course, a wider range of other actors involved in tackling climate change and other environmental challenges. These include:

- **Industry and corporations:** the key polluters are the industries and corporations that operate within states. Of course, national governments encourage and often direct these industries (usually privately owned) to increase a state's economic power and international competitiveness. However, as climate change is a global problem, the role of MNCs is particularly important as both a cause and potential solution. Powerful MNCs can sometimes be an obstacle to state action against climate change, particularly in poorer or developing states, which are reluctant to turn down foreign direct investment to uphold strict emissions targets.
- **National laws and taxes:** states can act alone in deciding to tackle climate change, particularly the harmful effects on their immediate home environment, even if not as part of specific global governance initiatives. They can create their own national laws, which require companies to reduce their emissions (the UK's Clean Air Act was passed in 1956, decades before

any international attempts to clean up the environment were seriously entertained). Alternatively, states may punish companies or citizens that pollute through higher taxes (again, UK taxes on petrol introduced in the early 1990s were aimed at taxing and punishing environmentally harmful behaviours). States can also try to encourage good behaviour or investment in cleaner technologies.

- **IGOs:** these play a vital role in providing states (and all other global actors listed here) with a forum in which joint action to tackle environmental challenges can be discussed, negotiated and agreed fairly. IGO-chaired talks can often appear more neutral and inclusive, as the IGO has to serve the interests of all the member states. The UNFCCC (see page 221) has provided the international basis for discussions on climate change since 1992. Increasingly, other IGOs discuss and take action on environmental matters. The EU has been particularly active in this area, introducing EU-wide regulations on air and water quality, for example.

- **City administration:** given that it is people living in cities who suffer most from pollution, many city administrators (such as mayors with limited powers to govern a city) have taken decisions and implemented policies to reduce emissions or adopt cleaner energy. For example, London's Congestion Charge, introduced in 2003, charges all vehicles entering central London and has reduced traffic to 27% lower than before the charge was introduced and seen cycling increase by over 60%. The cities of Delhi and Beijing have introduced bans on alternate days of vehicles with registration plates ending in odd or even numbers.

- **The international science community:** a key part of environmental global governance. The UN created the Intergovernmental Panel on Climate Change (IPCC, see page 223) as a means of both pooling international expertise and also ensuring that the given scientific advice was seen to be legitimate and neutral, rather than influenced by any one state.

Different viewpoints on tackling climate change

Deep and shallow ecology
Ecologism is a political ideology that places considerable importance on states' and other actors' impact on the natural environment. Ecologists believe that actors in global politics should take steps to protect the natural environment. They also believe that protecting the environment is a moral responsibility, and they criticise human behaviours that selfishly do not take into account environmental concerns.

Politicians, as opposed to scientists alone, became more concerned with environmental issues between the late 1960s and early 1970s. During this period, some politicians began to champion environmental concerns, regarding them as something only individual and collective action could solve.

Deep ecology
The Norwegian philosopher Arne Naess introduced the idea of deep green ecology as a way of thinking about humans and the environment. It is both a scientific and philosophical, and even a spiritual, argument. Its aim is to preserve and protect the natural environment for the benefit of the natural environment itself, seeing this

as an end in itself rather than something which will be of self-interested benefit to human beings.

Deep ecologists therefore argue that:

- all living things – plants, animals, humans – are of equal moral value. Any action that failed to preserve this equality would be morally wrong
- human beings are not more important than other living things (rejecting the idea of 'anthropocentrism', which believes that human beings are superior in the natural world). Human beings and nature are one and the same and should live with each other holistically
- individualism should be rejected. Human beings should always consider how we live in harmony with the rest of nature
- nature is not something to be exploited for human gain.

Few actors in global politics express the views of deep ecology. Even the most committed NGOs and environmental campaign groups follow the ideas of shallow ecology, and try to persuade governments and others of the need to protect the environment for the sake of human security and wellbeing.

Shallow ecology

Conversely, shallow ecology aims to conserve the natural environment in the interests of humankind. Actions taken to reduce the use of fossil fuels, for example, are good because they will enable humanity to live sustainably and to further human development.

Shallow ecologists therefore argue that:

- it is acceptable to approach environmental issues from the perspective of what will benefit humankind
- sustainable development (see page 217) is a priority as it combines conserving the natural environment with advancing human development, actively protecting the interests of future generations of humans
- human instincts and priorities can be modified to reduce harm to the environment, but it is still acceptable to prioritise human needs.

The idea of green politics emerged in the late 1970s, and with it the first references to 'green' political thinking and political parties. The first 'green' political parties were founded in Belgium and Germany. In the UK, the Ecology Party became the Green Party in 1990. A further distinction within shallow ecology is the differing viewpoints of 'light' and 'dark' greens. Light greens view the environment as one in which individuals should take primary responsibility through modifying their behaviour and personal impact on the environment. Dark greens view the environment as part of a global structural challenge, one requiring fundamental global political reform.

Green parties have generally struggled to gain enough electoral support to form governments, though in some European states (for example, Germany and Latvia) they have governed as junior partners in a coalition government.

The differences between developing and developed states

As the international community has tried to find solutions to climate change and ways of reducing its impact, at various points developing states have argued that the pressure put on them to take steps to reduce climate change is not fair. The differences of opinion between developed and developing states have reduced considerably in recent years. Nevertheless, we will see that during key international environmental negotiations, developing states have raised grievances, including the following:

- Developed states did not have to consider protecting the environment when they were industrialising. They did so unrestricted by environmental regulations. Now that developing states are industrialising and aiming to catch up with developed states, they are having to do so while under international pressure to agree to rules, for example that limit the types of energy they are able to use. Developing states argue that they are being held accountable to a higher standard than was required of developed states when they were developing.
- Environmental restrictions may impact the speed and success of developing states' progress. Such restrictions were not part of the modernisation theory that currently developed states followed.
- Developing states still have large populations living in poverty. Industrialisation is one way of reducing poverty, with expanding industry providing jobs and energy production to enable more people to enter employment, develop skills and earn better wages. Developing states argue that their development journey is just beginning. For some states, development through carbon energy is seen to be a cheaper alternative to investment in more expensive, cleaner sources of energy.
- Developed states caused much of the impact of pollution and climate change during their period of industrialisation. In its submission to the Paris climate change conference, India estimated that it was responsible for only 3% of historic cumulative emissions, whereas the US and EU were responsible for 16% and 15% respectively. China, the EU, Japan, Russia and the US together have been responsible for two-thirds of the world's historic carbon dioxide emissions. The argument goes that current restrictions on developing states are a result of the historical emissions and damage caused by developed states.

On the other hand, it is argued that developing states should play a significant role in tackling climate change:

- Emissions in developed states are stable, while those in developing states are rapidly increasing. Scientists have estimated that if India's economic growth continues at the rate of 8.5% per year, its emissions will soon reach one-fifth of the total world emissions that scientists believe the world can cope with before exceeding a harmful 2°C temperature increase.
- It is the poorest states that are the most vulnerable to the impact of climate change, such as through natural disasters or food production difficulties. Natural disasters, such as devastating floods, have a short-term impact on human security and safety, but a longer-term impact on economic development when crucial infrastructure is destroyed.
- Large population growth makes the potential challenge more pressing in developing states. Emissions are currently increasing and, if no action is taken, will increase dramatically as populations and energy demands rise.

The global population is expected to keep growing – some estimates have put the total population at 9.6 billion by 2050

In recent years, however, developing states have come increasingly to accept the need to take action on climate change. The largest developing countries responsible for global emissions, Brazil and India, and the African Union (AU) have all made clear commitments:

- India signed and ratified the Paris Agreement in 2016. It promised to generate 40% of energy from non-fossil fuels by 2030, although it was clear that it would need help from the international community to achieve this. It estimated that the cost of meeting its commitments to reduce climate change would be over US$2.9 trillion. India's population is likely to grow from 1.2 billion to 1.5 billion by 2030, making its future energy needs very high.
- Brazil has both signed and ratified the Paris Agreement, making it the third-largest country responsible for global emissions, after China and the US, to ratify the deal. It has said that it will increase renewable energy sources to 45% of all energy consumption by 2030. Brazil's contribution to climate change is somewhat different to other states, in that deforestation in the Amazon rainforest is the main cause of its emissions, rather than the burning of fossil fuels. Brazil made a commitment as part of the Paris Agreement to cutting illegal deforestation in the Amazon basin. However, after a decade of decline, the rate of deforestation once again increased after the election of President Jair Bolsonaro in 2019, increasing by as much as 34% in 2019 alone. Forest fires have also been on the increase, which are particularly damaging as they make reforestation very difficult.
- The African Union has been supportive of the most recent climate change negotiations in Paris. As of 2021, 90% of African Union states had ratified the Paris Agreement, with 52 submitting Nationally Determined Contributions (NDCs) under the Paris Agreement. Climate change is frequently on the agenda

of AU summits. The World Bank is an example of an IGO that supports African states in meeting their climate change commitments, for example by funding US$22 billion of investment through the Africa Climate Business Plan by 2025. The World Bank estimated in 2015 that Africa would need US$5–10 billion per year to meet the Paris climate change targets, and that these costs would only rise by the middle of the century.

Equally, there has been increasing agreement that developed states should help developing states to take action on climate change, and that they will not be able to fund meaningful action on their own. The first commitment came in the first international summit on the environment, the 1972 Stockholm Declaration on the Environment. Here, it was agreed that developing states needed financial assistance to safeguard the environment. This has been a continuing theme, amounting to more specific help in the Paris Agreement in 2016, where it was agreed to provide US$100 billion a year in climate finance to developing countries by 2020, with a commitment to further finance in the future.

The UN states that it provides 'enabling support' to those countries that otherwise might find it difficult to take action alone. There are several key areas of support.

- **Science for decision making:** in addition to the scientific support the IPCC provides (see page 224), the UN provides funding and training for research within states, particularly developing states. Developing this expertise helps to build a knowledge base of information and science on the extent of climate change and how it impacts specific regions and communities.
- **Low carbon technologies:** shifting from a reliance on fossil fuels to cleaner energy can be expensive for developing states. The UN works to bring together different stakeholders, such as renewable energy companies, governments and scientists, to help link the needs of governments and societies with a private sector that is developing cleaner energy technology, so that both are better able to understand these needs and challenges.
- **Education and training:** the UN has funded education in schools and universities as a way of driving economic and social change. Training has also focused on helping people develop professional skills, such as carrying out accurate assessments of the environmental or the health impact of pollution or other economic activity. The UN has also provided technical advice when governments are developing national climate change plans to help with mitigation and adaptation.
- **Data and information:** tackling climate change effectively relies on accurate data, to allow for accurate measurement of future impacts. The UN has helped by advising states on how they can use population surveys (census) to measure the impact and potential risk of climate change. Studies have also been carried out to analyse the impact of climate change on migration, where families and communities have been forced to move for climate-related reasons.

> ### Topic link
>
> it is arguable that more progress has been made on economic global governance than environmental global governance because states have more of an incentive to make progress on economic matters. This is explored in detail in Chapter 4.

Debate

Is it fair to ask developing states to do more to tackle climate change?

Yes

- Pollution from developing states is increasing. This will eventually overtake the pollution from developed states, so now is the time to act to reduce future emissions.
- Protecting the environment is essential, rather than an impediment, to states' development. Former Indian prime minister Indira Gandhi put forward this idea as early as 1972.
- Developing states are most likely to be affected by the negative impact of climate change, in terms of natural disasters and extreme weather events.
- The right to develop need not be incompatible with developing in a way that does not harm the global commons. This is in line with the concept of sustainable development, which argues that economic development and protecting the environment is not a zero-sum game where one comes at the expense of the other.
- Developed countries that went through their own periods of industrialisation in the nineteenth and twentieth centuries didn't have access to the same renewable energy options currently available to developing countries. It is not unreasonable to ask developing states to use this technology now that it is accessible.

No

- Pollution from most developed states is not increasing, but currently developed states do pollute more than developing states. Developed states should therefore concentrate on reducing their emissions. They are also in a better position to do so, as they remain economically powerful.
- Economic growth is more stable and industrialisation is well established in developed states, making them better able to fund and innovate ways of tackling climate change. The benefits of this innovation could then be transferred to developing states.
- Developing states have a right to develop. Dependency theory (see page 149) and the unequal spread of globalisation benefits both already mean that developing states face huge challenges in catching up to developed states. Asking developing states to take action on climate change while they develop merely makes their catching up harder to achieve.
- Historically, developed states have contributed hugely to the emissions that have caused harm to the planet. It is unfair for developing states now to be asked to contribute to a problem largely caused by developed states.

Evaluation tip: What would the consequences be for climate change if developing states did not do more to tackle climate change? Would these consequences be 'fair' both globally and within developing states themselves?

Activity

Research the actions that both developed and developing states have taken to reduce climate change, before comparing and contrasting these actions. You can use the following examples.

- Emerging economic powers: China, Brazil, India
- Established economic powers: Germany, the UK, the US
- Less developed and less powerful states: Ghana, Nigeria, Sudan

Do you think that all of these states are doing enough to combat climate change?

Sustainability

The tragedy of the commons (see page 207) is a theory which argues that natural resources will inevitably be depleted due to the incentives of the market and a human desire to maximise income. The counter to this is the idea of sustainable development, where a system is built in which resources do not run out and are protected for future generations. The United Nations aims to harmonise three elements: economic growth, social inclusion and environmental protection – with all three making progress. It links closely to the ideas of shallow ecology (see page 213).

Key term

Sustainable development
A form of development that seeks to conserve the natural environment so that the requirements of the present do not compromise the needs of the future.

The idea of **sustainable development** was first put forward in the United Nations' Bruntland 'Our Common Future' Report in 1987, which argued against the idea that protecting the environment would damage economic development. Instead, it argued that protecting the environment and reducing poverty could both be achieved at the same time. This strategy has gained increasing prominence over recent decades and sustainable development is now the main focus of efforts to reduce poverty (see page 329).

It has been given a major focus by the United Nations, through the Sustainable Development Goals (SDGs) agreed in 2015, replacing the largely successful Millennium Development Goals (MDGs), which did not give the same importance to climate change or the environment. Sustainable development plays an important role in tackling climate change – SDG 13 focuses on 'taking urgent action to tackle climate change and its harmful impacts'.

SDG 13 does not attempt to replace any of the UN's existing agreements or forums on climate change, such as the UNFCCC (see page 221), but the SDGs as a whole do offer the UN a means by which it can support nation-states in tackling climate change. States and MNCs can, of course, take the most meaningful action, but the SDG programme provides a framework of meaningful assistance for them to achieve their goals.

Examples of sustainable development projects include:

- Helping states and communities to adopt clean and affordable energy, including increasing the spread of renewable energy sources such as hydro, wind and solar power. With 13% of the global population lacking access to electricity, there is a need to close this gap with clean energy. Investment in new renewable technologies has the potential to create new jobs, with some governments seeing opportunities to boost employment. In India, nearly 100,000 new jobs have been created in solar and wind power since 2014.
- Focusing on cities, which demonstrate the challenge of sustainable development given that they are responsible for 60% of global economic growth, but 70% of global carbon emissions. Projects aim to help cut emissions from industry and transport, increase green spaces and create more compact communities reducing the need to travel within cities.
- Helping states to become more resilient to the impacts of climate change, through adaptation and mitigation measures. This includes strengthening river embankments, improving drainage and setting up early warning systems.

Overall, despite the considerable attention now being given to sustainable development, there remain significant challenges across each of the Sustainable Development Goals, set against a background of global population growth which brings with it an ever-increasing challenge to the supply and fair distribution of global resources.

Climate change scepticism and denial

Of course, there is still not universal agreement that climate change exists or that it is having a serious impact. There are three main groups that oppose scientific opinion on climate change:

1 Those who do not believe that climate change is happening at all and believe that the Earth is not warming.

Activity

Look at the UN's progress on the Sustainable Development Goals, which can be found on the UN website.

1 Which of the goals seems the most challenging?
2 Which of the goals is seeing the most progress?
3 What do you think is:
   a) holding back progress
   b) enabling success?

2 Those who believe that the Earth may be warming, but that this is happening naturally and is not caused by human activity.

3 Those who accept that the Earth is warming, but question the speed at which this is happening and the impact it is likely to have.

Given that climate change denial and scepticism still exist, and that some states have historically used them to avoid taking action, many early climate change summits focused on the need to get states to agree that the science is correct and that climate change does, indeed, exist. This was a necessary first step before later summits could agree upon exactly what action states could and should take.

In 2021, the UN published its largest global study of public opinion on climate change. The survey showed widespread support (62% of people) for the view that climate change was an 'emergency', with consistent results across all continents. Only 10% of those polled thought that the world was currently doing enough to tackle climate change.

Case study

Trump administration – how much did it hold back global progress on climate change?

The high-profile withdrawal of the US from the Paris Agreement in 2020 has, for many, exemplified a lack of US leadership on climate change during the Trump presidency. But did this have any wider impact on the choices that other major polluting states made during this period?

While the Trump administration received prominent criticism by withdrawing from Paris, there is not much evidence that other states – notably China and India – did much in this period to fill the gap in global leadership. The period after the Paris Agreement has seen something of a realisation that individual countries' pledges were not ambitious enough.

- **China:** there had been hopes that it would take more of a global lead, but also stalled on some of its commitments. Its investment in renewable energy decreased by around 50% from 2017 to 2019. It reversed a decision to ban new coal plants and has increased its coal plant capacity.
- **India:** while it is generally considered to still be on track to meet its Paris Agreement pledges, India also planned for more coal capacity during this period. Permission was also given to drilling for oil and gas in forested areas, with some environmental laws made less stringent.
- **Russia:** as the fourth largest producer of carbon emissions after China, the US and India, it had made unambitious nationally determined contributions in Paris which it is likely to meet. Investment in renewable energy stalled during this period and Russia's new energy plan showed continued reliance on its liquid natural gas (LNG) sector; itself a major supplier of non-renewable energy to other states (notably in Europe). While LNG emits less carbon dioxide than coal, this demonstrates continued prioritising of non-renewable energy.

How do realists and liberals view climate change?

Realists

- It is important to address climate change, but not before other states also address it. All states should move forward at a similar pace and at a similar level of seriousness – one state must not take more action than another.
- Any action must take into account the economic impact – actions must not harm the economy and allow other, rival states to take economic advantage.
- National interest drives all thinking on appropriate state action. If a measure is likely to be harmful to a state's economy and development, that state may not be persuaded to take action. If inaction is likely to be harmful, for example through increased risk of natural disasters, a state may be persuaded to take action.

Liberals

- Climate change is a collective action problem and global governance is required to fix it. The global commons is a resource from which all states benefit and all should protect, and individual states must not harm it through their own self-interest.
- IGOs provide a useful forum for states to discuss climate change and to agree international law, to hold states accountable for their promises on climate change.
- Developed states should help developing states to take action on climate change, since their contribution to climate change will be most dramatic. If unchecked, climate change will also have the most serious impact on poorer, developing states, so they must receive assistance to act.

Evaluation tip: Is the realist view or the liberal view the default position of most states? What evidence can you find of a more liberal approach to climate change?

Activity

The commitments that powerful states make to combat climate change are always a work in progress. Assess the recent commitments to global environmental governance by the world's super-polluters (Brazil, China, India and the US).

1 What promises have they made?
2 Have they kept to their promises?
3 Which of the super-polluters is doing the most to tackle climate change?
4 Why are some states doing more than others?

Global governance efforts

The first global governance efforts to protect the environment began in the 1970s. Since those early days, states have agreed upon a whole range of new agreements, institutions and laws by working together in international bodies (see Box 6.1). It is important to assess the impact these global governance efforts have had. Where has progress been made? What has delayed progress?

Global governance of environmental matters has been focused on the following key areas:

- **Agreement on the need to protect the global commons:** without this, states would not agree on or wish to become involved with global efforts to protect the global commons. They would either do nothing or be discouraged from acting if other states didn't also play their part.
- **Agreement on the scientific evidence for environmental threats affecting the global commons:** crucially, this involves agreeing on the causes of harm to the environment in order to take action against them. If states were to disagree on the causes, they would either avoid action or target the wrong issues, thereby reducing their impact. The IPCC is the main international body responsible for

providing the UN and states with rigorous and impartial scientific evidence, in response to which states can make the most suitable decisions.

- **Providing a negotiating framework for states and non-state actors to take action:** the idea of a negotiating framework may sound like a vague concept. However, states have signed up to the UNFCCC, in which they agree to be part of ongoing negotiations and discussions to tackle climate change. Without this guiding process and commitment to continual efforts to reach ever better and more comprehensive agreements, global environmental governance efforts would be rudderless. Within this framework, more specific agreements can be made (such as the Paris Agreement).
- **International summits to agree specific principles and action to be taken:** gatherings of world leaders and other actors, such as NGOs, MNCs and scientists, are required to give focus to – and sometimes to revive – international efforts.

Box 6.1

Key international meetings on climate change

There have been several key international meetings in relation to climate change.
- **Stockholm UN Conference on the Human Environment (1972):** members agreed on the principle of the need to protect the global commons. There was an emphasis on states taking individual, rather than collective, action.
- **Rio Earth Summit (1992):** the UNFCCC was agreed as part of three so-called Rio Declarations. The convention requires that states agree to work together to reach more specific international agreements on future climate change.
- **Kyoto Summit (1997):** set internationally binding targets to reduce carbon emissions. The targets applied only to industrialised states. Over 100 industrialising states, including Brazil, China, India and South Africa, were exempt from emissions targets. The US signed but did not ratify the Kyoto Protocol. The protocol came into full legal force nearly a decade later, in 2005.
- **Copenhagen Climate Change Conference (2009):** included the 15th Conference of the Parties (COP 15), but did not agree legally binding commitments. A key challenge in the negotiations was the problem of fairness between targets for developed and developing states. Unlike Kyoto, it agreed that developing states would do more to combat climate change and that developed states would also help raise US$100 billion by 2020 for developing states to invest in tackling climate change.
- **UN Climate Change Conference/Paris COP 21 Summit (2015):** the agreement was the first to achieve commitment from all states to cut carbon emissions. Fewer differences were allowed between developed and developing states. The agreement was partly legally binding and partly voluntary. States agreed to an ambitious pledge to prevent global temperature from rising above 2°C this century. There was more funding to help developing states play their part in tackling climate change.

The UN Framework Convention on Climate Change

The **United Nations Framework Convention on Climate Change (UNFCCC)** was agreed in 1992 at the Rio Earth Summit and provides a pathway for international cooperation. The UN Secretariat manages and organises summits and convention negotiations (see page 89). States which signed the UNFCCC committed to beginning a journey together where they, under UN guidance and encouragement, would work towards international agreements and ever more detailed and ambitious commitments. The UNFCCC's overall focus has been to work to limit global average temperature rises.

(see page 89)

Key term

United Nations Framework Convention on Climate Change (UNFCCC) An international treaty that set up a process through which future international negotiations on climate change could take place.

A total of 197 states – including all of the UN's member states – are 'parties' to (or members of) the UNFCCC. Climate change summits – such as the Paris summit – are therefore known as a Conference of the Parties (COP).

As a direct result of the UNFCCC, there have been two major further agreements:

- **The Kyoto Protocol (see page 229):** set legally binding targets for reducing emissions.
- **The Paris Agreement (see page 233):** strengthened the global response to climate change and states pledged to keep global temperature rises this century below 2°C and to aim to limit global temperature rises to 1.5°C.

The UNFCCC commits member states to the following principles, through which they can take more specific action in the future:

- It requires member states to agree to act in the interests of human safety, even in the face of scientific uncertainty.
- It identifies reducing dangerous greenhouse gases as the primary focus. It pledges to keep greenhouse gases at a level that prevents human-caused harm to the climate and to ensure that food production 'is not threatened, and to enable economic development to proceed in a sustainable manner'.
- It specifically asks developed countries to do the most to reduce climate change, since 'they are the source of most past and current greenhouse gas emissions' and 'are expected to do the most to cut emissions on home ground'.
- It requires developed states to commit to helping developing states to tackle climate change through financial support.
- It asks developed states to report their progress on climate change policies annually and to publish figures on their greenhouse gas emissions. These country statements began to provide a useful means by which the UN could monitor the promises and progress individual states were making. These state reports could then be independently monitored, praised or criticised. This was the first step towards states being more accountable for the actions they take to reduce climate change.

From the beginning, the UNFCCC recognised the need to treat developed and developing states differently. It does not state that developing states should do nothing to tackle climate change, but recognises that they should have financial help from more industrialised states. The UNFCCC also acknowledges that economic development is vital to developing states, and that achieving this is difficult, even without the requirements to take steps to reduce climate change. However, it does not let developing states off the hook, but instead promises to help them reduce their emissions in a way that prevents any adverse effects on their economic development.

Table 6.3 Different status of countries' responsibilities under the UNFCCC

Examples of 'Annex 1 & 2' countries, expected to do the most to cut domestic emissions and to give financial assistance to other countries	Examples of 'economies in transition' – not receiving or expected to provide financial assistance to other countries	Examples of 'Non-Annex 1' countries, which can expect financial support from 'Annex 1 & 2' countries
US	Russia	China
United Kingdom	Turkey	India
France	Ukraine	All African Union member states
Germany	Poland	Saudi Arabia
Canada		
Australia		

The UNFCCC's strengths are that it has extremely wide membership, with 197 states as parties to the treaty. Before the UNFCCC, international meetings on environmental matters were infrequent and unfocused, and there was no way of ensuring that states would continue to participate in regular climate change discussion. The UNFCCC therefore provides its principles as a roadmap for negotiations between all of the world's current major polluters and future polluters, all of which have participated consistently and annually since 1992. No state has subsequently decided to leave the UNFCCC. It has continued to act as the international driving force behind future agreements. However imperfect they may be, future agreements in Kyoto and Paris would have been much harder to achieve without the negotiating structures and agreements on principle set out in the convention.

When the government of a state signs and ratifies an international treaty, such as the UNFCCC, future governments of that state are bound by that treaty unless they decide to withdraw from it. Withdrawing from an international treaty, particularly one with such international legitimacy and recognition as the UNFCCC, is politically controversial and places more pressure on new governments to stick with commitments made by their predecessors. The UNFCCC has, therefore, encouraged successive governments to continue with international discussion and negotiations, some of which have been highly successful (for example, when legally binding emissions targets were agreed at Kyoto).

The Intergovernmental Panel on Climate Change

In the 1970s and 1980s, the scientific evidence for climate change was at a very early stage of development. It was clear that greenhouse gases were having a harmful impact on the environment and that human activity was the most probable cause. Just as action to combat environmental harm existed only at national level (and in some cases not at all), scientific research and investigation was similarly uncoordinated. Scientific investigations required international funding and knowledge needed to be pooled and maximised.

A further problem was that scientific advice and research risked becoming associated with individual states and their governments, or at the very least with the economic world view of a particular state. There was a need for the scientific advice to be seen as impartial and neutral, rather than advancing the interests of any one state and its economy.

By the late 1980s, the Stockholm Declaration had agreed much on the principles of collective action to prevent global environmental harm. The declaration had, in many ways, been achieved based on very little scientific evidence. In order to achieve more meaningful global action, it was clear that states required scientific advice of the highest quality and credibility.

The **Intergovernmental Panel on Climate Change (IPCC)** was created in 1988 to address these difficulties. Its aim is to provide governments and other decision makers with expert advice through the following principles.

- **Regular assessments of the impact and extent of climate change:** this has been especially important since states have begun, individually and collectively, to take steps to reduce climate change. Regular tracking of global and national progress, including emissions levels, is essential for progress in the right areas.
- **Regular assessments of the causes and risks of climate change:** with each international conference on climate change, the evidence base improves. A

Key term

Intergovernmental Panel on Climate Change (IPCC) An international panel of climate change experts set up by the UN to provide states and policymakers with expert advice on the causes of, impacts of and possible solutions to climate change.

reliable and well-researched evidence base is essential in order to persuade states to make commitments and prove the link between human activity and climate change. A weak evidence base would fail to persuade nations to act and leave them unaware of the potential risks and dangers.

- **Possible solutions to reduce the impact or manage the effects of climate change:** for some states, investing in renewable energy sources will be costly. International research into new technologies is more efficient than states conducting their own research. In this way, the IPCC has helped to propose clear and viable solutions for actions and initiatives that can reduce climate change.

Just as the responsibility for addressing climate change is a collective action problem, so too is the scientific assessment of the issues. Also, pooling the expertise of scientists from across the world ensures that evidence for climate change is not seen to come from any one state.

The IPCC operates in the following ways:

- It advises governments but does not, and cannot, force them into upholding its advice.
- It aims to provide both balanced and rigorous advice and assessments.
- Hundreds of scientists from many countries are involved in developing IPCC assessments and advice. This allows for many different views on climate change to be fed through to the IPCC in an open and transparent manner. For example, 721 experts from 90 countries were selected to take part in the Sixth Assessment Review, to be published in 2022. These experts have been selected through nominations from states and designated observer organisations (including agencies such as the UN Development Programme and NGOs such as Greenpeace and the Worldwide Fund for Nature). 44% of the authors come from what the IPCC refers to as 'developing states' and 'economies in transition'.
- It has produced regular reports since its founding (see Box 6.2). These Assessment Reports are major pieces of scientific research, which help to inform international meetings under the UNFCCC. There are several other reports published within each reporting cycle on specific issues, for example on climate change and its impact on land and food security.

The IPCC has largely been very successful at establishing a credible, trusted and neutral evidence base. It has been highly inclusive, with scientists from both developed and developing states participating in its research. In doing so, it has helped to build the capacity and skills of scientists in developing states so that they can better assess the impact of climate change, not just internationally but at a national level.

The pooling of such a wide range of expertise has also been a form of academic compromise. When states negotiate with each other on matters of policy, they put their views across, debate them and reach a compromise that is not just one state's view but one on which they can all agree. Similarly, the IPCC takes into account a wide variety of scientific research and ensures that a compromise is reached in its advice and assessments. This reduces the risk that the scientific advice provided to states is unbalanced, or too sceptical or extreme in its views. Consulting a group of scientists numbered in the hundreds ensures that all theories and research are taken into account.

Box 6.2

Key IPCC reports

The IPCC has produced a number of key climate change reports:

- First Assessment Report (1990): confirmed that increased greenhouse gases were causing climate change and that human activity had caused an increase in greenhouse gases. It predicted global temperature rises of 0.3°C per decade.
- Second Assessment Report (1995): showed that greenhouse gases were continuing to rise, with global temperature rises per decade remaining as predicted in 1990.
- Third Assessment Report (2001): some ecosystems and species would be irretrievably lost if action to reduce climate change was not taken. Some counter-measures were recommended, for example flood defences, which may reduce the impact of climate change, but these measures cannot be guaranteed.
- Fourth Assessment Report (2007): many of the impacts of climate change can be reduced, delayed or avoided through mitigation. The report was 90% certain that global warming is caused by human activity. Unmitigated climate change would, in the long term, be likely to 'exceed the capacity of natural, managed and human systems to adapt'.
- Fifth Assessment Report (2015): produced using the expertise of over 800 experts. It was likely that the period between 1983 and 2013 was the warmest 30-year period for 1,400 years. It confirmed the loss of ice sheets in Antarctica and Greenland, concluding that it was 95–100% certain that human activity had caused global warming. The projection for global mean temperature rises by 2100 was more than 1.5°C in each of the modelled scenarios.

International summits

International summits bring together states and other actors, ranging from MNCs to NGOs and scientists, to agree steps they can jointly take to protect the environment. The first summit – the Stockholm Conference on the Human Environment – was held in 1972.

The aims of international summits can be broadly summarised as follows.

- **Identifying and agreeing the problem and the need for collective action:** the Stockholm Conference on the Human Environment (1972) and the Rio Earth Summit (1992). These summits clarified the idea that humans had a right to a healthy and clean environment, linked with the idea of third generation human rights.
- **Agreeing specific action to be taken and making collective action a reality:** Kyoto (1997), Copenhagen (2009) and Paris (2015). These summits began to hold states accountable for binding commitments to reduce the causes and impact of climate change.

The United Nations Conference on the Human Environment (1972)

This summit, held in Stockholm, Sweden (and hence sometimes referred to as the Stockholm Conference) agreed 26 key principles, at a very early stage both in the development of scientific evidence for and international responses to climate change. However, it did not amount to international law or any binding commitments – the only requirement at this stage was for a majority of states to agree that there was a problem and that the problem could only be solved through international cooperation (see Box 6.3).

The conference came about after the UN Economic and Social Council (ECOSOC, see page 101) and the UN General Assembly (see page 98) voted in favour of a UN-led international conference on the human impact on the environment.

Some of the key principles of the Stockholm Declaration included:

- natural resources must be safeguarded
- non-renewable resources must be shared and safeguarded
- pollution must not exceed the environment's capacity to clean itself
- development is needed to improve the environment
- developing countries need financial assistance to develop environmental safeguards
- science and technology must be used to protect the environment
- each nation must establish its own standards.

Box 6.3

Indira Gandhi

India's prime minister Indira Gandhi gave an important speech at the 1972 Stockholm Conference. For the first time, the leader of a developing state made an explicit link between successful development and the need to protect the environment. Gandhi argued that both were needed for states to develop properly:

> There are grave misgivings that the discussion on ecology may be designed to distract attention from the problems of war and poverty ... We have to prove to the disinherited majority of the world that ecology and conservation will not work against their interest but will bring an improvement in their lives. The environmental problems of developing countries are not the side effects of excessive industrialisation but reflect the inadequacy of development.

Former Indian prime minister Indira Gandhi

Unlike the climate conferences of today, impartial and comprehensive scientific research, such as that conducted by the IPCC, was not yet readily available for assessment in Stockholm. The scientific evidence and the political process were still acting in isolation from each other and had not yet been fully joined up.

Furthermore, there was still the sense at this stage that nation-states should develop their own policies to react to climate change, rather than agreeing to international standards – in fact, one of the declaration's principles was that 'each nation should develop its own standards'. This is very different to the idea today that states should adopt common standards. Stockholm's key objective was to ensure that states began acting independently to protect the environment. It was a leap too far to expect collective action at this point – that would come later.

The Montreal Protocol (1989)

The Montreal Protocol (full name the Montreal Protocol on Substances that Deplete the Ozone Layer) has been celebrated as one of the earliest successes of environmental global governance. Its achievements are all the more impressive given that both the scientific and the political institutions supporting environmental global governance were not yet fully developed.

The protocol aimed to protect the ozone layer (the layer in the Earth's atmosphere that absorbs much of the sun's radiation, reducing excessive warming of the planet). Key measures included the banning of chlorofluorocarbons (CFCs) and other chemicals, whose emissions harmed the ozone layer and exposed the Earth to the risk of significant temperature rises.

A total of 197 states have now ratified the Montreal Protocol. Other Montreal successes include the following:

- It was the first example of an environmental global governance treaty where a certain number of states were required to sign and ratify the treaty before it would come into force. This principle, designed to encourage collective action, would later be used to full effect in the Kyoto Protocol and the Paris Agreement.
- The Montreal Protocol saw the first use of the precautionary principle. This is an agreement to take action as a precaution even if the science underpinning the need for action is not yet fully proven. The burden lies in proving that there are not harmful effects, rather than proving that there are.
- The protocol recognised the need for states to take different types of action, with some states needing to do more than others. This was another key principle to which later summits would adhere, sometimes to their cost (in the case of the Kyoto Protocol) and sometimes to their benefit (in the case of the Paris Agreement).

The success of the Montreal Protocol perhaps lies in the fact that states did not feel that their economic interests would be harmed through ratifying and implementing the treaty. Unlike later requirements to reduce carbon emissions and move to cleaner energy, moving away from CFCs was far less costly and did not have any wider impact on economies as a whole, unlike in the case of moving a fossil fuel reliant economy to cleaner energy.

Another Montreal success was the widespread feeling among states that they were sharing the burden of action equally, something that was missing at the notably less successful Kyoto Summit.

The Rio Earth Summit (1992)

The UN Rio Earth Summit was the second major meeting of nation-states working in a forum to discuss global protection of the environment.

There had been a gap of 20 years since the Stockholm Conference and Declaration. In the interim period, states had mostly been left to their own devices in terms of their response to dealing with climate change. The Stockholm Declaration had agreed the principles of protecting the global environment but had not set out a pathway for future, more detailed discussion and agreement. There was a need to give fresh international impetus and revive environmental global governance efforts. Above all, there was a need to establish a process by which states and the UN could continue to work together.

The summit met for 2 weeks and 172 governments were in attendance, including 112 heads of state. This gave the summit considerable legitimacy and made the negotiations more impactful. NGOs were also represented in their thousands. Alongside meetings between world leaders, there was a people's summit, with 17,000 ordinary citizens from across the world attending. It was the most comprehensive global environment conference that had ever taken place.

Unlike more recent summits, which have focused on precise actions that can be taken to reduce climate change, the key goal at Rio was to get states to agree to a framework for future action. In this way, it was continuing the work of the Stockholm Declaration. The major success of the Rio Earth Summit was agreeing to the UNFCCC (see page 221).

Alongside the UNFCCC, the Rio Declaration set out some very important key agreements on the principles at stake in protecting the global commons:

- Economic progress is only ensured if it is linked with the protection of the environment. Economic progress would, ultimately, be harmed if the environment were not protected.
- The international community should aim to develop further international agreements in order to protect the global environment and ensure responsible development.
- People are entitled to a healthy and productive life. This, for the first time, introduced a strong link between human rights and the environment. Human rights had long protected the rights to, for example, food and shelter, but not clean air.
- The future basis of sustainable development – development today should not threaten the needs of present and future generations.
- States have the right to exploit their own resources, but not by causing damage to the environment beyond their borders.
- Scientific knowledge of the problem needed to be improved. States agreed to share knowledge and technologies to manage climate change.

How successful was the Rio Earth Summit? The UNFCCC is undoubtedly the major success of the summit, as it locked in signatory states to a process of annual negotiations and, ultimately, legally binding agreements.

In terms of specific actions to tackle climate change, there was little achieved. But, arguably, the Rio Summit and Declaration represented a major success, because it led to the international community agreeing that there was indeed a problem and that the problem needed to be solved through collective action and continued commitment.

These agreements did not exist before the Rio Summit, and future action would not be possible without states coming together on these two basic principles.

Kyoto Conference of the Parties (COP) Summit and Protocol (1997)

The next major international conference on climate change was held in 1997 in Kyoto, Japan. The Kyoto meetings marked a shift in environmental global governance, from agreeing the existence of the problem, to identifying specific actions that states could take in order to reduce climate change. It was also the first attempt to hold states accountable for their actions via legally binding commitments.

During the Kyoto Summit, industrialised states made a commitment to reduce global greenhouse gas emissions

The Kyoto Protocol endorsed the following principles:

- There would be legally binding targets to reduce emissions (known as quantified emissions limitation and reduction objectives). These would only be required of 37 industrialised states and the EU. Coverage was not comprehensive and not all states agreed to these legally binding targets.
- Industrialised states were committed to reducing emissions of greenhouse gases by around 5% between 2008 and 2012 (known as the first 'commitment period').
- To try to encourage a critical mass of states to participate, the Kyoto Protocol would not legally come into force until enough countries (which together were responsible for at least 55% of the world's carbon emissions) had ratified it. Additionally, a total of 55 states were required to ratify the treaty before it came into force. This principle of collective action would reassure states that others were also taking action, they would not be acting alone and meaningful global action through many states acting together would have the greatest impact, making any national sacrifices (for example, to economic development) easier to justify.
- Brazil, China, India and South Africa were granted exemption from emissions targets. In total, 100 developing states were exempt from the treaty.
- States were required to submit reports on their progress and these were monitored by the United Nations.

- The Kyoto Protocol was also time-limited, with an expiry date set in 2012. Further commitments were made by a small number of states to a second 'commitment period' (concluding in 2020) to reduce emissions by 18% compared with 1990 levels.
- The treaty set up an international trading system, by which states could earn 'carbon credits' towards meeting their emissions targets by investing in reducing emissions in other states.

While the Kyoto Protocol was a major step forward in terms of agreeing specific global steps to combat climate change and legally binding targets, these stringent targets were beset with problems.

- The protocol did not come into force until 2005, nearly a decade after the Kyoto Summit and nearly halfway through the lifetime of the treaty (the original time period for meeting targets being 1997–2012).
- While states deliberated, emissions increased by as much as 40–50% between 1990 and 2009.
- The agreement was not comprehensive, with Brazil, China, India and South Africa exempt. This was a key factor in the US deciding to reject the treaty. Canada also withdrew from the protocol, having missed its emissions target.
- The protocol's inconsistencies created too many grievances, with states questioning whether others were being asked to do enough. It would take a more comprehensive and universal approach to reassure states that a majority was making a broadly equal and fair contribution. Both China and Russia were also not covered by legally binding targets. Russia did later ratify the treaty, but only 7 years after the summit. China did not sign the treaty, and it is estimated that its emissions have increased by nearly 300% during the treaty's lifetime.

In spite of the obvious failures of the Kyoto Protocol, there were some successes:

- Some regions and states did indeed stick to their commitments to successfully reduce emissions. The EU reduced its emissions by around 8% during its compliance with the protocol. The EU's success perhaps reflects its ability to create law through its institutions that applies to a group of states while reassuring European countries that they are all acting together, rather than bearing the burden alone.
- Kyoto influenced the EU to create the world's first carbon emissions trading scheme, which set an overall cap on greenhouse gases which is gradually reduced. Companies can then trade emissions allowances with each other. If one company exceeds the cap, it can buy credits from companies that have not exceeded the cap, thereby incentivising companies to keep below the cap.
- 37 countries pledged to stricter emissions targets from 2013 until 2020 in a second 'commitment period'. The UN estimated that these states had, by 2018, reduced their emissions by 25% as part of the Doha extension to the Kyoto Protocol.

Copenhagen COP 15 Summit (2009)

By 2009, the Kyoto deal was also set to expire in 2012 and a new deal was needed to replace it.

The key challenge was the need for collective action and a comprehensive agreement. Therefore, the main objective of the Copenhagen Summit was to get the largest polluters, especially the US, to agree on collective action. It also needed to address the question of those contributions expected of developing states, in order for developed states to agree to the deal. Developing states required help, but not exemptions.

Politically, the Copenhagen Summit was timely. There had been a change of US president that same year, and Barack Obama came to office pledging that the US would commit to international collective action in order to tackle climate change. In fact, President Obama committed considerable personal effort to the talks, directly leading negotiations with representatives from Brazil, China, India and South Africa. Obama recognised that at the heart of Kyoto's failure was a perceived lack of equality, which needed resolution in this fresh round of negotiations.

The key principles to come out of the Copenhagen Accord included:

- an agreement that there was a need to limit global temperature rises to less than 2°C
- a method for verifying industrialised nations' reductions in emissions, resulting in greater transparency – China, in particular, had been opposed to this
- the promise of new resources for developing states, with an annual total of US$100 billion provided by 2020
- the introduction of the Green Climate Fund, to help with climate change-related projects in developing states
- a requirement that states would make public their plans for reducing carbon emissions by 2020
- the requirement that the implementation of the Copenhagen Accord would be reviewed in 2015 (this eventually took place at the Paris Summit).

Crucially, the Copenhagen Accord did not include:

- any legally binding targets, either for developed or developing states
- any plan for the agreements made in the Copenhagen Accord to become legally binding in the future
- approval by member states – rather states 'recognised' the principles of the Accord. Unanimous support for the deal was also not achieved – it was not clear whether or not the Accord represented a formal UN agreement in international law
- a promise to take action to ensure global temperature rises remained below 2°C – there was merely agreement on the scientific evidence and the need to limit global temperature rise
- penalties for states that did not meet their commitments, even in the case of less ambitious requirements, such as publishing plans for cutting carbon emissions by 2020.

The key weaknesses of the Copenhagen Accord were that it did not include any legally binding targets, nor was it clear whether the accord itself carried the weight of international law. There was therefore very little scope for holding states accountable for the pledges they had made. The UN secretary-general Ban Ki-moon criticised the deal for these oversights and urged parties to make the deal legally binding at future meetings.

However much enthusiasm President Obama showed, it was unlikely that the US Congress would ratify any more comprehensive, legally binding treaty. Obama was muted in his praise for the Copenhagen Accord, stating that it was 'not enough' and the discussions were 'extraordinarily complex and difficult … laying the foundations for international action in the years to come'.

The so-called BASIC group (comprising Brazil, South Africa, India and China) and the US negotiated with each other almost entirely behind the scenes, as the most significant polluting states tried to hammer out a deal. Obama announced that the five states had reached an initial agreement, including on the 2°C temperature rise limit. Other states complained that they hadn't even seen the deal the US and BASIC group had negotiated.

Consequently, the negotiations were hardly inclusive or comprehensive. Arguably, states were not yet ready to negotiate in a group of 190. Rather, they still needed to achieve agreements within powerful blocs of states. As Kyoto had proven, without the commitment of these states, any overarching agreement would be worthless. The lack of agreement on legally binding targets further suggests that the most powerful states remained unwilling to accept legal targets and preferred, instead, less formal commitments.

In defence of the Copenhagen Accord, world leaders said that any deal was better than no deal – China and India had, after all, agreed to reduce carbon emissions for the first time (even if the targets were not legally binding).

Overall, the Copenhagen Summit was a failure. The accords lacked legal force. The challenge of unifying states into collective action remained elusive. The negotiations had been fractious and highlighted divisions between developed and developing states, and between powerful developing states (the BASIC group) and less powerful developing states (the G77). The head of the G77 stated that, for Africa, the deal was 'a suicide pact, in order to maintain the economic dominance of a few countries'.

Greenpeace's closing statement labelled Copenhagen:

> a crime scene tonight, with guilty men and women fleeing to the airport. There are no targets for carbon cuts and no agreement on a legally binding treaty. Too few politicians are capable of looking beyond the horizon of their narrow self-interest, let alone caring much for the millions of people who are facing down the threat of climate change.

Box 6.4

US presidents on climate change

Ronald Reagan (1981–89): Reagan was president during the early period of global environmental governance, during which time the world was still waking up to the challenge and was only beginning to organise itself to tackle this collective action problem. Reagan did champion the Montreal Protocol in 1988, calling it 'a monumental effort of science and diplomacy', and the US Senate unanimously ratified the protocol. Within the US, critics say that the Reagan administration was weak in its enforcement of anti-pollution regulations and was too keen to allow private industry to exploit land for mining and other resource extraction.

George H. W. Bush (1989–93): President Bush's speech at the Rio Earth Summit in 1992 set a far more positive tone towards global environmental action than we would hear during the later presidency of his son, George W. Bush. Bush Snr directly challenged the notion that environmental protection put economic growth at risk, stating that 'those who say that economic growth and environmental protection cannot be compatible [should] come to the US, where in the 20 years since Stockholm, our economy has grown by 57% and yet we've cut the lead going into the air by 97%, the carbon monoxide by 41%'. However, Bush Snr's presidency lasted only one term and, while the US signed and ratified the Rio Declaration and joined the UNFCCC during this time, little more was asked of the US beyond agreeing to the declaration's principles.

→

Bill Clinton (1993–2001): the first Democratic president in the modern era of environmental governance signed, but did not ratify, the Kyoto Protocol, as US Congress would not approve it. Despite this failure, Clinton voiced his strong support for the Kyoto Protocol. This is an example of a US president negotiating at an international summit with his hands tied – Clinton still negotiated in support of the protocol, knowing that Congress would be unlikely to give its support and ratify the treaty. He voiced concern that developing states 'must participate in a meaningful way if we are to truly tackle this problem', and defended the protocol against claims in Congress that it would hurt the US economy.

George W. Bush (2001–9): Bush Jnr withdrew support for the Kyoto Protocol, stating that it was unfair that developing states were not required to commit to emissions targets. However, while withdrawing from the protocol, President Bush did implement a national plan to reduce carbon emissions by 18%, and the pace of US emissions did slow during the Bush Jnr administration. During this period, the Kyoto Protocol was the subject of frequent efforts to revive it, but the US's position on the protocol did not change.

Barack Obama (2009–17): Obama negotiated the Copenhagen Accord in 2009, early in his presidency. He was criticised for negotiating with the BASIC countries (Brazil, South Africa, India, China) 'behind closed doors', although by that stage no agreement would have been possible without key states hammering one out. Obama also campaigned to reverse the Bush administration's rejection of the Kyoto Protocol. At national level, Obama was much more successful – highlights include the Clean Power Plan, which set the US's first national limit on carbon pollution.

Donald Trump (2017–21): Compared with his predecessors, Donald Trump has been the most sceptical towards climate change. He described global warming as 'invented by and for China in order to make US manufacturing non-competitive' and made an early pledge to withdraw the US from the Paris Agreement (successfully delivered in his final months in office). Trump scrapped Obama's Clean Power Plan and replaced it with less stringent regulations to limit carbon emissions. Despite campaign promises to protect the coal industry, jobs in this sector actually fell by nearly a quarter.

Activity

Using Box 6.4 and your own knowledge and research, discuss how US policy on climate change has changed over various presidencies.

1 What have been the most significant steps US presidents have taken either in tackling climate change or in rejecting pressures to act?
2 Which president do you think was the most successful in protecting the global commons?
3 Is it fair to make comparisons between presidents in different decades? Has it become easier or harder for US presidents to take action on climate change?

Paris Summit (COP 21, 2015)

COP 21 was hosted amid high security after the 2015 terrorist attacks in Paris. Once again, attendees were conscious of the need to put right the failures of previous summits, including the lack of:

- a comprehensive and unified approach, both to the negotiations themselves and the solutions proposed – no more behind-the-scenes deals among a small group of states, with many developing states sidelined

- legally binding targets applying to all states, with no exemptions given to major polluters. Previous summits had failed to agree comprehensive, legally binding targets: either failing to set any legally binding targets (Copenhagen) or only having a small number of states agree to targets (Kyoto).

The result was the first international climate change treaty that committed all states to legally binding emissions reductions. By 2021, 190 states had joined the agreement, with those states collectively responsible for over 95% of global carbon emissions. Crucially, for the first time both the US and China (responsible for nearly 40% of global emissions) had both signed up to legally binding targets. Key parts of the Paris Agreement were:

- an agreement to keep global temperature increase 'well below' 2°C and to pursue efforts to limit it to 1.5°C
- a commitment to so-called 'pledge and review' whereby states agree to cut emissions according to national plans or 'Nationally Determined Contributions' (NDCs) and have those plans and commitments reviewed by the UN. States were required to put forward these plans to the UN by 2020
- to collectively review progress every 5 years. States are required to make renewed, stronger pledges (the so-called 'ratchet' mechanism). Alongside this, a global stocktake is built in to assess whether action taken is having an impact and what further action might be needed
- a fund of US$100 billion a year by 2020 in climate finance for developing countries, with a pledge to increase this over time
- once the deal came into force, countries that ratified it would have to wait a minimum of 3 years before exit. This became important as the Trump administration could not legally exit the Paris Agreement immediately, and only formally withdrew in November 2020 – three years after first signalling its intentions and the day after President Trump lost the 2020 presidential election. President Biden reversed this decision on his first day in office, just two months later.

NDCs were the Paris Agreement's method for resolving the disagreement between developed and developing states that had seen previous summits fail in their objectives. States themselves would outline contributions, which the UN would then review, rather than any other authority imposing them. These pledges are not legally binding, with no penalties for missing targets.

This signalled a change from the Kyoto proposals, where industrialised states were subject to enforced emissions targets decided by a higher authority, and where industrialising states would need to take 'nationally appropriate mitigation actions'. With NDCs, both developed and developing states would be required to cut emissions and produce their own national plans for how they would achieve this.

Of course, one weakness of states agreeing their own national targets is that their planned actions may not be sufficient. More than five years on from the Paris Agreements, the UN reported that:

- Worldwide, greenhouse gas emissions were still rising – though there is some evidence that the rise is slowing.
- The Covid-19 pandemic had contributed to a short-term reduction in carbon emissions and states should not go back on their climate change commitments in their economic recovery plans.

- An increasing number of states were committing not just to reductions but to becoming carbon neutral. Early commitments came from the UK, France, EU, Japan and – most encouragingly – China.
- G20 states, which account for approximately 78% of greenhouse gas emissions, were not on track to meet their NDCs.
- Overall, NDCs were not on track to meet the Paris target of keeping global temperature rises to below 2°C; but rather to an increase of 3°C by the end of the century.

Distinguish between

The Kyoto Protocol and the Paris Agreement

The Kyoto Protocol (1997)

- Only a small number of developed states participated, with China and India exempt and the US (and eventually Canada) choosing not to participate.
- If targets are missed, then states would be required to make up the shortfall in a future commitment period.
- A critical mass of states was needed for it to enter into force, meaning that it did not come into force until 8 years after it was initially agreed.

The Paris Agreement (2015)

- NDCs – all states participate, making their own plans for reducing carbon emissions.
- The agreement took legal effect in 2016.
- There is a legally binding commitment to collective action. Individual states do not face penalties if they fail to meet targets.

Table 6.4 Nationally determined contributions (NDCs) of key states and their progress

State	Nationally determined contribution (NDC) pledge in 2016	Progress	2021 NDC commitment
US	26–28% below 2005 levels by 2025.	In 2020, the UN judged that the US was not on track to meet its 2016 NDC pledge and that if all states adopted a similar level of commitment, global temperature rises would reach 4°C, missing the Paris target of 2°C by some distance.	President Biden announced in April 2022 that the US would cut net carbon emissions by 50% below 2005 levels in 2030, saying that 'this was a decisive decade for tackling climate change'. Commentators said that this doubled previous US commitments.
China	China proposed to reduce its ratio of carbon emissions to GDP to 60–65% below 2005 levels by 2030.	The UN 'Emissions Gap' report in 2020 judged that China was on track to meet its NDC pledge by 2030 and the rate of emissions is slowing, nearing its peak. China accounts for half of the world's coal capacity and a quarter of overseas fossil fuel infrastructure development. Overall, China's NDC was judged to be not enough to reach the Paris goal of keeping global temperature rises below 2°C.	In 2020, China pledged to reach peak emissions by 2030 and become carbon neutral by 2060.
European Union	The EU promised to cut carbon emissions by 40% by 2030.	The UN 'Emissions Gap' report in 2020 judged that the EU 27 was on track to meet its NDC commitments. However, this NDC commitment was unlikely to be enough to contribute to keeping global temperature rises to below 2°C.	In 2020, the EU pledged a 55% net reduction of emissions by 2030 and to be carbon neutral by 2050.

The success of the Paris Agreements has been that nearly every country in the world has now signed up to emissions reductions, whereas in the Kyoto Protocol only a small group of developed states had done so. This is a significant achievement in reducing the divisions between developed and developing states in terms of sharing the burden of collective action.

The treaty also set out a clear pathway for the future, through its five-year review mechanisms. This was vital given the long-term nature of the problem and the need to keep states committed, given how quickly the scientific assessment of the measures required changes and the difficulty of renegotiating an entirely new agreement.

However, the Paris Agreement could be criticised for being a compromise too far. In order to gain full participation from states, it was necessary to give states the freedom to set their own targets. The result of this freedom has been that states have not set rigorous enough NDCs and so, collectively, the goal of keeping temperature reductions to below 2°C is unlikely to be achieved. The Paris Agreement opened up future challenges in ensuring that states' promises are both sufficient and are delivered, given the lack of penalties and the non-binding nature of the NDCs.

Glasgow Summit (COP 26, 2021)

The UK hosted the first major meeting of world leaders on climate change after a hiatus imposed by the Covid-19 pandemic. The key challenge of the summit was to deliver more ambitious commitments from states to their NDC pledges made after the Paris Agreement, which required states to make new commitments after 5 years.

After two weeks of negotiations, the key pledges that emerged included:

- States expressed 'alarm and utmost concern that human activities have caused around 1.1°C of global warming to date' and resolved to pursue efforts to keep to 1.5°C.
- There was agreement to 'phase down' coal power. India and China were powerful states arguing against a pledge to 'phase out' coal. This was the first decision on coal power to feature in a COP agreement.
- Developed states agreed to provide $100bn per year annually until 2025 to help developing countries to tackle climate change. The agreement acknowledged that the same funding commitment had not been met in 2020.
- The Paris Agreement set up a carbon market and the COP26 deal finally agreed how this would work in practice, with states trading emissions reductions.
- 100 states committed to stopping deforestation by 2030, collectively amounting to 85% of world forests.
- The US and China made their own, bilateral, agreement to cut methane gas emissions. Separately, 100 states agreed to cut methane emissions by 30% by 2030.
- With the renewed global focus on a climate emergency, especially amongst prominent campaigners and NGOs, did the Glasgow summit deliver necessary progress?

Strengths:

- New ground was broken with the first agreement on reducing coal power — even if the commitment was watered down from 'phasing out' to a more nuanced 'phasing down'.
- The Paris framework has seen an increasing number of states now moving to 'net zero' pledges, with an estimated 90% of the world economy now covered by such pledges.
- There was a first commitment also to reducing deforestation and reducing methane emissions, which account for a third of greenhouse gases.

- There was a renewed commitment from developed states to helping developing states, but an admission that this was a second attempt at delivering on a promise broken once before.

Weaknesses:

- Perhaps the most important assessment of progress was from scientists. Analysts from the Climate Action Tracker estimated that no major economy had agreed to emissions reductions which would keep temperature rises below 1.5°C.
- A majority of states had strengthened their NDC pledges, but these have yet to be delivered and the track record from the first round of NDC pledges at the Paris COP summit is that many states, including those which pollute the most, made insufficient NDC pledges immediately after the Paris Agreement, many of which were not even kept to.
- Although 100 countries agreed to cut methane emissions by 30% by 2030, major emitters like China, India and Russia have not made pledges.
- The agreements reached at Glasgow, as at previous COP meetings, are non-binding. There are therefore no enforcement mechanisms to ensure compliance.
- The analysis shows that, on the most important measure of success, global temperature rises – after two weeks' of negotiations in Glasgow – are on course to rise by 2.1°C.

Future challenges

The leadership of the key polluting states – notably China and the US – will always be critical to the success of any environmental global governance initiatives. The US's withdrawal under President Trump has left the US playing catch-up with its pledges and reflects a pattern of inconsistent US support for climate change agreements dating back to the Kyoto Protocol.

The UN, scientists and campaigners agree that the Paris Agreement has been the most successful international agreement so far, but that it remains insufficient and unlikely to meet its target.

The story of UN climate change summits has been one of steadily trying to resolve outstanding issues and plug gaps in previous agreements. Greenpeace has strongly criticised national governments for their 'completely inadequate responses' to the Paris Agreements.

Challenges for future summits include:

- ensuring that states propose more ambitious nationally determined contributions, that will collectively meet the target of limiting global temperature rises
- encouraging more states to commit to becoming carbon neutral and to reducing reliance and investment in fossil fuel
- ensuring that states keep to those targets, when there is no means of enforcement in the Agreement (and states would be unlikely to accept one in the future)
- the Paris commitment to a 2°C temperature rise limit is now out of date and it is widely recognised that an even more challenging limit of 1.5°C is necessary. Given that the previous round of NDCs was not sufficient to limit temperature rises to 2°C, this is a considerable challenge
- proposals in the Paris Agreement for carbon trading were not implemented in the first five years of the treaty
- keeping pace with the scientific evidence and recommendations – the politics moves slowly and the scale of the problem moves quickly, creating a critical challenge. There is a worrying track record of the political process reaching agreements too slowly, which are then deemed to be insufficient.

Topic link

The different power dynamics between states has a key impact on the success or otherwise of international climate change conferences and is explored further in Chapter 7.

A net zero future

Over recent years, it has become clear that pledges to reduce carbon emissions are unlikely to limit global temperature rises to below 1.5°C, as recommended by the Intergovernmental Panel on Climate Change. Instead, the UN is now urging states to commit to 'de-carbonisation' and 'net zero' carbon emissions. This shows how difficult it is for international agreements to keep up with the pace of the scientific evidence, as the Paris Agreement contains no specific reference to the de-carbonisation that is now deemed necessary.

States are beginning to pledge to become carbon neutral by 2050, but how feasible are these promises?

- The UK was the first major economy to pass domestic law requiring it to cut emissions to net zero by 2050. This Act of Parliament would be difficult (though not impossible) for future governments to roll back on and provides a degree of accountability for government promises. The Institute for Government judged that the UK was likely to find its net zero commitment very challenging, given that it was already behind on meeting its previous target of cutting emissions by 80% by 2050. There will need to be significant de-carbonisation of household energy supplies and transport, where emissions have not been reduced significantly in recent years. The Johnson government brought forward the deadline for phasing out the sale of petrol and diesel cars to 2030 and promised over £1 billion in investment to increase access to zero emissions vehicles.

- In 2020, the European Union also pledged to become carbon neutral by 2050. Meeting this target will be similarly challenging, with some member states (such as Poland) still heavily reliant on coal. The pledge will require the EU to radically accelerate its current rate of emissions reductions. Between 1990 and 2017, the EU cut 35 megatons of carbon dioxide and will need to see reductions of as much as 130 megatons by the end of 2030 to stay on track. Focusing on renewable energy for power supply will probably lead to the quickest reductions, given that solar and wind technology are readily available. As with the UK, changing transport usage to zero emissions vehicles will be a slower challenge in reducing emissions.

Are changing dynamics of power helping to overcome difficulties in global environmental governance?

Yes

- Global civil society movements are using social media and increased global connectivity to spread global campaigns, emphasising the 'climate emergency' and putting more pressure on countries to deepen their commitments.
- With emerging powers such as India and China becoming increasingly confident economic powers, they have agreed to make emissions reductions for the first time in the Paris Agreement.
- There is increasing demand within democratic states for their leaders to take action. The European Union, in particular, has seen coordinated action among its member states.

No

- The realist desire to maximise economic power is still prevalent and is leading to countries making commitments that lack ambition and that, collectively, even in the Paris Agreement are not sufficient to limit global temperature rises enough.
- International organisations still lack real power in not being able to force states to take enough action and to hold them accountable if they do not keep to their promises. Hard power will never be a feasible option, so international organisations have to rely on soft power of negotiation and 'naming and shaming'.
- With some states still non-democratic or semi-democratic, there is insufficient accountability. Even in democratic states, it is difficult to hold governments accountable for promises that are judged over many decades.

Evaluation tip: If progress is being held back, is this due to new dynamics of power that represent a change – or challenges that have always existed and are likely to exist in the future?

Table 6.5 Climate change conferences since Paris

Summit	Key outcomes
2016 – Marrakesh	A UN report warned that the existing Paris pledges would be likely to result in temperature rises of 2.9°C to 3.4°C by the end of the century.
	The existing NDCs were to remain in place until states were required to update them in 2020.
2017 – Bonn	States continued to negotiate the rules for reporting and checking of emissions targets, without reaching a final agreement. The Paris Agreement had set a deadline of 2018 for agreeing these.
2018 – Katowice	Agreement was reached on the reporting processes for the Paris Agreement.
	IPCC report updated its recommendations, urging states to limit global temperature rises to 1.5°C.
2019 – Madrid	UN secretary-general, António Guterres, urged states to go further and commit to becoming carbon neutral by 2050.
	The summit attempted to move forward another unresolved issue from the Paris Agreement, on establishing a carbon credit scheme. No agreement was reached.
2020 – Online conference (due to Covid-19 pandemic)	The full COP summit postponed due to the Covid-19 pandemic and was replaced by a Climate Ambition Summit hosted by the UN, UK and France.
	States began to put forward new NDCs (due by 2021), with the UK and EU setting emissions targets of 68% and 55% respectively. 24 states made long-term pledges to become carbon neutral.

Table 6.6 Strengths and weaknesses of international climate change summits

Summit	Major strengths	Major weaknesses
Rio Earth Summit 1992 – the UNFCCC was agreed as part of three so-called Rio Declarations. The convention requires that states agree to work together to reach more specific international agreements on future climate change.	Set up the framework and principles for all future summits (UNFCCC), which have enabled states to make more detailed progress.	Did not agree any specific actions beyond agreeing to principles.
Kyoto Protocol 1997 – set internationally binding targets to reduce carbon emissions. The targets apply only to industrialised states. Over 100 industrialising states, including Brazil, China, India and South Africa, are exempt from emissions targets. The US signed but did not ratify the Kyoto Protocol. The protocol came into full legal force nearly a decade later, in 2005.	A minority of states did set useful emissions targets and successfully cut emissions.	Major emitting states were either exempt (China) or withdrew (US). Participation very weak.
Copenhagen 2009 – a key challenge in the negotiations was the problem of fairness between targets for developed and developing states. Unlike Kyoto, it agreed that developing states would do more to combat climate change and that developed states would also help raise US$100 billion by 2020 for developing states to invest in tackling climate change.	New financial support for developing states and agreement in principle to limit temperature rises to 2°C.	Did not set up any new emissions targets or resolve any of the participation problems of Kyoto.
Paris Agreement 2015 – the first to achieve commitment from all states to cut carbon emissions. Fewer differences were allowed between developed and developing states. The agreement was partly legally binding and partly voluntary. States agreed to an ambitious pledge to prevent global temperature from rising above 2°C this century. There was more funding to help developing states play their part in tackling climate change.	Widespread participation and agreement on action by both developed and developing states.	States setting their own emissions targets has been difficult to monitor and commitments have been insufficient.

Imagine that you are producing the agenda for the next international summit on climate change.

1 What actions do states need to take next?
2 Should states be encouraged or, as Greenpeace recommends, forced to take more action?
3 What do you think could be the biggest obstacle to making progress on climate change at the next summit?

Activity

1 How effective do you think international campaigners have been on climate change issues?
2 What have been the most effective campaigns and tactics?
3 What have been the least effective campaigns and tactics?

Box 6.5

Climate change activists

Greta Thunberg: Came to global attention in 2018 for successfully organising a series of strikes among schoolchildren in Sweden. These strikes quickly gained global attention and spread to other countries, culminating in two major strikes in March and September 2019. It is estimated that a million children from over 100 countries were involved in these strikes. In 2019, Thunberg took a year off school and became a regular advocate at major international climate change summits. She first spoke at the UN Climate Action Summit in New York in September 2019.

Varshini Prakash: Founded the US youth climate political action movement, Sunrise Movement, in 2017. The movement has campaigned for a 'Green New Deal' in the US, aiming to 'mobilise every aspect of American society to 100% clean and renewable energy' and linking environmental policies with job creation and a transition to guaranteeing 'living wage' employment for all. Prakash was appointed to President Joe Biden's climate task force shortly after his election.

Vanessa Nakate: Rose to prominence in Uganda in 2018 after staging a solitary protest outside the national parliament in the capital Kampala over successive months. She has spoken at many international summits and has highlighted the climate crisis as a racial issue, arguing that 'you cannot have climate justice without racial justice. It isn't justice if it doesn't include everyone' and has criticised the exclusion of Black and African perspectives from climate change debate. Her Green Schools Project in Uganda has been working to shift schools to solar energy.

Greta Thunberg speaks at the United Nations Climate Action Summit, 2019

Debate

Is the Paris Agreement the best deal yet on climate change?

Yes

- Allowing states to make their own commitments, rather than forcing states to take legally binding steps, has encouraged every state to pledge emissions targets. This is better than a minority of states committing to targets but a majority (especially the biggest emitters) committing to no targets.
- States such as China and India no longer need to be persuaded of the need to take action. They have set themselves stretching targets because they are acutely aware of the dangers climate change poses.
- Both developed and developing states agree that they need to take action. There are no exemptions, and states have the freedom to decide what action is most appropriate – but they do not have the choice of whether or not to cut their emissions.

No

- The pledges that states have made, and have been allowed to set themselves, are insufficient in limiting global temperature rises to below 2°C.
- Giving states the power to set their own targets enables them to make decisions where they may prioritise their economic interest above environmental interests.
- Too much trust is placed on states taking action, without any means of punishing or holding them accountable if they do not keep their promises.
- There is too little power within the treaty to even question whether states are proposing sufficient action in their INDCs. Once again, a major polluter and world power has failed to remain committed to the agreement, with President Trump announcing in June 2017 that the US would withdraw from the agreement.

Evaluation tip: Your conclusion will rest on whether Paris can claim to have made more progress than other summits. Progress may be judged in terms of political progress in resolving stumbling blocks in the negotiations and in terms of translating into action that actually tackles climate change.

What you should know

Having read this chapter you should have knowledge and understanding of the following:

→ Global environmental governance efforts have taken place under the United Nations Framework Convention on Climate Change, which has allowed for a succession of international summits and agreements to be reached. The United Nations has played a key leadership role.

→ Protecting the global commons is a key part of global governance. It is impossible for the international community to take meaningful action if states do not discuss and negotiate the collective action they can take together. States are unlikely to be persuaded to act alone and the actions of lone states will not solve serious problems such as climate change.

→ Developed and developing states have disagreed about how to tackle climate change. Developing states feel most at risk, particularly from natural disasters, and have felt that developed states have been the primary cause of global warming and should do the most to reduce its impact. Since the Paris Agreement, there is increased willingness among developing states to take action.

→ Environmental global governance efforts have tended to fail when states have been forced to act or when states have felt that contributions are not fair.

→ Global civil society organisations and NGOs can be useful advocates for change and put pressure on national governments and international organisations. But progress in persuading states is slow and they sometimes lack the power to force states to take more effective action.

Further reading

Attenborough, D. (2020) *A Life on Our Planet: My Witness Statement and a Vision for the Future*. Ebury Press.

Berners-Lee, M. (2021) *There Is No Planet B*. Cambridge University Press.

Gadsby, J. (2019) 'Global governance and the environment', *Politics Review*, Vol. 29, No. 2, November.

Gates, B. (2021) *How to Avoid a Climate Disaster*. Allen Lane.

Heywood, A. (2010) 'How deep is deep ecologism?', *Politics Review*, Vol. 20, No. 4, April.

Thunberg, G. (2019) *No-one is too Small to Make a Difference*. Penguin.

Practice questions

Section A

1 Examine the criticisms that can be made of the UN Framework Convention on Climate Change and the Intergovernmental Panel on Climate Change. *[12 marks]*

2 Examine the reasons why shallow green ecology has become more mainstream than deep green ecology. *[12 marks]*

3 Examine the main reasons why sustainable development has been put forward as a solution to the tragedy of the commons. *[12 marks]*

Section C

1 Evaluate the extent to which there are still competing views about how to tackle environmental issues. *[30 marks]*

2 Evaluate the extent to which global civil society and non-state actors are successfully influencing nation-states to change their environmental policies. *[30 marks]*

3 Evaluate the extent to which international action on climate change has been blocked by conflict between developed and developing states. *[30 marks]*

4 Evaluate the extent to which the states have been responsible for holding back progress on environmental issues. *[30 marks]*

5 Evaluate the extent to which international climate change summits may be described as making progress. *[30 marks]*

7 Power and developments

Learning outcomes

By the end of the chapter you should understand:
- → the meanings of hard, soft and smart power, and how they can be used in global politics
- → different forms of state power, including superpowers, great powers and emerging powers, with examples
- → different types of polarity, including unipolar, bipolar and multipolar, with examples, and be able to discuss these in relation to each other and global stability
- → how to identify different systems of government, including democratic, semi-democratic, autocratic, failed states and rogue states, and be able to explain their characteristics and consequences for the global order
- → different 'spreads and developments' in global politics, including trends like the spread of liberal economies and democracies, and developments in the rule of law
- → how developments in global power have impacted different global issues, including conflict, poverty, human rights and the environment, allowing you to make synoptic links across topics

Getting you started

On 3 November 2020 the US's global position was once more questioned by an election which resulted in Joe Biden becoming the 46th President of the United States of America. The election was unusual in many ways, not least because of the Covid-19 pandemic. Not only did the election take much longer to call (because there were many more postal votes cast, delaying the counting of results), but it also meant the election appeared very close, until some of the last states were called. Trump publicly disputed the outcome throughout the process. Biden's inauguration also looked very different against the backdrop of a global pandemic with social distancing, masks, heavy security and no large crowds. Trump did not attend Biden's inauguration: it is highly unusual for a former president not to witness the swearing-in ceremony of the new president.

The counting of the electoral votes was hotly contested by Trump and his supporters, which dramatically culminated in the storming of the Capitol on the 6 January 2021. Trump met with widespread criticism for not discouraging these actions and there was a subsequent impeachment trial for incitement of insurrection, at which he was acquitted. The insurrection was a significant threat to liberal democracy in a country that has long been heralded as 'the leader of the free world'.

The inauguration of Joe Biden in January 2021

The polarisation between the two candidates can further be seen when comparing their very different inauguration speeches. This indicates that a Biden presidency will be a different era and might once more change global power structures. All of this has given the US a very different image on the global stage; question marks remain over just how influential this will be in international relations. The rhetoric of the Biden administration following the 2020 election was very much one of rebuilding the US, especially domestically, though Biden is also concerned to improve the US's foreign policy relationships and repair its global image.

This is vastly different from the Trump administration's tag line 'America first', which he used in his inaugural address:

> Together, we will make America strong again. We will make America wealthy again. We will make America proud again. We will make America safe again. And yes, together, we will make America great again.

Trump's apparently realist approach stood in stark contrast to Biden's emphasis on a much more cooperative and accountable approach in his inaugural address:

> Politics doesn't have to be a raging fire, destroying everything in its path. Every disagreement doesn't have to be a cause for total war. And we must reject the culture in which facts themselves are manipulated and even manufactured.

The US was for a long time seen as a global leader, but in more recent years there have been questions over whether its power has been in decline. Other states are starting to demonstrate a significant challenge to the US's position. In addition, there have been new forms of power balance emerging, in a multipolar world, with regional bipolarity appearing and states vying to be regional hegemons.

In this chapter we will consider what represents power in global politics, the extent to which the balance of power is changing and also the political realities between then and now.

Different types of global power

'Power' is a frequently used term in global relations. However, it can be hard to define. At its essence, power means the ability to exert influence through various means over others. In the case of global politics, this relates to the methods nation-states use to exercise control and achieve the outcomes they want.

Realists suggest that nation-states exist in a global 'self-help' environment and therefore their focus is on survival in an anarchic world order in which there is no supranational authority capable of enforcing global standards of behaviour. The so-called 'billiard ball model' (see page 10) helps us to visualise this: states are constantly colliding with each other as they seek to protect their own interests. As a result, conflict is inevitable. This also demonstrates another way that realists often see states as accumulating power through the structural dynamics of a system of international anarchy.

For liberals, power in the international system is interwoven and interconnected, especially now, with the advance of globalisation. The cobweb model (see page 20) illustrates this approach, whereby the interests of states are so closely intertwined that they gain more from cooperation than from competition. These two models help us begin to establish how the balance of power affects the global political system.

Topic link

The ideas of international anarchy and complex interdependence are covered in Chapter 1. Power and developments have been one of the focal areas of interest for these theories.

Case study

The BRICS countries: Brazil, Russia, India, China, South Africa

The BRICS countries: Brazil, Russia, India, China, South Africa

Jim O'Neill, the former chairman of Goldman Sachs Asset Management, coined the term 'BRICS' as shorthand for the five major emerging economies of Brazil, Russia, India, China and South Africa. The BRICS have met annually since 2009, taking turns to host the event in a different location in the same 5-year cycle, starting with Russia and ending with South Africa. The latter first attended in 2010 as a guest, and first hosted as a full member in 2013.

The initial BRIC country grouping was controversial, with some of the countries in the group more developed than others, particularly economically. It was also controversial that the group did not initially include any African countries, especially considering that it was supposed to represent newly emerging global powers, and therefore intended to contest the traditional global power hierarchies. This is one of the main reasons behind South Africa's admission. Nigeria, another African country with dramatic potential for growth, has since been added to the MINT countries, also a term O'Neill coined. The MINT countries represent a similar but more recent grouping to the BRICS, and comprise Mexico, Indonesia, Nigeria and Turkey.

The rise of the BRICS and MINT countries demonstrates the way in which the landscape of international politics is changing. In recent history, the Global North has dominated economic development. However, the twenty-first century may see economic and, with it, political influence shifting from West to East. The G20, unlike the G7, represents developing as well as developed nations and is increasing in global influence. In 2015, China established the AIIB, providing a rival centre of economic structural power to the Western-dominated World Bank and IMF. China has one of the biggest economies in the world and is a serious competitor to the US for the world's largest economy.

Activity

1 Research the economic power of the BRICS and the MINT countries in terms of GDP, foreign direct investment, and influence in global and regional organisations (economic structural power).
2 Make a table showing which of these countries is the most/ least economically impressive.
3 Do you agree that Jim O'Neill included appropriate emerging countries in his acronyms?
4 To what extent do you think economic influence brings political influence?

One way to consider the power of a nation-state is in terms of its key capabilities. A state's strength can be measured based on several fundamental capabilities:

- **Economic power:** often measured in GDP, or GDP per capita, but it may also include factors such as trade balances, levels of debt, stability of economic growth, influence over trade rules and contributions to international programmes and organisations, including NGOs, international aid, and research and development (R&D, see below).
- **Military power:** this not only includes the size of a nation's standing army, but crucially its global reach (a criterion for being a superpower) – that is to say, a state's ability to deploy anywhere at any time. This includes naval strength, air force capacity and, importantly, technological capacities, including nuclear weapons, drones, intelligence and increasingly cyber technology.
- **Cultural power:** this represents a state's global cultural outreach, for example through television, film, food, fashion, celebrities and brand names. This is a more controversial and complex characteristic, which is harder to measure. Some argue that the world is becoming increasingly homogenised (see Chapter 2), while others argue that the world has become a 'melting pot', with many different cultures competing for global influence. Whichever approach you agree with, there is no doubt that a nation-state's cultural appeal can provide it with important soft-power influence in international relations. Globalisation has, for example, traditionally been seen as a way in which the US has been able to globally expand its influence through the appeal of its political values and culture. This is often referred to as Americanisation or, more negatively, 'McDonaldisation' or 'Coca-Colonisation'.
- **Diplomatic power:** this includes a number of features, including elements of structural power, the reach of its foreign policy, and the global impression a state makes, together with its ability to utilise its power of influence. For a state to exert diplomatic strength it should be prepared to provide global leadership on issues such as conflict resolution, the environment, the global economy, poverty and development.
- **Population power:** although on face value this is a relatively straightforward measure, it does have underlying complexities. A large population can give a state significant power and influence, but it can also create problems. This is because if a state has a large population, many of whom live below the poverty level, it may be preoccupied with the internal social and economic problems this creates. It is also important to note whether or not the population of a state is ageing and how fertile its population is. Russia has very poor fertility levels

and has a declining population. Japan has also suffered from its resistance to immigration, which, some critics argue, has reduced its capacity for innovation. In contrast, the US has an expanding and youthful population – by 2050, it is estimated that the US population will be 438 million. If present trends continue, the Russian population could sink to 132 million by then.

- **Structural power:** this represents a state's capacity to influence intergovernmental organisations such as the UN, the Bretton Woods Institutions (the IMF, World Bank and WTO), the Asian Infrastructure Investment Bank (AIIB), and the G7 and G20. The US, for example, provides the largest share of funding for the World Bank and IMF, while China financially dominates the AIIB.
- **Regional power:** some states have significant influence in their respective regions. They may pool sovereignty to enhance their influence, which may give them a greater level of structural and diplomatic pressure, especially in terms of their influence over IGOs and NGOs. The US, for example, is the dominant force on the Organization of American States and Russia is by far the most important member of the Eurasian Customs Union. Indeed, some critics have suggested that Russia is using the Eurasian Customs Union (Armenia, Belarus, Kazakhstan, Kyrgyzstan and Russia) to reassert authority within its immediate zone of influence.
- **R&D power:** the amount that a state spends on R&D (research and development). R&D refers to innovation in developing products and services – some states may develop a reputation as being at the forefront of developments in certain technologies. This serves as a status symbol and can provide a state with strategic advantage, especially in terms of new technology.
- **Natural resource power:** states that are resource-rich can possess significant bargaining power. They can also be harder to sanction due to other states' reliance on their resources. Furthermore, a resource-rich state may be able to act more independently, since it does not need to rely as heavily on other states. However, being resource-rich is a hindrance to some states, particularly those in Sub-Saharan Africa. This has been described as the 'resource curse', since it can encourage powerful states to try to economically dominate poorer countries, relegating them to a state of neocolonial dependency.

Hard and soft power

According to liberal theorist Joseph Nye, the two main types of power tactics (as opposed to resource power, as outlined above) in global politics are **hard power** and **soft power**. Power tactics are about how a state uses the resources that it has.

Often realists will give more weight to hard power, while liberals will argue that soft power is just as significant, especially in a more globalised world.

Hard power

Hard power sits well within realism, as illustrated by the billiard ball model in which states fight, and often collide, with each other in their attempts to maximise their influence. It is defined by the more physical elements of military and economic power. For example, a powerful state is more likely to have the military strength to both physically defend itself and to attack or intervene in another state. A state with a strong economy will also be able to place sanctions on another state. Both military and economic actions are considered to be a form of command power, through which a state can change the actions of a rival state. Hard power therefore focuses on those ways in which a nation-state can compel obedience to its will.

Activity

Think of an example and provide evidence for a country that is powerful in each of the key areas of global power. You should find that different countries are powerful in different ways.

Key terms

Hard power A state's military and economic power. This can involve threats and coercion.

Soft power A state's diplomatic or cultural power. This can involve persuasion and attraction.

Soft power

Soft power is best understood as the way in which a nation-state achieves its objectives through the attractiveness of its culture and political system. Soft power therefore focuses on those non-military and non-economic ways in which a state can persuade other states to emulate its world view. Given the massive expansion of the internet and the spread of globalisation, the opportunity for states to advance their cultural and political values has never been greater, and so soft power provides a cheaper, less risky and potentially more effective way by which a state can seek to achieve its political objectives by winning friends and achieving positive global recognition.

As Joseph Nye puts it, the important thing in global relations is 'whose story wins'. The US's cultural appeal therefore played a significant role in the ending of the Cold War, since totalitarianism could not compete with the materialistic/consumer appeal of free-market capitalism. As the US journalist and satirist P. J. O'Rourke puts it, communism collapsed 'because nobody wanted to wear Bulgarian shoes'. Instead, the world turned towards US brands.

A more recent example of soft power has been seen with so-called 'vaccine diplomacy': while the West has generally vaccinated its own populations first, countries like China, Russia and India have been focusing on sharing vaccine stocks with poorer countries to improve their soft power.

Case study

Vaccine diplomacy

Vaccine diplomacy is an example of soft power. In the Covid-19 pandemic, vaccines were used to improve diplomatic relations (soft power). While the West focused on vaccinating its own populations, some emerging powers harnessed the vaccines to increase their international influence.

Serbia has the fastest vaccination rate in continental Europe and became a hub for vaccinations, supplying vaccines that it acquired from China and Russia to its neighbouring countries. Many of the citizens of countries like North Macedonia, Bosnia-Herzegovina and Montenegro travelled to Serbia for their vaccinations. There has even been so-called vaccination tourism from countries like Turkey. Serbia saw this as an opportunity to improve its geopolitical standing and also to bargain between the West and non-Western powers.

Meanwhile Russia and China sent vaccinations across the globe. Russia capitalised on Europe's delays in rolling out the vaccine and sold vaccines to Hungary. China publicised its vaccine generosity and even incorporated it in the Chinese Belt and Road Initiative framework, using middle eastern and African summits to offer vaccines along with investment opportunities. Even where traditional spheres of influence exist, vaccine diplomacy has operated differently; while America used an 'America first' rhetoric, China focused on selling vaccines in Latin America. Russia and China also worked on licensing deals to allow manufacturers in some countries (such as Indonesia and the United Arab Emirates) to produce vaccines themselves. This was publicly supported by the WHO and UNICEF which appealed for more such deals, giving Russia and China some soft power in these institutions.

India was also influential in supplying vaccines to its neighbours in South Asia, competing with China for diplomatic sway. However, some of India's soft power could be offset by the heavy negative publicity of the Indian government's mismanagement of the Covid crisis, particularly in the Ganges region.

The West focused first on vaccinating its own populations and then channelling any extra vaccines into programmes like COVAX, which distributed them to the most vulnerable people in the poorest countries. They also handed more power to pharmaceutical companies to decide where vaccines should go, which could be determined by highest bids. This might suggest that for Western governments, their domestic popularity is more important to them than improving their global soft power.

Smart power

Joseph Nye also coined the term 'smart power', which refers to a state using both hard- and soft-power methods to achieve its aims. For example, smart power was a key feature of President Obama's administration, and further popularised by former US secretary of state Hillary Clinton.

Obama's use of smart power was most clearly demonstrated in his approach to the middle east. In his 2009 Cairo speech, early in his first presidential term, he focused on the benefits of Islamic culture and emphasised the need for cooperation and co-existence. This marked a significant break from the rhetoric of the previous Bush administration, which had emphasised the neoconservative approach of hard power through the War on Terror. Through Obama's acknowledgement that the West had been antagonistic to the Arab world in the past, and his demonstration of cultural understanding, he was presenting a softer approach.

However, during his first term, and certainly his second, Obama also demonstrated a clear willingness to use hard power where necessary. Even during the Cairo speech, Obama stated that the US would not tolerate extremist threats to its national security. Furthermore, his rhetoric towards terrorism changed over time, in light of events such as the beheading of US hostages by ISIL, and his administration increasingly focused on drone strikes against militant targets. Therefore, the Obama administration exhibited the use of both hard and soft power.

Millions protested President Obama's 'hard power' use of drone strikes in regions such as Pakistan and Syria

What type of power is the most effective in international politics?

Hard

- Without a strong military power, states do not have the capacity to defend themselves, or to use military force as a threat.
- Economic power is essential to be taken seriously on a global scale and to be influential in punishing other states, e.g. with economic sanctions.
- Hard power enables countries to be more self-reliant and therefore less at the mercy of other states' behaviours; they are more able to act in their own national interest as they see fit. Hard power is generally more effective at getting quicker results.
- For democratic governments, hard power is appealing to their electorate, with many voters seeing importance in feeling economically secure and protected by a strong military. For autocratic states, hard power is important to maintain, or even enforce, stability.
- Hard power can provide quick intervention.

Soft

- Antagonistic behaviour can only get states so far without them isolating themselves. The most powerful states tend to have strong alliances and therefore a popularity in global politics.
- Soft power enables states to be more influential in the long term, with the spread of culture, ideas and values. This can enable states to win over hearts and minds abroad too, creating a stronger leadership position.
- Avoiding the need for military intervention or economic sanction enables states to grow stronger in other ways and focus their attention on other interests.
- In an increasingly interlinked world, alliances are more and more important for fulfilling common interests. Soft power is essential to this.
- Soft power needs to be built up over many years.

Evaluation prompt: Consider the contexts in which hard and soft power would be more effective. This will depend on the state's national interests and its main objectives. Liberals and realists will take different views on how effective hard and soft power are.

Activity

See if you can develop one point from the two sides of the debate into an evaluative paragraph. Try to add the following:

- Which theory would argue that hard power is more effective and why? Which theory would argue the opposite is true and why? Use key concepts where you can.
- Consider which type of power you think is more effective in relation to this point and explain why. Justify your answer by adding some evidence (an example) to support what you are saying.
- Try to make sure your counter point relates directly to and evaluates specifically your initial point. For example, Point 1: Hard power is essential for states to be able to effectively defend themselves. Counter point: Soft power can help promote peace and stability which is more beneficial in the long run, reducing the need to be as defensive.

'Carrots and sticks'

Often realists illustrate the concept of power within the international system with reference to 'carrots and sticks'. The carrot is a reward or an incentive (this could be cultural, political values, foreign policies, aid incentives), while the stick represents punishment (usually expressed through the withdrawing of aid, the imposition of sanctions and possible military strikes). For example, in the past the US has offered North Korea the 'carrot' of energy and food aid and the 'stick' of economic sanctions in relation to its testing of nuclear weapons – North Korea can have its 'carrot' if it stops testing but will face the 'stick' (in the form of economic sanctions as well as the US offering military and economic support to its neighbour, South Korea, in order to temper North Korea's aggression) if it continues with its nuclear programme. President Theodore Roosevelt put this principle succinctly when he said, in regard to US foreign policy, 'Speak softly and carry a big stick'.

Table 7.1 summarises the types of power, along with examples and theoretical links.

Table 7.1 Types of global power and theoretical links

Type of power	Theoretical links	Examples
Hard: economic and military strength	**Realist:** the idea of 'carrots and sticks'. For realists, hard power is by far the dominant form of power and is most significant in defining a state's strength. They argue that without sufficient hard power a state's sovereignty is weakened. Hard power is crucial in an anarchic system in which every state is competing, and conflict is inevitable. Hard power is seen as a coercive force and is generally used unilaterally.	Bush's neoconservative approach during the War on Terror. The US used its military power to lead a coalition of forces in Afghanistan and Iraq. Obama ordered drone strikes in various countries, including Afghanistan, Iraq and Syria. Russia's invasion of Crimea in 2014 (and ongoing presence in various parts of Ukraine) has been a clear challenge to Ukraine's sovereignty through the use of hard power. The economic sanctions placed on Russia by various countries as a result of its actions in Crimea, including Australia, Canada and the US, and regional blocs and organisations such as the EU and NATO. In April 2017 President Trump launched 59 Tomahawk cruise missiles against the Assad regime to deter further chemical attacks.
Soft: cultural, economic and diplomatic strength	**Liberal:** soft power is the way in which a nation-state achieves influence through persuasion. This can be manifested through its cultural and diplomatic appeal. For liberals this is an increasingly important form of power in an ever more globalised world, where interconnectedness is a common feature and systems of global governance are a necessity. Soft power is generally used multilaterally, and liberals see it as a way to promote stability.	Obama's Cairo speech marked a move towards the increased use of soft power in US foreign policy, especially in relation to the Arab world. States may use foreign aid as a means of soft power to attract, persuade and influence. Biden's inauguration speech indicated a greater focus on soft power with sentences like 'Much to do, much to heal, much to restore, much to build and much to gain'. Arguably the formation of the BRICS was a move to increase their soft power by bolstering their diplomatic influence, especially within IGOs (the G20, the IMF, the World Bank). The US has often been said to have a significant global cultural influence, with globalisation even sometimes called 'Americanisation', seen in its influence over popular culture, fashion, music, fast food, etc. Germany arguably exerted its soft power during the 2015/16 migrant crisis in Europe, taking a leading role on the issue and accepting large numbers of refugees. The popular international appeal of heads of state in the way they have dealt with 2020's global pandemic, notably New Zealand's Jacinda Ardern, could be seen as soft power.
Smart: hard and soft power used in combination	**Liberal/softer realist:** mostly a liberal idea, although some softer realists may also see the merits of using soft power to reinforce hard power (although they ultimately give hard power precedence). Joseph Nye coined the term.	The Obama administration's approach to the middle east used soft power (e.g. in the Cairo speech) in combination with hard power (e.g. drone strikes). The UN can also be seen to use smart power, e.g. it offers large amounts of aid and humanitarian relief (forms of soft power), but it also enforces sanctions and military intervention in certain instances.

The changing balance of global power

As well as understanding the different types of power, it is important to consider how states are viewed as powers within the international system, and their varying significance to global affairs. It is important to understand how and why this power is classified. This means considering how we might describe the most powerful states – or states where the power is spread across several significant but not ultimate powers – or those states that have only recently become more powerful. We will describe power in relation to the types of power we have explored above.

In global politics, this is often seen within the changing historical context. Prior to the First World War there were several **great powers**, including Great Britain,

Key term

Great power A state that wields significant global influence militarily and economically and through its leading role in IGOs such as the UN, G7, G20 and the Bretton Woods Institutions. It therefore has a forward foreign policy and plays an influential role in global issues.

Key terms

Superpower A state that possesses all the characteristics of a great power, but will be able to make its influence felt anywhere in the world through advanced nuclear and cyber technology (and the means of delivering a devastating military response anywhere in the world at any time), diplomacy and influence over its allies, which share its ideological beliefs.

Emerging power A state that has started to acquire great power status, but has not yet met all of the criteria to become a great power. Generally, it is becoming rapidly powerful in certain areas and will be likely to have a significant level of regional influence, while in other areas it may still be developing.

France and the Austro-Hungarian Empire. The emergence of new powers during the interwar period, such as fascist Italy, Japan, Nazi Germany, the communist Soviet Union and the US, meant that global power was now shared more equally. But after the Second World War, power shifted again to the war's victors, the dominant Allied powers (China, Great Britain, France, the Soviet Union and the US). This is reflected in the many international institutions that were formed by and contained representatives of these powers, for example the UN Security Council (UNSC).

The balance shifted again in the Cold War era, during which time there were two clear **superpowers**: the Soviet Union and the US, which were engaging in a superpower rivalry based around ideology. These two superpowers were unrivalled by any other state, and both had their own clear ideological and regional spheres, with the US dominating the Western world with capitalism and the Soviet Union dominating the Eastern world with communism. Virtually every other world state was aligned to either the US or the Soviet Union and their respective ideologies during this period.

When communism collapsed in eastern Europe, leading to the fall of the Soviet Union in 1991, the US, as the sole remaining superpower, possessed global hegemonic status. No other power came close to matching its influence, and leading US political commentator Charles Krauthammer coined the phrase America's 'unipolar moment'. However, especially since the bloody aftermath of the Iraq War and the global financial crisis, **emerging powers**, such as China and Russia, pose a challenge to US hegemony. This has led some political philosophers, like John Mearsheimer, to predict that we are once again entering a period of power transition, which is likely to lead to a more multipolar balance of power.

Topic link

Balance of power is discussed in Chapter 1, when considering the inevitability of war.

Distinguish between

Great powers and superpowers

Great powers

- Great powers must have significant regional influence within their 'near abroad'.
- They should have the capacity for significant military outreach.
- They should possess a major role in international organisations, providing them with significant structural power.
- They will have some of the strongest economies in the world.

Superpowers

- A superpower must have significant global power and 'global reach'. This is particularly true in the case of military power.
- It must have nuclear weapons, although recent developments in cyber technology may reduce nuclear importance.
- It should exert dominant structural power within important institutions of regional and global governance.
- It should be able to assert its global influence anywhere in the world at any time.
- It will possess a world view and the willingness to proactively enforce that world view in international relations.
- As US foreign policy professor W. T. R. Fox put it in 1944, a superpower will possess 'great power plus great mobility of power'.

Table 7.2 The BRICS powers

	Brazil	Russia	India	China	South Africa
2020 GDP ranking (IMF)	12	11	6	2	43
2019 population ranking (World Bank)	6	9	2	1	24
Nuclear weapons	No – Brazil has the technology but has signed the Treaty on the Non-Proliferation of Nuclear Weapons	Yes	Yes	Yes	No – it has done in the past but dismantled them when it signed the NPT
2020 military expenditure rank by GDP (Stockholm International Peace Institute)	15	4	3	2	not in top 40
Natural resources and trade	Brazil has many natural resources, including gold, iron, uranium and petroleum, among many others. It also has a significant amount of hydropower. It trades heavily in agriculture (especially coffee, beef, soya and sugar). Brazil is also a big supplier of timber and oil. It has significant textiles and electronics industries.	Russia has significant natural resources, including oil, gas and coal (especially in the Ural Mountains). It also has uranium. Natural resources dominate Russia's exports. It also has a significant proportion of the globe's fossil fuels.	India has lots of major mineral resources, including coal, iron ore and bauxite, as well as natural gas, diamonds and limestone. It also has nuclear reserves in uranium and thorium. India has been famous for its telecommunications industry, with lots of MNCs outsourcing to India.	China is behind only the US and Russia in terms of the proportion of natural resources it holds. It has significant resources of coal, iron, tin, copper and zinc, among various others. China is renowned for its electronics exports.	South Africa has many natural resources, including diamonds, gold and silver. It also has salt, iron, cobalt, copper, uranium and bauxite, among others. Its main exports are tropical fruit, sugar, wool, gold and diamonds. South Africa is yet to unlock the full extent of its natural resources.
IGO membership	Member of the G20. Member of the sub-regional bloc Mercosur.	Member of the G20. Permanent member of the UNSC. Was a G7/8 member until suspension for its invasion of Ukraine.	Member of the G20. India is not a UNSC permanent member but has been a key contender whenever there have been talks to expand the permanent membership base.	Member of the G20. Permanent member on the UNSC.	Member of the G20. Member of the African Union (AU).

A good way to learn the types of power each state has and how they compare with each other is to make Top Trumps cards. You could do this with classmates, or ask your teacher to do it in a lesson so you don't have to make all the cards yourself. If you don't know how to play Top Trumps, use the following instructions:

1   Make your cards using the criteria in Table 7.2, or applying the criteria to another group, such as the G20. Each member of your group should make several cards and cut them out. You will then have a deck. (Note: for categories that don't have a clear 'value' you might need to rank them based on which country you think is the best and worst in that particular field.)

2   To start, shuffle and deal all the cards evenly between all players, face down. Each player should shield his or her cards from opponents.

3   The player to the dealer's left begins. They choose a category (e.g. GDP ranking) from their card and read out the value. Each player then reads their value for the category. The player with the highest value wins and takes all the other players' top/front cards and puts these cards to the bottom of their pile. It is then their turn to choose a category from the next card.

4   If the cards share the same value or there are no data for that category, all the 'in play' cards are placed in the middle and the same player chooses from the next card in his/her deck. The winner of this next hand also wins the cards in the middle.

5   The person holding all the cards at the end wins.

Key terms

Polarity The way in which power is distributed in the international system, into unipolarity, bipolarity and multipolarity.

Unipolarity A single pole of power, meaning one state dominates all others. To be hegemonic, a state must therefore possess ultimate power in all its capabilities and be able to engage in unilateral action anywhere in the world at any time.

Bipolarity Two competing poles of power. This is best characterised with the superpower rivalry between the US and Soviet Union during the Cold War. For true bipolarity, the two powers are evenly matched and there is a clear balance of power.

Multipolarity Multiple poles of power, in which several states compete with each other. They may have different strengths and weaknesses in terms of their power, but each wields relatively equal influence on the international stage.

Polarity

Polarity refers to 'poles of power'. There are three main forms of polarity: **unipolarity** (a single pole of power), **bipolarity** (two poles of power) and **multipolarity** (multiple poles of power).

Bipolarity: the Cold War era

One of the key questions polarity raises is to do with how stable the international system is/was during a certain power dynamic.

The Cold War provides a classic example of a bipolar system, in which there were two key and equally matched superpowers competing for global influence. During this period, the UN became largely redundant, since the Soviet Union and the US, as permanent members of the UNSC, would veto any perceived threats to their own interests (see Box 7.1). Each superpower also had its own military alliances and client states whose support it could rely upon. The US was the leading member of NATO and the Soviet Union dominated the Warsaw Pact. In addition, Israel had close ties with the US and Cuba with the Soviet Union, while both superpowers continually sought to reduce the other's influence in non-aligned states, such as Egypt, India and Indonesia.

Box 7.1

Key events of the Cold War

Some key events of the Cold War that demonstrate the debate over bipolarity and stability:

1962   The Soviet Union places nuclear missiles in Cuba, provoking the Cuban Missile Crisis. President Kennedy responds with a 'quarantine' of Cuba, which takes the superpowers to the brink of nuclear war. This was the most unstable time of the Cold War.

$\rightarrow$

1975	President Gerald Ford and Soviet leader Leonid Brezhnev agree to the Helsinki Accords, which guarantee the borders of Europe. This is often seen as being the high point of détente. This arguably demonstrates that mutually assured destruction (MAD) can be effective in creating stability.
1980	Election of President Ronald Reagan. The first Reagan administration (1981–85) dramatically increases Cold War tensions – cruise missiles are placed in western Europe and plans are developed for the Strategic Defence Initiative ('Star Wars') to protect the US from Soviet missile attack. This is another example of heightened tensions.
1986	The Reykjavik Summit between Gorbachev and Reagan significantly reduces Cold War tensions. Realists might use this as another example of stability.

Mutually assured destruction acted as a disincentive for conflict between the two superpower nations (the Soviet Union and the US) during the Cold War

What are the implications of bipolarity for global stability?

Liberals and realists have very different opinions on whether or not this system of Cold War bipolarity created global stability.

According to realists such as Kenneth Waltz, the Cold War promoted peace, since the existence of two evenly balanced powers meant that neither side was capable of eliminating the other. As a result, both sides appreciated the limits of what they could achieve and so a balance of power was established, which it was not in the interests of either side to try to undermine. If one side had risked war, the results for both would have been catastrophic. As we will see later in the chapter, there are some parallels here to regional bipolarity we have seen more recently, for example in Saudi Arabia and Iran.

This therefore created an equilibrium that neither side was prepared to break, since by destabilising the equilibrium it would have created conflict due to the threat of mutually assured destruction (MAD). Indeed, some political commentators have even argued that Cold War bipolarity actually encouraged understanding and conflict resolution, since both sides understood that often the best way of advancing their own interests was by working with the other. For example, following the death of Joseph Stalin in 1953, diplomatic relations briefly improved between the secretary-general of the Soviet Union, Nikita Khrushchev, and President Dwight Eisenhower. In 1959 in Moscow, for example, Khrushchev and Vice-President Richard Nixon engaged in an informal and jocular exchange about the relative merits of their two world views. Soon after, Khrushchev visited Eisenhower in Washington, DC to further try to develop trust between the two sides.

During the 1970s, President Richard Nixon and Secretary-General Leonid Brezhnev established a period of détente between the US and the Soviet Union. One consequence of this was the Strategic Arms Limitations Treaty (1972), which slowed the arms build-up between the two powers. The 1975 Helsinki Accords, which were signed between Nixon's successor, Gerald Ford, and Leonid Brezhnev, provide the best example of the sort of cooperation that can be achieved in a bipolar world. Not only did Helsinki involve each side, guaranteeing the borders of the other, it even included commitments to increase economic, technical and cultural relations between them.

However, according to liberals, bipolarity is destabilising and dangerous. This is because both sides will continually be advancing their military, diplomatic and economic interests at the expense of the other, so creating fear, suspicion and latent hostility. It, therefore, does not provide the conditions for a lasting or meaningful peace. According to the Ancient Greek historian Thucydides, it was actually the inherent dangers of bipolarity that led to the Peloponnesian War between Athens and Sparta (431 BCE–404 BCE), since 'what made the war inevitable was the growth of Athenian power and the fear which this caused Sparta'.

Therefore, liberals claim that the Cold War was much more defined by very long periods of mutual distrust and antagonism, as illustrated by US paranoia about a 'missile gap' in the 1950s or the ease with which the Cuban Missile Crisis could have provoked nuclear war as the Soviet Union sought to pull ahead in the arms race by placing nuclear missiles in Cuba.

The early 1980s were also profoundly unstable as President Ronald Reagan dramatically increased spending on nuclear weapons in order to prove US superiority over the Soviet Union. In 1983, as we have seen, the Soviet Union shot down a South Korean airliner, which could have provoked a military response from the US. In the same year, the Soviets came close to a military strike on the West when they made the mistake of thinking that the NATO military exercise Operation Able Archer was the real thing. The way in which both events came very close to provoking direct military confrontation was, of course, due to the profound distrust between the two adversaries. Indeed, according to Robert S. McNamara, who served as US defence secretary from 1961 to 1968, 'Cold War: hell it was a hot war!'

Proxy and peripheral wars

During the Cold War, both sides also tried to extend their global influence at the expense of the other through 'hot wars'. In the Vietnam War (c.1963–75), the Soviet Union and the US were not in direct combat, but they took opposing sides and backed these sides (North Vietnam and South Vietnam respectively) to win. Each saw a victory as furthering their position in the superpower rivalry.

Activity

1 To what extent do you think the nuclear bipolarity of the Cold War made direct military confrontation between the superpowers more or less likely?

2 Do you agree with the realist political philosopher Kenneth Waltz that the Cold War was a period of stability? Explain your answer fully. You may want to consider whether peace is simply the absence of war.

Alternatively, peripheral wars were fought between one superpower and another country (but the superpower's opposition would be allied to their superpower rival). For example, during the Korean War (1950–53) the US fought alongside South Korea to restrict communist advance in the Korean peninsula.

Debate

Was the Cold War system a stable system?

No

- Liberals generally hold this view, since they see the Cold War as a dangerous and turbulent time.
- Although avoiding direct conflict throughout the entire period, both sides tested the resolve of the other through global proxy wars.
- MAD was far from stable – it nearly ended in nuclear war during the Cuban Missile Crisis in 1962. According to Robert S. McNamara, who was John F. Kennedy's defence secretary at the time, 'We lucked out. It was luck that saved us.'
- There were no stabilising checks and balances on the superpowers, given the UN's ineffectiveness at this time.

Yes

- Realists mostly hold this view. The balance of power between the Soviet Union and the US created a stable equilibrium, which meant that neither side would gain from waging all-out war against the other.
- In his 1987 book *The Long Peace*, key realist proponent John Lewis Gaddis argued that the Cold War was a time of relative stability because although there were lesser conflicts, there was no direct conflict between the two main powers. Conflicts between other powers were also ultimately less likely because all states revolved around the two main ideologies (communism and capitalism).
- The principle of mutually assured destruction (MAD) meant that neither power would launch a military or nuclear attack on the other. Both sides therefore had an incentive to avoid war.

Evaluation prompt: Decide whether you agree more with the liberal or realist viewpoint and then why you think that, using the most compelling piece of evidence you have to justify this position. Try to write that into a paragraph: 'I agree with the ... position because ... The example that best supports this view is ...'

The rise of US hegemony

During Ronald Reagan's presidency (1981–89) the US achieved a commanding lead in the Cold War. The economic pressures of competing with the US undermined the Soviet economy and under Secretary-General Mikhail Gorbachev, economic and political reforms were introduced. According to the nineteenth-century French historian and political theorist Alexis de Tocqueville, the most dangerous time for a dictatorship is when it begins to reform, since that reform is likely to be too slow to please its restive population. This was certainly the case with Gorbachev's reforms. As the momentum behind reform gathered pace, he gave more and more power to the constituent parts of the Soviet Union, the biggest of which, by far, was Russia led by Boris Yeltsin. When communist hardliners tried to overthrow Gorbachev in 1991, it was Yeltsin who rallied the nationalist opposition, defeated the coup and then, by declaring Russia independent, led to the dismantling of the Soviet Union. The union was formally dissolved on 26 December 1991.

The break-up of the Soviet Union established 15 new independent states. Russia was, of course, the biggest, but many of the others were extremely weak economically and left politically fragile from years of oppressive communism. They also faced struggles in terms of divided ethnic identities, particularly as state borders were being redefined.

Case studies

Georgia

- Georgia has had a tumultuous history with Russia. It was part of the Soviet Union and became independent in 1991.
- There is still tension between the US and Russia over Georgia, since Russia still regards it as within its sphere of influence.
- After the break-up of the Soviet Union, Georgia went through a period of sharp economic decline.
- Georgia has expressed its desire to be part of both the EU and NATO, which is a source of tension for Russia. The 2003 Rose Revolution, which marked the end of pro-Russian leadership in Georgia, was a clear demonstration of pro-Western feeling.
- Georgia regards South Ossetia and Abkhazia as rightfully belonging to it. However, in 1993, Abkhazia declared itself an independent state. In 2008, as a result of war between Georgia and Russia, South Ossetia also declared itself independent. Both now look towards Russia for protection.
- Russia joined the WTO in 2012 after long-standing opposition from Georgia and a compromise, which involved close monitoring of the disputed territories of South Ossetia and Abkhazia.

Ukraine

- Ukraine has had a similar experience to Georgia since the break-up of the Soviet Union. It also became independent in 1991.
- It was left in economic ruin after the break-up of the Soviet Union.
- It is also internally divided. Many Ukrainians are pro-West, while others are fiercely loyal to Russia.
- The 2004 Orange Revolution saw mass demonstrations in the capital, Kiev, against corruption.
- Ukraine's government has close ties with the EU and would like eventual membership.
- The annexation of Crimea in 2014 saw tensions flare up once more between Russia and the West. There have also been significant tensions in the Donbass region. The unrest in Ukraine is ongoing and has seen various flare-ups in recent years. Russia's actions resulted in international economic sanctions, as well as Russia's suspension from the G8. Tensions are ongoing.

Evaluation prompt: In the case of both Georgia and Ukraine, the Cold War history and context are important for understanding more recent events and the ongoing tensions, so they remain good examples of both the tensions that have resulted from bipolarity and regional tensions, with former Soviet States redefining their positions.

Case study

Russia and hard power today

Military power

Russia's hard power in terms of military strength is significant. Following what Russia considered to be an unsatisfactory experience in the 2008 Georgian war, the military underwent reform in 2009 and now has the fourth highest military budget in the world. Military activity has expanded well beyond its periphery (e.g. Ukraine and Georgia), including since 2015 a military presence in Syria. Russia has taken part in joint military ventures, such as in 2019 when Russia and China sent naval vessels to South Africa to engage in military exercises.

In 2020 Russia demonstrated its military hard power by sending two nuclear-capable Blackjack bombers to Venezuela for training purposes, which the US considered a provocative gesture. Russia's recent display of hard power has demonstrated that it is capable of a military global presence, albeit of a different nature to the US's. Russia cannot compete with the US in regard to aircraft carriers or number of military bases, but it does have regional dominance, nuclear capabilities (the biggest nuclear stockpile in the world), a strong ground force (one of the largest forces in the world which still uses conscription, and includes the most significant tank force) and strategies such as resource coercion.

→

Economic power

Russia's economic power does not match its military power, though it is still significant. Russia is considered to be an upper-middle-income country and while it has a significant GDP (ranking eleventh globally), given its global position its economy isn't as strong as might be expected. Russia is one of the founding members of the Eurasian Customs Union, which was established as a counterweight to the EU in Russia's 'near abroad'.

Energy revenues account for the largest part of Russia's economy, making it a resources superpower: it is very reliant on natural resources, specifically the export of natural gas and oil, and the government controls both of these. However, Russia has experienced a number of financial crises: it struggled in the 1990s, and although it picked up briefly in the early twenty-first century, it fell into significant decline following the global financial crisis. Recovery since has been unstable. Russia has also experienced significant economic sanctions following its annexation of Crimea, as well as losing its position in the G8. Russia's economic development is extremely uneven across the country, with Moscow contributing a much higher proportion to economic growth than elsewhere, and wealth distribution being very uneven.

What are the implications of unipolarity for global stability?

When the Soviet Union collapsed in 1991, the US achieved hegemonic status, since there was now no other state that could globally compete with it. The resulting world order that characterised the ending of the Cold War was therefore unipolar. According to Joseph Nye, 'not since Rome has one nation loomed so large above the others'. Charles Krauthammer has referred to this period as representing the US's 'unipolar moment'. One aide of George W. Bush is even alleged to have gone so far as to claim that 'we're an empire now, and when we act, we create our own reality'.

According to the hegemonic stability theory, a hegemon that is perceived by most other global players as being benign can act as a global police, and this will therefore encourage and promote global stability. The awesome and unchallengeable power of Rome provided stability in the ancient world for centuries, since no other power could challenge its authority. This long period of peace therefore became known as the Pax Romana. In the second half of the nineteenth century, the naval outreach of Great Britain also provided international stability, as British ships patrolled global sea lanes and no other power was prepared to seek to displace Great Britain as global hegemon.

At the end of the Cold War, a similar Pax Americana was also achieved. American ideals of free-market liberal democracy, as Francis Fukuyama pointed out in *The End of History*, were triumphant and the global popularity of the US's economic, political and cultural identity was assured. Other powers 'bandwagoned' behind the US in order to secure their protection, share its ideals and avoid its wrath. The US was seen as a 'benign leader'.

The dangers of unipolarity

However, according to realists like Kenneth Waltz, a unipolar world can also be highly unstable. This is because the hegemonic status of one state can encourage dangerous resentment among emerging powers. Waltz argues that because states are security-maximisers, in their attempts to protect themselves, they will feel constrained by another power's claims to global hegemony. This will be particularly dangerous and destabilising when a hegemon is declining in power and influence. Such a state of affairs has been referred to as power transition and can make international relations extremely volatile.

It has been argued that this provoked the First World War, since a rapidly growing Germany, emboldened by British failures in the Boer War, decided to challenge what had been the hegemonic status of Great Britain. According to this principle, US hegemony encouraged stability, so long as her position was unrivalled. However, the US's failure to achieve its objectives in either Afghanistan or Iraq, followed by the collapse of the US bank Lehman Brothers, has more recently highlighted US military and economic weakness, so undermining the US's claims to global leadership.

The attitude of emerging powers towards the existing hegemon is therefore vital. If the hegemon is resented and emerging states decide that they can achieve more by challenging it, this can create the environment for destabilising power transition. Until recently, for example, China has been prepared to accept US hegemony. However, its increasing assertiveness in its 'near abroad', represented by its building of reefs in the South China Sea in defiance of US-led regional condemnation, suggests that it feels able to challenge US dominance. Equally, the Russian annexation of Crimea from Ukraine in 2014 in defiance of an onslaught of Western criticism indicates that Russia may also begin to probe US weakness. The way in which President Barack Obama also refused to provide global leadership during the Arab Spring and then stood by as Russia militarily intervened in Syria on behalf of President Assad further suggests the limitations of US power.

The radical political philosopher Noam Chomsky has also argued that the possession by one state of hegemonic power is very dangerous, since a lack of constraints on what it is able to do can encourage it to act in defiance of international norms of behaviour. This can therefore create the potential for malign hegemony, in which one state becomes so powerful that it no longer takes into account the views of other states. Chomsky argues that a unipolar world can encourage a hegemon to become a 'rogue superpower', pursuing its own interests at the expense of international law. The way, for example, in which the US invaded Iraq in 2003 without a UN mandate demonstrates the danger of one power having such pre-eminent power that it can ignore the wishes of other states and international organs of global governance.

Topic link

Chapter 2 discusses US hegemony in relation to globalisation. There is debate as to whether globalisation can actually be seen as Americanisation, and whether a decline in American hegemony and a rise in multipolarity could be part of the globalisation process.

Noam Chomsky has warned about the danger of a malign hegemony

Debate

Is the US still the global hegemon?

Yes

Economic

- The US remains the largest economy in the world. US GDP in 2020 was US$20.8 trillion.
- The US dollar is the main form of international currency.
- Wall Street is the world's central global trading hub.
- The US has huge amounts of structural power in important organs of global economic governance, such as the World Bank, IMF and WTO.
- The US has an expanding population that is estimated to reach 439 million by 2050.
- Six of the world's top ten most valuable brands in 2020 were American (Amazon, Google, Apple, Microsoft, Facebook, Walmart).

Cultural

- The US is pre-eminent in terms of soft-power influence. It is world-renowned in television and film and has globally leading fashion and corporate brands. The US has produced many of the world's most famous films and for a long time dominated the global box office.
- The dominance of American cultural values has encouraged some political commentators to argue that 'globalisation' is another word for 'Americanisation'.

Political

- The US possesses important structural power in many IGOs. It is the most proactive permanent member of the UNSC and plays the dominant role in IGOs such as the IMF, World Bank, G7 and NATO.

Military

- The US has the world's largest military budget. In 2020 the annual defence spending of the US was $778 billion. The US remained the largest defence spender in 2019 representing 38% of global military spending. The US's nearest rival is China, whose annual defence spending was $208 billion in 2020.
- The US has 800 military bases in more than 70 countries across the globe and so can deploy troops anywhere in the world at any time.
- The aggregate tonnage of the US navy, which forms the basis of US outreach, is greater in size than that of the next 13 navies combined. The US has 11 operational aircraft carriers compared with the UK (two), China (two, one under construction) and Russia (one). The US is also building two more aircraft carriers.

No

Economic

- China is expected to eventually overtake the US in terms of its GDP and foreign direct investment. China is said by some to already have overtaken the US in terms of purchase power parity.
- US debt to China amounted to over $1 trillion in 2020.
- China has overtaken the US as the biggest investor in Africa and South America.
- The AIIB (Asian Infrastructure Investment Bank) is based in Beijing. China proposed the implementation of the AIIB which came into being in 2015 and has the potential to rival the World Bank as a lender to the developing world. This can be seen as a response to the structural domination that the US has traditionally had in the Bretton Woods Institutions.
- Of the top ten of the most valuable brands in 2020, three were Chinese (ICBC, Ping An, Huawei).
- The Chinese Belt and Road Initiative (BRI) is an example of Chinese economic power and influence given that it will mean investment in over 70 countries and IGOs (see Chapter 1).

→

Cultural

- Other cultures are becoming more influential on a global scale. Bollywood and Nollywood are in direct competition with Hollywood. Association football is the most popular sport in the world and the most popular sports teams in the world are Manchester United and Real Madrid. In 2020 China became the world's biggest box office territory.
- The US's global soft-power influence has been dramatically undermined by controversies such as the Iraq War, waterboarding and Guantánamo Bay and more recently Trump's 'Remain in Mexico' policy (which has now been formally ended). Meanwhile, China has been expanding its global cultural influence by opening Confucius Institutes across the world, which spread Chinese values.

Chinatown in New York: due to immigration, there are a number of 'melting pots' in Western countries

Political

- There are rivals to the US's structural power, with many of the emerging powers taking on increasingly significant roles. China and Russia are also permanent five members of the UNSC. India is fast becoming a significant actor for the Global South. Many of these emerging powers hold significant regional power. Furthermore, the Bretton Woods Institutions have increasingly come under criticism for their Western (and, in particular, US) dominance. This has been a key feature of the anti-globalisation movement.
- President Donald Trump's 'America First' rhetoric may have alienated other countries, therefore undermining the US's soft-power global influence. His withdrawal of the US from the Paris climate change agreement in June 2017 provided China with the opportunity to seize global leadership in combating climate change. Biden has seemed to express a hard-line approach with China so far, albeit for different reasons to Trump, suggesting relations may not significantly improve.

Military

- Russia and China are both beginning to challenge US military might in terms of the global reach of their forces and the sophistication of their weaponry.
- China is developing short- and medium-range missiles, and Jin and Shang nuclear-powered submarines, in order to have the dominant military force in the South China Sea.
- In 2016, Russia announced that it had constructed the world's most lethal nuclear weapon: the RS-28 Sarmat, which can dodge radar, travel up to 10,000 km and carry up to 12 warheads. In June 2020 Russia released an Executive Order reinforcing its intention to continue to use nuclear weapons as a deterrent to threats. This was the first time in over 30 years Russia had made this kind of statement public.

In what ways is the world becoming more multipolar?

Multipolarity is a system of global power in which there are a number of relatively evenly matched powers. This means that no one power can claim hegemonic influence over the others. As a result of the changing balance of economic and military global power, the consequences of globalisation and advances in military technology, it has been claimed that the contemporary world is increasingly multipolar. This is because no one power can dominate all others, as was the case during the Roman Empire and was, briefly, the case at the end of the Cold War when the US was the unchallenged hegemon. Today, power is much more evenly distributed between states, IGOs and NGOs, and there are so many more constraints on a state's freedom of action that even the US cannot make its presence felt everywhere in the world.

Activity

Decide whether you think the US is a true hegemon.

Use the debate box to help you write a paragraph explaining whether you think the US is a true hegemon (economically, culturally and politically), justifying it with evidence.

Economic and cultural dominance

Although the US is still the world's pre-eminent power, its economic dominance is being challenged not only by China but also by the rise of other emerging powers, such as Brazil, India, Russia and, perhaps most notably, the EU, which is now the most lucrative single market in the world. Global brands are challenging US brands and China has become the world's greatest neocolonial power, investing massively in Africa and South America – regions that were traditionally within the US's economic zone of influence. The fact, too, that China controls so much of the US's debt further illustrates how the economic balance of power has shifted eastwards, while the Washington Consensus of free-market liberalism is increasingly being challenged by the Beijing Consensus of state-orientated capitalism, which weathered the 2008 financial crisis surprisingly unscathed. The establishment in 2015 of the AIIB as a rival to the World Bank in influencing the developing world provides a further example of the way in which economic power is moving eastwards.

The 2016 election of Donald Trump demonstrated extraordinary class and racial divisions within the US – a divide that was largely repeated in the Biden election. These divisions contrast with the popularity of Russia's Putin (who has one of the highest approval ratings of any leader although not as high as it was in his first presidency) and the nationalist self-confidence of Recep Erdoğan's Turkey and Xi Jinping's China. The way in which global news networks such as Al Jazeera and RT (formerly Russia Today) increasingly challenge the US's traditional dominance of global news has also fostered this greater sense of empowerment among emerging powers. Germany and the UK also regularly compete with the US for pre-eminence in global soft-power influence.

Widespread coverage of human rights abuses, such as waterboarding, has also eroded the US's global cultural influence. President Trump even admitted that the US is no better than any other country in terms of human rights violations. This has therefore undermined the US's traditional claim of moral exclusivity, indicating that the US may now see itself more on a par with other powers. Biden has been outspoken about promoting human rights and the administration has been critical of China's human rights record, as seen with Secretary of State Blinken at their 2020 meeting in Anchorage. Similarly Biden has been very critical of Putin. However, American foreign policy does not always match its rhetoric, given there is a balancing act between the values of human rights and reaching agreements, especially around climate change, which could necessitate working alongside other countries regardless of their human rights records.

Military and cyber technology dominance

Militarily, the rise of China is also challenging the US. China is investing heavily in long-range bombers, nuclear submarines and medium-range missiles in order to stake its claim as the pre-eminent power in the Pacific. President Obama's tactical decision to militarily focus on the Pacific rather than the Atlantic has been seen by some political commentators as a tacit admission that the US is no longer prepared to fight on both these fronts. The ability to fight such a two-front war has traditionally been seen as defining hegemonic status. However, in 2021 at the G7 Summit in Cornwall Biden agreed a 'New Atlantic Charter' with the UK, which can be seen in part as a response to the threat from their autocratic rivals Russia and China.

Humiliations in Afghanistan and Iraq also demonstrate that there are severe limitations on what the US is militarily able to achieve. President Obama's unwillingness to provide either a diplomatic or military lead during the Arab Spring, as well as his failure to intervene in the Syrian civil war, has enabled both Russia and Turkey to take the initiative in developing the peace process. Furthermore, Trump's foreign policy and the US's continued withdrawal from the global arena have suggested less military focus overseas. Russia has also been emboldened by its success in regaining Crimea from Ukraine and so is now flexing its military muscles outside its 'near abroad' for the first time since the end of the Cold War.

In addition, the growing significance of cyber technology further illustrates that any power with a sophisticated computer cadre (easily achieved with the globalisation of human ingenuity and free passage of computer scientists across borders) could make the US's hegemonic status as the world's most powerful nuclear state redundant. This is in part a further reason for the 'New Atlantic Charter' and one of the areas the Western alliance wants to focus on. This is because a cyber-attack could enable a relatively weak state to bring a significantly more powerful one to its knees.

Therefore, as the US progressively finds its military, economic, diplomatic and cultural influence challenged by emerging powers, it is likely that the world will become increasingly multipolar. This dispersal of power to the BRICS, MINT and regional power blocs, such as the EU, will prove difficult to reverse, while on the UNSC, the US increasingly finds itself confronted by a more assertive Russia and China. Some have also suggested that globalisation has more widely dispersed power to non-state actors, such as global pressure groups, powerful multinational corporations and IGOs. This means that as the centrality of the state in global relations is challenged, so this will make it progressively harder for one state to dominate the rest of the global community.

Do Russia or China post a significant challenge to US hegemony?

There is certainly a challenge to US power from both Russia and China. Russia has been involved in various conflicts including Georgia, Ukraine and Syria, which have strained US relations. It has also had protracted disputes with the UK over the poisoning of Alexander Litvinenko in 2006 and Sergei and Yulia Skripal in 2018. There was also alleged interference from Russia in the 2016 US presidential elections. The US and Russia currently have mutual sanctions in place.

Meanwhile China is the US's biggest economic rival. The US has taken much more economic interest in Asia recently, which can be seen from Obama's 'Pivot to Asia' (e.g. the Trans-Pacific Partnership in 2011). Arguably this was an attempt to temper China's increasing influence in the area. The US has also experienced tension with

China over what it sees as unfair trading of raw materials, and raised these issues in the WTO. Characteristically, Obama's presidency marked more cooperation with China (e.g. over the environment), while Trump was more antagonistic, entering into a trade war with China.

China also poses a threat in terms of its military expansion into the South China Sea. China uses the South China Sea for patrolling its nuclear ballistic missile submarine which is a nuclear deterrent against the US, and for a buffer zone in the event of a US attack. The Sea is also significant to China in terms of maritime trading routes, natural resources and food security (as it is a significant fishing ground), which has encouraged China to claim sovereignty of much of the area. Both China and the US have accused each other of acting in an antagonistic way in this region.

Case study

Pivot to Asia

One of the most important foreign policy decisions of the Obama administration was the 'Pivot to Asia'. Born in Hawaii, Obama saw himself as the first Pacific–American president and he strongly believed that the US must ensure that China does not achieve regional hegemony across Asia. US military resources and diplomatic initiatives were, therefore, increasingly focused on countering the growth of Chinese influence. As a result, Obama provided no global leadership when the Arab Spring broke out: during the Libyan rising, for example, he urged the European leaders Prime Minister David Cameron and President Nicolas Sarkozy to provide the military lead.

In 2013, when President Assad used chemical weapons against his opponents in Syria, Obama again chose not to act, encouraging an emboldened Putin to then intervene on behalf of Assad. Obama was similarly unfocused on Europe, and when Russia annexed Crimea from Ukraine in 2014, many accused his administration of providing insufficient leadership.

Obama at the East Asia Summit, 2012

The US position as 'leader of the free world' has been a big part of the US's soft power and played a part in its hegemonic status over time. Obama promoted the idea of the US being a leading liberal democracy that advocated for human rights, but Trump's election saw a shift in attitude that resulted in significant threats to international human rights. For example, in 2018 the Trump administration received widespread national and international criticism for separating children from their parents at the

Activity

1 Using the evidence above and your own research, what have been the consequences of President Obama's 'Pivot to Asia'?
2 To what extent does President Obama's 'Pivot to Asia' suggest that the US's claim to global hegemony is coming to an end?

Activity

Make a table headed 'Is the US in decline?' and include Yes and No columns.
1 Using the case study above, what arguments can you find on both sides of this debate?
2 Can you add anything else from what you have read elsewhere in the chapter?

Topic link

Chapter 1 refers to
the Pivot to Asia when
discussing realist views of
power dynamics between
China and the US.

Mexican border as part of US immigration policy. As a result of Trump's different approach to human rights, arguably China and Russia saw an opportunity to pull back from human rights agendas in the UN.

What are the implications of multipolarity for global stability?

A multipolar system is likely to have five or six centres of power, which are not grouped into tight alliances. Each state therefore follows its own perceived best interests and so the distribution of power continually shifts between them.

The realist viewpoint

Realists like John Mearsheimer argue that multipolarity represents the most unstable distribution of global power. This is because the system is much more fluid than bipolarity and unipolarity, since there is a constantly shifting balance of power as a number of relatively evenly matched states seek to maximise their influence at the expense of others. This creates fear and uncertainty among the states involved and, since there are so many players, the risk of possible conflicts is increased. Mearsheimer argues that regional conflicts are examples of why we might miss the 'stability' of the Cold War era. In the absence of two superpowers competing, we are more likely to see multiple smaller-scale regional conflicts, ultimately creating a more volatile and unpredictable international system. His example centred on Europe but the same could be said to be true of India and Pakistan or Iran and Saudi Arabia.

According to this theory, in a bipolar world two evenly matched superpowers will not want to risk open conflict and, when politics is unipolar, the global hegemon can deter the aggressive impulses of lesser powers. However, a multipolar world encourages risk-taking by states, so undermining the potential for a long-lasting balance of power. It could be argued that the Second World War broke out because global politics had become multipolar in the 1930s and so the Axis Powers (Germany, Italy and Japan) were prepared to take the risk of rebalancing global relations in their favour. Should the US become just one among a number of relatively equal states, then the great power rivalries of the mid-twentieth century could well be replayed in the twenty-first century (see Figure 7.1).

The liberal viewpoint

However, liberals are more optimistic about the consequences of multipolarity for global peace and stability. They argue that in the absence of a global hegemon or a superpower rivalry, states are more likely to cooperate in multilateral organs of global governance. The existence of more evenly matched states therefore provides greater opportunities for cooperation than either bipolarity or unipolarity.

Therefore, it could be argued that the relative security of a multipolar world depends upon whether the leading players are prepared to work through international agencies of government, or whether they prefer to compete within alliance structures. The latter is, of course, much more dangerous for peace than the former, and characterised the period of the two world wars. Liberals therefore argue that for multipolarity to provide peace, nation-states must set aside state egoism and be prepared to cooperate through organisations such as the G7, G20, UN and WTO.

The idea of polarity can largely be understood chronologically:

| The Cold War (bipolarity) 1948–91 | A 'liberal moment'/ New World Order? | US hegemony (unipolarity) | c.21st-century world order (multipolarity?) |

Liberals and realists have different ideas on how these forms of polarity relate to stability:

Realists argue that this was a time of stability, and that there was a balance of power, which was ensured by MAD. Liberals argue that this was far from the case — the world came close to nuclear annihilation and the period was characterised by proxy and peripheral wars.

Liberals were optimistic at the end of the Cold War that there was potential for greater peace and stability. The UN was now more functional with the US and Russia (formerly the Soviet Union) no longer at loggerheads. For liberals, this was a time of global cooperation, which was characterised by more humanitarian operations. Realism's view of bipolarity as stable was, for now, discredited.

Realists saw the rise of US hegemony as a new form of stability. They viewed the phase of international anarchy and therefore instability to be over with the clear dominance of a global leader (hegemonic stability theory). Liberals viewed the rise of US hegemony in part as a time for the spread of Western ideas and values, such as democracy. Liberals like Ikenberry have even called for unipolarity with a benign hegemon. However, overall Liberalism tends to argue that there would be greater stability from more of a diffusion of power (i.e. greater multilateralism and multipolarity).

Some say US hegemony is over and the world is more multipolar, with the rise of the emerging powers. For liberals, this is a good thing, as it will give rise to more democratic and diplomatic measures and a greater focus on supragovernmentalism (linked to democratic peace theory). For realists, a decline in a clearly dominant hegemony leads to more instability as the international system descends into anarchy once more. Some argue that we may be seeing the dawn of a new phase of bipolarity between China and the US. There has also been a rise in regional bipolarity, with state interests lying in becoming regional hegemons, e.g. the rivalry between Saudi Arabia and Iran.

Figure 7.1 **Polarity**

Debate

Is there multipolarity in today's system?

Yes

- There are new emerging powers, such as the BRICS nations, which are becoming increasingly powerful on the global stage, challenging the idea that there is one clear hegemon. This suggests that the US's economic hegemony is in decline.
- China has a dramatically expanding economy and is now more prepared to assert itself in diplomatic relations.
- Russia is more self-confident following its interventions in Crimea (2014) and Syria (2015).
- The world is now a global civil society through increased cosmopolitanism – globalisation is no longer limited to 'Americanisation'.

No

- The US remains a hegemonic power in terms of its economic strength and military outreach.
- China's military outreach is only regional compared with the US's global military outreach.
- Russia lacks allies, and socially and economically it has many of the characteristics of a developing state. Its military outreach is insignificant compared with that of the US.
- Arguably, Americanisation remains more pervasive than cosmopolitanism, with US culture still incredibly influential.

- There is increasing competition from violent non-state actors to states, representing a diffusion of power. ISIL and al-Qaeda are examples of this new power challenge.
- There has been a trend for states to vie for regional power (e.g. the regional bipolarity of Iran and Saudi Arabia or of Pakistan and India). This can be seen as a part of a multipolar system as there are a number of different significant poles of power operating at once.

- Regional power could be simply be seen as a way of organising global relations, with the US retaining a global role that is still hard for others to compete with, and which still has a significant impact on its regional relations. For example, the US has a clearly influential role in the bipolar struggle between Iran and Saudi Arabia.

Evaluation prompt: The question of whether we have moved to a more multipolar world from a unipolar one of American hegemony is complex and in flux. Consider to what extent you think the US's hegemony has now been challenged, and in what ways, how and by whom. Justify your answer using examples.

Key term

Failed state A state whose government is no longer able to provide its citizens with protection. Law, order and central government have collapsed, the economy no longer functions and there is a descent into anarchy. It is no longer a viable political unit and therefore will not be able to engage in diplomatic relations with other states.

Case study

New wars

In 1999, Mary Kaldor published *New and Old Wars: Organized Violence in a Global Era*. According to Kaldor, the increasing number of **failed states** would lead to new sorts of wars in which outside powers would be forced to intervene in order to stop the failed states becoming a magnet for violent extremism and terrorism. These wars would be different from traditional wars in which nation-states battled each other. The advance of military technology, together with the interconnectedness of globalisation, made this type of war less likely, since neither side would be likely to benefit. Both sides would suffer economically (see Thomas Friedman and the Dell Theory of Conflict Resolution, page 49). Militarily they would also be irrational. Either one side would be so militarily dominant as to quickly crush the other, as happened when the UK and the US invaded Iraq in 2003, or they would be so equally matched that the destruction wrought by both sides would ensure there could be no winner.

The characteristics of 'new wars' include the following:
- Warfare will be within a failed or failing state.
- The fighting will involve irregular forces rather than the armies of nation-states fighting each other.
- The fighting will generally be classed as an insurgency, in which irregular forces often linked to criminal gangs and terrorists will seek to take over control of what is left of the state.
- New wars can be termed 'asymmetrical', since regular forces (often from outside powers) will be likely to have superior military equipment, but will not be able to deploy it effectively against the insurgents.
- Civilian casualties will be very high. This is because the insurgents may use terror tactics and regular troops will find it difficult to distinguish between insurgents and civilians.
- There will be no set-piece battles – fighting is much closer to guerrilla warfare.
- Old wars have a clear beginning and end. In new wars, the descent into anarchy is gradual and, as there is no defined rival army or government to surrender, new wars are likely to be prolonged indefinitely without an obvious end point.
- Historians will appreciate that such wars are not entirely new. Similar insurgencies occurred with Spanish partisans against French occupation during the Peninsular War (1808–14), the Irish War of Independence (1919–21) and the Vietnam War.

Topic link

The concept of new wars is discussed in relation to human rights interventions in Chapter 5.

Regional bipolarity

Arguably there has been more of a shift towards regionalism in recent years and this has come with new power struggles. It has become perhaps more important and realistic for states to be a leader in their region than to vie for global power. Consequently, there are increasing elements of regional bipolarity within a more multipolar global system.

One notable example of regional bipolarity is between Pakistan and India, whose nuclear standoff has echoes of the Cold War era. Another key example is between Iran and Saudi Arabia, which have been fighting proxy wars in the Middle East that have led political commentators to also describe this as a new cold war. Arguably now the pursuit of international power has moved from that of global hegemony to regional hegemony.

Pakistan and India

Since their partition in 1947, India and Pakistan have had a tumultuous relationship. This division caused many millions to be displaced along religious grounds, creating a refugee crisis.

The two states share certain demographic characteristics, with both speaking a number of common languages and having significant Hindu and Muslim populations. India declared itself a secular state but has a Hindu majority and significant Muslim minority, while Pakistan subsequently became an Islamic republic but also has a significant Hindu minority (2.4% in 2019).

One of the most notable areas of tension has been the territorial conflict over Kashmir (which China has also been a third party in). This dispute is ongoing, remaining contested since India and Pakistan's partition. Within the Kashmir region, India has control over the highest proportion of the land, followed by Pakistan and then China holding the smallest share. There have been many clashes resulting in several ceasefires and ceasefire lines including the 'line of control', which operates as a de facto border between Indian and Pakistani territories. Former US President Clinton once described the line of control as being one of the most dangerous places in the world.

Various other conflicts have occurred since independence and there have been attempts at summits and improving bilateral diplomatic relations. In 2001, a terrorist attack on the Indian parliament by two terrorist groups with connections to Pakistan created the potential for nuclear conflict between India and Pakistan. The 2007 Samjhauta Express bombings and the 2008 Mumbai attacks strained relations yet further, killing both Indian and Pakistani civilians. In later years tensions have remained high, but have perhaps improved. In 2015 Modi became the first Indian prime minister to visit Pakistan since 2004. However, there remains significant distrust between the two countries.

> ## Activity
>
> 1 Provide as many examples as you can of modern-day insurgencies. Why do they share the characteristics of new wars?
> 2 Explain why insurgencies are so difficult to defeat.

> ## Topic link
>
> Chapter 6 notes the relationship between climate change and conflict, with conflict being more of an issue in countries that are politically or economically fragile, with the example of water supplies being a tension between India and Pakistan.

Middle east

One of the more recent shifts in terms of power and developments has been the rise of regional bipolarity in the middle east. Since the end of the Second World War in 1945 and the beginning of the Cold War, the middle east has been wrapped up in the Cold War politics of the USSR and the US. Both Russia and the US remain intertwined in the geopolitics of the middle east today.

In the early 2010s, a movement across the Arab world known as the Arab Spring or Arab Spring marked a significant transformation in the region. Widespread protests called for more freedoms from oppressive regimes, which had a destabilising effect in an already volatile region. Prior to the Cold War, Egypt, Syria and Iraq acted as regional leaders, but they are now reliant on international support to 'prop up' the state. In Egypt the protests were intent on ending the Mubarak regime and ultimately resulted in his resignation in February 2011, after which a number of politically unsettled years ensued. Syria also experienced protests against the Assad regime: there was a hard-line military crackdown by the authorities, resulting in the emergence of a number of militant groups and leading into a complex civil war. Therefore, the balance of power in the region has shifted towards Saudi Arabia and Iran, which can now be seen to be competing in a regional bipolarity. Both see each other as significant threats and are vying for influence in the region.

While Iran and Saudi Arabia have never actually declared war on each other, they have fought a number of proxy wars in Iraq, Syria and Yemen. Given that they haven't been involved in direct conflict, this has been described as a cold war. However, unlike the previous Cold War their aim is for control of the middle east, as opposed to hegemonic global dominance.

Saudi Arabia has large oil reserves and has historically had strong ties with the US. Iran also has significant oil reserves but has had a more politically tumultuous past, with outside involvement from the US, UK and Russia and more domestic unrest within its leadership. In 1979 the Shah of Iran was overthrown in a widespread uprising. This dramatically increased tensions with Saudi Arabia, whose own autocratic government feared a similar popular rebellion. Saudi Arabia felt similarly uncomfortable with the Arab Spring, concerned that they would cause domestic unrest. Saudi Arabia has long had a desire to maintain the status quo of the region.

There is also a religious divide between the two countries, with Saudi Arabia having a mostly Sunni Muslim population and Iran a mostly Shia Muslim population. While this divide is often overplayed in the West, it does serve to further distinguish the two groups from each other. Furthermore, both countries have vied for religious leadership in the area, with tensions over the fact that the two holy sites in the region are in Saudi Arabia (Mecca and Medina).

Activity

Create your own timeline of the main events in this conflict in Yemen, from the Arab Spring onwards. Try to think about this in terms of Iran and Saudi Arabia acting in a bipolar way.

Case study

Proxy wars

Iraq

The Iraq–Iran war in the 1980s was a point when tensions increased between Iran and Saudi Arabia too. The full-scale war between Iraq and Iran had a heavy civilian death toll, trenches and chemical warfare. When Iran began to win the war, Saudi Arabia feared that Iran would gain a foothold in Iraq, which had acted as a buffer between them. Therefore, Saudi Arabia started to support Iraq in non-military, mostly financial ways to fight back against Iran. The war continued until 1988 under a UN ceasefire.

In 2003, the US, an ally of Saudi Arabia's, also got involved in this conflict with the result of overthrowing Saddam Hussein. Saudi Arabia had not supported the US in doing this. It feared the potential for a security vacuum, worrying it would destabilise things further. The US's intervention resulted in Iraq being left as a failed state, and to this day there is still low-level insurgency – an outcome that concerns both Iran and Saudi Arabia. This has led both countries to support various rebel groups within Iraq, mostly on the basis of religious grounds, with Saudi Arabia supporting (by sending money and weapons) Sunni groups and Iran the Shia groups. This is a pattern that continued into the Arab Spring, with Iran and Saudi Arabia supporting different sides in the various protest movements across the region.

Syria

The Syrian civil war, which began in 2011 as part of the Arab Spring, is another conflict that can be seen as a proxy war between Iran and Saudi Arabia, as well as having a complex history of Western intervention. Russia backed the Assad regime, given that Syria is its main ally in the region. Iran has also supported the regime on religious grounds. Meanwhile Saudi Arabia and possibly the US (long-term allies) and Turkey backed the rebel groups in overthrowing the Assad regime. This led to a protracted and ongoing civil war.

Yemen

In the wake of the Arab Spring, Yemen has suffered a long civil war (2014–present) and a devastating famine. Yemen is now a failed state. The uprisings forced Saleh (who became leader, when the northern and southern states of Yemen were officially united as one country) to step down and hand over power. The Houthi movement, which had been working to undermine Saleh over the previous decade, took advantage of this time to take control of the northern heartland of the Saada province and neighbouring areas. Iran was backing rebellion groups to do this, which antagonised Saudi Arabia which (along with other Sunni Arab states) began air strikes on these groups in an attempt to uphold Hadi's government. This was also backed by Western powers. Meanwhile other groups like al-Qaeda and IS have been regaining territories elsewhere in Yemen. The conflict is ongoing, at great human cost.

Systems of government: characteristics

There is a wide variety of ways in which states are governed (see Table 7.3). **Democratic states** have elected leaders and regular elections, which a variety of political parties contest. This provides the electorate with choice so that the government that is elected has a genuine mandate from the people and therefore enjoys democratic legitimacy. In liberal democracies, the rule of law means that the rights of all citizens are equally protected. The separation of powers between the executive/legislature and the judiciary ensures this. As a result, the government is expected to act within the law and the judiciary can hold it accountable for legal breaches.

Key term

Democratic state
Characterised by free, fair and regular elections in which governments are elected that are accountable to the public. They value liberal rights and freedoms and place a higher emphasis on the empowerment of individuals. A democratic state derives its legitimacy from the popular consent of the public.

Key terms

Semi-democratic state
A state that superficially possesses the features of a democracy but has underlying authoritarian features, ensuring the government won't willingly relinquish power. The rule of law is limited, since the government is not fully committed to democratic principles of justice, fairness and tolerance.

Non-democratic state An autocratic or authoritarian state, in which power is concentrated in the hands of either an individual or a select few. They vary in the despotic tendencies of their governments, with totalitarian states the most ruthless in their crushing of internal dissent.

Authoritarian state A state in which power is concentrated solely in the hands of a single, usually unelected, person or party. Power is hereditary and sometimes seized, and is unlimited, given the lack of accountability.

Table 7.3 Countries and their systems of government

Country	System of government	Category of government
China	Communist, authoritarian (one-party state), military dictatorship (People's Liberation Army)	Authoritarian
India	World's largest democracy (note that India's democracy has recently been challenged by Modi)	Democratic state
Russia	In practice an authoritarian state, but claims to be a multiparty state	Authoritarian
South Africa	Democratic, but with a level of corruption, arguably semi-democratic	Semi-democratic state
UK and US	Liberal democracies	Democratic states

Semi-democratic states superficially possess democratic characteristics, but on closer examination also contain authoritarian tendencies. The government is not constrained by the rule of law and so can put its own interests before those of its citizens. This is often achieved through amending the constitution in favour of the government, discouraging dissent, only allowing certain political parties to contest elections and limiting the freedom of the media. Electoral fraud and the intimidation of opposition parties are characteristic of elections and so the transfer of power is unlikely to be smooth. Semi-democratic states can also be referred to as 'majoritarian' (rather than liberal) democracies. This is because the interests of the majority are placed above those of the minority.

The governments of **non-democratic states** lack any democratic legitimacy. Since a non-democratic government is not accountable to its citizenry, it therefore lacks a popular mandate. These sorts of governments are classed as authoritarian. This means that those in government have sole authority for the running of the country. They are permanent and do not, therefore, need to seek the electoral endorsement of their citizens.

Authoritarian states place power with one individual or one ruling party. They rule in an autocratic fashion, since political dissent is not tolerated. The government controls the media and the judiciary acts according to the government's wishes, so threatening human rights. Alternative political parties are banned and state control is total. Authoritarian leaders do not willingly relinquish power and so the government perpetuates itself without ever seeking legitimisation from its citizens. The most repressive of authoritarian states are generally referred to as totalitarian states. For example, North Korea is best termed a totalitarian state.

Distinguish between

Autocratic and democratic states

Autocratic states

- In autocratic states, power is centralised in the hands of a single, dominant party or individual.
- There are no elections. Referendums (plebiscites) may be allowed but they are not fair and are a way of providing the government with popular acclamation.
- The judiciary lacks independence from the government, so undermining the principle of the rule of law.
- There is heavy state control over political institutions and the populace at large.

Democratic states

- In a democracy, power is distributed across society, with various checks and balances.
- There are free and fair elections, so providing the government with democratic legitimacy.
- The government is regularly made accountable to the public and so can claim a popular mandate.
- There is a greater emphasis on individualism.
- The rule of law ensures that there are limits on what the government can do, so protecting citizens' rights.

Case study

Failed and rogue states

Democratic Republic of the Congo: a failed state

A good example of a failed state is the Democratic Republic of the Congo (DRC).

- The country is characterised by civil war, which brought about the end of President Mobutu Sese Seko's brutal dictatorship in 1996.
- It suffers from significant ethnic and provincial divides (see Figure 7.2), which were arguably exacerbated by particularly oppressive Belgian colonial rule, the legacy of which perpetuates to this day.
- It has had a tumultuous relationship with some of its neighbours in what has historically been an unstable region (the DRC borders both Rwanda and Uganda, both of which also have recent histories of appalling human rights abuses).
- There is deep-seated corruption, both at the highest levels of authority and in the lower echelons, with militias being prominent in the country's history.
- Rape has been used as a widespread weapon of war and there is massive recruitment of child soldiers.
- It has arguably been a victim of the West in terms of colonialism, the exploitation of its resources through black markets and Western interference (or lack thereof) in this part of Africa.

Democratic People's Republic of Korea: a rogue state

The Democratic People's Republic of Korea (DPRK), or North Korea, is an example of a **rogue state**.

- North Korea's significant nuclear arsenal is a key feature of its 'rogue' status. Its readiness to both test and threaten the use of nuclear weapons poses a threat to international stability and directly threatens other nation-states.
- North Korea and its neighbour, South Korea, have had a long-standing, hostile history (see Figure 7.3). This was perpetuated by the Cold War, during which Korea was drawn into a lengthy and costly peripheral war, in which the US supported the more liberal South and the Soviet Union the communist North.
- The US continues to have a tense relationship with North Korea. Trump's negotiations with North Korea during his presidency failed to improve the situation. North Korea wanted the end of economic sanctions and withdrawal of US nuclear power from South Korea before any denuclearisation begins, and the US wanted North Korea to begin denuclearising and allowing inspections, and with neither willing to compromise a stalemate was reached.
- North Korea does not cooperate in the international system and has frequently flouted international laws. It has one of the worst human rights records, directly contravening the UN Charter, and has failed to uphold international agreements even when it has signed them, for example the Treaty on the Non-Proliferation of Nuclear Weapons.

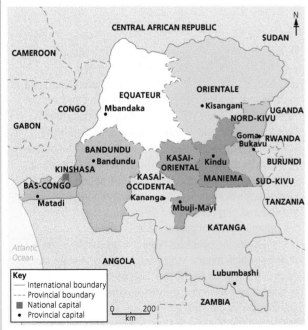

Figure 7.2 Provincial boundaries, the DRC

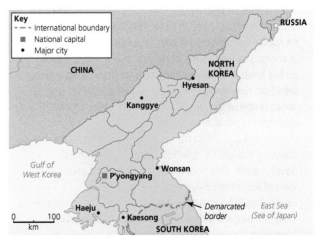

Figure 7.3 The DPRK (North Korea)

- It has suffered from the 'resource curse', whereby its being very rich in many natural resources has actually left the country in a dire position. Colonial powers first exploited these resources, followed by brutal dictatorships. The country is also rife with civil war, corruption and militia groups using the black market for their own gains. Given the DRC's lack of infrastructure and development, it has lacked the amenities it needs to benefit from harnessing these resources itself.

- North Korea's population is deliberately isolated from the rest of the world and its government pursues a deeply isolationist foreign policy.

Key term

Rogue state A state that acts in defiance of international norms of behaviour by threatening regional and global stability, through the development of weapons of mass destruction in defiance of international agreements and/or its connections with global terrorism.

Topic link

Rogue states and failed states are also discussed in Chapter 3 in relation to global governance.

Democracy

This chapter has already examined the impact of democracy on stability. Liberals generally argue that increased globalisation leads to global governance, multilateralism and cooperation, as well as the spread of liberal democratic values, and that overall this creates stability (democratic peace theory, see page 280). But there are many wider advantages and disadvantages to the democratic system and democratic governments.

Debate

Is democracy the most effective form of government to promote peace and minimalise conflict?

Yes

- Democracy is good for political development, as it empowers the populace. This empowerment will also create stability since people are less likely to want to rebel against the system.
- Democracy goes hand in hand with liberal values and freedoms and liberal democracy is the system that, according to Fukuyama, brings us to 'the end of history' as the ideal form of government. This fits with the liberal idea that democracy encourages multilateralism and cooperation, with relationships that become mutually dependent, accountable and transparent.
- Democracy complements capitalism and free trade, meaning it is also a significant factor in economic development. This enables a more peaceful and stable form of sustainable development.
- Democracies bring peace and stability to the international system. They are better at multilateral cooperation (democratic peace theory).

No

- Democracy shouldn't be seen as 'one size fits all'- a benign dictator can benefit a relatively new or underdeveloped country through strong leadership. In a country that has had a volatile history this could create more stability, especially during stages of transition.
- Democracy is unsustainable if implemented too early. Economist and author Dambisa Moyo argues that states first need a strong economy before they can implement a successful democracy. Therefore, the notion that democracy will always promote peace and stability is short-sighted and perpetuates a Western bias that it is always the optimum form of government.
- Many developing countries benefit from protectionist policies (which require strong leadership and state control) as they are a good way to stabilise economic growth. In turn, strong economic growth is more likely to create stability and avoid conflict.
- Western liberals assume that democracies always provide the best form of government and that

→

- Democratic governments are held to account and are, therefore, more transparent, both of which are essential to upholding human rights. This means there is more likelihood of reaching global agreements and reducing corruption and conflict.

authoritarian governments impede development. However, some authoritarian countries have achieved impressive growth rates and domestic stability and are able to play a constructive role in global politics. China is based on one-party rule and its government has dramatically reduced Chinese levels of poverty. By around 2028, China is set to overtake the US as the world's biggest economy. Singapore is a one-party state and so is far from the Western ideal of a liberal democracy, and yet in terms of crime, economic freedom and life expectancy, Singapore is a much better place to live than the US.

Evaluation prompt: Which side of the debate do you agree with? Try to support your argument with real examples of where democracies have been good or bad and use the key theoretical ideas (especially of liberalism) to add to the debate.

Topic link

This question has strong links to the idea of Western imperialism and so it overlaps significantly with poverty and development, human rights, global governance and political theory such as Fukuyama's idea that liberal democracy is the end of our political evolution.

Case study

A false spring?

The Arab Spring began in Tunisia in 2010, when the populace mounted protests against President Zine El Abidine Ben Ali's oppressive regime. This sparked a revolutionary wave of support for the installation of democracy across the Arab world, with varying degrees of violence and success. The revolution resulted in extended violence in Egypt, Iraq, Libya, Syria and Yemen.

A key feature of these protests was the use of technology. Globalisation has allowed technology to spread the idea of liberal values and freedoms across the world. People are therefore much more aware than ever before of the freedoms experienced in other nations. Arguably, this was one of the major triggers for the Arab Spring. In particular, Facebook and Twitter played a key role in mobilising populations against their governments, so challenging the repressive governments that had often been in power for decades.

Liberals initially saw the Arab Spring as a 're-run' of the fall of communism in eastern Europe in 1988–89. Repressive dictatorships would be replaced with people power, so establishing a surge of liberal democracy throughout the Arab world. History, however, does not always progress the way we may want it to. It was not only pro-Western liberals who wanted to see the back of repressive dictators, such as Hosni Mubarak of Egypt and Muammar Gaddafi. Radical Muslims, who fear and resent Western liberalism, also often led the protests against these dictators and so when tyrannies were

challenged, the results were much more bloody and anarchic than anticipated. In Libya, for example, anarchy reigns, and the Syrian civil war has led to hundreds of thousands of deaths. Estimates vary considerably among activist groups, but the Syrian Observatory for Human Rights estimated that between March 2011 and December 2020 the number could be as high as 593,000. Many of these casualties have been civilians, including a high number of children. In Egypt, the military has reimposed order with the tacit acknowledgement of the West and in Yemen a brutal civil war has involved both Saudi Arabia and Islamist militants in a struggle for control.

Therefore, the consequence of the Arab Spring has not been the rise of new democracies. Instead, there is a greater threat than ever before of failed, rogue and authoritarian states defining the future of the region. According to the British historian A. J. P. Taylor, the liberal revolutions in Germany in 1848 ended up simply reinforcing authoritarianism: 'German history reached its turning point and failed to turn.' The same may, unfortunately, be true of the Arab Spring today.

Since the Arab Spring we have seen Iran and Saudi Arabia fighting numerous proxy wars across the Arab world, with Iran generally in favour of the uprisings and challenging the status quo and Saudi Arabia trying to uphold current regimes and maintain its position, ultimately with the aim of firming up a place as a regional hegemon.

How has the global balance of power changed since the end of the Cold War?

To what extent is China a superpower?

In 1972, President Richard Nixon became the first US president to visit the People's Republic of China. His meeting with Chairman Mao provided the initial foundation for China's decision to develop trade with the rest of the world. The consequences of this for China's seismic economic growth have been profound. In 1994, the year he died, Nixon presciently warned that:

> Today, China's economic power makes US lectures about human rights imprudent. Within a decade it will make them irrelevant. Within two decades it will make them laughable.

China's economic outreach is certainly global. For almost 30 years, China's annual growth rate has been between 8% and 10%, though this has slowed down in recent years to around 6% in 2019. China's state-run capitalist model weathered the global financial crisis in 2008 significantly better than the models of Western powers and, by 2010, the Chinese economy was 90 times greater than it had been in 1978. With the world's largest population (1.45 billion in 2021), China has massive reserves of cheap labour, making it the manufacturing and export heart of the world.

China has also demonstrated its growing power with the Belt and Road Initiative (see Chapter 1), a massive infrastructure initiative that will invest in over 70 countries and international organisations. Similarly, the so-called 'String of Pearls' initiative (the concept of China building a network of commercial and military bases in ports across many countries, which has been seen as a particular threat to India) has demonstrated China's expanding geopolitical influence. It is anticipated that the global pandemic will significantly slow down China's growth, however it seems unlikely this will disproportionately impact China.

Although still considered to be a developing nation (due to the levels of poverty and the lack of development of significant parts of the country, especially in rural areas), China has also become the most successful neocolonial power in the world. It is Africa's biggest trading partner and the value of China–Africa trade in 2019 was $192 billion, up from $185 billion in 2018. In defiance of the Monroe Doctrine, which regards South America as firmly within the US's sphere of influence, China has dramatically increased investment in the region. From 2000 to 2013, trade between China and South America increased 22 times. China is now the second largest trading partner of Latin America (the US is the largest). President Xi Jinping has made numerous visits to the continent in order to further develop economic and diplomatic ties.

Chinese investments are also global. Chinese investors own Birmingham City Football Club, House of Fraser, Pizza Express, Volvo and Weetabix. A Chinese investment of £6 billion is financing the proposed Hinkley Point C nuclear reactor in Somerset. Chinese investors are also financing the Nicaragua Canal, which will cost US$50 billion and is designed to challenge the Panama Canal.

China's structural economic power is dramatically increasing, further extending its global outreach. Since 2001, China has been a member of the WTO and, in 2015, Beijing established the AIIB, which provides loans to developing countries in the Asia-Pacific region. China also heavily invests in the US in the form of foreign direct investment. This demonstrates how China has grown, given that it used to rely on foreign direct investment from the West.

In 2019, the Chinese government reported an official defence budget of just under $178 billion, however other estimates are higher. This is second only to the US. China has purchased an aircraft carrier from Ukraine and completed construction of its own in 2017, with another completed in 2021. It is also attempting to militarise reefs in the South China Sea and is building up its submarine and missile capability in the region. In 2014, for example, China deployed the Jin-class ballistic missile submarine in the South China Sea. Each submarine is armed with 12 JL-2 nuclear missiles.

Limitations

However, these developments do not confirm that China is close to becoming a superpower. Some critics have likened China at the beginning of the twenty-first century to Prussia at the end of the nineteenth century. In short, China is great and powerful in its 'near abroad'. However, its military and diplomatic outreach does not match its economic outreach. The US, for example, has almost 800 military bases in 70 countries as well as alliances across the globe. Only in 2016 did China open its first overseas military base, at Djibouti in the Indian Ocean.

China's global influence is also arguably limited by its communist ideology. American democratic values have, especially since the Second World War, had a global appeal, which China's more authoritarian approach lacks. In its immediate zone of influence, Japan, the Philippines, Singapore, South Korea and Taiwan all look to the US for both ideology and protection, therefore affecting its soft power on a local and a global scale. ASEAN also provides an alternative model of development. India, as the world's largest democracy, represents a potential barrier to China's global influence. Even Russia, which is increasingly authoritarian and understands the value of courting China, shares a 4,000 km disputed border with China, making its friendship unreliable.

In addition, China still has issues with its human rights record, which has come under heavy criticism from the international community, once more affecting its soft power. A recent example of this has been the claim that China has been committing a crime against humanity and possibly genocide against the Uighur Muslim population in the Xinjiang region. China denies these allegations and claims it is trying to combat separatism and extremism in the region.

Biden met with Xi Jinping as Vice President in 2011

There is also the question of whether China actually wants to be a superpower. In order to be a superpower a nation-state needs to have a clear world mission and be willing to take on a global leadership role. Rome in the ancient world had this sense of mission, as did Great Britain in the nineteenth century, and in recent years so has the US. However, China has generally viewed world affairs according to Westphalian principles, by not seeking to impose its values on other states and jealously protecting its sovereignty from outside influence. In 2015, President Xi Jinping announced at a military parade commemorating the 70th anniversary of the end of the Second World War that, 'China will remain committed to peaceful development. We Chinese love peace. No matter how much stronger it may become, China will never seek hegemony or expansion.'

However, China's more recent geopolitical actions have suggested a shift in this behaviour, and it could now be argued that China is at least vying for regional hegemony. After all, there has seemingly been a global move towards regional hegemony as opposed to global hegemony, and we have seen similar in the middle east with Saudi Arabia and Iran's battle for dominance in the Arab world. Other signs point to China's ambitions being even greater: the Belt and Road Initiative and the String of Pearls concept suggest an increasingly global range of influence. In 2017, in the wake of President Trump's abandonment of the Paris treaty, China quickly positioned itself as the global leader on climate change.

To what extent does the rise of China threaten global stability?

According to US historian Robert Kagan in *The Return of History and the End of Dreams*, 'Power changes nations. It expands their wants and desires; increases their sense of entitlement'. According to the offensive realist John Mearsheimer, the rise of China is unlikely to be peaceful. The US still jealously guards its hegemonic status and, according to power transition theory, will even be prepared to fight to preserve it. As Mearsheimer puts it, 'if China continues to rise you better be very careful, because that will drive the US stark raving crazy'.

China's expansion of its military influence in the South China Sea could therefore bring it into conflict with other regional powers, such as Japan, South Korea and Taiwan. These powers have strong military and diplomatic support from the US and so China's attempts to achieve regional hegemony could provoke a showdown with the US, which also sees itself as a Pacific power and as the guarantor of these states' independence. A particularly contentious issue is North Korea. The US has felt threatened by North Korea's nuclear programme while China has been a long-standing ally of North Korea. China and North Korea have experienced particularly good relations in recent years with Kim Jong-un and Xi Jinping meeting numerous times. However, North Korea's nuclear programme and unilateral action in the region remain contentious with China.

China and the US depend on each other for trade and investment, and it is not in the economic interests of either country to provoke a war with the other. Niall Ferguson has even coined the term 'Chimerica' to emphasise the depth of their economic dependency on each other. China has also shown that it can work closely with the US: for example, their joint climate change deal in 2014, which paved the way for progress at the Paris Climate Conference in 2015. At his first meeting with President Trump, President Xi Jinping noted that, 'We have a thousand reasons to get China–US relations right, and not one reason to spoil the China–US relationship.' However, since then Trump pulled out of the Paris climate change agreement in a move that has been seen as globally antagonistic and that has received large-scale bad press.

President Trump agreed with China in other areas, stating that both countries had a similar interest in de-escalating tension in Korea by stopping North Korea's nuclear missile programme. As Henry Kissinger has pointed out, viewing China as a threat to peace could simply end up being 'a self-fulfilling prophecy'. That said, more recently Biden has rejoined the Paris Climate Agreement and signed a series of Executive Orders to address climate change. Biden's approach to the relationship with China is still not entirely clear, but early in his term he has already challenged China on its human rights record. The relationship between the US and China remains tense but also very significant to both countries and global politics.

In what ways has the changing balance of global power impacted contemporary global issues?

Synoptic links are key to this section of the Power and developments component. You need to be able to identify the extent to which changing relationships and state actions relate to various developments in power, and how they impact contemporary global issues. These include conflict, poverty, human rights and the environment. The impact of power and development on these global issues is inextricably linked to globalisation.

How have attitudes towards human rights changed since the end of the Second World War?

The Cold War

At the end of the Second World War, the UN took the moral lead in trying to establish an international community in which the **rule of law** and respect for human rights would challenge aggressive nationalism and racism. The Charter of the United Nations (1945) laid the foundations for a new world order based upon cooperation between nation-states rather than conflict. In 1948, the Universal Declaration of Human Rights (UDHR) for the first time established an international standard of human rights to which all states should aspire.

Tragically, 1948 also coincided with the Soviet takeover of Czechoslovakia and the Berlin Airlift, so that the beginning of the Cold War soon overshadowed the fine cosmopolitan ideals of the UDHR. The resulting deterioration in relations between the Soviet Union and the US therefore meant that the UN generally became gridlocked, as each superpower vetoed the resolutions of the other. In addition, it was in the interests of each superpower to advance its tactical interests at the expense of the other. This meant that each state became engaged in proxy wars to advance the interests of its allies, often exacerbating and prolonging military conflicts. The protection of human rights was therefore considerably less important to the leaders of East and West than advancing strategic self-interest and guaranteeing their security.

> **Key term**
>
> **Rule of law** The principle that the legal system in a nation-state should provide impartial justice for everyone, so no individual can claim to be above the law and the government is bound to obey the rule of law. The government (executive) is therefore separate from the judiciary. A liberal democracy, like the UK, is governed according to the rule of law, in contrast to an authoritarian state.

> **Topic link**
>
> The Cold War is a good example of how the Security Council can be a limiting factor to the UN passing resolutions, with the P5 having absolute vetoes. This is discussed further in Chapter 3.

Case study

Rule of law

The rule of law refers to the principle that the legal system should provide impartial justice for everyone within a nation-state. This means that no individual can claim to be above the law and that the government is itself bound to obey the rule of law. The government (executive) is separate from the judiciary, ensuring that the judiciary is not simply a tool of the government as it is in totalitarian states. The powers of the government are therefore limited, so protecting the civil liberties of the public from arbitrary interference.

A liberal democracy, like the UK, is governed according to the rule of law, in contrast to an authoritarian government in which there are no constraints on how the government acts.

The US's 'unipolar moment', c.1991–c.2003

When the Soviet Union collapsed in 1991, the US became the only remaining superpower. US power was unchallengeable and so the US achieved hegemonic status. President George H. W. Bush referred to a 'New World Order', which would now be defined by free trade, the spread of democracy, greater cooperation between nation-states and a greater commitment to human rights.

When Iraq invaded Kuwait in 1990, Bush succeeded in winning global support for a UN-backed invasion force to expel the forces of Saddam Hussein. For Bush, this was a crime of 'naked aggression' that had to be stopped. In 1992, he sent US troops into Somalia in order to ensure that humanitarian relief efforts reached famine victims. His successor, Bill Clinton, was also keen to associate the US with the global promotion of human rights.

- In 1995, the US played the leading role in NATO's bombing of the Bosnian Serbs following the Srebrenica Massacre. At the subsequent Dayton, Ohio Peace Talks, the then-US secretary of state Warren Christopher succeeded in brokering an end to the civil war.
- In 1999, the US led the NATO bombing of Serbia to stop the ethnic cleansing in Kosovo.
- During the 1990s, the US played a key role in encouraging the peace process in Northern Ireland and Palestine.

In addition, the end of the Cold War persuaded scholars of international relations, like Francis Fukuyama, that the future now lay with liberal democracies. According to liberals, when there are more democracies there is greater international stability (democratic peace theory). According to this principle, democracies are hesitant to go to war since they are inherently more peaceful than other political systems. In recent history, for example, there are virtually no examples of two liberal democracies in conflict on the battlefield.

Democratic peace theory has its beginnings in the ideas of German philosopher Immanuel Kant, who argued that through democracy and cooperation we can attain perpetual peace. During the 1960s the theory became more cohesive, developing the principle that democracies are more accountable and transparent. Arguably, therefore, democracies are more amenable to multilateral engagement and tend to be less prepared to take destabilising unilateral action in order to achieve more power. These features allow for more effective global governance, which is better for peace and stability in general.

However, we should beware of looking back on the 1990s as a golden period for human rights protection and humanitarian intervention. According to former New York Governor Mario Cuomo, 'You campaign in poetry. You govern in prose.' In other words, even the most liberal democratic leader often has to act according to realist self-interest and accept that there are limits on what he/she can do to advance a human rights agenda.

- In 1993, following the battle of Mogadishu in which 18 US soldiers were killed, President Clinton withdrew US military forces from Somalia, sternly informing the UN General Assembly on 28 September 1993 that, 'If the American people are to say yes to UN peacekeeping, the United Nations must know when to say no.'
- In 1994, as Rwanda was sliding into anarchy, the Clinton administration failed to provide either moral or military leadership. Instead, its priority was to evacuate foreign nationals and UN peacekeepers, allowing the genocide of 800,000 Tutsis and moderate Hutus.

Therefore, even when the US enjoyed global prestige and unrivalled hard- and soft-power outreach, there were clear limits on what it was prepared to do to advance human rights.

The limits of US power, c.2003–

The War on Terror further undermined the US's commitment to a human rights-based foreign policy. During his first few months in power, President George W. Bush scribbled on a report of the Clinton administration's failure to intervene to stop the genocide in Rwanda: 'not on my watch'. However, the way in which the US conducted the War on Terror, often in defiance of international norms of behaviour, severely undermined its reputation as a bastion of human rights.

In addition, the rise of more authoritarian governments, such as those of China and Russia in the early twenty-first century, has further challenged the ongoing importance of human rights in international relations. President Putin has militarily intervened on behalf of President Assad in Syria in order to protect Russian interests in the region and stop the further spread of Islamist terrorism. That the Assad regime has an appalling record on human rights has not deterred Putin's enthusiastic support. China has also continually condemned criticisms of its own record on human rights. In 2017, a Chinese report on human rights went on the offensive against the US, claiming that the US was too ready to wield 'the baton of human rights' in spite of 'paying no attention to its own terrible human rights problems'.

The dramatic events of 2016 have also made many liberals question the extent to which human rights is under greater threat than at any time since the early Cold War. The 2016 Brexit referendum unleashed significant anti-immigrant feeling and leading European politicians, such as Nigel Farage, Viktor Orbán, Geert Wilders

The debates surrounding Brexit centred on anti-immigration and British sovereignty

and Marine Le Pen, have won considerable acclaim for their denunciation of 'outsiders'. Much of this could be seen as a backlash against the so-called refugee crisis. During his election campaign, Trump also offended many liberals with his ruthlessly pragmatic campaign, which promised to build a wall on the Mexican border and 'bring a hell of a lot worse than waterboarding'. Recently the global pandemic has also meant that attentions have been focused on tackling this new global threat. That said, Biden has refocused on human rights so we may begin to see a shift in the global rhetoric once more.

However, we should be careful not to argue that human rights were once a global priority and have now become an irrelevance because of the rise of authoritarianism and populism. Arguably the human rights agenda has always been fraught. It took four years (from 1991 to 1995) for NATO to intervene in Bosnia to stop the carnage. In 1994, the world community did nothing as genocide engulfed Rwanda. Since the end of the Cold War, appalling human rights abuses have also gone unpunished in Darfur and Zimbabwe. President Obama won the Nobel Peace Prize in 2009, but the drone strikes he launched caused numerous civilian casualties, while he steadfastly refused to intervene in the Syrian civil war since vital US strategic interests were not at stake.

To suggest, therefore, that the protection of human rights has suddenly become an irrelevance to a new breed of authoritarian and nationalist leaders is misleading. After all, it was the alleged arch-realist Donald Trump, rather than the supposed liberal Barack Obama, who launched missile strikes on Syria in April 2017 for its use of chemical weapons on civilians.

> **Topic link**
>
> There are clear parallels here with Chapter 5, and the concept that universal human rights may have actually been quite a Western-centric idea. This has also been linked to the alleged hypocrisy of the West in how it has addressed human rights.

How has the changing balance of world power affected conflict?

As we have seen, challenges to US hegemony may encourage greater possibility of conflict. Realists fear that conditions of power transition can lead to conflict as emerging powers, keen to expand their influence, challenge the hegemon's attempts to retain its global standing. Since realists argue that states seek power and security, the uncertainties of power transition are, therefore, highly unstable, as aspiring powers are more likely to take risks in order to achieve greater power and influence.

On the other hand, liberals have argued that a more multipolar world can encourage states to work together if they are prepared to cooperate through organs of global governance. In a more evenly balanced world no one power is able to unilaterally impose its will on the others (the malign hegemony theory) and so countries can more effectively resolve their differences through dialogue.

Neither interpretation is wholly satisfying, since each is based upon a different interpretation of what motivates states. If states are motivated solely by the desire for power, then the first interpretation holds. If, however, states are communitarian in their outlook, then the second interpretation will be truest. In reality, states, like people, are neither entirely realist nor entirely liberal in their attitudes and so the best we can predict is that the changing balance of world power will bring with it both dangers and opportunities.

However, what is more certain is that the challenges of failed and rogue states are unlikely to disappear. The extent to which the global community succeeds, or fails, in dealing with failed states like Syria, or rogue states like North Korea, is therefore likely to determine the sort of direction in which global politics progresses in the twenty-first century.

How has the changing balance of world power affected poverty?

Globalisation has led to an increase in free-market capitalism. This has dramatically reduced global poverty, since it has enabled developing countries to take advantage of the opportunities for growth that global trading presents. As a result, there has been a significant convergence between the Global North and the Global South, challenging the utility of the concept of a North/South divide. The share, for example, of the developing world's population living on less than US$1.25 a day (the international definition of poverty) fell from 30% in 2000 to below 10% in 2014. In 2015 the international poverty line was raised (reflecting cost of living) by the World Bank to $1.90, with around 9.4% of the world's population below that in 2020.

However, it is estimated that due to the Covid pandemic, we will now see a rise in absolute poverty for the first time in 20 years, with estimates indicating that 150 million people could be pushed into extreme poverty in 2021. One of the main reasons why the Millennium Development Goals (2000–15) achieved the success they did was because globalisation provided greater opportunities for extreme poverty reduction than ever before.

A number of developing countries have achieved remarkable success in lifting their citizens out of poverty. In 2020, South Korea had the 10th biggest economy in the world, ahead of Russia in 11th place. Among the top ten biggest economies in the world in 2020, two were in the developing world – China (2nd), India (6th), with Brazil falling into 12th. African countries with the most spectacular growth rates are those that have focused on taking advantage of new opportunities in global trade, such as Ethiopia (textiles and coffee) and Côte d'Ivoire (the world's largest exporter of cocoa beans). Across Africa, too, Chinese investment is providing massive opportunities for the development of infrastructure. Estimates suggest that in 2019 China's FDI in Africa was over $100 billion and had contributed to 20% of Africa's economic growth.

However, although millions have been lifted out of poverty in emerging economies such as China, India and the East Asian Tigers (Hong Kong, Singapore, South Korea and Taiwan), the changing balance of global power has had much less of an impact on what Paul Collier has called 'the Bottom Billion'. Often located in Sub-Saharan Africa, the billion people living in poorly resourced, landlocked and poorly governed states are more likely to be victims of globalisation, as cheap manufactured products are 'dumped' on them, undermining their potential for achieving initial-stage industrialisation. Neo-Marxists, such as Immanuel Wallerstein in his 'world systems' theory, also argue that even those developing states that seem to be expanding as a result of globalisation are actually being exploited. Neocolonial powers utilise their cheap labour and raw materials so that the profits from globalisation go to the core (colonising) rather than the peripheral (colonised) power. Furthermore, their growth rates can be misleading, given they are starting from a very low baseline.

Amy Chua has also argued in *World on Fire* (2002) that the sudden imposition of free markets can dramatically increase inequality and resentment. Globalisation does have the potential to raise all boats but not equally, and so in increasing numbers of states (both North and South) the gap between rich and poor is becoming worryingly extreme. The election of Donald Trump in 2016 was due, in part, to his victory in the 'rust-belt' states such as Michigan, Pennsylvania and Wisconsin, where manufacturing jobs have steadily been lost to the developing world, so creating a new poverty underclass.

Topic link

This overlaps with the issues discussed in Chapter 6 regarding the environment and sustainable development, with clear overlaps to the tragedy of the commons debate.

Distinguish between

Free trade and protectionism

Free trade

- Trade is largely left to its own devices, with little government regulation. This means that it is free and is sometimes referred to as 'trade liberalisation'.
- There is little interference from the government in the form of taxes, tariffs or quotas.
- Adam Smith, one of free trade's key proponents, argued that if left to their own devices, economies would self-regulate (the 'invisible hand'). The laws of supply and demand therefore create an equitable share and price for produce.
- Often (but not always), free trade goes hand in hand with democracy, since there is less government authority over the economy.
- Free trade promotes competition and innovation. It therefore boosts profit and, in turn, GDP.

Protectionism

- In a protectionist system, governments more tightly control the operation of the free market.
- There is greater government intervention in markets, for example through subsidies, taxes, tariffs and/or quotas, which boost domestic production at the expense of foreign competition.
- Governments promote domestic trade as far as possible so that there is less reliance on imports.
- Protectionism is sometimes associated with more authoritarian regimes, since these sorts of governments are more likely to be controlling and interventionist.

How has the changing balance of world power affected the environment?

The changes in the global order have had a mixed impact on the environment. On the one hand, the increased focus on trade, global travel and industrialisation has taken a massive toll on the environment. On the other, the increased cooperation that has come with globalisation, together with greater emphasis on global governance, has led to climate change and environmental protection gaining greater prominence in international debate.

The rapid economic growth of emerging powers has led to significant environmental damage due to heavy industrialisation, deforestation and increasing pollution, all of which have significantly increased carbon emissions. The focus of the developing world on lifting its populations out of poverty has made it difficult to address the problem of climate change. This has meant that the developing world has prioritised economic growth over sustainable development. The way, too, in which the developed world has criticised the developing world for its use of cheap, carbon-emitting fuels, like coal, might also be seen as hypocritical. After all, during the last two centuries, the developed world became rich by polluting the atmosphere and now it could be seen as trying to deny the developing world the opportunity to become wealthy. The difficulty of achieving a consensus between the developed and developing worlds on how best to limit carbon emissions is one of the key reasons why the Copenhagen Conference (2009) was not more successful (see Chapter 6).

The political economist Thomas Malthus pessimistically argued that population growth was unsustainable and that we do not have the global resources to continue to support growth at current rates. In other words, there is a 'limit to this growth'. While we have now passed Malthus' predicted time of crisis, many have adopted the ideas of neo-Malthusianism, arguing that without a significant focus on resource management and sustainable development, we will reach a crisis point characterised by famine, disease and civil war. Arguably, we are already witnessing these effects in certain parts of the world.

However, the Danish economist Ester Boserup argued that the challenges created by population growth necessarily force us to come up with new and better solutions. There will be a growth in the creation of new technologies and this will enable us to better manage resources, so that population growth will once again be sustainable.

In addition, the Paris Climate Change Conference (2015) demonstrated that the developing world is becoming much more aware of the dangers of unrestricted economic growth. The conference succeeded in getting nearly all of the 200 states represented to agree that temperature rise in the twenty-first century should be kept as close to 1.5°C as possible. Nation-states will also accept regular reviews of their efforts to limit carbon emissions and the developed world will provide 'climate finance' to help the developing world transfer to greener technology.

Furthermore, in 2017 the attitude to climate change of the leaders of the developed and developing worlds seemed to 'flip'. China reversed plans for 104 new coal plants and President Xi Jinping expressed regret that President Trump had not lived up to the global aspirations of the Paris treaty. In March, the Trump administration reversed the restrictions President Obama had put on the extraction of fossil fuels. This looks likely to change under the Biden administration. Biden appointed John Kerry as the US's first full-time climate envoy, describing him as being a climate leader who will have a 'seat at every table around the world' and will be able to ensure that the climate crisis is an issue once more on the security council.

Biden rejoined the Paris accord as one of his first acts as president. He has also made clear that the US will commit to the Paris Agreement's target for zero carbon emissions by 2050. Furthermore, Biden cancelled the Keystone XL pipeline initiative which was due to extend an existing oil pipeline from Alberta to Nebraska, and which had come under significant opposition from environmentalists. It is still difficult to predict the way in which the changing balance of world power will continue to impact the environment. However, the issue has become significantly more of a focal point to the US under Biden and environmentalism has been part of a global movement lately with various protests and movements, including Extinction Rebellion, putting it on centre stage.

Debate

Multipolarity is conducive to more effective political global governance than unipolarity

Yes

- Increasingly, global problems that transcend state borders, for example environmental issues and trade agreements, need global solutions. This makes cooperation politically more likely. There is therefore an incentive for states to cooperate with shared goals.
- Increasingly, multipolarity has marked a move to multilateralism and liberal democracy (Fukuyama), therefore the international stage is now more amenable to cooperation.
- Globalisation has made it possible and necessary for global governance to work effectively. Improved technology, better sharing of information and more inter-reliance are all good for global governance.

No

- States will still act in their own self-interest and while there may be a use for global governance where there are shared goals, states will ultimately ignore it when they need to act in their own self-interest (Bull).
- There are many states that continue to flout the rules of global governance and act in their own self-interest. Many states have even been seen to act in ways that have been described as hostile in recent years (China and Russia being good examples, not least since they are part of the P5).
- Globalisation has only made the situation more complex, with more to play for, but ultimately it will not mean states cooperate unless it benefits them. A key example has been in getting agreements on environmental issues – ultimately very few states have been willing to halt their economic development sufficiently to reach the 'shared goals'. It has also created an unequal playing field, which only increases instability.

Evaluation prompt: Liberals and realists will take different positions here. Liberals will argue that multipolarity is good for global governance and realists will argue that ultimately states will all want to be the most powerful and will continue to act in their own self-interest, therefore multipolarity is inherently unstable as there is no dominant power. You then need to decide which position you agree with more and support it with your strongest arguments, justifying your view with evidence.

What you should know

Having read this chapter you should have knowledge and understanding of the following:

→ 'Power' is a frequently used term in global relations. At its essence, power means the ability to exert influence through various means over others. In the case of global politics, this relates to the methods nation-states use to exercise control and achieve the outcomes they want.

→ The two main types of power in global politics are hard power and soft power. Often realists give more weight to hard power, in which states fight, and often collide, with each other in their attempts to maximise their influence. Liberals argue that soft power, best understood as the way in which a nation-state achieves its objectives through the attractiveness of its culture and political system, is just as significant, especially in a more globalised world.

→ Joseph Nye also coined the term 'smart power', which refers to a state using both hard- and soft-power methods to achieve its aims.

→ Since the rise of the nation-state in the nineteenth century the global balance of power has continually shifted between the great powers, superpowers and emerging powers, with important repercussions for peace and global stability.

→ Polarity refers to 'poles of power'. There are three main forms of polarity: unipolarity (a single pole of power), bipolarity (two poles of power) and multipolarity (multiple poles of power).

The Cold War provides a classic example of a bipolar system, in which there were two key and equally matched superpowers (the Soviet Union and the US) competing for global influence. When the Soviet Union collapsed in 1991, the US achieved hegemonic status, since there was now no other state that could globally compete with it. The resulting world order that characterised the ending of the Cold War was therefore unipolar. As a result of the changing balance of economic and military global power, the consequences of globalisation and advances in military technology, it has been claimed that the contemporary world is increasingly multipolar, with some arguing that China is on the verge of claiming superpower status.

→ There is a wide variety of ways in which states are governed, including democratic, semi-democratic, non-democratic and authoritarian states. The Democratic Republic of Congo and the Democratic People's Republic of Korea are modern examples of failed and rogue states, respectively.

→ Liberals tend to regard democracy as the best form of government, however some authoritarian countries have achieved impressive growth rates and domestic stability, and are able to play a constructive role in global politics (e.g. China, Singapore).

→ Changing relationships and state actions relate to various developments in power and have impacted contemporary global issues, including conflict, poverty, human rights and the environment. The impact of power and development on these global issues is inextricably linked to globalisation.

Further reading

Chomsky, N. (2003) *Hegemony or Survival: America's Quest for Global Dominance*. Henry Holt and Company.

Fukuyama, F. (1992) *The End of History and the Last Man*. Free Press.

Gadsby, J. (2019) 'Is US hegemony under threat?', *Politics Review*, Vol. 28, No. 3, February.

Jefferies, J. (2020) 'The resurgence of the nation-state', *Politics Review*, Vol. 30, No. 2, November.

Kaldor, M. (1999) *New and Old Wars: Organized Violence in a Global Era*. Stanford University Press.

Kissinger, H. (2015) *World Order: Reflections on the Character of Nations and the Course of History*. Penguin.

Laycock, S. (2021) 'Is hard power making a comeback?', *Politics Review*, Vol. 30, No. 3, February.

Practice questions

Section A

1 Examine the factors that account for the increased use of soft rather than hard power.   *[12 marks]*
2 Examine the main controversies associated with rogue states and non-democratic states.   *[12 marks]*
3 Examine the main implications of multipolarity and bipolarity.   *[12 marks]*
4 Examine the main factors that account for the rise of democratic and non-democratic states.   *[12 marks]*

Section C

1 Evaluate the extent to which the current world order conforms to a multipolar distribution of power.   *[30 marks]*
2 Evaluate the extent to which failed and rogue states present the greatest threat to world stability and security.   *[30 marks]*
3 Evaluate the extent to which hard power is the most effective means for states to achieve their desired outcomes.   *[30 marks]*
4 Evaluate the extent to which the changing nature of the world order since 2000 has impeded political global governance.   *[30 marks]*

8 Regionalism and the European Union

Learning outcomes

By the end of the chapter you should understand:

→ what regionalism is and its various different forms, including economic, political and security

→ the significance of regionalism within the context of globalisation, political regionalism and regional governance

→ the impact that regionalism has on sovereignty, alongside the theoretical debates on this issue

→ various regional organisations (or regional blocs), other than the European Union, and explain their developments, including the United States-Mexico-Canada Agreement (formerly NAFTA), the African Union, the Arab League and the Association of Southeast Asian Nations

→ the various factors that have fostered European integration and explain the patterns of major developments that have led to this

→ the formation, role and objectives of the European Union, including its key institutions and processes of enlargement, key treaties and agreements, economic and monetary union, and supranational and intergovernmental approaches

→ the significance of the EU as a global actor, including the constraints and obstacles that affect it as well as the political, economic, military and structural influences the EU has in global politics

→ the ways in which regionalism addresses and resolves global issues, including conflict, poverty, human rights and the environment

Getting you started

On 31 January 2020 at 11 p.m. (midnight in Brussels), the UK became the first and only country to leave the EU after its 47-year membership in the regional bloc. In the 2016 referendum, the UK had voted to leave the **European Union (EU)**, the 'Leave' campaign having won the nationwide referendum by 51.89% to 48.11%.

Subsequently David Cameron, who had supported the 'Remain' campaign, resigned and was succeeded by Theresa May, who in March 2017 formally triggered Article 50 of the Treaty of Lisbon. Article 50, a paragraph in the Lisbon Treaty agreed by EU member states in 2007, sets out the steps a country needs to follow to leave the EU. These include notifying the European Council, negotiating a withdrawal deal and specifying legal terms for the future relationship with the EU. Theresa May was responsible for negotiating the Chequers agreement which resulted in the Brexit withdrawal agreement. Theresa May resigned in 2019 after failing to have her withdrawal agreement approved by Parliament, and Boris Johnson became prime minister. Johnson was returned to power after the 2019 general election: he was a key figure in the 'Leave' campaign and has been intent on leaving the EU.

Key term

European Union (EU) A collection of 27 European nation-states with both intergovernmental and supranational institutions designed to promote cooperation around its shared values, aims and agreements.

The EU flag: the blue represents the sky of the Western world, the 12 stars the peoples of Europe (12 being the symbol for completeness and perfection)

In January 2020 the UK officially ceased to be a member state of the EU and entered a transition period to enable the UK and the EU to negotiate a new political and economic relationship including trade, immigration, the movement of people, and counter-terrorism. At this time the UK remained in the Customs Union and the Single Market, and was still subject to EU rules. This all changed in January 2021 when the UK officially withdrew from these with a new trade deal.

The EU is widely agreed to be the most advanced example of **regionalism**, due to the unique level of integration among its member states and its expanding membership. It is now a collection of 27 European countries with both intergovernmental and supranational institutions and is designed to promote cooperation centred on its shared values, aims and agreements.

The UK's decision to leave is the first decision of its kind from an EU member state. During the run-up to the referendum, the 'Leave' campaign argued that membership of a regional organisation like the EU resulted in a loss of power and sovereignty and made the case for the UK 'taking back control' of its borders and decision making. The 'Remain' campaign argued that in a globalised and interconnected world, EU membership gave the UK influence and access to free trade with its nearest neighbours on a wide range of shared interests.

The debate over whether membership of regional organisations has a negative or positive impact on a member state's power and sovereignty is one of the central questions when considering the significance of regional organisations. We will explore this debate in this chapter.

The growth of regionalism

The EU is an example of a regional bloc that focuses on economic and political union. Its member states have integrated so widely (in terms of member state numbers) and deeply (in terms of the EU's functions and powers) that it can arguably be seen as an example of **federalism**.

Key terms

Regionalism A group of countries in a given geographic region, also known as a bloc, that share common features, aims, incentives or goals. Different regional blocs can differ quite significantly in their powers and functions.

Federalism Regionalism theory suggests that a centralised federal body exercises power, acting on behalf of the regional bloc. It therefore advocates supranationalism and deeper economic and political integration.

Topic link

Regionalism and global governance are clearly interwoven in how they relate to each other, the issues they deal with and how they have emerged alongside increased globalisation.

In a federal system, power is shared between a central authority above nation-state level (in this case, where member states have given up power over some decisions to central institutions of the EU, such as the European Commission) and state-level authority (in this case, where states retain power over other decisions in their national governments). This contrasts to the process of devolution which can be seen as less permanent and where ultimate power still remains with the state. Instead, federalism works more like the US system of federal government whereby there is a constitutional division of power. This means there are two levels of government, and at both levels there is the power and authority to make laws. Therefore the federal subdivisions in a system like that in the USA have a much greater degree of autonomy than devolution would allow. One can see that the EU system could be seen as more federal because there are regional laws as well as ones at the national level, so there is a significant degree of autonomy for nation-states.

Regionalism grew in significance in the late twentieth century. Just as states have looked for means of global governance at international level, for example through the UN, states have also tried to find ways of working together at regional level, for example through the EU, the USMCA and ASEAN. This has had an impact on the world order and reshaped the international stage, making international relations less state-centric. Regional organisations were founded to give states a smaller, more focused and less cumbersome means of working together than is sometimes possible at international level with larger memberships.

Regionalism and power

A key consideration when analysing regionalism and regional organisations is the amount of power these organisations, such as the EU or the AU, have over their member states. These powers are usually decided in the treaties that states signed when the organisations were founded (see Table 8.1). These treaties set out the rules and legal basis for how the organisations work. For example, the Treaty of Lisbon sets out in Article 50 the legal process by which a member state voluntarily leaves the EU.

Table 8.1 Timeline of regional organisations and treaties

Date	Organisation	Purpose
1945	Arab League	The Arab League was set up in March 1945, initially with six countries (Egypt, Iraq, Transjordan (now called Jordan), Lebanon, Saudi Arabia and Syria, with Yemen joining a few months later. It now has 22 members, but Syria is currently suspended. The aims are to promote economic growth and trade, as well as to maintain sovereignty and encourage political stability in the region.
1950	Council of Europe and the European Convention on Human Rights (ECHR)	Created a mechanism for human rights to be agreed and protected above nation-state level, enforced by the European Court of Human Rights (ECtHR). The ECHR and ECtHR were founded as part of the Council of Europe, which now has 47 members, including Russia and Turkey, and is separate from the EU.
1951	Treaty of Paris, founding the European Coal and Steel Community (ECSC)	Created a common market for coal and steel between Belgium, France, Italy, Luxembourg, the Netherlands and West Germany. One of its founders, former French foreign minister Robert Schumann, said that it would 'make war [between its member states] not only unthinkable but materially impossible'.
1957	Treaty of Rome, founding the European Economic Community (EEC)	The six members of the ECSC signed a treaty creating the EEC, which committed its members to making 'ever closer union among the peoples of Europe'. The treaty formed the main institutions of today's EU, the European Commission, the European Court of Justice, the European Parliament and the Council of Ministers.

→

Date	Organisation	Purpose
1963	Founding of the Organisation of African Unity (OAU)	The first attempts to create regional governance in Africa. The OAU was founded as former colonies gained their independence and was designed to strengthen and defend newly independent states' sovereignty.
1967	Founding of the Association of Southeast Asian Nations (ASEAN)	The first members of ASEAN were Indonesia, Malaysia, the Philippines, Singapore and Thailand. ASEAN's aim was to enhance economic cooperation in the region.
1973	Caribbean Community (CARICOM)	Set up in 1974, CARICOM now has 15 members; their main aim is to promote economic cooperation and integration, but they also work to coordinate foreign policy. CARICOM is an official United Nations Observer.
1985	South Asian Association for Regional Co-operation (SAARC)	Founded in 1985, SAARC has eight members and was set up to promote regional integration and economic development. In 2006 it created a South Asian Free Trade Area. It is an official United Nations Observer and has various multilateral links including with the EU.
1993	Maastricht Treaty – the European Community becomes the EU	By now, the EU had developed into a common market of 12 members (the UK joined in 1973), with free movement of people, goods and services. The treaty began the process for creating a single European currency. The euro came into circulation in 2002 in 13 member states.
2001	Organisation of African Unity becomes the African Union (AU)	The AU has seen African states cooperate on both security and development issues. It has sent peacekeepers to Somalia and, as a bloc, has also threatened to withdraw from the ICC, stating that the ICC is biased against Africans.
2009	Treaty of Lisbon	Created a constitution for the EU and included moves to make decision making simpler (by reducing the policy areas where unanimous agreement was needed), given that the EU had seen its biggest enlargement in 2005 with ten new member states, including many former Soviet states in eastern Europe. The treaty also created the position of President of the European Council (as of 2017, Donald Tusk) and a High Representative for Foreign Affairs, designed to strengthen the EU's independent voice on the world stage.
2015	Eurasian Economic Union	From the 1990s the first treaties were signed for Eurasian economic union. The Treaty of Eurasian Economic Union came into force in 2015. The EAEU has its own Single Market and Customs Union. Its membership includes Armenia, Belarus, Kazakhstan, Kyrgyzstan and Russia.
2016	Brexit	The UK voted to leave the EU and, in 2017, triggered Article 50, the first member state to do so.
2018	United States–Mexico–Canada Agreement (USMCA)	A free-trade agreement between the United States of America, the United Mexican States and Canada which replaced NAFTA. NAFTA was agreed in order to eliminate tariff and non-tariff barriers to trade in the North America region. While the USMCA largely maintains the provisions in NAFTA, it includes changes to intellectual property and digital trade, additional environmental and working regulations, increased incentives for car manufacturing in the US, greater access to Canada's dairy market and a greater duty-free limit for Canadians buying US goods online.
2020	Brexit Withdrawal Agreement	The UK officially left the EU in January 2020, entering into a transition period until leaving the Customs Union fully in January 2021.

There are two ways in which power and decision making work within regional organisations:

1 **Intergovernmentalism:** member states make all of the decisions. Decisions are not delegated to separate institutions and no institution can force states to do something that they do not agree with (as is the case with the African Union (AU)). With this type of decision making, states retain more control over decisions and therefore the impact on sovereignty and the sacrifices that states make are lessened. It can also be said that this type of decision making is more democratic, if elected national governments are taking decisions themselves.

> **Key term**
>
> **Intergovernmentalism**
> Governments work together to come up with mutually beneficial agreements, but their sovereignty remains intact.

Key term

Supranationalism
Certain institutions take decisions above the level of domestic governments, therefore diminishing the sovereignty of those states. Certain forms of regionalism have significant aspects of supranationalism, which is controversial, given the impact it has on state sovereignty.

2 **Supranationalism:** the regional organisation makes all of the decisions and imposes them on its member states (supranational literally means 'above nation-state level'). In the case of the EU, the European Commission is the only part that can propose new laws, and in many policy areas the law will be agreed if at least 55% of the member states representing at least 65% of the EU population agrees it in the Council of Ministers (this is known as 'qualified majority voting', where each member state's voting power is not equal but is weighted according to the size of its population). This type of decision making is often criticised as resulting in states giving up too much power and sovereignty. It is also argued that supranationalism is undemocratic and, within the EU, this is often referred to as the organisation's 'democratic deficit', meaning that decisions are taken that member state populations have not voted for.

Why a European Union?

The EU was originally founded to further economic and political cooperation within Europe between states that had fought two world wars only two decades apart.

The EU has had most impact in terms of:

- peace and security (between its member states)
- economic and monetary union
- political union (including social and environmental policy)
- human rights (although the ECtHR and ECHR are separate from the EU)
- police and judicial cooperation
- common foreign and security policy.

Peace and security

The EU has been very successful in preventing violent conflict between its member states.

In 1951, France, West Germany and the Benelux countries (Belgium, the Netherlands and Luxembourg) signed the Treaty of Paris, which established the ECSC. The coal- and steel-rich regions between France and Germany, particularly in the Ruhr valley, were key natural resources fought over during both world wars.

The ECSC subsequently became part of the EU, which was formally established with the Maastricht Treaty on 1 November 1993. Therefore, while the initial reasons behind the EU were economic, it came into being at a time when Europe was keen to promote peace and stability, having just emerged from the Second World War. The initial trade agreement was a way to ensure this peace and stability by encouraging cooperation and reducing competition and conflict, particularly between France and Germany. However, it has left the EU with a legacy and clear mission to promote the liberal values of democracy and freedom (the liberal idea of 'democratic peace theory' (see page 280)). Over time, the level of integration has become so deep between EU member states that the idea of war between European nations is now unthinkable. The EU was awarded the Nobel Peace Prize in 2012 in recognition of its 'six decades' contribution to the advancement of peace and reconciliation, democracy and human rights in Europe'.

Economic union

The core of the EU project has been a deepening of economic and monetary union between its member states. In 2002, the euro came into circulation. Before this, the EU in its various preceding forms had created a common market with freedom of movement for people, goods and services. The EU has therefore focused on removing tariff and non-tariff barriers to trade between EU member states.

The 'four freedoms' of movement are a key feature of the European Single Market.

- **People:** under the Schengen Agreement (1985), 26 European states (including non-EU member states) have created a travel zone in which there are no border or passport checks. This allows for free movement of people, while EU member state citizens are free to live and work without restriction in other EU member states. The Schengen Area has been under pressure in recent years, with some states reinstating border controls to deal with the migrant crisis caused by conflict in the middle east (notably Syria) and terrorism threats (in the case of the state of emergency, which France imposed in 2015).
- **Goods:** Single Market member states have removed all customs checks and restrictions within the Single Market region. This allows for free movement of goods between member states.
- **Capital:** large amounts of money used for payments or investments can be moved freely without restriction within the Single Market.
- **Services:** companies within the EU are free to set up companies and provide services (for example, any service from banking to car hire) in other EU countries.

Distinguish between

Tariff and non-tariff barriers

Tariff barriers	Non-tariff barriers
• Taxes and charges that the government of the state receiving imports adds to these imports.	• Other barriers to free trade, which include a government setting a limit or quota on imports of particular goods or services, or other measures that restrict trade.

Another key element of the EU's economic activities has been the creation of a single European currency, the only regional currency of its kind in the world. States gave up their national currencies, such as the French franc or the German Deutschmark, for the euro, which was introduced in 1999 (for financial transactions, but not in notes and coins) and fully introduced as notes and coins on 1 January 2002. In 2021 the Eurozone had 19 member states using its currency.

Key challenges for the euro have included the following:

- The creation of new EU institutions for the Eurozone in the form of the ECB, which has the power to set monetary policy for the Eurozone area (including centrally imposed interest rates).
- Ensuring that members of the Eurozone all tax and spend responsibly (known as fiscal policy, the amount states tax and spend). The Eurozone sets non-binding guidelines for states to follow. These guidelines came under severe pressure after the 2008 global financial crisis, during which Greece, in particular,

experienced a debt crisis and required the ECB and other Eurozone member states to provide financial assistance to 'bail out' its economy. Governments feared that, without this assistance, the Greek economy would collapse, causing considerable damage to all Eurozone member states and the potential collapse of the euro. In 2012, the European Fiscal Compact was signed as a legal intergovernmental treaty requiring states to keep their national budgets in balance or in surplus.

Political and social union

Another key pillar of the EU has been social and political union, which has seen the creation of a huge number of laws. The EU has also created a forum for its member states to work together in order to agree laws and other measures to tackle the challenges facing all member states.

In terms of social policy, the European Social Fund gives money to projects aiming, for example, to reduce unemployment. Around 10% of the EU budget is spent on the Social Fund. The EU has also harmonised labour laws through individual EU laws, known as 'directives'. These laws harmonise social policy on matters as diverse as working hours and unemployment rights. The European Commission proposes EU directives, and the EU's Council of Ministers and the European Parliament agree them. The European Court of Justice interprets the law and ensures that EU law (including directives) is applied fairly across all EU member states (see page 318).

EU directives are agreed on a wide range of matters, ranging from social policy to trade and the environment. Indeed, a key argument of the UK's 'Leave' campaign was that the EU was creating too many directives and imposing them on member states. Directives have been agreed relating to industrial emissions, regulation of pharmaceuticals, standardising weights and measures of produce into the metric system, and bans on appliances that use too much power. A frequently debated EU directive focuses on the shape of bananas, and states that bananas should be 'free of malformation or abnormal curvature' – although nothing is actually banned under this directive, it does outline different classes of 'curvature'.

Judicial and policing

The EU has also introduced close cooperation on justice and policing matters between member states, including coordination of law and enforcement on matters such as international terrorism and organised crime.

The European Arrest Warrant allows for a police force in one member state to issue an arrest warrant and for a police force in any other member state to arrest the individual wherever they may be in the EU. This removes the need for states to negotiate extradition of a suspect back to his/her home state.

Human rights

The EU has been a persuasive advocate for human rights. The European Convention on Human Rights (ECHR) was created in 1950, therefore coming into existence before the European Community (later the EU). It was one of the earliest elements of the European agenda, aimed at preventing a repeat of human rights abuses committed during the Second World War. The ECHR has a wider membership than the EU, being made up of member states of the Council of Europe (which includes non-EU member states such as Russia and Turkey). The EU has also established its own Charter of Fundamental Rights, which sets out the specific rights (economic, social, political) that should be in place for all European citizens.

The EU has often been criticised for lacking the means and the will to intervene militarily to uphold human rights. For example, it did not play a major role in responding to the genocide that took place in former Yugoslavia in 1995 (see Chapter 5), Europe's only genocide since the Second World War. With little power of its own to conduct a coordinated foreign policy, the EU did not intervene, while the UN and NATO led the military response through a UN Protection Force and NATO air strikes.

Arguably, this prompted the EU to do more in terms of promoting human rights. In 1992 (notably, in the midst of the crisis in the former Yugoslavia), the European Commission established the Directorate-General for European Civil Protection and Humanitarian Aid Operations (ECHO). ECHO provides humanitarian aid money and emergency aid workers, and responds to natural disasters and crises. It also works closely with several NGOs and currently has a strong presence in Syria, among other regions.

The environment

In the international community, the EU has been at the forefront of global governance efforts to protect the environment. In 2020 the EU pledged to be carbon neutral by 2050. In order to achieve this the EU will need to radically accelerate current emissions reductions. The EU has introduced environmental laws at regional level that address issues such as acid rain, air and water quality, noise pollution, harnessing sustainable energy and protecting the ozone layer. These policies may not have been possible to agree at international level, and therefore have been achieved so much earlier than any international climate agreements. These successes are due in large part to the EU's small size (compared with the number of parties involved in international agreements) and the similar levels of economic development among its member states (compared with international agreements needing to balance the demands made of both developed and developing states).

The creation of trade laws as part of the Single Market has allowed the EU to develop laws protecting the environment as part of the same process. Sustainable development, that is to say developing trade and protecting the environment at the same time so as not to put future generations' development at risk, has been a consideration throughout the Single Market's development. For example:

- EU member states agreed to legally binding targets on reducing emissions and developing renewable energy technology. These went further than the non-binding targets that nation-states agreed at the Paris Summit in 2015. The EU has been committed to these goals. The EU aimed to achieve the following so-called '20-20-20 goals' by 2020:
  - a 20% cut in greenhouse gas emissions
  - finding 20% of EU energy from renewables
  - a 20% improvement in energy efficiency.
- The data suggests that the EU has been on target with these goals and has managed to meet them, undeterred by Trump's withdrawal from the Paris Agreement in 2017. In order to stay on track with the 2030 targets the EU will need to see reductions of 130 megatons of carbon dioxide. It is likely much of this change will come from renewable energies.

- The EU has agreed a wealth of environmental protection directives, harmonised across the EU and enforceable by the European Court of Justice. These include a directive requiring public and private sector organisations to carry out an environmental impact assessment before any new building or infrastructure projects.

The EU has committed to reach carbon neutrality by 2050, with the set target to reduce greenhouse gas emissions by at least 55% of the 1990 levels by 2030 as part of the European Green Deal. For now, these targets remain very ambitious, with some countries in the EU still heavily reliant on non-renewable energy (e.g. Poland and coal). While the Covid-19 outbreak has had a negative impact on agreeing environment policy it has also had a positive impact on air quality and has encouraged more of a focus on outdoor spaces. It has also become apparent that President Biden has pledged similar goals for the US, which may encourage the EU in its efforts. By July 2021, the Commission will review its progress and where necessary review and revise policies.

One area in which the EU has especially maximised its structural power has been in international environmental talks and governance. For example, the EU has used its observer status in the UN and its role in the G20 to promote environmental causes on the international stage. The EU has been integral to the development of various international environmental agreements (for example, the 2009 Copenhagen Agreement on climate change) and has been fundamental in promoting and upholding them. The EU has seemed to continue to take a lead in negotiations in carbon emissions and promoting the Paris 2015 agenda. However, they took less of a front seat in the recent COP26 negotiations. The spotlight was instead on the US and China's role, and the role that developing countries will have in combating climate change.

Poverty

The EU has had a significant role in encouraging development outside of its borders and has been a key factor in the global mission to eradicate poverty. It is also remains the world's leading donor of Official Development Assistance, providing 75.2 billion euros of aid in 2019.

This money has gone to different regions around the globe but, significantly, the largest sum has gone to areas in Europe itself. The aid has not been limited to any one sector, covering everything from service provision and infrastructure development to humanitarian aid.

However, some have criticised the EU's Common Agricultural Policy (CAP) for making it harder for farmers in developing states outside the EU to sell their produce into the EU. This is because the CAP provides subsidies for EU farmers (see page 134), which enable them to keep their prices lower (and therefore more competitive) when they sell their produce to the developing world (the CAP covers approximately half of the EU's budget, costing 54 billion euros in 2020).

> ### Topic link
>
> There are clear links here with the global governance topics. It is worth considering how part of global governance is the reliance on regional organisations coordinating nation-states in order to make an effective response easier - this links to the idea of building blocks. Regionalism can arguably make global governance more effective.

Case study

The EU Covid Recovery Fund

An interesting way to consider the impact of Brexit in Europe has been by examining the response to Covid-19. One area where the EU has tried to create a unified response has been the provision of a Covid recovery fund, which was included as part of the 2021 budget. The deal for this was struck at the end of 2020 after delays caused by Hungary and Poland's objections to the funding being tied to the rule of law. If the UK had still been in the EU, it would have been the second largest contributor to the recovery fund. There is a good chance it would have been significantly reluctant to go ahead, potentially preventing the fund from happening.

The budget included a sizeable Covid-19 stimulus fund of 800 billion euros and required unanimous support. Without this deal, the EU would have needed to resort to an austerity budget for 2021. It is expected that the funds will come into effect from July of 2021. The first country to get a green light on spending was Portugal with its recovery and resilience plan.

The budget's agreement comes a year on from the EU's historic decision to pool debt in order to fund recovery and continues this trend, with the largest joint issuance of debt the Union has seen to date. The EU's recovery package is significant but when compared to the US's $1.9 trillion infrastructure plan, as well as its advanced vaccination programme, it is expected the EU's economic recovery will be somewhat slower than that of America.

The EU recovery fund will prioritise green and digital projects, in line with the EU's 2050 targets for net zero greenhouse gas emissions and its digitisation targets. For the EU, the recovery fund intends to renew confidence in its capabilities after what has been seen as a poor early response to the crisis and a patchy vaccine rollout.

Angela Merkel, Emmanuel Macron and European Council President Charles Michel discuss the EU's Covid-19 recovery plan

Topic link

The Covid-19 pandemic has also been on the agenda of the UN (see Chapter 3), but the focus has been different, with the emphasis more on tackling development and poverty while the EU has arguably had a more strategic focus in tackling the spread of the virus.

Regionalism

Regionalism refers to the idea that nation–states in a certain geographically defined area are united by common:

- goals
- incentives
- interests
- aims.

These geographically defined areas are often referred to as 'regional blocs'. Regionalism has arguably existed since the end of the Second World War and is therefore not necessarily a new phenomenon, but it has grown and intensified in recent years, much the same as globalisation.

The Cold War was a time of bipolarity rather than regionalism – the world was divided into two halves around the ideologies of capitalism and communism, meaning there were only two real regional alliances during this period (centred on the US and western Europe on the one hand, and the Soviet Union and Warsaw Pact states on the other). However, with the increase of social, political, cultural and economic interconnectedness, it has become ever more important for states in a more multipolar world to form alliances and agreements with one another.

Table 8.2 The differences between economic, political and security regionalism

Economic regionalism	Political regionalism	Security regionalism
Focuses on economic progress, free trade and removing barriers to trade within the region.	Needs longer-term strategic aims.	Focuses on defence and security against shared threats.
Must have interdependent economies and economic interests.	Focuses on resolving challenges and maximising opportunities that two or more states face (e.g. climate change or terrorism).	Often there will be shared political ties too.
Does not necessarily need a common cultural interest.	To some extent, relies on shared values and so there need to be cultural similarities.	Territorial borders are especially important and these states have a common interest in protecting this area (e.g. a common threat).
Does not need longer-term strategic aims.	Is likely to be more inward looking and acting in the region's self-interest.	This may have some impact on sovereignty because of the emphasis on a common defence policy, but this might be quite specific and so limited to a certain context.
Tends to be more outward looking than political regional blocs, including reaching trade deals as a bloc with other states outside the region.	The emphasis on pooled sovereignty and deeper integration means there is more of an erosion of sovereignty.	
Involves limited erosion of sovereignty, except in the case of a single regional currency like the euro, which involves considerable impact on sovereignty.	Enables states to form common positions and achieve greater influence through pooling sovereignty (particularly in the case of smaller states).	

Regional alliances are often appealing to states and make practical sense if states within a region have shared interests that they wish to advance or defend (for example, advancing free trade in the case of the EU or tackling internal violent conflict in the case of the AU). In this way, regionalism and globalisation are intertwined, but they can also work against each other.

Types of regionalism

There are several different forms of regionalism, most commonly characterised through states wishing to work together on developing their economies, shared political challenges and/or security (see Table 8.2). Regional blocs may follow only one of these types of regionalism or a combination of all these types.

Economic regionalism

States that have shared economic aims and, therefore, incentives to cooperate may form a regional bloc, often based around trade deals (see Box 8.1). An example of an economic bloc based solely on trade was NAFTA, now the USMCA. This agreement between Canada, Mexico and the US enables these states to trade freely with one another through the reduction of trade barriers.

Box 8.1

Multilateral regional trade agreements

There have been several major regional trade agreements under negotiation in recent history, including the following:

- **Comprehensive and Progressive Agreement for Trans-Pacific Partnership:** this originally was the Trans-Pacific Partnership (TPP), a regional trade deal agreed in 2016 between the states of the Pacific rim, but excluding China and the US. President Barack Obama had championed the trade deal, but his successor President Donald Trump withdrew the US from the TPP on 28 January 2017. The remaining countries replaced it with the Comprehensive and Progressive Agreement for Trans-Pacific Partnership.
- **The United States–Mexico–Canada Agreement (UMSCA):** agreed between Canada, Mexico and the US originally in 1994 (as NAFTA) and updated in 2018.
- **African Free Trade Area (AfCFTA):** a free trade area founded in 2018, with trade commencing in 2021 (postponed by Covid-19). It was created by the African Continental Free Trade Agreement, including 54 or the 55 African nations, and it is the largest free-trade area in the world since the formation of the WTO.

Topic link

Regional economic governance has some obvious overlaps with global economic governance and feeds into the building blocks versus stumbling blocks idea (see page 304). On the one hand, regional trade agreements can open up the global market and increase international trade and multilateral cooperation (building blocks), however on the other they can act as stumbling blocks to global integration by making regional areas more insular.

Often states make mutually beneficial trade agreements, which enable them to maximise their own economies. This may be via a free-trade agreement, whereby states liberalise trade by reducing or removing restrictions between the regional states, such as taxes, tariffs, quotas and embargoes.

States also use regional protectionist policies to protect domestic trade. For example, they may place limitations on quotas from outside their region, which fortifies their own economies – by restricting imports, domestic populations are encouraged to buy products produced within the region. The EU, for example, is protectionist over its agricultural industry. The CAP offers farmers subsidies, which enable them to produce cheaper goods, thereby encouraging EU citizens to buy these goods over more expensive products from outside the region.

President Barack Obama famously intervened in the 2016 referendum on the UK's membership of the EU by stating that if the UK decided to leave the union, it would be 'at the back of the queue' when it came to negotiating a new trade deal with the US. At the time, Obama was focusing on agreeing a trade deal – the TTIP – between the US and the EU bloc, which is now obsolete. The 'Remain' and 'Leave' campaigns differed on their views as to whether it was in the UK's interests to negotiate with the US as part of a united regional bloc or whether seeking the UK's own bespoke trade deal with the US would better defend the UK's economic and trading interests.

Key term

Sovereignty The principle of absolute and unlimited power that a nation-state exercises over its population and territory, and the defining characteristic of a state. Some forms of regionalism weaken sovereignty due to states handing over some power to international bodies.

Political regionalism

Political regionalism tends to focus on tackling collective action problems that two or more states within a particular region are faced with. It can be a deeper form of integration because it requires shared cultural ties and a common value system, both of which give a regional bloc a more distinct identity. Often there will be longer-term strategic aims and a broader political vision. Countries that enter into political regionalism will generally gain an advantage from pooling **sovereignty**, because they are more influential collectively than they are individually (see Box 8.2). Therefore, political regionalism can significantly increase states' structural power within international organisations and informal forums. For example, the EU is a member of the G20 and is an observer state of the UN.

Box 8.2

Examples of regional political alliances

There are several major regional political alliances in existence today, including the following:

- **Arab League:** this was founded in 1945 and comprises 22 member states (as of 2017, Syria's membership was suspended) across the middle east and north Africa region. The Arab League does not have its own institutions that operate in the same way as those of the EU. Rather, it conducts its business primarily through Arab League summits, in which it aims to agree common positions on any policy area of shared interest.
- **Alliance of Small Island States (ASIS):** established in 1990 with no formal constitution, ASIS was created to give a unified voice to small island states at risk from climate change. It comprises many small states, including the Maldives, Nauru (one of the world's smallest states) and the Seychelles. ASIS allows these states to work together in organisations such as the UN and at major climate change conferences to achieve greater influence than they would alone.

Figure 8.1 depicts how different regional blocs might fit into the various forms of regionalism. In practice, this will not always be clear-cut and some of these definitions are open to debate.

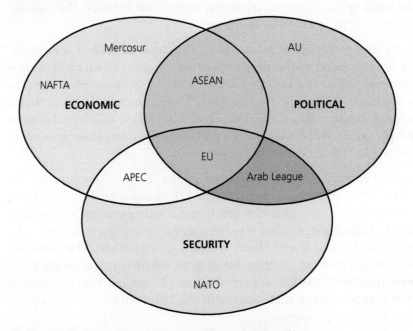

Figure 8.1 Regional blocs and various forms of regionalism

Over time, regionalism has evolved to include both a widening and a deepening of regional relations. Widening refers to the expansion of regional blocs, a good example being the steady growth of the EU, with many countries still wanting to join the union. Deepening refers to the idea that there is a greater involvement of states in the regional bloc, or that sovereignty is pooled. When integration is deeper, states necessarily see some of their internal sovereignty eroded (but importantly not taken away) in order for it to be pooled.

Regionalism has both intergovernmental and supranational aspects and, depending on the type of regionalism, it may be one or a combination of the two. If there are supranational elements within a regional bloc, we can expect to see deeper integration and pooled sovereignty.

Security regionalism

In the case of security regionalism, states make an alliance to better strengthen their regional borders. Often this involves militaristic alliances or agreements that if an outsider attacks any of the states within the regional bloc, all regional members will react. Therefore, security regionalism directly relates to defence policies, while the alliance of such states may be centred on a common threat.

The EU has tried to gain more influence over security policy through its Common Foreign and Security Policy (CFSP). The Lisbon Treaty signed in 2007 agreed more powers for the EU to project its own unified foreign and security policy through the appointment of a High Representative of the Union for Foreign Affairs and Security Policy and the President of the European Council. In reality, however, despite the EU gaining more of a unified voice than had previously been the case, NATO remains the most influential security organisation for European states – the majority of the EU's member states are also members of NATO. The EU's CFSP confirms that NATO is the principal organisation responsible for the territorial defence of Europe.

Case study

Operation IRINI

Operation IRINI (Greek for peace), launched in 2020, is an example of the EU's efforts towards security regionalism. Run by the European Union Naval Force under a new CDSP (Common Security and Defence Policy), it aims to enforce the UN arms embargo to Libya following the Libyan civil war in order to help the peace process in the country. Using aerial, satellite and maritime resources, IRINI is able to inspect vessels off the coast of Libya that may be carrying arms. It can also gather information about smuggling and human trafficking, and can help train the Libyan coastguard and navy.

IRINI replaced Operation Sophia, the EU's previous military operation launched in 2015 that focused on preventing human trafficking across established routes in the Mediterranean.

Topic link

NATO is discussed further in Chapter 3, where the focus is more on its role as an IGO rather than its security regionalism.

NATO is discussed further in Chapter 3

Key terms

Widening The expansion of regional blocs and their spread to incorporate more member states, e.g. the EU's expansion to include Warsaw Pact states from eastern Europe in 2004 and 2007.

Deepening The level of integration becomes increasingly more comprehensive in terms of the number of policy areas on which states cooperate and the powers of independent decision making that any alliances or organisations have. With deeper integration, states are moving towards a more federal-style system.

Pooled sovereignty The idea that regional co-operation does not necessarily weaken an individual state's sovereignty at a global level, rather it can strengthen it by combining its power with other nation-states, enabling them to share resources and influences to greater effect.

Sometimes security alliances are centred on the movement of people. Some states consider relatively free movement between regional members to be safe, but they maintain a common policy to restrict immigration from further afield or to prevent illegal asylum seekers. There has been significant discussion within the EU throughout the so-called migrant crisis, which was exacerbated by discussions over immigration during Brexit. The Arab League also has a principle to protect the sovereignty of its member states and help procure stability in the region against a backdrop of historical political tensions.

> **Topic link**
>
> The way we talk about types of regionalism is quite similar to how we talk about types of globalisation (Chapter 2), given that there are similar economic, political and cultural processes at play.

Debates and significance of regionalism

There has been much debate over the extent to which regionalism has been significant and in what ways it has impacted global politics. One of the key debates is the extent to which regionalism is compatible with globalisation. Some argue that the two are integral to one another, while others argue that they are incompatible.

Furthermore, there has been much discussion over the impact that regionalism has on sovereignty and governance, at both regional and global levels. Many observers argue that the impact of both globalisation and regionalism has challenged the idea of Westphalian sovereignty to the extent that it is no longer the defining feature of international relations.

> **Topic link**
>
> The role of state power, and the debate over whether states remain the most important global actors, is discussed in Chapter 1, in relation to realist views. The idea of Westphalian nation-states is also a crucial element of the globalisation topic (Chapter 2), given that globalisation can be seen as a threat to sovereignty.

Regionalism and globalisation

There is significant debate over whether regionalism works with, or against, globalisation. On the one hand it can be argued that regional blocs merely act as a way to better organise global relations – in other words, they are *building blocks*. Since states group together based around common features, it is far easier to conduct international affairs. Arguably, this makes global processes easier to manage and therefore can enhance globalisation, because these processes become more efficient.

Others have argued that regionalism acts as a *stumbling block* to the globalisation process, as regional blocs become more inward looking – they focus their efforts on their own part of the globe and lose interest in the global picture.

Debate

Does regionalism act as a stumbling block or building block to globalisation?

Stumbling block

- Inwardly looking regional blocs display a 'regional egoism', in that they are only really interested in the concerns of their own region and are therefore fairly isolationist in policy.
- Regional blocs may cut off economically through the implementation of protectionist policies that impinge on the free movement of global trade.
- Regionalism is incongruous with globalisation because instead of enhancing a global community and a global civil society, it further divides the world into segments. This leads to the restriction of global cosmopolitanism.
- Regional blocs are all quite different in character, meaning they cannot effectively act together to organise global relations.

Building block

- Regional blocs enhance globalisation by essentially compartmentalising the globe, making it 'smaller' and more manageable. This has been termed the 'global village argument', meaning the 'global' and 'local' begin to merge.
- Regional blocs organise states into those that have similar goals, making the processes of global governance more efficient.
- Regionalism is compatible with globalisation – it involves similar processes of cooperation, multilateralism and governance, just on a smaller scale.
- Outwardly looking regional blocs want to make the most of global networks and are simply acting as a larger unit than a nation-state.

Evaluation prompt: Regionalism and globalisation can be seen as quite distinct at times, and at others they can appear to be part of one process. Where they are distinct you might find it easier to think of regionalism acting more as a stumbling block, and where they seem to be acting as part of one process you might see it as more of a building block. Decide which one you think is *more* the case and then explain why with examples.

Activity

Do you think that regionalism and globalisation work together? Are they part of the same process (building blocks) or do they merely move power divides from nation-states to regional blocs? Write down the strongest argument (in your opinion) on each side of this debate, then add your own conclusion explaining your reasons.

Think about this within the context of multipolarity. Find three pieces of evidence (theory/ statistics/examples) to support your view.

Topic link

With increased multipolarity comes increased regionalism. Often multipolarity and multilateralism can be seen to go together, and we might therefore argue that regionalism can help to act as a building block for globalisation because it enhances the effectiveness of supragovernmentalism. However, we might also argue that states are much more inclined to focus on regional hegemony than global hegemony, as we have seen with the bipolarity between India and Pakistan or Saudi Arabia and Iran. In cases such as these regions can be seen to look more inwardly and create more global divides.

Prospects for political regionalism and governance

Political regionalism has clear ramifications for governance at a state, regional and global level. Regionalism has generally progressed from simple and mutually agreeable deals of a mostly economic nature to a much more involved system. In the case of political regionalism, this has also seen the rise of regional governance, to the extent that some blocs now act almost as federal powers. For example, the EU has often been seen to have confederate or federal aspects to it, particularly where it acts supranationally. The

ECJ is one area that can be seen to act quite federally, it resolves conflicts between two levels of government (European institutions and its member states) with community law overriding national law. It has even led to the debate of whether, due to this level of integration, we could consider a regional bloc, such as the EU, to be a superpower.

There is also debate over whether or not regional blocs are a help or a hindrance to global governance. This returns to the idea of building blocks and stumbling blocks. On the one hand, regional blocs offer more easily manageable groups of actors, which make for easier negotiations and more probable agreements. Furthermore, they are naturally allied groups with a more unified voice. This can enable smaller, or weaker, states to have a greater influence, both within their region and on the global stage. Arguably, this has gone some way to redressing many of the structural imbalances in international organisations with supranational elements (for example, the UN) – many observers agree that regional blocs have enabled previously sidelined states, such as those from the Global South, to become empowered in a way they never could as lone states.

Impact on state sovereignty

Regionalism has also had a clear impact on sovereignty, but the extent to which this is the case depends on the way regionalism is conducted. If regionalism is predominantly intergovernmental, the impact on sovereignty is minimal – states retain their sovereignty in intergovernmental agreements that are mutually beneficial to all. If regionalism is supranational, then there must be a necessary erosion of sovereignty for it to succeed. However, states can ultimately still choose to leave a supranational agreement (as has been demonstrated by Brexit) or to ignore it. Therefore, it can be said that states ultimately remain as sovereign entities and continue to act predominantly in their own self-interest.

Distinguish between

Intergovernmental and supranational sovereignty

Intergovernmental

- Nation-states make mutually beneficial agreements but act independently and in their own self-interest.
- Sovereignty remains fully intact.
- States can still easily opt out of agreements at an intergovernmental level.
- Intergovernmentalism may go beyond decision-making bodies and include scrutinising and steering bodies, etc.

Supranational

- Refers to international institutions of law that can act above state level.
- State sovereignty is eroded through supranationalism.
- States are not acting on their own behalf but rather as part of a bigger organisation.
- Usually, the erosion of sovereignty is voluntary and related to specific areas, e.g. trade.
- Supranationalism generally refers to decision-making bodies. Interdependence is given institutional recognition.

Topic link

Chapter 3 discusses how global governance is intergovernmental, and it is only on the regional scale (most notably the EU) where there is supranationalism.

Liberals and realists have different views regarding the impact regionalism has had on sovereignty, and indeed whether the implications are of a positive or negative nature. For liberals, cooperation is always good, whether on a regional or a global scale, as long as one does not impede the other. States are strengthened through cooperation and liberals argue that governance on a regional and a global scale is the only effective way to deal with a more interconnected world, given that some issues simply cannot be addressed by states acting alone. Issues such as human rights, movement of people, global trade and climate change all increasingly require strong relationships between states if we are to tackle them.

On the other hand, realists argue that ultimately regional and global governance is futile because states will continue to act in their own self-interest, with strong states still able to abuse the system, or even ignore it entirely. Therefore, while strong states can ultimately reclaim their sovereign power, there is little point in the whole exercise.

> ## Topic link
>
> The idea of sovereignty acting as a barrier to more action against issues such as human rights (Chapter 5) and the environment (Chapter 6) is a recurring theme in terms of the effectiveness of intergovernmentalism and supranationalism.

There are three main regionalism theories in relation to sovereignty:

1 **Federalism:** regionalism can and should be seen as a federal-style system with a central authority. There will be a significant impact on sovereignty, as it is pooled.
2 **Functionalism:** regional blocs develop to fulfil specific functions only, rather than as broader entities. There will be a more limited impact on sovereignty.
3 **Neofunctionalism:** falls somewhere between the two – while there may be initial functions for the regional bloc, these may well 'spill over' into other areas. There will be a mixed impact on sovereignty.

These theories consider how regional blocs are integrated and help us to understand how regionalism emerged in the first instance, and the impact it has since had on sovereignty. They highlight that there is a clear relationship between the level of integration and impact, in that the deeper the regional integration, the greater the supranational element and, therefore, the greater the impact on sovereignty. We will examine these theories in more detail later in the chapter in regard to the EU, given that it is the most established and deepest form of regionalism in the world.

Further to the above established theories, there is also the idea of 'new regionalism'. This refers to the substantial increase in regionalism in the 1990s, which saw it have a global, rather than local, effect, much of which was based around economic integration.

The development of regional organisations (excluding the EU)

There are many examples of regional organisations representing different types of regionalism. Regional blocs are the most significant and they vary in terms of character and type of regionalism (either economic, political or security). Some of the key regional organisations (excluding the EU) to consider are the USMCA (formerly NAFTA), ASEAN, the Arab League and the African Union.

United States–Mexico–Canada Agreement (USMCA)

The USMCA is a form of economic regionalism. It is a free-trade agreement ratified in 2020, which replaced NAFTA, which had been implemented in 1994. It followed a year of negotiation at a time when President Trump was making a number of trade relations changes such as ceasing negotiation on the Trans-Pacific Partnership and increasing tariffs with China. NAFTA was focused on reducing trade barriers and tariffs in particular areas: textiles, agriculture and automobiles between the US, Mexico and Canada. It had the intention of increasing trade, integrating Mexico (bringing it in line with the higher wages of North America and discouraging migration) and promoting manufacturing in the region in order to increase productivity. Various administrations supported this agreement until the Trump era. This is a form of economic regionalism but it does not seek deeper political regionalism and even its free-trade agreement does not extend to a fully free-trade area like the EU does.

The USMCA maintains a lot of the original elements from NAFTA but with some important updates, including an agreement to review it every 6 years and for it to expire after 16 years. The most notable areas of change included a focus on regional protectionism of automobile exports (0% tariffs on cars where 75% made in North America), changes to steel and aluminium tariffs, greater access to the Canadian dairy market, Canadians receiving duty-free on American goods they buy online, and 40–45% of all auto content to be made by workers earning at least $16 per hour. There were also modernisations to the old policy around digital trade and intellectual property. As well as a focus on working regulations, there were more environmental regulations.

Association of Southeast Asian Nations (ASEAN)

ASEAN is primarily a form of economic regionalism with a clear aim to promote trade in the region (particularly to protect against Chinese domination but also as a counterweight to Japan). It does have some broader social aims such as protecting and improving health. It also has a limited political element via the aim to defend member sovereignty. ASEAN's focus is on promoting economic growth as well as peace and stability in the region and it has the aim of becoming a full economic community. It is aiming for an EU-style single market. There is also a security aim, with the ASEAN Regional Forum (ARF) aiming to resolve conflicts peacefully. ASEAN allows visa-free travel in the region and its security cooperation involves sharing intelligence. ASEAN's headquarters are based in Jakarta. It has six major members, ten countries in total, including Indonesia, the Philippines and Thailand, but not China or Japan.

How it operates:

- ASEAN held its first East Asian summit (EAS) in 2005. The EAS groups, ASEAN countries and China, Japan, South Korea, India, Australia and New Zealand meet biannually.
- The highest decision-making body is the annual summit of heads of state and government.
- There are also ASEAN ministerial meetings for foreign ministers, which coordinate activities and create guidelines.
- The standing committee is chaired by the foreign minister of the summit host country. It includes the secretary-general and directors general of the ASEAN national secretariats.
- The Secretariat-General runs ASEAN activities and implements policies headed by the secretary-general.
- There are many other committees, ministerial bodies and technical groups in the organisation.

Successes:

- The South East Asian Nuclear Weapon-free Zone Treaty was signed in 1995.

- AFTA Asian Free Trade Agreement was signed in 1992; any country that has joined since has had to sign the agreement.
- In 2008 a landmark agreement was ratified which all ten members eventually agreed on. It deepened economic integration, turned ASEAN into a legal entity and committed members to promoting human rights and democratic ideals.
- ASEAN has put pressures on Myanmar to adopt reforms (although it could be argued this has not been sufficient).

Failures:

- It has been criticised for all talk, no action. It relies on consensus and non-interference which has reinforced authoritarian governance in the region.
- The Bali Summit saw members back a general democratic principle that is somewhat incongruous with some of its member states.
- ASEAN has been criticised for its lack of action against the regime in Myanmar.
- International terrorism has been high on the agenda for ASEAN, but it has come under criticism for limiting its role to mediation and resolution.
- ASEAN has been unsuccessful so far with regard to conflict in the South China Sea. It has tried to establish a code of conduct in the area, but to no avail.

The Arab League (AL)

The Arab League is primarily a political and security alliance, founded in 1945. It aims to encourage cooperation between member states in order to promote their interests and affairs. There is a significant security element, with the aim to protect member state sovereignty and to promote peace and stability. Its focus is on coordinating policy. It hopes to unite Arab states and strengthen ties between them. Originally it was intended to free the remaining Arab states from colonial rule and prevent a Jewish state in Palestine. Now it is more focused on maintaining stability in the region. Its headquarters are in Cairo and it has 22 members (with Syria currently suspended) from north Africa and the Middle East, including Egypt, Iraq, Jordan and Saudi Arabia.

How it operates:

- Its highest body is the Council, which includes representatives of each member state.
- All member states have a vote irrespective of their size.
- It meets twice annually but can convene at special sessions requested by two states.
- The daily running is done by the General Secretariat, which headed by the Secretary-General. This is the administrative body of the league and executive body of the council and specialised ministerial councils.
- It reaches intergovernmental agreements by consensus, and there are no supranational elements.

Successes:

- Greater sense of purpose since the Arab Spring: backed UN action against Gaddafi in Libya, suspended Syria over its repression of protests (however, subsequent actions here have dwindled).
- Agrees over supporting Palestinians (but rarely beyond making declarations – with the exception of an economic boycott in some countries; also there has been some shift in attitudes to Israel, with the UAE, Bahrain and Sudan now recognising Israel).
- Success has perhaps been at lower levels, e.g. school curriculums, protecting manuscripts, creating a regional telecommunications union.
- Suspending Libya under Colonel Gaddafi, and Syria during the Arab Spring. It also supported the UNSC air strikes on Libya.

Failures:

- Leadership rivalry.
- Division between traditional monarchies and 'revolutionary' states.
- The decisions made by the League are only binding for countries that voted for them, which has made some parts of the League completely redundant, e.g. Treaty of Joint Defence and Economic Cooperation and key bodies such as the Joint Defence Council.
- There are limitations to its strength. It was not able to offer a unified response in the 1991 Gulf Wars; there were divisions over the Iraq war; it failed to agree a wider response or recovery programme for Libya during the Arab Spring; it failed to broker peace agreements with Syria during the uprisings and continued Sunni/Shia tensions in the region have cause disunity.
- Its collective security policy (attack on one being seen as an attack on all) is somewhat weakened by internal conflicts in the region.

The African Union (AU)

The AU, established in 2002, is mainly a form of political regionalism, uniting Africa to give its nations a bigger voice on the global stage. It can be seen as a backlash against colonial and neocolonial interference in Africa, and therefore has security elements. The AU has a developmental goal centred on economic growth and peace and stability in the region. It aims to reduce poverty and increase growth as well as to improve human rights and to empower Africa by acting as its own peacekeeper. Its headquarters are in Addis Ababa and its membership includes all African countries that are not disputed territories.

Rwandan soldiers boarding an aircraft in support of an AU effort to quell violence in the Central African Republic

How it operates:

- It is loosely modelled on the EU.
- It has intergovernmental decision making.
- It has a Pan-African Parliament which debates continent-wide issues and advises heads of state.
- It also has a Peace and Security Council.
- Plans for the future include a human rights court, central bank and monetary fund as well as an economic community with a single currency by 2023.
- The Chairperson post rotates annually, and is elected by the assembly.
- The assembly includes the head of state of all member countries which meet annually. This is the main decision-making body.
- The executive council comprises the foreign ministers of the member states, who advise assembly members.
- The commission is the administrative branch. It has ten commissioners with their own individual portfolios. This is where policy is implemented, and activities are coordinated. A chairperson is elected by the commission to serve a 4-year term.

Successes:

- The African Union has got rid of the non-interference policy that its predecessor the OAU followed and set up the Peace and Security Council in 2004, which allows the council to intervene in conflicts, with force where necessary. AU peacekeepers have been used in Sudan, Burundi and Somalia.
- The AU has a New Partnership for African Development (NEPAD) which is an anti-poverty initiative. They have an agreement with the West to promote good political and economic practice in return for aid and investment.
- Various states have been suspended over coups d'état and only readmitted when they have returned to constitutional rule.
- Increasingly its peacekeepers have replaced UN peacekeepers on the continent, for example in Somalia and Darfur. Troops within the region have a greater legitimacy and so tend to command more respect. While many of the missions are still funded by the UN, the greater range of active operations undertaken by the AU is a substantial help to the UN. In addition, there has been a focus on peacebuilding, which if effective is more sustainable.

Failures:

- Morocco left after a disagreement over the decision to allow the disputed territory of Western Sahara to join the AU, but rejoined in 2017.
- The AU's predecessor was criticised for a lack of action. The AU has sometimes been said to also be ineffective as certain people were seen as 'dictators' within the organisation.
- Failure to act earlier over civil war in Libya and its lack of backing of a South African-sponsored peace plan, as well as lack of pressure on Gaddafi to step down.
- Some of the AU's plans have been too financially ambitious for its poorer countries to fund, meaning it has looked to China. China has made significant investments in the AU, including paying for its headquarters. Given China's increasing economic presence in Africa, this has caused some concern.
- There is a lack of cohesion between the AU promoting democratic principles when many of its members aren't democratic.
- The AU threatened to pull out of the ICC in 2017 which could have negatively affected its international image.
- The AU has failed to control Ethiopian forces in internal conflict (2020).

Organisation	USMCA	ASEAN	AL	AU
Type of regionalism				
Summary of what it does				
Key successes				
Key failures				

Key term

European integration
The level to which the EU is integrated legally, economically, culturally and socially, considering the deepening and widening elements of its formation.

Regional blocs

Regional organisations outside the EU do not have the scope or level of **European integration** that makes the EU such a unique example of regionalism. While these regional blocs are still developing and their integration is in some instances deepening and widening, it does seem unlikely that they will ever come to rival the EU model. However, there are arguments on both sides of this debate (see Debate box).

Debate

Do rival blocs challenge the EU?

Yes

- The EU has gradually expanded and developed its role since its origins as the European Coal and Steel Community in 1951. Given that the rise of 'new regionalism' did not emerge until the 1990s, perhaps it is still early days for other regions that may decide to go down a similar path. Organisations like the African Union and ASEAN have modelled themselves on the EU and since they were established later they may still develop into something more like the EU.
- Other regional blocs have moved to expand their remit. Many regional blocs have evolved from being purely economic in nature to now sharing political and security aims (e.g. ASEAN, AU, Arab League).
- The African Union is substantial, with 55 member states, which unites the entire continent (unlike the EU).
- The EU has arguably started in a stronger position than the other regional blocs. It doesn't have to contend with postcolonial recovery like the AU, the political conflict and turmoil that the AU suffers, or the rising power of China on its doorstep as in ASEAN. Therefore, it is possible that with time and with these issues addressed, these blocs could begin to rival the EU.

No

- The EU has had a unique role in promoting cultural values and ideals. It has a clear identity in promoting democracy, peace and security. Arguably this is unique to the EU, given its foundation in the wake of the Second World War, its role in addressing the long-standing rivalry between France and Germany and the all-pervasive feeling of 'never again' regarding the conflict. This indicates the EU has a structural and soft power other blocs cannot rival.
- The EU has played a unique role in promoting certain policies on a global scale, arguably making it more of a global political actor than other regional blocs. It has pioneered human rights, adopting the ECHR and establishing its own judicial system for its administration (the European Court of Human Rights). Together with its member states, the EU is the largest provider of climate funding in the world, using the funds for climate-related projects in the developing world to facilitate their green transitions (in 2019 it provided 23.2 billion euros).
- The EU has a balance of strong powers, but not superpowers, which enables it to 'pool sovereignty' in the absence of a dominant superpower. It is the only regional bloc that uses supranationalism to the extent that some have argued it has confederate or federal qualities.

→

- External factors like globalisation could incentivise other regional blocs to become more competitive, as they may react in response to power plays in the broader international system. For example, the rise of the AU could be seen as a feature of multipolarity (see page 254) or as a rise in the power of the Global South. Regionalism has become more commonplace and can even be seen as a feature of globalisation, with a newer form of regionalism moving on from just agreements between states to also include more non-state actors.

- The EU has strong structural power, being a member of the G20 (along with a number of its member states) and organisations like the WTO. It is also an observer member in the UN.
- The EU has a much deeper regionalism that encompasses economic, political and security factors than any other regional bloc. There is the potential for this to go even further still; in this way the EU is the most complex and established regional organisation.

Evaluation prompt: Other regional blocs do not yet rival the EU, but there is an argument that they could do one day. You should consider what impact Brexit might have – not just on the EU's power but on regionalism more generally. Either it could have a negative impact on regionalism and push states more towards nationalism and protecting their sovereignty. In this case we could see a return to the nation-state as the key actor in global politics. Alternatively it might make states feel as though they are better off in a regional alliance. This could be especially true as we see the emergence of non-Western powers starting to become increasingly influential. Also, it is worth considering the obstacles other regional blocs might need to overcome in order to legitimately rival the EU. Decide on your position and justify it with examples and theory (liberal and realist perspectives).

Regional blocs such as ASEAN have evolved from being purely economic to having political aims

Topic links

- The role of regionalism has links to the polarity topic (Chapter 7) in terms of whether nation-states remain the key players in polarity and power balances or whether these have shifted to include regional blocs, IGOs, NGOs and MNCs.
- The realist and liberal views of IGOs are also discussed further in Chapter 1.
- The ability of non-state actors to act outside of the parameters of nation-states has also had implications for issues like the environment (Chapter 6) because it only makes global agreements more complex.

Activity

Answer the questions below:

1 Have other regional organisations been influenced by or modelled themselves on the EU? Can you give examples of which ones and how they have done this?
2 Do all regional organisations have a similar impact on sovereignty? Try to use examples to justify your answer.

European integration: major factors and developments

There are currently 27 members of the EU, now that the UK has left.

EU formation, its role and objectives

Formation

The EU's formation is best understood chronologically (see Table 8.3). It was formally established in 1993 with the Maastricht Treaty but, as we have seen, its roots lie in the formation of the European Coal and Steel Community (ECSC). From here the group progressed into the European Economic Community (EEC) and finally the EU.

Case study

The UK's new trade partnership with the EU

Background

After the UK left the EU, there was a need to create a new trading partnership between them. This would be a complex free-trade agreement considering trade in goods and services as well as a broad range of other areas like interests, investment, competition, aid, taxation, air and road transport, energy and sustainability, fisheries, data protection and social security. For the UK, this was particularly important since the EU is its largest trading partner. The agreement applied from January 2021 after the UK's transition phase ended.

The agreement includes:
- zero tariffs and quotas on goods that comply with appropriate rules of origin. Limited mutual market access to services was also agreed
- commitment to environmental protection and fighting climate change, social and labour laws, taxation transparency. There is a binding dispute settlement mechanism in place, with the newly established Partnership Council now responsible for this
- an agreement over joint management of fish stocks in the EU and UK waters. The UK can continue to develop British fishing activities, while the activities of European fishing are safeguarded along with sustainability regulations. EU fishing quotas in UK waters will reduce to 75% of the pre-Brexit rate over the 5.5-year transitional period, but both parties can continue to fish in each other's waters. Given the UK left the EU Common Fisheries Policy, this was an area of considerable negotiation

- social security is coordinated to ensure certain rights for both UK and EU citizens, which includes UK citizens working in the EU and EU citizens working in the UK
- transport agreements enable access to markets, but there are more restrictions under the Single Market
- the UK remains able to access some of the EU's flagship programmes if it financially contributes, an example being Horizon Europe (research and innovation)
- the free-trade agreement is not fixed for ever and will involve both parties sticking to the agreement. If the rules shift too far either way then tariffs could be introduced
- the UK and EU made separate agreements about the exchange of classified information and cooperation over nuclear energy.

What ended for the UK?
- Free movement of people.
- Membership of the Single Market.
- Participation in most EU programmes.
- Defence and foreign policy cooperation.
- The authority of the ECJ in dispute settlement (with the exception of the Northern Ireland Protocol).
- The UK no longer needs to follow EU rules on product standards (new checks are in place).
- Strict EU laws on animal products mean some UK products can no longer be exported.
- The UK is no longer automatically part of trade deals negotiated by the EU. At the time of the UK's departure, the EU was part of about 40 trade deals involving more than 70 countries. (The UK has now negotiated deals with 66 of these countries.) Any agreements not reached would be subject to WTO terms (therefore tariffs). The UK has established new trade deals too, with Japan and with Norway, Iceland and Liechtenstein.

Table 8.3 Timeline of EU formation

Year	Events
1945–51	The first steps: after the Second World War there was a need for integration and a desire for peace and security. The ECSC was formally introduced in 1951. France and Germany made the initial proposal in an attempt to ease the competition between them by fostering greater cooperation. This community comprised the 'Inner Six' (see page 319). The ECSC was designed to reduce trade barriers on coal and steel and to better coordinate policies over these resources.
1957	The Treaty of Rome (1957) was crucial to European integration and provided the legal basis for the modern EU. This saw the formation of the EEC, essentially the beginning of the common market. Key agreements came into force, such as the Common Agricultural Policy (CAP) and the Common Fisheries Policy (CFP).
1973–79	The UK joined the EEC in 1973. This was the first period of enlargement, with Denmark and Ireland also joining at this time.
1986–92	The Single European Act (1986) prepared for establishing the Single Market, which was completed in 1992. This also saw the abolition of national vetoes in most areas and a monetary union (some erosion of national sovereignty). The Berlin Wall fell in 1989.
1992–93	The Maastricht Treaty (1993) set up four freedoms of movement: people, goods, capital and services. It also saw the completion of the Single Market. The euro was introduced (although Denmark and the UK opted out of the single currency). Key features of the Maastricht Treaty include: • the establishment of the Common Foreign and Security Policy (CFSP), which promotes cooperation in justice and home affairs • certain institutions in the EU are strengthened, with more power going to the European Parliament and the European Court of Justice • a cohesion fund is set up to help poorer countries to meet the costs of convergence criteria of monetary union (see page 321) • the establishment of the subsidiarity principle (upon former prime minister John Major's insistence), which is a general principle of EU law whereby the EU can only act where the action of individual countries is insufficient to the interests of the EU as a whole (a measure to protect the sovereign interests of EU member states)
1992–2002	The euro was introduced in 11 countries and then in Greece in 2001. At this point it was used for commercial transactions only (currency in the form of notes and coins came later, in 2002). This created the Economic Monetary Union (EMU), with the exception of Portugal, Scandinavia and the UK. The European Economic Bank regulates the euro.
2003–08	In 2003, the Treaty of Nice made amendments to both the Maastricht Treaty and the Treaty of Rome. It reformed the institutional structure of the EU, in part to deal with eastward expansion. In 2004, ten more countries joined, with a further two in 2007, making this a notable period of expansion. In 2008, the financial crisis hit Europe.
2009	The Treaty of Lisbon was ratified and came into force in 2009. This was significant in modernising the key EU institutions and making them more efficient. The reforms decreased the number of policy areas in the Council of Ministers where unanimous decisions were needed in order to pass EU laws, representing for some an increase in EU powers and a negative impact on state sovereignty. The treaty also created the positions of President of the European Council and High Representative for Foreign Affairs, which aimed to give the EU more of an independent and influential voice on the world stage.
2008–9, global financial crisis	Portugal, Italy, Ireland, Greece and Spain were in a deep sovereign debt crisis brought on by the global financial crisis and bank bailouts. This led to a crisis of confidence and there was panic on the international market because of the gravity of these debts and the bailouts required to resolve them.
2012–17	In 2012, the EU won the Nobel Peace Prize. In 2013, Croatia joined the EU (the most recent member to be accepted). In 2016, the UK held a referendum to leave the EU and on 29 March 2017 Article 50 was triggered. This period also saw multiple terrorist attacks on EU nation-states and the emergence of the European migrant crisis, putting pressure on the EU's Schengen freedom of movement area.
2020–21	The UK officially ceases to be a member state of the EU in January 2020 and enters its transition period while the final terms are negotiated. In January 2021 it leaves the Customs Union and the Single Market.

Activity

Conduct research into the economies of Portugal, Ireland, Italy and Spain. How was the situation in these countries similar to or different from that in Greece?

Roles and objectives

The EU's role has changed over time – it began very much as an economic organisation and has increasingly become far more political. As we can see from the timeline of its formation, the EU always had the intention of promoting peace and stability, but in its initial stages it was focused on the trade of coal and oil. Realists argue that this initial focus could be seen as promoting state self-interest, since the objective was clearly primarily economic. However, for liberals, the economic incentive also had a political advantage, with the added bonus that increased economic cooperation would help to create stability, particularly between the long-standing rivals France and Germany, in order to reduce the threat of future conflict.

As time progressed and the economic ties became deeper through the adoption of the Single Market and monetary union, it was clear that the EU was increasingly taking on more of a political role. Various treaties, especially the Maastricht Treaty (1993), saw developments in the EU's key institutions and systems of governance. Increasingly there was a common political agenda and a growing feeling that its institutions should be acting on behalf of the EU as a single entity. During this period, questions of sovereignty were up for debate, with measures such as subsidiarity (the idea that a central authority should perform only those tasks that cannot be performed at local level) demonstrating the clear adoption of a more political role.

The EU has also increasingly taken on more of a security role. After the Treaty of Lisbon (2009) the External Action Service was established, which is the EU department that formally implemented the European Security and Defence Policy (ESDP), later called the Common Security and Defence Policy (CSDP). This covers EU defence and military aspects, as well as civilian crisis management, and falls under the jurisdiction of the EU itself.

Furthermore, particularly since the early 2000s, the EU has been increasingly involved in humanitarian work, and has performed operations in Europe itself (the former Yugoslavia), Africa and Asia. While the EU has no standing army, it does have the European Union Force (EUFOR) and the European Union Naval Force (EUNAVFOR), both of which have been involved in interventions with a military focus.

Increasingly, the EU's various intelligence services and armed and police forces are also working collectively in response to the increased terrorism threat. For example, the 2016 attack on Berlin's Christmas market saw Italian police authorities arrest the perpetrator within Italian borders. This has led to a growing and symbolic sense of a shared European identity, with various landmarks across Europe being lit in the colours of the national flags of those nations affected.

In response to the increased terror threat, there was a growing and symbolic sense of a shared European identity: London's Tower Bridge was lit up in the red, white and blue of the French flag after the November 2015 Paris terrorist attacks

Federalism

Federalism suggests that there should be a move towards a centralised federal body that acts on behalf of the regional bloc. It therefore advocates supranationalism, and deeper economic and political integration. This fits the EU model well, since it argues that regionalism under a federalist model is a good way to promote peace and stability, as it prevents state-centrism (states acting purely in their own interests). If states transfer some of their sovereignty to a higher federal body (pooled sovereignty), they reduce the risk of the pursuit of self-interest creating an anarchic system.

The EU is an excellent example of this form of federalism, as it was designed initially to reduce the tensions between France and Germany. It has since developed to such an extent that war between these two nations is now unthinkable.

However, one could argue that the EU is not integrated enough to be considered a federal system − for example, not all EU states have adopted the euro. This alone is incongruous to a truly federal system. Furthermore, states can opt out of agreements or even remove themselves entirely from the system (as seen with Brexit).

Functionalism

The functionalist model arose as a challenge to the idea of federalism. It argues that blocs such as the EU did not emerge to become federalist, but rather to serve specific functions. We can see from the stages of the EU's formation that functionalism is an applicable model. The EU was set up to establish an agreement over the trading of coal and steel. While it has continued to develop as an economic institution, it has also grown to meet various political and security functions. These functions are better met with collective action, as opposed to individualistic state action. Functionalists are generally positive about the EU's ability to meet these needs effectively.

However, others have argued that, in practice, states have been very reluctant to hand over power to functional bodies, and that these bodies have lacked the legitimacy of sovereign bodies. Furthermore, one could argue that the model is too simplistic and short-sighted in relation to the EU, and that the EU has always had longer-term visions than functionalism.

Neofunctionalism

The theory of neofunctionalism sits somewhere between the previous two theories, and argues that regionalism does indeed meet some functional needs but that this spills over into other, broader areas. Usually neofunctionalism begins by addressing economic functions, but leads to some political spillover. We can certainly see this right from the beginning of the EU, in the form of the coal and steel trade agreement, which had primarily economic goals but also aimed to promote stability within Europe.

Furthermore, the European defence policies of recent years demonstrate that when there is a functional need, the EU develops new policies (for example, to combat terrorism) but that these often morph into longer-term strategic aims (for example, fostering a cosmopolitan identity and encouraging much of Europe to 'band together'). This approach suggests that there is a complex interplay between the economic and political aspects of regionalism.

Establishment and enlargement of the EU's key institutions

Establishment

Figure 8.2 represents the organisation of the key EU institutions (aside from the European Council) and how they interrelate. The role of voters in both national governments and the European Parliament is significant when we consider how democratic the EU is. In addition, considering its legislative, executive and judiciary roles helps us to explain how the EU system can be seen as federalist, and to decipher whether or not the EU works intergovernmentally, supranationally or as a combination of the two.

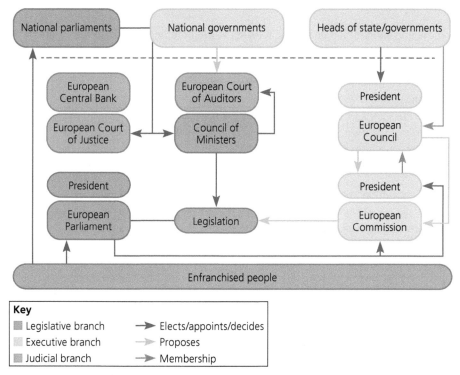

Key

■ Legislative branch   → Elects/appoints/decides

■ Executive branch   → Proposes

■ Judicial branch   → Membership

Figure 8.2 **How the key EU organisations interrelate**

Table 8.4 summarises the major EU institutions and their features.

Table 8.4 **The major EU institutions and their features**

Institution	Key feature
European Council	Informally known as the European Summit.
	One of the EU's intergovernmental institutions.
	A decision-making body, focusing on longer-term decisions.
	Comprises heads of state and foreign ministers. It also includes the president and vice-president of the European Commission.
	Has a permanent full-time president (Charles Michel).
	Meets four or more times a year.
	Offers strategic leadership and is responsible for the EU's longer-term vision, including setting policy guidelines, resolving disputes between member states, agreeing reforms of treaties and steering the EU's foreign policy. The Council was responsible for signing off the Brexit deal.
	States have a veto.
Council of Ministers	One of the EU's intergovernmental institutions.
	Also, a decision-making body, focusing more on day-to-day or shorter-term decisions.
	Comprises ministers from all 27 member states. These ministers are accountable to their own governments.
	The ministers change depending on the issue under discussion and so act almost like a cabinet.
	The president is a country, not a single person, and this rotates among the members every 6 months.
	Decision making is through a voting system (this has to be unanimous for decisions on some policy areas, but for other issues is based on a majority voting system known as 'qualified majority voting'). The Treaty of Lisbon increased the number of policy areas where qualified majority voting applies.
	States have no veto and can be outvoted.

→

Institution	Key feature
European Commission	Often seen as the main executive institution of the EU. It exists to promote and defend the interests of the whole EU.
	The only part of the EU that can propose new laws.
	The laws are voted on by the Council of Ministers and European Parliament.
	A supranational organisation.
	The bureaucratic arm of the EU.
	Based in Brussels, Belgium.
	Comprises 27 commissioners, one from each EU member state, and a president (Ursula Von der Leyen). Commissioners are duty bound to defend and promote the EU's interests, rather than the interests of their home state.
	Responsible for processing legislation and acts as a watchdog for policy implementation.
European Parliament	Made up of Members of the European Parliament (MEPs) from the 27 member states. It is the only elected body of the EU, with countries directly electing MEPs every 5 years.
	A supranational organisation.
	Mostly located in Brussels, Belgium.
	Organised by political group as opposed to nationality. For example, the Europe of Freedom and Democracy political group comprises Eurosceptic parties from across the EU.
	Its role has expanded over the years, but its main function remains to scrutinise, rather than create legislation.
European Court of Justice	Acts as a judicial body, interpreting and adjudicating EU laws and treaties.
	A supranational organisation.
	Comprises 28 judges (pre-Brexit), one for each member state, and eight advocates who advise the courts.
	EU law has primacy over national law, which means that the European Court of Justice has the power to disapply domestic laws.
	The Court of First Instance handles certain cases brought by individuals or companies.
European Central Bank	Responsible for the economic governance of the euro, specifically its purchasing power and therefore its price stability (similar to the Bank of England's role with the pound sterling in the UK).
	A supranational organisation.
	Based in Frankfurt, Germany.
	Represents the 19 countries that are in the Eurozone.

Activity

Explain why each EU institution in Table 8.4 can be seen as either intergovernmental or supranational. Remember to explain this in relation to sovereignty. You can check your answers later in the chapter, when we discuss the level of integration in the EU and whether the EU has more of an intergovernmental or supranational element.

Activity

It is easy to confuse the Council of Ministers and the European Council, but they are quite different.
1 Using Table 8.4 initially, distinguish between the two and then highlight their key differences from memory. Note, there are fewer similarities than differences!
2 Construct a table, with the Council of Ministers in one column and the European Council in the other, and list the similarities and differences within the columns.

Enlargement

Current president of the European Council Charles Michel

As well as deepening integration (which considers the loss of sovereignty for the wider interests of the EU), there has been much discussion in relation to the widening integration of the EU, in particular to its expansion to include additional member states. As the timeline of the EU's formation demonstrates (see page 313), there have been various waves of enlargement throughout the regional bloc's history.

When it was established, the EU had only six original members (known as the Inner Six), in contrast to the 27 members of today. Since then, it has seen several waves of enlargement, prior to the UK's withdrawal in 2020:

- **Inner Six (1951):** Belgium, France, Germany, Italy, Luxembourg and the Netherlands.
- **First Enlargement (1970s):** Denmark, Ireland and the UK (including Gibraltar).
- **Mediterranean Enlargement (1980s):** Greece, Portugal and Spain.
- **Northern Enlargement (1990s):** Austria, Finland and Sweden.
- **Post-communist/Eastern Enlargement (2000s):** Czech Republic, Cyprus, Estonia, Hungary, Latvia, Lithuania, Poland, Slovenia, Slovakia (2004), Bulgaria, Romania (2007) and Croatia (2013).

There are many states that are still waiting to join the EU, with the Balkan states, in particular those of the former Yugoslavia, being the main contenders. Some argue that it would be easier for the EU to absorb these states, given that EU funding already makes contributions towards their development. One of the more controversial applicants is Turkey, which has been under negotiation to join since 1987.

Enlargement on this grand scale has been controversial – Russia, in particular, has seen the EU's growth as antagonistic, given that the EU's border looks increasingly similar to that of NATO's and many of the newer eastern European members were former Russian allies or satellite states. Therefore, the EU, designed to promote peace and security in the region, has had to consider the wider impact of allowing eastern European countries to join and how this could cause conflict with Russia. Furthermore, newer members often have weaker economies, putting pressure on the existing members' economies.

Another issue relates to the significant cultural differences of possible new EU members. Given that the EU has grown to have more of a collective cultural identity, accepting countries that have quite different outlooks (such as Turkey) could prove to be problematic.

Finally, there is the issue of effectiveness – the larger the EU, the larger the base of interests it needs to coordinate. This may make it harder for the EU to form cohesive policies, especially in regard to foreign policy. This is especially problematic when unanimity is called for, for example in the Council of Europe.

Key treaties and agreements

Many of the key treaties and agreements within the EU are used as evidence of deepening integration within the regional bloc. They have also evolved the key institutions and extended their powers. However, some agreements have meant that nation-states have had to compromise their national interests for the sake of wider EU interests. This loss of sovereignty is evidence of federalism.

However, one can argue that member states still act in their own interests, in that they can either opt out of certain agreements or ultimately withdraw from the EU, as we have seen with the UK and Brexit. The fact that numerous states opted out from the euro (including Denmark, Sweden and the UK) is evidence that member states retain sovereign control and, therefore, that the EU is not a truly federal system. While this is changing (since the Treaty of Lisbon (2009), it has been mandatory for new member states to adopt the euro), it is still significant that several EU states have been able to maintain this position. Furthermore, certain countries have negotiated their way out of various other agreements, or renegotiated the terms (as the UK did in the 1980s with the CAP).

Finally, the law of subsidiarity states that the EU can only act when individual nation-states are incapable of acting – in other words, it cannot otherwise impinge upon state sovereignty.

Table 8.5 is a summary of the EU's key treaties and their agreements.

Table 8.5 The EU's key treaties and agreements

Key treaties	Key agreements	Implications
Treaty of Rome (1957)	European Economic Community Common Agricultural Policy and Common Fisheries Policy	This introduced a commitment to the common market and the customs unions. The EEC (economic integration) was created and key institutions were founded (European Parliament, European Council, European Court of Justice). The Common Agricultural Policy introduced subsidies and the Common Fisheries Policy introduced quotas.
Single European Act (1986)	Set the deadline for the Single Market Strengthened EU's Parliament	The Single Market deadline was set for 1993. Given recent enlargement, qualified majority voting (QMV) was put in place to speed up decision making. Integration was also deepened with new powers for the European Parliament, which laid the basis for European foreign policy.
Maastricht Treaty (1993)	The freedom of movement of goods, services, people and money The principle of subsidiarity European Monetary Union (including the formation of the European Central Bank)	This formally created the European Union; it moved the EU on from being purely economic regionalism and trade agreements. The freedom of movement was introduced for the 'four freedoms'. It also paved the way for a common currency: the EMU involved three stages of integration, with a common currency being the final most involved stage. The euro was introduced in 1999. The principle of subsidiarity was introduced to protect the sovereignty of the EU member states for matters considered to be out of the EU's parameters. The project of a common foreign and security policy was introduced, and more powers were given to parliament.

Key treaties	Key agreements	Implications
Treaty of Nice (2003)	Amended Maastricht Treaty and Treaty of Rome Facilitated recent EU widening	The EU saw its biggest widening to date with ten more states joining, leading to an adjustment of the EU Commission, with states now only having one seat each. QMV was extended in Council of Ministers, with bigger states given more weighting in QMV voting. Defence policy cooperation was also deepened.
Treaty of Lisbon (2009)	Common Security and Defence Policy European Constitution President of the European Council External Action Service and High Representative for Foreign Affairs	Significant new powers were given to the EU Parliament (up to 75% of legislative areas). It introduced the Common Security and Defence Policy in its current form. The idea of a codified European constitution was abandoned. More power was given to EU Parliament, EU legislation was sent to national parliaments to decide if proposals need deciding at EU level (principle of subsidiarity). A permanent role as President of the European Council was created as was a High Representative for Foreign Affairs, designed to give the EU an independent voice.

Activity

1 Write down what you can remember about the treaties and agreements shown in Table 8.6, and then go back to the EU formation section (page 313) to see how much you have remembered.
2 Try to identify an example of an agreement that contributed to political, economic and security regionalism, and make a note of the treaty under which it happened.

For example, the EMU was agreed on under the Maastricht Treaty and helped strengthen economic regionalism in the EU.

The Economic and Monetary Union

The process of European integration broadly followed three stages:

1 economic union
2 monetary union
3 political union

As the middle stage of integration, the EMU clearly had both economic and political elements.

The origins of the EMU go back to 1978, when the European Exchange Rate Mechanism (ERM) was established. The ERM was designed to tackle one of the biggest issues with trade in the EU: fluctuating exchange rates. The ERM would reduce exchange rate variability and achieve monetary stability in Europe.

In 1992, the pathway to EMU was agreed under the Maastricht Treaty. It represented a clear move beyond stabilising exchange rates to establishing a single currency. In practice, the EMU is a group of policies aimed at converging the economies of EU member states in three stages (the euro convergence criteria), with each stage designed for progressively closer economic integration. Only once a state participates in the third stage can it adopt the euro as its official currency.

Some EU member states opted out of the single currency (namely Denmark and the UK), but those that qualify today have to meet the euro convergence criteria set out by the Maastricht Treaty as, after the enlargement of the EU in 2004–7, all new EU member states must commit to participate in the third stage in their treaties of accession.

As part of the 1996 Dublin Summit, the Stability and Growth Pact (SGP) was established, which was designed to ensure that EMU members had a strict budgetary discipline and to maintain the EMU's stability. However, the SGP was non-binding and some member states did not comply with the need for budgetary discipline.

The euro is the official currency of the Eurozone, which consists of 19 of the 27 EU member states

The EMU: economic benefits
Membership of the EMU has clear economic benefits:

- It removes obstacles to trade by extending the Single Market. Traders and travellers are free of the constraints of currency conversion rates. This creates a certainty in trade prices, enabling traders to trade on lower profit margins and therefore creating savings and reducing prices.
- There is greater transparency over prices, which benefits producers, cross-border traders and consumers alike.
- The SGP ensures economic stability and low inflation.
- The EMU is, in theory, less vulnerable to the world currency markets, allowing the EU to have a greater financial and economic global influence, to the extent that within organisations like the World Bank and IMF, the EU is able to counterbalance the US.

The EMU: political benefits
There are also many political benefits to membership of the EMU:

- Pooling sovereignty arguably strengthens, rather than weakens, EMU member state sovereignty. This is especially true in an increasingly globalised world in which national monetary sovereignty is already challenged.

- Before the EMU was established, the Bundesbank (the German Federal Bank), rather than the ECB controlled EU monetary policy. Many other European countries (especially France) were unhappy with Germany's economic control of the union. The EMU redresses this imbalance.
- Many see the euro as a further step towards a federalist political union, leading to greater integration. This could include harmonising taxes or larger budgets to offset the negative impacts of depressed areas. Furthermore, it also helps to foster the EU's cosmopolitan identity and creates a stronger European identity.

The EMU: drawbacks

Nonetheless, the EMU does have its drawbacks:

- There are economic risks, including the capacity for the ECB to misjudge monetary policy and the potential for EMU governments to ignore, or sidestep, SGP rules. In fact, both France and Germany flouted these rules in the mid-2000s by overspending and exceeding the 3% of GDP limit on a state's budget deficit.
- Policies won't always benefit all states. For example, interest rates that suit some have a negative impact on others.
- The SGP gives EMU member states the ability to employ measures traditionally used to boost weakened economies, for example raising public spending to tackle unemployment.
- Politically, there is the cost to national sovereignty over some key areas of economic and monetary policy, as well as an element of hypocrisy as to how this is enforced among EMU members.
- There is a democratic deficit issue, given that sovereign responsibility to regulate monetary policy is removed and transferred to an unelected independent central body (the ECB).

Debate

Is EMU membership positive or negative?

Positive

- The euro has made free trade even easier within the EU member states that are part of the Eurozone. Exchange rate costs are eliminated when trading between the Eurozone member states and for foreign investors with operations in more than one Eurozone member state.
- The ECB can regulate monetary policy across the EU, making financial conditions more stable and predictable.
- The ECB can offer more stability through the ability of states to pool together to help states that encounter economic difficulty. If Greece had not been a Eurozone member, it is doubtful it would have received so much financial assistance during its recent debt crisis.

Negative

- Some states lose out, as they are supporting weaker economies (perhaps even responding when weaker economies have made poor decisions in respect of managing their own economies and getting into debt).
- There is a loss of sovereignty for EMU members. Individual member states are less able to change their monetary policy in order to respond to economic conditions within their own state (for example, by raising or lowering interest rates).
- There is a democratic deficit, given that domestic citizens of EMU member states do not have a direct say over monetary policy. The Fiscal Compact also limits states' choices on their public spending, by requiring states to balance their budgets.

Evaluation prompt: The benefits and drawbacks of EMU membership are intertwined with the pros/cons of supragovernmentalism. For this debate, decide if overall the EU benefits from the EMU as a supragovernmental element and justify this with examples.

Supranational vs intergovernmental approaches

When arguing whether the EU is a supranational or intergovernmental organisation, it is worth considering how its key organisations fit into the two categories (see Table 8.6).

Table 8.6 EU organisations: intergovernmental or supranational?

Organisation	Intergovernmental or supranational?
European Council	Intergovernmental, because each member state is represented within the European Council and is acting on its own behalf. Therefore, heads of state and foreign ministers retain a reasonable amount of control in steering the overall direction of the EU on behalf of their own sovereign interests. They are each able to use a veto.
Council of Ministers	Intergovernmental, since ministers represent their own country and therefore their country's sovereign interests in shorter-term decision making within the EU and on specific issues.
European Commission	Supranational, given that it proposes EU laws, something that member states cannot do. The laws and policies it oversees act in the interests of the EU as a whole as opposed to its individual sovereign members.
European Parliament	Supranational, since while member state domestic populations elect MEPs to office, the parliament's role is to scrutinise legislation on behalf of EU, rather than national, interests.
European Court of Justice	Supranational, given that it has the ability to make judgments that can override the laws of national governments.
European Central Bank	Supranational, since it sets interest rates on behalf of EMU countries, which is traditionally seen as a key role for sovereign states.

The European Parliament building in Strasbourg

Is the EU a supranational/federal institution?

Yes

- There are more supranational organisations in the EU. Their powers are significant (e.g. the European Court of Justice can make judgments that have primacy over national laws, the ECB controls monetary policies for EMU members).
- EU institutions gain more power through its various agreements and treaties.
- There is now a clear EU figurehead (Charles Michel, former President of Belgium and current President of the European Council).
- The EU's role has adapted and moved from a primarily economic agreement to more of a political and strategic alliance.
- It acts on a global stage with a significant amount of structural and diplomatic power. It has a significant influence over certain global issues (e.g. the environment, human rights) and an important role in various IGOs and NGOs.

No

- The most significant organisations are intergovernmental – that is, the decision-making bodies (the European Council and the Council of Ministers). Ultimately these bodies steer the direction of the EU as a whole, while ensuring that national interests are represented.
- The principle of subsidiarity ensures that states retain their sovereignty in most situations.
- States can ultimately withdraw from certain agreements (e.g. not all states are party to the single currency), or decide to withdraw from the EU altogether, which demonstrates that ultimately the EU is still state-centric.
- The EU lacks the central authority required of a federalist system.
- It lacks a cohesive foreign policy and, due to its diverse membership, is unlikely to form one.

Evaluation prompt: You might decide that the answer is somewhere in the middle, for example the EU is a partially supranational organisation. However, you should be able to summarise in what ways it is/is not supranational and make an argument. For example, it is not entirely supranational because it lacks central governance and states remain ultimately sovereign but in terms of economic alliance and trade agreements, we might argue it does operate in a supranational way.

The EU as an international body/global actor

The former US secretary of state Henry Kissinger (in office as secretary of state between 1973 and 1977) once asked the question, 'Who do I call if I want to speak to Europe?' on a matter of international importance. Traditionally, the US has relied heavily on France, Germany and the UK as the most powerful voices in Europe and therefore the most reliable and influential European governments to work with on issues of major significance.

The EU has increasingly attempted to expand its role from a regional body coordinating policy within Europe to a regional body with power and influence as a **global actor** in its own right. For some, the idea that the EU acts as a spokesperson for the peoples and governments of EU member states is a controversial one, and represents a threat to individual member states' sovereignty and their ability to conduct their own, independent foreign policy. Others see a useful role in the EU gaining influence as a more independent and unified voice on the world stage. The EU now has a clear figurehead for the world stage too, in the form of the President of the European Council (Charles Michel) who also acts as the EU's figurehead on the world stage, perhaps at last answering Kissinger's famous question.

Constraints and obstacles affecting the EU's influence in global politics

Political

The EU has had a number of political obstacles to contend with. While there have been some clear political benefits, the EU as a regional bloc and organisation has faced significant challenges.

> **Key term**
>
> **Global actor** A power or entity (e.g. a collection of states) that has a significant presence on the international stage, participates or acts in international affairs and is considered to have influence over states and the international system in general.

The most obvious political challenge is the impingement of sovereignty. This issue was especially brought to the fore when the UK voted in the 2016 referendum to leave the EU, but it has been an element of tension throughout the EU's history. The issue of state sovereignty fuels the debates around freedom of movement, particularly in the wake of the European migrant crisis.

There is also the issue of a democratic deficit, in that the EU lacks basic democratic principles. As citizens of democratic countries, EU citizens should have the ability to vote over its more supranational elements and institutions, but in reality they do not – the European Parliament is the only elected body within the EU and it has to make decisions alongside the Council of Ministers, so does not have the final say. This is especially problematic given that the EU promotes the liberal values of democracy and freedom, and some would argue that this aspect of EU governance has even damaged its soft power.

Economic

In many ways, the EU has been a great economic success, but there have also been some significant economic drawbacks. The 2008 global financial crisis hit Europe especially hard (in particular Portugal, Italy, Ireland, Greece and Spain), and demonstrated that the EU was not immune to fluctuating global markets. The economies of Portugal, Italy, Ireland, Greece and Spain have still not yet fully recovered, and the bailout of these national economies has been expensive for other EU member states.

Furthermore, expansion has created an economic strain on EU countries because the newer members tend to have weaker economies, thereby creating an economic burden on the stronger states. Additionally, not all EU member states have accepted the euro and of those that have, there have been winners and losers. Germany has done well from having a devalued currency, which has made its exports more appealing to the global market, while other countries, such as Italy, which would ordinarily have used methods such as devaluation to overcome recession, have been prevented from doing so. There has also been significant disagreement over policies such as the CAP, demonstrating the difficulty in an organisation of 28 member states (pre-Brexit) of reaching agreement on matters of trade. More recently, it has been indicated how complex the trading relationships and agreements are with the UK's withdrawal, since this has led to protracted negotiations.

Structural

There are some obvious overlaps with broader political obstacles when it comes to the EU's structural power. How much political power does the EU really have on the global stage? Can it be seen as a superpower? Many have argued that it cannot, given that there is a lack of a central authority or a clear figurehead in the same way as exists in superpower nation-states.

Furthermore, the EU has such a diverse set of interests (both politically and culturally) that at times it has been a challenge to agree on cohesive policies – this is especially true in the case of foreign policy. This again hampers the EU's ability to act as a unified player on the global stage. Its continued expansion has exacerbated this issue and arguably made it less effective.

It can also be argued that the UK's decision to leave the EU has proved detrimental to the EU's structural power, especially when seeing Europe as a counterbalance to the US in organisations such as the World Bank and the IMF. The UK is one of the key EU powers, and its 'special relationship' with the US has helped to bolster the EU's overall influence on the international stage. While President Trump had indicated he would like a US–UK alliance, rather than an EU alliance, which in part formed the rationale behind the 'Leave' campaign, Biden's position is less clear. The UK's willingness to cooperate with Trump may well push Biden away from the UK. The extent of Brexit's impact on the EU's global influence remains to be seen.

Military

One of the EU's most significant weaknesses is its lack of a central military power. The EU employs forces primarily for humanitarian intervention, but it does not have a central standing army. The EU relies on NATO (which has a very similar membership to the EU) for defence, but this has led to some seeing the EU as the US's military puppet. This was highlighted during the war in the former Yugoslavia, and especially in Kosovo, during which NATO had to step in to end the conflict. The EU was largely seen as weak for allowing the largest genocide since the Second World War to happen in its own backyard.

Furthermore, the EU has developed a common security policy, but it has been susceptible to national security failures, with a number of terrorist attacks taking place across Europe in recent years.

Debate

Can the EU be considered to be a superpower?

Yes

- **Economic power:** the EU has significantly increased its economic power by unifying its currency and establishing the largest free-trade area in the world.
- **Structural power:** the EU has been highly influential in global institutions, particularly in relation to certain issues such as human rights and the environment.
- **Soft power:** the EU has a significant influence over other states, with many countries still very keen to join it (e.g. other Balkan states, Turkey).
- **Organisation:** the EU has made changes to its structure in efforts to become more efficient, strengthening the role of its institutions and giving it a clear figurehead.

No

- **Economic:** the EU has not been immune to fluctuating global markets and was a major victim of the global financial crisis.
- **Lack of military power:** the EU has no standing army and has been seen as the US's puppet, given its reliance on NATO for defence.
- **Lacks cohesion:** given its diverse range of members and therefore interests, the EU does not have a clear foreign policy, which also hampers its structural power within global organisations.
- **Lack of central authority:** arguably there is no clear central authority and its 'leaders' act more as chairpersons or managers.

Evaluation prompt: It is good to weigh up this question in terms of the credentials of a superpower. You might then need to determine whether you believe that only nation-states can be superpowers. There is an argument that traditional superpowers would need to operate as a single sovereign entity but you could conversely also argue that in an increasingly globalised and multipolar world new forms of actor are behaving like superpowers.

Topic link

This links to the power and developments topic in terms of what constitutes as a superpower, but it also links to ideas about globalisation and the decline of the nation-state. If we consider that the EU is a superpower, state sovereignty of its member states would be significantly weakened.

Activity

'Evaluate the extent to which the EU is a superpower.'

Think back to the key features of a superpower and write a conclusion to the above essay question. You should try to include the key features of a superpower in your answer and justify (back up) your argument with what you believe to be the most compelling argument. Try not to sit on the fence - there is no right or wrong answer, as long as you can evidence it.

Regionalism and global issues

Increasingly, regionalism has a part to play in global issues. This is partly due to the supranational element of regionalism, and the role that regional blocs play in governance (at state, regional and global levels). Some key synoptic areas to consider are conflict, poverty, human rights and the environment. It is important to consider what influences and impacts regionalism has had in these areas.

Conflict

Regionalism can generally be seen to promote peace and security. It can be associated with the liberal idea of democratic peace theory, given that where there is political regionalism, there is a tendency towards multilateral cooperation, which goes hand in hand with democracy. As globalisation and regionalism have spread, there has been a simultaneous spread of democracy, leading political scientist Francis Fukuyama to say that liberal democracies are the end of political evolution, as they are the ultimate political system. Democratic peace theory argues that democracies are unlikely to go to war with one another. The EU is an excellent example of this, with countries such as France and Germany – former long-standing rivals with complex histories of conflict – now so unlikely to go to war with one another that we can describe it as unthinkable.

Furthermore, some regional organisations have gone to lengths to promote peace and security. For example, the African Union has its own Peace and Security Council which responds to conflicts in Africa. This can go beyond just peacekeeping: it also has the power to undertake peacemaking and peacebuilding missions in Africa. The AU has carried out numerous peacekeeping missions under the UNSC authority (e.g. its peacekeeping mission in Somalia, which remains active at the time of publication). The African Union's peacekeeping force is often felt to have more legitimacy on the continent and can command more respect than outside forces. This has been very useful for global peace and security. Not all regional organisations have followed suit here though, with ASEAN and the Arab League doing very little in this regard.

The reduction in conflict is not just down to political regionalism – we could also make the neoliberal argument that economic cooperation is a very effective way to promote peace and stability. If states are economically reliant on one another there is very little incentive for them to go to war with each other. Indeed, this feeds into the arguments of British academic Mary Kaldor, who highlights that increasingly war is not centred on states in the traditional sense (the 'New War' thesis, see page 200). Regionalism tends to unite like-minded countries, but it can also create alliances between states that might not otherwise cooperate.

That said, regional blocs can be quite inward looking, with isolationist agendas that could arguably lead to conflict. For example, ASEAN is keen to temper China's dominance in Asia. Furthermore, if regionalism becomes increasingly linked to ideology, there is potential for conflict – the Cold War was essentially a conflict between two ideologically focused regional blocs.

Poverty

Regionalism has had an impact on poverty in terms of how regional blocs have addressed this concern, both within their own regions and globally. First, there is greater cooperation and both economic and political incentive to tackle the issue of poverty within regional blocs. A good example has been the EU and its attempts to address issues of poverty, particularly in the former Yugoslavian states, to better align those state populations and economies with the rest of Europe. Second, regional blocs dealing with significant levels of poverty (for example, the AU) have a voice in global institutions in regard to their own development. Furthermore, greater economic integration could arguably help improve poverty levels in regional blocs, particularly for organisations like ASEAN where there is a significant divide in its member states' GDPs.

Regionalism can also be seen to promote international cooperation in the areas of aid and development external to regions (demonstrating the 'building blocks to globalisation' argument, see page 302). The EU has a clear identity of promoting liberal values and has therefore invested heavily in funding aid programmes abroad, and is deeply involved in global strategies to reduce poverty. Initiatives such as the UN's Sustainable Development Goals can be much more effective if regional alliances can help implement them, which has also encouraged regional coordination with NGOs.

Human rights

In theory, regional cooperation could be advantageous to human rights at both the regional and the global level. However, there is perhaps less incentive to combat human rights violations regionally than there is to combat poverty. The EU has encouraged freedom of movement and has had a significant role in taking in asylum seekers from north Africa and the middle east (albeit controversially). The EU has also incorporated regulations over workers' rights. Within the EU the European Council has a set of (non-binding) guidelines and is arguably influenced by the ECHR's role in the region. However, precisely because the ECHR has a strong role in this regard one could argue the EU does not prioritise human rights in its own right.

There has also been a benefit to human rights on a global scale, with regionalism helping to promote a more global appreciation of liberal values and freedoms, thereby reinforcing the UN's Charter of Human Rights. This fits in with ideas of cosmopolitanism and identities that extend beyond nation-states. That said, overall, it could be argued global governance is more effective at promoting human rights than regionally.

Regional organisations have caused issues for human rights on a global scale too. For example, the African Union has long taken issue with the ICC for what it sees as a Western bias in its prosecutions. The African Union has threatened to withdraw from the ICC and has also got a poor record of arresting those indicted when they

Activity

Plan an answer to the essay question:

'Evaluate the extent to which regionalism inevitably weakens state power and sovereignty.'

travel within the AU. Other regional organisations have come under fire for not putting enough pressure on their members to address human rights issues, as was the case with ASEAN and Myanmar. While the Arab League does have an Arab Charter on Human Rights, the region as a whole has been criticised for its human rights record, especially around women's rights. This has led to discussion over whether the Arab League has a compatible understanding of human rights to the UN Charter.

> ### Topic link
>
> There are significant overlaps with elements of global governance here with conflict issues linking to political global governance, poverty to economic global governance and human rights and environmentalism. This also links to the stumbling blocks and building blocks debate, since regionalism and globalisation can either work together or against each other in tackling these issues.

The environment

Climate change is a modern-day concern that has posed a challenge to state-centric politics, given that it cannot be tackled at state level. Action is needed at state, regional and global level, and regionalism has offered a crucial link between the state and the global in that it can help to make global governance more effective (this again forms part of the 'building blocks' argument). The EU has led the way in terms of agreeing at regional level what could not be agreed at international level. It has also been highly influential at international summits such as the 2015 Paris Agreement, which was a UN initiative within which the EU played a fundamental role.

Arguably, another advantage of a regional approach to environmental issues is that there is potential to better deal with the different needs of regions when developing international environmental policies. This is a liberal argument, and one that realists would see as unrealistic. Many have argued that it is unfair to impose the same climate change restrictions as those on already-industrialised nation-states on developing countries that are still industrialising. Some even see this as part of a neo-imperialistic agenda to maintain an international hierarchy and prevent these states from developing. Others have argued that as we have seen a progression in technology, scientific collaboration and access to evidence, we can better react to climate change, in a way that we could not during the period in which developed countries were industrialising.

In any case, if these issues are to be reconciled, it may well be easier to do this through collective regional voices, as opposed to employing a state-based approach. That said, it has become clear that to truly tackle climate change a global approach will be needed.

Other issues

Globalisation

There is a clear link between regionalism and globalisation. While there is debate over the extent to which regionalism is a help or a hindrance to globalisation, there is no doubt that it has emerged alongside globalisation and that the two are most certainly intertwined.

Activity

Draw a concept map of the links in this topic in order to see how much you can remember, or if there is anything that you can add to the links. Once you have listed as many items as you can, go back and check your concept map against the links presented in the textbook – are there areas you were unsure on? This should help you to form a plan for revision.

Therefore, we see the same debates that relate to globalisation coming up in the topic of regionalism, including:

- widening and deepening integration
- the challenges to state sovereignty
- the implications for issues larger than the state.

Power and developments

There is a clear link between regionalism and the Power and developments component. It is important to consider the role that regional blocs play in international relations, which is becoming an increasing feature of a globalised world. As the world has become more interconnected, we have seen a decline in the traditional, state-centric approach to international relations and an increased move towards pooled sovereignty.

Topic link

This feeds into ideas of multipolarity and multilateralism. There are clear links to globalisation too and the idea of whether regionalism acts as a building block or a stumbling block.

Debate

Does regionalism inevitably weaken state sovereignty?

Yes

- Political regionalism is likely to weaken state sovereignty to some degree, especially where there are supranational elements.
- Even in economic alliances it could be argued sovereignty is weakened, as was seen in the debt crisis in the EU. Some states were expected to bail out others, while those states most in debt were subjected to SAPs. Also, if the economic integration involves shared currency, there is an impact on sovereign power.
- There have been various moves to nationalism and isolationism for states in recent times, which could be seen as a reaction against perceived erosion of sovereignty by IGOs. The 'Leave' campaign in the UK argued the impact on its sovereignty was a main reason to leave the EU, claiming it wanted to regain power from Brussels. Furthermore, the US could be seen to be more isolationist and under Trump it removed itself from a number of regional groups, e.g. the Trans-Pacific Partnership.
- Regionalism tends to go hand in hand with intergovernmentalism and more multilateral approaches for dealing with global issues. Inevitably this has meant working with non-state actors and has arguably diminished the significance of the nation-state as a sovereign power.

No

- If political regionalism is purely intergovernmental then regionalism is likely to be negligibly weakened. Even where there are supra-governmental elements, states can still maintain their sovereignty and ultimately withdraw if they wish, as we have seen in the EU.
- Economic and security regionalism are less likely to weaken sovereignty, and in some instances are there to fortify it. For example, the Arab League has it high on its agenda to maintain sovereignty in the region.
- It has been argued that by pooling sovereignty states can in fact enhance their position, meaning that this could be in their national interests. Regionalism can help tackle issues in a way that is mutually beneficial, thereby strengthening the position of its members.
- There has been a shift towards regional hegemony as opposed to global hegemony, with some states seemingly prioritising regional power over global power. This has been seen, for example, with regional bipolarity in Saudi Arabia and Iran. This would suggest these countries have no intention of weakening their sovereignty, rather they are hoping to become regional leaders. However, part of this process has meant forming alliances, agreements and organisations which lend themselves to regionalism.   .

Evaluation prompt: Realists and liberals have traditionally seen this in quite absolute terms. For realists, any supranational element erodes sovereignty and should be avoided or is simply ineffective. For liberals, cooperation can lead to mutually beneficial outcomes and in an increasingly globalised world is unavoidable. You might decide if you agree wholeheartedly with one position, or if there are elements of both that you agree with, then justify your answer with examples.

Further reading

Gadsby, J. (2017) 'The European Union, too much regionalism or too little?', *Politics Review*, Vol. 27, Issue 2, November.

Smith, P. (2020) 'The African Union and global politics', *Politics Review*, Vol. 30, No. 1, September.

Sobolewska, M. (2020) *Brexitland: Identity, Diversity and the Reshaping of British Politics*. Cambridge University Press.

Usherwood, S. (2018) *The European Union: A Very Short Introduction*. Oxford University Press.

Wall, S. (2020) *Reluctant European: Britain and the European Union from 1945 to Brexit*. Oxford University Press.

What you should know

Having read this chapter you should have knowledge and understanding of the following:

→ Regionalism has been increasing in the post-1945 world order, as states try to find ways of cooperating with their nearest neighbours on issues of common concern. Regionalism can often be less prone to gridlock and disagreement than global governance on an international level.

→ The European Union (EU) is the world's most comprehensive and extensive regional organisation in terms of both the number of member states and the amount of policy areas that it deals with ('widening and deepening' throughout its history). The EU's primary role has been to deepen economic and trading partnerships with Europe, through a single market and single currency.

→ Regionalism can present challenges for state sovereignty, particularly in regional organisations that have supranational decision-making powers, because in these cases the organisation can force member states to comply with decisions that a member state might not have agreed to. The EU is the most powerful regional organisation in terms of the powers that it has over its member states. Arguments that the EU represented an excessive loss of control and sovereignty were a key part of the successful 'Leave' campaign in the 2016 referendum on the UK's membership of the EU.

→ Regional organisations can focus on economic matters and trade, security, development or human rights. Most regional organisations focus on economic and trade cooperation, such as the United States–Mexico–Canada Agreement (formerly NAFTA) and the Association of Southeast Asian Nations. Regional blocs, such as the Arab League and the African Union, are useful ways for states within a region to have more influence together than individual states would alone. This pooling of sovereignty can be argued to increase, rather than decrease, a state's power and influence on the world stage.

Practice questions

Section A

1 Examine the differences between economic and political regionalism. *[12 marks]*
2 Examine the main challenges associated with both intergovernmentalism and supranationalism. *[12 marks]*
3 Examine the main factors that account for the rise of regionalism in both political and economic terms. *[12 marks]*
4 Examine the main differences between the regionalism of the African Union and ASEAN. *[12 marks]*

Section C

1 Evaluate the extent to which the EU has been a model for regionalism around the world. *[30 marks]*
2 Evaluate the extent to which regionalism can be seen to address global issues such as poverty and the environment. *[30 marks]*
3 Evaluate the extent to which the EU is a federalist system. *[30 marks]*
4 Examine the extent to which regionalism can help to promote global stability in a more multipolar world. *[30 marks]*
5 Examine the extent to which economic regionalism is the most significant form of regional alliance. *[30 marks]*
6 Evaluate the extent to which regionalism inevitably weakens state power and sovereignty. *[30 marks]*

Index

see also internet
social policy 294
society of states theory 22–3
soft power 18, 247–8, 250–1
Somalia 148, 178, 185, 191, 198
South Africa 96, 113, 150, 229, 245, 253, 272
see also BRICS countries
South Asian Association for Regional Cooperation (SAARC) 291
South Korea 42
sovereignty 22–3, 34–5, 37, 55, 66–9, 74, 159, 173, 199, 300–1, 304, 331
Srebrenica 107, 109, 116, 165, 179, 190, 195, 280
Stability and Growth Pact (SGP) 322
Stalin, J. 256
states
developed/developing 214–17
failed 81, 148, 192, 268, 273
great powers 251–3
nation-states 33–5, 40, 67–75, 80
as primary actors 5, 12, 18, 80, 205
rogue 81, 273–4
system of government 271–5
see also sovereignty; world systems theory
Stockholm Conference on the Human Environment 1972 221, 225–7
Stockholm Declaration 1972 216, 223, 226
structural adjustment programmes (SAPs) 37, 126
subsidies 44, 133–5, 148, 284, 296, 299, 320
superpowers 252, 260, 276, 280, 327
supranationalism 292, 304, 315, 324–5
sustainability 38, 47, 217, 312
sustainable development 218
Sustainable Development Goals (SDGs) 38, 83, 86, 99, 102–3, 122, 146, 153–4, 156, 218
Syria 11, 23, 25, 55–6, 95, 100, 108, 155, 188, 194, 196, 198–9, 260, 265, 270–1, 290, 307

T

Taiwan 30, 42, 277–8
Taliban 55, 63, 107, 186
tariffs 12–13, 37, 41, 44, 122, 132–5, 140, 150, 152, 284, 291, 293, 306, 312
taxation 12–13, 36, 67, 126–8, 152, 155, 211–12, 312

terrorism 3, 20, 36, 63, 70, 194, 204, 249
Thatcher, M. 45, 151
Theory of International Politics 6, 16
Thirty Years' War 1618–48 34–5
Thunberg, G. 38, 68, 73, 203, 210, 240
totalitarian states 272
trade 12, 19, 24, 36, 37–8, 41–4, 121, 131–6, 292–4, 298–9, 305–6, 322–3
see also tariffs
trade wars 121, 135
tragedy of the commons 207, 217
Trans-Atlantic Trade and Investment Partnership (TTIP) 67
transformationalists 66
Trans-Pacific Partnership (TPP) 12–13, 69, 123, 299
treaties 82–3, 111–18
bilateral 82, 111
multilateral 82, 85, 111
Treaty of Lisbon 2009 67, 288, 291, 301, 313, 321
Treaty of Nice 2003 321
Treaty of Paris 1951 290, 292
Treaty of Rome 1957 112, 290, 320
Treaty of Westphalia 1648 34–5, 111
see also Westphalian principles
Treaty on the Non-Proliferation of Nuclear Weapons (NPT) 37, 83, 107, 112–13, 159
Trump, D. 1, 8–9, 13, 17, 25–6, 34, 45, 48, 56, 62, 68, 115, 162, 190, 209, 219, 233, 244, 251, 278, 282, 284, 285, 299

U

Uighur Muslims 197
Ukraine 9, 72, 93, 115, 258, 277
underdevelopment 149
unemployment 21, 124, 128, 155, 294
unipolarity 110, 254, 259, 267, 280, 286
United Nations (UN) 1, 3, 11, 28, 37–8, 79, 83–111
Charter 84–5, 88–9, 160, 329
climate support 216
Convention on the Law of the Sea (UNCLOS) 206
Economic and Social Council (ECOSOC) 88, 101–3, 210
effectiveness of 105–11
Environment Programme (UNEP) 206
Framework Convention on Climate Change (UNFCCC) 38, 85, 206, 221–3

General Assembly (UNGA) 88, 98–101
International Children's Emergency Fund (UNICEF) 153
membership 88
peacekeeping 86, 106–10, 179–85, 183
and poverty 153–4
primary institutions 87–8, 111
Responsibility to Protect (R2P) 27, 54, 100, 182–3
Security Council (UNSC) 3, 7, 9, 11, 12, 23, 28, 51, 69, 83, 86–7, 90–7, 112
Trusteeship Council 88
United Nations High Commission for Refugees (UNHCR) 37
United Nations International Children's Fund (UNICEF) 38
United States (US)
climate commitments 235
as global leader 244
hegemony 257–67, 280
inequality 45
'pivot to Asia' 9, 264–6
power and tactics 17, 25–6
system of government 272
War on Terror 84, 107
United States–Mexico–Canada Agreement (USMCA) 38, 291, 298–9, 305–6
Universal Declaration of Human Rights (UDHR) 18, 50–2, 82, 86, 160–1, 173–5, 279

V

vaccines 103, 248
Vietnam War 1963–75 256

W

Waltz, K. 6, 16, 255, 259
war and conflict
Arab Spring 2010–12 20, 40, 68, 108, 270, 275
Bosnian Civil War 1991–95 51, 54, 109, 179, 190–2
chemical weapons 56
Cold War 1945–91 15–16, 33, 53, 107, 115, 178, 254–7, 279, 298
disarmament 7, 86, 94, 102, 113
Gulf War 1991 178
Iraq–Iran War 1980–88 271
Iraq War 2003 7–8, 13, 25, 186, 190–1, 198, 271
military intervention 27, 54–6, 178–201, 295
nuclear weapons 16, 37, 71, 86, 112–13

Photo credits

Photos reproduced by permission of: **p.2** Reuters/Alamy; **p.7** US Army Photo/Alamy; **p.15** Sueddeutsche Zeitung Photo/Alamy; **p.21** Wenn Ltd/Alamy; **p.26** ZUMA Press, Inc/Alamy; **p.30** White House Photo/Alamy; **p.34** Sputnik/Topfoto; **p.40** jamdesign/Fotolia; **p.43** Richard Human/Alamy; **p.47** Penny Tweedie/Alamy; **p.54** brianeuro/Alamy; **p.68** Europa Newswire/Alamy; **p.70** Denis Charlet/Getty; **p.72** 360b/Alamy; **p.79** Chris J Ratcliffe/Getty; **p.84** Sean Pavone/Alamy; **p.90** Xinhua/Alamy; **p.104** Picture Partners/Alamy; **p.116** 508 Collection/Alamy; **p.120** Norman Chan/Fotolia; **p.124** Photomac/Fotolia; **p.127** ullsteinbild/Topfoto; **p.138** White House Photo/Alamy; **p.151** Pictorial Press Ltd/Alamy; **p.154** Living Legend/Fotolia; **p.160** Fred Ramage/Stringer/Getty; **p.165** AWesleyFloyd/Fotolia; **p.166** REUTERS/Alamy; **p.175** jgolby/Fotolia; **p.184** Ben Flavell/Alamy; **p.190** MediaPunch Inc/Alamy; **p.193** john wreford/Alamy; **p.200** Photoshot/TopFoto; **p.206** Alexander/Fotolia; **p.208** Olli Geibel/Alamy; **p.215** estherpoon/Fotolia; **p.226** SPUTNIK/Alamy; **p.229** carabay/Fotolia; **p.240** UPI/Alamy; **p.244** UPI/Alamy; **p.245** gilbertc/Fotolia; **p.249** Xinhua/Alamy; **p.255** Romolo Tavani/Fotolia; **p.260** PA Images/Alamy; **p.262** Christo Sharpe/Alamy; **p.265** 506 Collection/Alamy; **p.277** Retuers/Alamy; **p.281** kamasigns/Fotolia; **p.289** Lulla/Fotolia; **p.297** Anadolu Agency/Getty; **p.308** US Air Force Photo/Alamy; **p.311** The Asahi Shimbun/Getty; **p.315** London pix/Alamy; **p.319** dpa picture alliance/Alamy; **p.322** eyetronic/Fotolia; **p.324** fotostock/Alamy.